Charles Whaley
September 1994

Yale Publications in the History of Art

Walter Cahn, editor

Speaking for Vice

Homosexuality in the Art of Charles Demuth, Marsden Hartley, and the First American Avant-Garde

Jonathan Weinberg

Yale University Press New Haven and London

Yale Publications in the History of Art are works of critical and historical scholarship by authors formerly or now associated with the Department of the History of Art of Yale University. Begun in 1939, the series embraces the field of art historical studies in its widest and most inclusive definition.

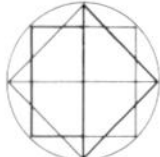

Series logo designed by Josef Albers and reproduced with permission of the Josef Albers Foundation.

Designed by Sonia L. Scanlon
Set in Bembo type by Tseng Information Systems, Inc., Durham, North Carolina
Printed in the United States of America by Thomson Shore, Inc., Dexter, Michigan

Library of Congress Cataloging-in-Publication Data
Weinberg, Jonathan, 1957–
Speaking for vice : homosexuality in the art of Charles Demuth, Marsden Hartley, and the first American avant-garde / Jonathan Weinberg.
p. cm. — (Yale publications in the history of art)
Includes bibliographical references and index.
ISBN 0-300-05361-4 (acid-free paper)
1. Demuth, Charles, 1883–1935—Criticism and interpretation. 2. Hartley, Marsden, 1877–1943—Criticism and interpretation. 3. Homosexuality in art. 4. Erotic painting—20th century—United States. 5. Avant-garde (Aesthetics)—United States—History—20th century. I. Demuth, Charles, 1883–1935. II. Hartley, Marsden, 1877–1943. III. Title. IV. Series.
ND237.D36W45 1993
759.13—dc20 93-18547
CIP

A catalogue record for this book is available from the British Library.

The paper in this book meets the guidelines for permanence and durability of the Committee on Production Guidelines for Book Longevity of the Council on Library Resources.

10 9 8 7 6 5 4 3 2 1

For Eugene Glynn and Marc Lida

There is a crusade against vice in Lancaster. . . . I am going home to speak for vice.

Charles Demuth

Contents

Acknowledgments

This book would never have been completed without the advice, encouragement, and criticism of friends and teachers. Given the initial doubts and hostility raised by my subject, that support was particularly needed and appreciated. I was graciously assisted by the professional staffs of the Archives of American Art, the Art Institute of Chicago, the Barnes Foundation, the Beinecke Library of Yale University, the Demuth Foundation, the Fogg Art Museum, the George and Helen Ladd Library of Bates College, the Hirshhorn Museum, the Houghton Library of Harvard University, the Kennedy Galleries, the Kinsey Institute, the Lancaster County Historical Society, the Library of Congress, the Museum of Modern Art, the Philadelphia Museum, the Yale University Art Gallery, the University Gallery of the University of Minnesota, and the Whitney Museum of American Art.

One of the great pleasures of doing the research on this project has been the many friends I have made in the process of learning about my subject. Charlotte B. Brown, George Chauncey, Jr., Michael De Lisio, Dorothea Demuth, Emily Farnham, Gerald Ferguson, Donald Gallup, Eric Garber, Barbara Haskell, Mervin Jules, Bruce Kellner, Ann Kibbey, Marilyn Kushner, Townsend Ludington, Michael Lynch, Carol L. Morgan, Linda Nochlin, James Saslow, Kenneth Quail, Gail R. Scott, Tom Sokolowksi, and Brian Wallis were all more than generous with material and information. Betsy Fahlman shared with me not only her research on Charles Demuth but her knowledge of the history of Lancaster and of American art in general. I wish to thank Ray Gerard Koskovich and Kermit Champa for sharing their unpublished writings on Charles Demuth with me. Lee Edelman, Henry Geldzahler, Ann Gibson, Jonathan Katz, Tom Lentz, Joe Litvak, John O'Brian, Chris Reed, Kenneth Silver, Virgil Thompson, Rhoda Wolf, Steven Watson, and Henri Zerner have all given me valuable advice. Jill Crabtree, Diane Dillon, and Laura

Katzman read through the manuscript and made valuable suggestions. Susan Lippman helped with the photographs. My closest friend, Marc Lida, was an essential editor and counselor on this project.

Judy Metro and Karen Gangel, my editors at Yale University Press, shepherded this book to its completion. I am grateful for their support.

My dissertation advisor, T. J. Clark, supported this project from its inception and nurtured it to completion. His work has been a great inspiration to me, and although he is in no way responsible for the flaws of this book, it would not have been written without his advice, his encouragement, and the model of his teaching and writing. My lover, Nicholas Boshnack, supported my work, kept me happy, and chauffeured me (I do not drive) across the Northeast in search of memories of Marsden Hartley and Charles Demuth. Finally, I wish to thank Maurice Sendak, who gave me my first watercolor set, and Eugene Glynn, who introduced me to art history and provided me with financial support to pursue it. I am also grateful to my colleagues in the History of Art Department at Yale University for their help and faith in my work. No one at Yale has meant more to me than Vincent Scully; his friendship and lectures have been an inspiration.

I am grateful to *Art in America* and to *Arts Magazine* for permission to reprint and rephrase parts of my articles on Charles Demuth and Paul Cadmus. The research and materials for this book were supported by a one-year Harvard Fellowship and an Enders Grant from Yale University.

Introduction

My focus is on homosexuality in American avant-garde paintings between the two world wars. Such a discussion necessarily involves analysis of how the dominant culture marks out the boundaries of acceptable behavior. It explores the connections between the practice of an avant-garde that is intent on testing the limits of such boundaries and the expression of a clandestine sexual subculture. I am aware that in certain quarters this book may be considered to press against the limits of what is considered the proper domain of art history. A subtheme of this work is the link between the division of behavior into the normal and the abnormal and the categorization of aesthetic experience into the essential and the nonessential. The desire to isolate the work of art from what is taken to be the polluting force of homosexuality is widespread among the sympathetic critics of Charles Demuth and Marsden Hartley. Even Marcel Duchamp, who himself, in a famous episode of avant-garde history, appeared in drag, insisted that the work of art was undermined by too-close scrutiny of the sexual identity of its creator. Indeed, as if in anticipation of this study, he warned specifically against giving too much weight to the issue of sexuality in discussing the work of Charles Demuth: "The little perverse tendency that he had was not important in Demuth's life. After all, everybody has a little perverse tendency in him. That quality in him had nothing to do with the quality of his work. It had nothing to do with his art."[1] The very terms *perverse* and *quality,* no matter how softened, echo a larger process by which society seeks to order behavior and define responses to experience. Given the range of sexual references in Duchamp's works, it is disappointing to find him acquiescing in a theory that excludes sexuality from the interpretation of art. Yet that he would so readily disallow such a crucial component of his own artistic production shows the degree to which dwelling on the issue of sexuality, and in particular homosexuality, is seen to threaten the integrity of the work of art. In this, Duchamp is merely joining the rest of Demuth's friends, family, and sympathetic critics in trying to disassociate Demuth's work from what I suspect they feel is the damning evidence of its subject matter: its repeated representation of homosexuality.

Ironically, the very vagueness of Duchamp's "perverse tendency" amplifies the "little" aspect of the artist's life that we are supposed to ignore. This quality of indirectly pointing to the artist's homosexuality while seeming to ignore it is typical of much of the writing on the artists discussed here. It is particularly prevalent in the Demuth literature, where innuendos like *effete, elegant, decadent, perverse,* are allowed to float over the discussions of his art. The ambiguity of such terms, with their allusions to a clandestine subject matter and life-style, sometimes serves to connect descriptions of very different kinds of art. The approach of the influential reviewer Henry McBride to the paintings of Charles Demuth and Paul Cadmus is almost identical. In his article "An Underground Search for Higher Moralities" he worries—half ironically, half in earnest—about the moral danger Demuth faces in his search for a certain kind of subject matter: "I don't know why it is, but the moment you go downstairs into a restaurant in New York you begin to see life. Or so I judge from Mr. Demuth's drawings. How revolting, for instance, must have been Baron Wilke's establishment? It has been closed by the police sometime since. Races of various colors intermingled, danced and drank there. Yet I hold it was entirely right of Mr. Demuth to have studied it, so evidently in the interests of higher morality."[2]

McBride falls back on the same terms when discussing a painting by Paul Cadmus:

> Very straight-laced people would back haughtily out of the rooms after taking one glance at Paul Cadmus's picture called *Seeing the New Year In*—if they could. . . . One assumes that Mr. Cadmus is a moralist, yet even so, it is difficult to get the intention back of his picture. The painting doesn't have the air of fantasy. There is a cold, hard restlessness in the drawing that suggests the artist has been determined to give you the facts and

> nothing but the facts, but at the same time the artist's complete absorption in every inch of wickedness in the picture attests too great an interest in wickedness for its own sake.[3]

Neither of these two descriptions speaks directly of the artists' sexuality. McBride pretends that the artists view the scene of decadence as outsiders, moralists, even as we are meant to know that they probably enjoy the same vices they depict, vices that are not fully described. Given his close friendships with the artists he wrote about, and his own homosexuality, it is likely that McBride knew that such saloons and private parties were among the few places where gay men could socialize openly. McBride protects himself from a too-close association with that morally suspect subject matter. In both cases the artist as moralist is a ploy, a very thin smokescreen that the critic expects his more knowing audience to see through.

Often, like crafty politicians who do not want to be charged with capitalizing on their opponent's misfortune, critics whisper scandals in one breath and loudly argue against their inclusion in art historical discussion in the next. I wish to replace the vagueness of this approach, which under the guise of protection implicates all aspects of the artist's work in unnameable corruptions, with one that makes specific the role homosexuality played in the paintings of key American artists. I shall show that homosexuality is at issue in certain works not merely by virtue of connections to particular events in an artist's life but because that artist has deliberately chosen it as a subject. I shall demonstrate that such representation of an illegal and dangerous form of love is tied to the artist's need to reveal an essential aspect of his life.

Constructivism versus Essentialism

The homosexual is not a trans-historical category. Although subcultures based on same-sex love seem to have existed at various times throughout Western history, their defining qualities were based on the particularities of their culture. The homosexual as a definition of a certain type is part of a larger process of society's ordering of itself—a process that is continually changing in history.

By stressing the historical transformation of the concept of the homosexual, I am relying on so-called constructivist theories put forth by those social historians who insist that sexual identities are *constructed* by the society and have meaning only in terms of a complex matrix of culturally determined roles. Many other histories of sexuality are possible, arising from different views of human character. Some of those histories might see "homosexuals" as a distinct type present in every historical period. Unquestionably, homosexual behavior—defined as sexual acts between partners of the same gender—has existed throughout time and in almost every conceivable culture, but it is heatedly debated in gay studies whether that behavior created in its actors a sense of self-difference and group identification equivalent to that shared by modern minorities. Jeffrey Weeks, a leading proponent of the constructivist point of view, writes: "We should employ cross-cultural and historical evidence not only to chart changing *attitudes* but to challenge the very concept of a single trans-historical notion of homosexuality. In different cultures (and at different historical moments or conjunctures within the same culture) very different meanings are given to same-sex activity both by society at large and by the individual participants."[4] In contrast, the so-called essentialists see human character, and therefore sexuality, as relatively immutable. At the turn of the century, both biological and psychoanalytic descriptions of homosexuality, for all their differences, were essentialist in their emphasis on sexuality as the crucial element in the development of character throughout the history of Western civilization. Such thinking, for example, allowed Freud to attempt an analysis of Leonardo da Vinci's sexuality in spite of the enormous cultural gap between fin-de-siècle Vienna and Renaissance Florence. It also allowed civil libertarians like Edward Carpenter to defend the rights of contemporary homosexuals by listing famous artists and political figures from the past who were believed to have engaged in homosexual relations. Validation of modern sexual practices was sought by counting off all the distinguished men thought to have had homoerotic inclinations rather than by examining the significance homosexuality had for specific individuals in history.

Nonetheless the essentialist approach cannot be dismissed simply by challenging it with the different meanings same-sex experience had for earlier societies. Although homosexuality may have differed in the past and various terms were used to define it, one should not necessarily conclude that it did not exist as a form of self-definition that has relevance to the experience of modern homosexuality. It is a question of emphasis as much as of ontology. Which is more interesting: to trace the constants of physical and mental oppression that seem to have been experienced by those who made love to someone of the same sex, or to insist on the particular response to homosexual acts during a given period? The latter line of questioning is in no sense merely academic. Indeed, it is precisely the mutability of those responses that draws attention to the arbitrariness of so many contemporary social restrictions against sexual behavior of all kinds.

Regardless of their disagreement over the validity of the category *homosexual* in discussing the sexual interactions of past societies, essentialists and constructivists are beginning to come together in acknowledging that sexual definitions do change, not only from century to century but from decade to decade and culture to culture. Mentioning the homosexual content of a work of art without giving the term its precise historical significance invariably brings to mind a confusing set of qualities familiar to us from our own contemporary experiences—qualities that may or may not have anything to do with an earlier attitude toward similar behavior. As Weeks succinctly put it: "The physical acts might be similar, but their social implications are often profoundly different."[5]

For my purposes, the essentialist-constructivist debate can largely be left to one side. There is little place here for trans-historical comparisons; instead I focus on a discrete period in which no one would dispute that the modern term *homosexuality,* and the character types and subcultures it has been used to describe, was already in place. Yet it is crucial that the debate be touched on, not only because it draws attention to the relatively recent appearance of sexuality as a significant—not to say determinant—factor in describing character formation, but because the arguments deployed about definitions and their significance emphasize the instability of the labels used to describe sexuality.

If one is to speak of the role of homosexuality at all—and such discussion in various forms has been going on for some time now—it is necessary to determine the status of homosexuality in the period in question. What did it mean for a work of art to have a homosexual content in 1914 or 1930? If such a content were disguised, what audience would understand it? What were the pressures exerted by the culture against the expression of homosexual desire and, given those pressures, why did certain artists find it necessary to produce this content?

Of course, merely correcting and expanding the limited discussion of homosexuality in the art historical literature still does not address Duchamp's anxiety, namely, that focusing on peculiarities of an artist's personal life necessarily impugns the quality of the art produced. There is a serious worry that emphasizing the marginality of an artist's range of interests also will marginalize his or her art. In a well-known book on twentieth-century American literature, John W. Aldridge writes: "Homosexual experience is of one special kind, it can develop in only one direction, and it can never take the place of the whole range of human experience which the writer must know intimately if he is to be great. Sooner or later it forces him away from the center to the outer edges of the common life of his society where he is almost always sure to become a mere grotesque, a parasite, or a clown."[6]

In the end, is not Duchamp merely wishing to protect Demuth's work from this kind of assessment? Yet Aldridge's claim is based on a mistaken assumption that "human experience" has a "center," and that that center is a privileged vantage point for "intimate" knowledge of the "whole range of human experience." For Aldridge, experience at the edges is too specialized, too focused, too directed, to provide access to the totality. Yet few artists, regardless of their sexual preference, have lived lives that approximate the lives of the majority of society or even of its ruling elite. Marginality, as the word is used here, is not Aldridge's measurement based on the scale of the common life of the society; it refers to a pervasive trope for the artist's perception of his relationship to that society. What is remarkable about Aldridge's statement is not just that in passing he seems to toss out the canonical works by Proust, Whitman, Stein, Rimbaud, Verlaine, Cather, Gide, and Genet, but that he so completely misunderstands the power that the theme of the artist as outsider had for the avant-garde as a whole. Actually, Aldridge's *grotesque, parasite,* and *clown* are not a bad catalogue of the heroes of much late nineteenth- and early twentieth-century art, and the culture as a whole does not seem to have regarded such heroes as irrelevant or unrepresentative.

Why limit the study to the decades 1910 through 1940? In one sense I am falling back on the convention of using the Armory Show as a convenient point for the onset of modernism in the United States, although New Yorkers got their first taste of Parisian avant-garde painting in Alfred Stieglitz's gallery as early as 1908. More important, the writers and painters of the small New York art world of the period—not always encompassed by the "Stieglitz circle"—took part in an extensive debate about art and morality that is documented in a variety of primary material, including extensive correspondence between the principals. This close contact between artists of different class backgrounds and sexual orientations offers an opportunity to focus on the relationship between the social and artistic transgressions that were so much a part of the avant-garde stance. The consciously marginalized life-style of many of the New York modernists, whether homosexual or heterosexual, seems directly opposed to the claim—often made at the time and since—that their art embodied the American experience. Stieglitz and his associates shared a desire to create an art that, though cognizant of European modernism, would be distinctly American, free from the Old World emphasis on classical associations and erudition. To a degree, Demuth and Hartley both believed they were making such an art. One of the questions I grapple with is this: How did they reconcile this production of the American with the representation of their marginalized status as both homosexuals and avant-garde artists?

The years 1910–40 can also be seen as a discrete period in the history of sexuality. By World War I the institutionalization of the homosexual was essentially complete, and homosexual characters were becoming commonplace in avant-garde literature. Not only was the term used increasingly in medical and legal literature, but there was a growing confidence that it described a specific type with discernible habits and characteristics. The Kinsey Report, which appeared just after World War II, provides an end marker to this stage in the changing status of the homosexual. Its claim that same-gender sexual acts were relatively common among the general public dramatically shifted the existence of homosexuality from the specialized medical, legal, and cultural realm to one of widespread public debate.

One last issue must be discussed before moving on. Limiting my discussion to the problems raised by the art of Hartley and Demuth requires leaving out a discussion of lesbian iconography and painters. One of the trickiest political issues of gay studies is whether to discuss homosexual men and women in the same category. If the focus is on subcultural interactions, then it is important to remember that up until the past twenty years, lesbian and male homosexual groupings were quite separate. Over the years a growing awareness of political identity has brought gay men and lesbians together in a struggle for human rights and against AIDS, but this does not mean that the two sexual orientations and their social ramifications are in any way equivalent. Although both groups share certain experiences in coping with victimization at the hands of the dominant culture, the lesbian experience is also shaped by oppression from a male-dominant society. For reasons of space and expertise, I shall avoid the great questions of the heterosexual matrix, the dynamics of male-female relationships that presumably provide the model for all sexual interactions in the period studied, even though such questions will have to be tackled in the larger project of an adequate sociology of homosexuality. The issue of lesbianism and art, however, cannot avoid such questions in however pragmatic or provisional a spirit, given its relationship to the general problem of the oppression of women. In any case, my subject is not all forms of same-sex love and its depiction but the way attitudes toward men having sex with each other created the modern homosexual, sustaining subcultures that in turn were represented in art.

This book is not an inclusive study of the subject. Instead of following the pattern of many recent histories of so-called minorities, which seem intent on asserting the importance of their approach through copious examples, I have purposely limited my scope. By working closely with the paintings of two important American modernist artists, Charles Demuth and Marsden Hartley, I hope to avoid the broad and often reductive generalities that surveys (whether of the minority or majority variety) must employ almost by definition. On the other hand, by not restricting my discussion to any single artist, I am able to explore certain crucial issues, such as the question of a shared subcultural code or tradition.

1 Who Is a Homosexual?

In Charles Demuth's *Three Sailors on the Beach* (fig. 1, pl. 2), a sailor, naked but for a tank top and black boots, sits spread-legged on the sand, revealing his erect penis. He stares directly at the genitals of a man who stands above him, dressed only in boxer shorts. The implication of the standing man's posture—he has one hand on his excited companion's neck and the other on his own genitals—is that we are witnessing the preliminaries of fellatio. The trinity is completed by a sailor who is turned away from the pair. Staring out at the ocean, he seems to pull his shirt over his head, taking the characteristic pose of a triumphant boxer. Although his state of undress is the model of decorum in comparison with the overt sexual display of the other two figures, his athletic stance reinforces the painting's quality of exhibitionism.

Three Sailors on the Beach and the other erotic paintings by Demuth have been discussed in terms of the artist's voyeurism.[1] Indeed, we might think of the wealthy, highly educated, and impeccably dressed Demuth as completely removed from the sailor's lewd display were it not for the initials C. D. inscribed within the traditional heart-shaped tattoo on the arm of the standing sailor. The placement of this erotic scene on an open beach (there are some bathers and sailboats in the background), where it is unlikely that even the most drunken military men would carry on in such an uninhibited manner, suggests that the picture does not record an actual event. Nor is there direct evidence that Demuth was ever sexually intimate with sailors, let alone with one who was so in love with him as to have Demuth's initials tattooed on his arm. Yet C. D. conveys a desire to be more than a voyeur, more than just an observer of the sailors' erotic play. The tattoo provides a way for the artist to

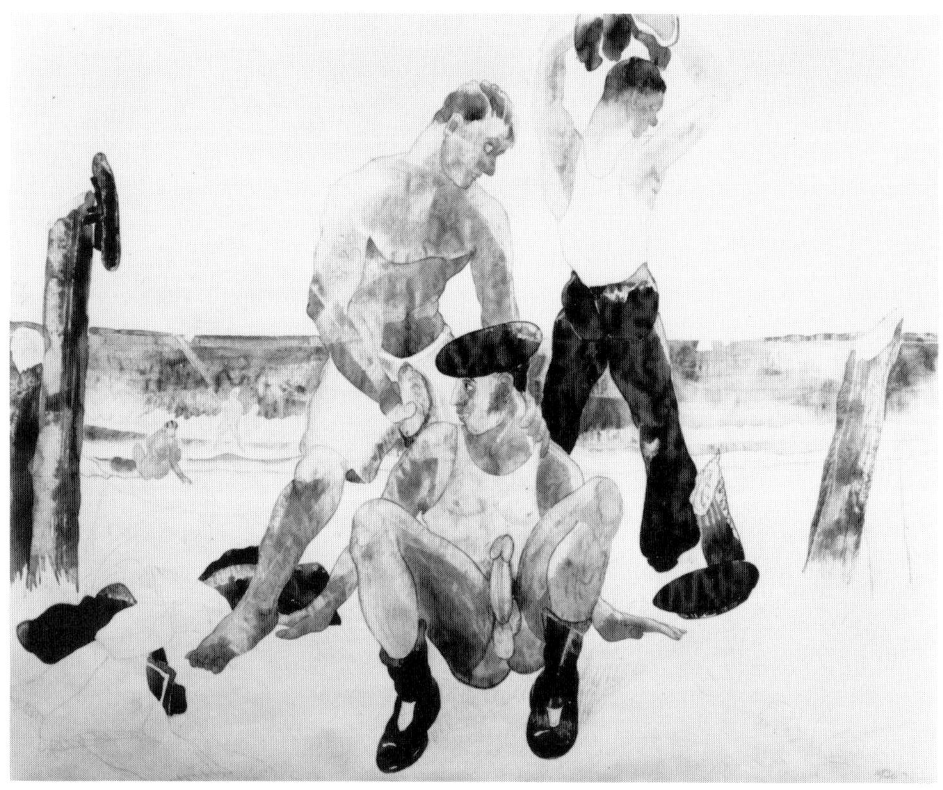

1. Charles Demuth, *Three Sailors on the Beach,* watercolor and pencil on paper, 13½ × 16½ in., 1930. Private collection. Courtesy Richard York Gallery, New York.

be in the picture without actually being depicted. More important, Demuth is not merely recording an imagined homosexual encounter; through the signature he is defining himself *as* a homosexual.

Initials are also at the center of another painting about homosexual love, Marsden Hartley's *Portrait of a German Officer* (fig. 2, pl. 1). Michael Lynch and Barbara Haskell both suggest that Hartley's image was meant not so much as a glorification of Germany's war effort as a memorial to a dead lover.[2] The work brings together the emblems rather than the harsh realities of war. A soldier's medal for some unknown deed, flags for raising in battle, numbers and initials for identifying the dead, are overlapped on a black field. Hartley was in love with a young German soldier, Karl von Freyburg, who died in the early stages of World War I. Freyburg's initials are clearly visible in the lower left corner of the painting, as is "24," his age at death. Hartley's name, though disguised, is also built into the symbolic language of the painting. An epaulet twists into the letter E, which stands for Hartley's given name, Edmund. (He had changed it to Marsden some ten years earlier.) Hartley, present at the center of the canvas by the name of his youth, is surrounded by the emblems of his would-be lover.

For all their obvious differences, *Three Sailors on the Beach* and *Portrait of a German Officer* both express two male artists' desire for men. But merely pointing to an artist's sexual orientation, whether homosexual, heterosexual, or bisexual, does not go very far in explaining his or her paintings. Overall, the discussion of homosexuality in relation to the art of either Hartley or Demuth has often been limited by a failure to link the term to its historical context. Those using the word *homosexual* assume the reader knows what is being referred to. Such confidence belies the inherent variability of the kinds of human relationships the term *homosexuality* is meant to describe. Rather than signifying specific sexual acts, or a state of being, meanings of the word have been unusually unstable since the beginning of its widespread use at the end of the nineteenth century. What exactly did *homosexuality* mean in Hartley's and Demuth's day? Who used the term and to what purpose? How were same-sex relationships treated by the American legal and medical establishment? What are the kinds of transgressions that congregate around the particular sexual practices that are

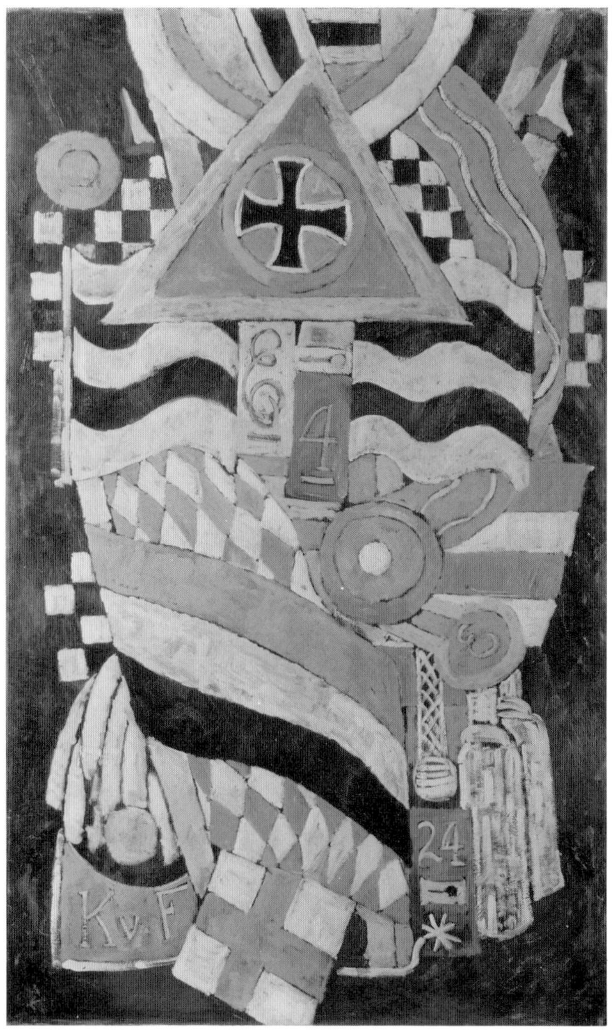

2. Marsden Hartley, *Portrait of a German Officer,* oil on canvas, $68\frac{1}{4} \times 41\frac{3}{8}$ in., 1914. Metropolitan Museum of Art, New York; The Alfred Stieglitz Collection, 1949.

defined by the term *homosexuality?* Above all, what did society have to fear from the acts of fellatio and sodomy as practiced between two men?

When Marcel Duchamp spoke of Demuth's homosexuality, referring to it cryptically as his "little perverse tendency," he no doubt meant to convey a sense that sexual desire was merely a matter of taste. Besides expressing the sexual tolerance typical of the New York intellectual and artistic circles he frequented in the 1950s, Duchamp was suggesting that focusing on an artist's homosexuality was as absurd as focusing on his choice of clothes or his love of fine chocolates. Yet such a view ignores the fact that since the mid-nineteenth century *homosexuality* (and its now-obsolete synonyms *inversion* and *uranism*) defined not only a set of physical acts or perverse pleasures but a variety of persons—almost a species. Some specialists went so far as to claim that it was a new gender altogether, a third sex. Certainly, homosexual acts had been considered crimes before the nineteenth century—sodomy had been punishable since the Roman Empire. Still, Western society before this time had recognized that all humans, given certain tastes, temptations, and circumstances, had the potential to commit sodomy, just as they had the potential to commit any heinous or petty crime. Sodomy, or buggery—and we should be clear that the term *sodomy* was used to define anal (and at times oral) intercourse between same-sex as well as male-female partners—was part of the general catalogue of sins to which the flesh was prone.[3] As Michel Foucault and his followers demonstrate, modern legal and medical authorities largely invented the concept of the homosexual and a long list of other deviant character types—the criminal, the psychopath, the hysterical woman, the masturbator, and so on. These terms participated in the creation of social "others," human beings who needed to be cordoned off in order to protect the rest of society from their "unnatural" behavior. Sexuality was now deemed a determining characteristic in the formation of the self, affecting how one walked, dressed, and even thought. Increasingly, in a variety of medical and legal texts, one's sexuality described not only with whom one had sex but also who one was.[4]

Medical descriptions of homosexuals began to appear in the United States in the 1880s, although there is much disagreement in these early texts over the extent of the behavior described. Some writers were unwilling or unable to recognize the social implications of the sexual phenomenon they discussed, seeing it only as a rare perversion represented by a few case histories. A frequent element in many of these accounts is the patient's surprise at being told there might be others like him. Yet as early as 1889 there were authorities who insisted not only on the pervasiveness of homosexuality but also on the existence of established communities of inverts in every American city, with their own specialized practices and codes. The Chicago-based physician G. Frank Lydston reported that: "There is in every community of any size a colony of male sexual perverts; they are usually known to each other, and are likely to congregate together. At times they operate in accordance with some definite and concerted plan in quest of subjects wherewith to gratify their sexual impulse."[5] A sensationalism often accompanied a physician's announcement that, unbeknownst to most average Americans, there were thousands of sexual deviants in their midst. Dr. William Lee Howard wrote: "The number of these sexual perverts in America is astonishing to one unacquainted with this most important branch of neuropathic studies. As I have said, they belong to the intellectual classes, and are found in pulpit [*sic*], at the editorial desk and in the studios, as well as before the bar and at the bedside."[6]

Of course, the inability of the medical establishment to conceptualize homosexuals socializing in groups, and its ignorance of establishments that catered to a gay clientele, does not mean that such practices and places did not exist in the United States before that era. In fact, records of police raids of male brothels indicate that homosexual activity was prevalent throughout the nineteenth century. Yet the recognition that such activity might reflect a pattern of interactions constituting a community wholly defined by its members' sexual tastes had to await a conceptual framework: *the homosexual*. In other words, homosexuals as a community were invisible not just because they wanted their activities to go unknown but because the discursive apparatus that documented such activities—the medical and legal categorizers—were not looking for such groups.

That process of identification and classification exploded at the end of the nineteenth century. In works by such writers as Benjamin Tarnowsky, Moll, and Richard von Krafft-Ebing, the invert was just one of many sexually abnormal types encountered in the human species. Same-sex relationships were taken as a kind of extreme biological or psychological aberration. Like the insane, inverts were considered to have little choice or control over their propensity. Dr. George F. Shrady, author of one of the earliest medical discussions of homosexuality in America, classified same-sex acts among the "lowest forms of bestiality and sensuousness exhibited by debased men" and counselled that "conditions once considered criminal are really pathological, and come within the province of the physician."[7] By 1904 another American physician, William Lee Howard, called homosexuality "a normal sexual feeling," because "most congenital perverts are *inverts,*" and "a congenital invert is not an individual whose sexual instincts are perverted, but one who presents an unfortunate anatomical anomaly."[8] Howard echoed a popular idea that the homosexual had "a female soul in a male body." The homosexual drive itself was not abnormal, just the context—the male body that contained that drive. Howard's view is a vulgarization of Havelock Ellis's important *Sexual Inversion,* in which he claimed that homosexuality was a biological variation, present in animals as well as in humans. (Ellis's study of homosexuality was issued first in the United States in 1897, the British edition having been withdrawn before publication.)[9] *Sexual Inversion* was a plea for tolerance—in part based on the assumption that homosexual behavior, although influenced by upbringing and environmental circumstances, was inborn, and that the invert could therefore do little to change his propensity. Such a view would suggest that, by and large, the average male child was not likely to slip inadvertently into homosexuality—he would have to inherit specific genes to develop an exclusive attraction to members of his own sex. Yet Ellis also claimed that human beings were bisexual. A homosexual was someone whose heterosexual impulses were in suspension. For Ellis, the "real distinction would seem . . . to be between a homosexual impulse so strong that it subsists even in the presence of the heterosexual object, and a homosexual impulse so weak that it is eclipsed by the presence of the heterosexual object." Although Ellis insisted on the importance of genetic inheritance, he recognized that there were no clear boundaries between homosexual, heterosexual, and bisexual behavior and that such terms, while useful as descriptions, could not be rigorously maintained: "The division into heterosexual, bisexual and homosexual is a useful superficial division, it is scarcely a scientific classification."[10]

The Freudians

Ellis's belief in the basic bisexuality of human beings parallels the writings of Freud and his followers. Yet in contrast to Ellis, Freud, whose theories were first introduced to the United States in 1909, stressed the importance of behaviorally acquired characteristics in the development of sexuality. The pervasive fear that a child might become homosexual as a result of an episode of seduction or some other traumatic event in rearing was a vulgarization of Freudian theories of sexual variance. One of the earliest articles on homosexuality to be published in the United States by a Freudian was A. A. Brill's 1903 essay "The Conception of Homosexuality." Brill has been called the "unofficial ambassador of psychoanalysis in America," and in his introduction to the popular 1938 Modern Library selection of Freud's works (which he also translated) he immodestly declared that "psychoanalysis was unknown in this country until [he] introduced it in 1908."[11] He became particularly well known by the circle around Marsden Hartley and Charles Demuth following a lecture he gave on psychoanalysis in 1914 at one of Mabel Dodge Luhan's celebrated evenings in New York.[12]

In his 1903 article, Brill wrote that there was little evidence to support the hypothesis of a genetic factor in the production of homosexuality: "There may be some congenital inverts, but of the forty-nine cases that I have analyzed I always discovered one or more early affective sexual impressions which favored the development of homosexuality. In others a fixation of the inversion took place earlier or later in life through external favoring and inhibitory influences, such as exclusive relations with the same sex in boarding-schools, in the army, in the navy, in prison, etc."[13] For Brill, cases of male homosexuality not produced by the absence of female companions, as in prison, were the result of an arrested development—usually because the mother or father failed to fulfill a proper role in the oedipal process. Brill followed Freud in claiming that "before the age of puberty the sexual feelings are usually unspecialized."[14] The male child was supposed to pass through the inversion phase on the path to finally choosing a female object. The homosexual was someone who, for several reasons—perhaps the absence of a parent, or a particularly cruel father, or a smothering mother—failed to reach the normal heterosexual stage.

Brill's essay is striking not so much in its now-familiar analysis of the possible causes of homosexuality in the male as in its further claim that homosexuality may be present in any number of neurotic conditions that the layman would never identify with deviant sexuality: "Every neurosis regularly shows some admixture of inversion, and during the analysis of a hysteria or compulsion neurosis one invariably finds some heterosexual and some homosexual roots."[15] A year later, Trigant Burrow, a colleague of Brill's who had studied with Carl Jung in Switzerland, read a paper before the American Psychoanalytic Association in which he declared that "latent homosexuality enters so universally into the repression that underlies neurotic disorders as to be practically synonymous with a neurosis."[16] The key word is *latent;* that is to say, those unconscious desires that the patient represses but that are expressed in his neurotic symptoms. Because of the latency of the patient's homosexual attractions, neither he nor his family and friends suspect that his neuroses might have an origin in homosexuality. According to the psychoanalytic model, homosexuality was not necessarily betrayed by obvious attributes, or even by sexual experiences with partners of the same sex. Sometimes even the psychoanalyst had difficulty diagnosing such cases. Brill writes: "Strange as it may seem, the diagnosis of homosexuality is not always an easy matter. In the first place it must be urged that a sporadic homosexual act does not necessarily mean homosexuality, nor does the absence of such acts signify heterosexuality. There is naturally no difficulty when one is confronted with an absolute invert who acknowledges his inversion. There are, however, a number of inverts who are really ignorant of their inversion."[17]

Brill's tone of tolerance and sympathy for homosexuals contrasted sharply with most previous writings by American medical authorities, yet his conclusion that homosexual desire might be hidden in a myriad of human relationships oddly mirrored the popular fear that the child, and even the adult, might slip into inversion. Built into the Freudian model of sexual development was the idea that the choice of sexual object was not a given—that it was socially determined and that any child had the potential to become a homosexual. The path to what Freud or Brill would have called normal sexuality, that is, heterosexuality, was dangerous—at any point in development the child might falter or be waylaid, although that early traumatic experience might not surface until years later. Perversions were constantly asserting themselves. In one of Freud's most famous formulas, he claimed that the "neuroses are, so to say, the negative of perversions."[18] The neurotic's symptoms—a tic, a paralysis, an inability to drink—were always the result of a sublimation of perverse desires which, because of "disgust" induced by social norms, could not be expressed directly. Such perversions almost always carried with them an element of homosexuality. And so homosexuality permeated the society, not in the form of obvious "pansies" who cruised the waterfront, but as an uncontrollable desire embedded in the unconscious, a desire to which anyone might be subject.

Brill's essay on homosexuality, based on Freud's *Three Essays on the Theory of Sexuality,* was crucially different from earlier discussions by American doctors in another important respect. By focusing on homosexuality as an object choice, that is, as a form of love, the Freudian point of view emphasized the similarity between homosexual and heterosexual attachments. Whereas earlier writers had viewed homosexuality as an extreme perversion and had therefore emphasized genital acts, or in some cases invented an entirely new kind of human being to explain inversion, psychoanalysts spoke of homosexuality as part of the great question of the dynamics of loving. In Freud's scheme of things, homosexuality and heterosexuality were not opposites—heterosexuality in fact contained the experience of an earlier homosexual period. Both were essential components of that Freudian struggle called the "family romance." Psychoanalysis, in focusing on the invert's re-creation of oedipal relationships in his attachment to companions of his own sex—in much the same manner as heterosexuals—brought the homosexual back into the orbit of everyday life. In a footnote to the 1910 edition of *Three Essays,* Freud wrote:

> Psychoanalytic research is most decidedly opposed to any attempt at separating off homosexuals from the rest of mankind as a group of a special character. By studying sexual excitations other than those that are manifestly displayed, it has found that all human beings are capable of making a homosexual object-choice and have in fact made one in their unconscious. Indeed, libidinal attachments to persons of the same sex play no less a part as factors in normal mental life, and a greater part as a motive force for illness, than do similar attachments to the opposite sex.[19]

In addition to the link between inversion and neurosis, even socially sanctioned behavior could be traced back to homosexual desire: for example, an ability to lead men in war or a hero's much-admired willingness to sacrifice his life for fellow soldiers on the battlefield could be attributed to sublimation of sexual attraction to males.

Freud's theories on sexuality thus served to question the idea of the homosexual as a clearly definable type. Although his theories challenged the stereotype of inversion as a problem of misplaced bodies—of women in the bodies of men and men in the bodies of women—they only increased the popular anxiety about the contagiousness of homosexuality.

If trained psychoanalysts like Brill were often uncertain of the diagnosis of inversion, how was the layman to identify the homosexual? What did he look like? The answer, according to the Freudians, would be that he looks like anyone else. Other medical authorities, however, insisted that distinct physical differences existed. From the late nineteenth century until the 1930s, various "scientific" evidence was presented to demonstrate the distinct body differences between homosexual and heterosexual men. As late as 1934 the prestigious *Psychiatric Quarterly* published an article by George W. Henry, who claimed that "the homosexual male is characterized by a feminine carrying angle of the arm, long legs, narrow hips, large muscles, deficient hair on the face, chest and back, feminine distribution of pubic hair, a high-pitched voice, small penis and testicles and the presence of a scrotal fold. Not uncommonly there is an excess of soft fat on the shoulder, buttocks and at the girdle." Oddly enough, Henry adds later—in contradiction to what comes before—that "occasionally the penis is very large and the hips are unusually wide."[20]

Edward J. Kempf's *Psychopathology* actually included a series of photographs that supposedly illustrate what he calls "homosexual panic," which he defines as "the pressure of uncontrollable perverse sexual cravings."[21] The cravings he has in mind are fellatio and anal intercourse with someone of the same sex. Kempf's patients betray their desires not merely in their confessions to him but in their facial and body features. But according to Kempf these subtle qualities cannot be adequately described and are best revealed in an image: "It requires genius to convey an accurate idea with drawings, painting or sculpture, hence descriptions by words, far more difficult, is beyond reach of the average psychiatrist."[22] Lacking such artistic ability,

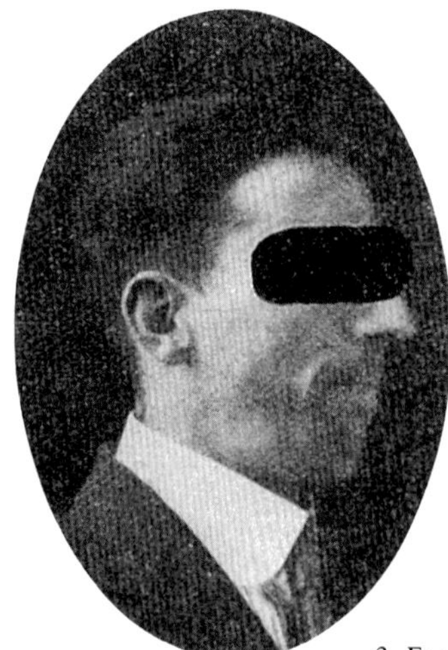

3. From Edward J. Kempf, *Psychopathology* (St. Louis: C.V. Mosby Co., 1921), fig. 81, p. 724.

Kempf falls back on the photograph to document homosexual panic. In a typical image (fig. 3), a man is shown in profile with his eyes blacked out. There is nothing unusual about the face except for a certain stiffness so often detectable in posed photographs. The profile format of the medical photograph, in its similarity to the mug shot taken by police, confers guilt irrespective of the man's features. But it is Kempf's caption—"The tensions about the mouth show tremendous striving as a defence against oral eroticism"—that labels this as the portrait of a deviant.[23]

Despite its status as evidence, the photograph reveals not the homosexual but the words of the "expert." Without the caption and the context of the medical textbook, the image of the young man is meaningless. Like many medical and legal authorities at the first part of the twentieth century, Dr. Kempf is confident that he is able to recognize the homosexual and that his features and mannerism allow him to be classified with precision. Essential to Kempf's construction is that the homosexual, independent of his actions, can be spotted. His peculiar stance, or the odd way he stares, or the tightness of his smile can be photographed or rendered into paint or stone by an artist of genius. Yet, clearly, homosexuality is not in Kempf's images but in the discourse that surrounds them—the caption, the text, and the wider medical and legal debate on the definition of homosexuality. The doctor's certainty that the homosexual betrays his sexuality in his image is less a matter of evidence—his photographs seem absurdly empty of anything like scientific evidence—than a symptom of a desire to be able to separate out homosexuality from the normal. But it is the very inappropriateness of Kempf's certainty that provides the point of greatest interest. Given all the conflicting descriptions and arguments, why are the experts so often confident they know "the homosexual"? Why are the diverse interactions, emotions, features, gestures, and voices of *homosexualities* so often replaced with rigid classification schemes and stereotypes?

Mary Douglas provides one answer. In her important study *Purity and Danger* she discusses the role of deviancy in both maintaining and threatening social boundaries. For Douglas, a culture's designation of a group of actions as deviant may arise from its need to establish clear order. To designate certain actions as acceptable or normal, it is necessary to know what is not acceptable, what is abnormal. The perception of the pattern of social ritual is dependent on a sense of disorder, on what the pattern leaves out. Although it is an old trope that the existence of widespread deviancy, particularly homosexuality, foreshadows the collapse of the social order (a classic example might be Edward Gibbon's analysis of the decline of the Roman Empire), the bounding of groups into clear "others" may instead be a sign that the mechanisms of social control are functioning well. Deviancy poses a true threat to the social structure only when it does not maintain its position outside the normal system—when it cannot easily be classified. Douglas writes: "Danger lies in transitional states, simply because transition is neither one state nor the next, it is undefinable. The person who must pass from one to another is himself in danger and emanates danger to others. The danger is controlled by ritual which precisely separates him from his old status, segregates him for a time and then publicly declares his entry to his new status."[24] Although Douglas uses examples from so-called primitive cultures or ancient societies, she is quick to suggest the relevance of her observation for modern society, speaking of the difficulty prisoners or mentally ill people have in returning to society after their confinement. The marginalization of homosexuality seems to follow this same pattern in early twentieth-century America. As long as the gay male was either secret about his sexuality or declared it in certain extreme and obvious situations, thereby mediating it through ritualized behavior, society was able to deal with his existence without upsetting its systems of social control. The more indeterminate his nature and social place, the more dangerous the homosexual became to societal boundaries.

Applying Douglas's theory, we might say that homosexuality was particularly threatening to early twentieth-century society not because it was such an obviously different mode of being, but because among variant forms of sexuality it was the one that most closely conformed to the heterosexual model. Regardless of the horrified tone of so many of the doctors who recorded case histories of homosexuals from this period, gay men then (and still) make love in much the same way that heterosexual couples do. (In fact the language of certain homosexual subcultures between the wars often mimicked the language of heterosexuality—for example, through the epithets that designated one partner male and one partner female during the sexual encounter.) The danger of homosexuality may have resided not in its otherness but in its not being other enough. Oddly enough, the very formation of visible homosexual subcultures at the end of the nineteenth century, which was so important for creating a gay identity and later the gay civil rights movement, was in part a result of the buttressing of the dominant culture's sense of its own order. At the same time that the ghettoizing of homosexual experiences contained the potential for group identification and protest, it also allowed society to point to particular persons with the certainty that they were other, and to particular places with the certainty that that was where the others went. The centrality of essential rituals like the marriage vows—and the sense that came with them of the nuclear family being not so much a social convention as something arising from that peculiar imperative, the "natural"—all this was dependent on an ability to recognize the marginal and to know where it lived. And so, in this crucial issue of sexuality, the culture seemed to be turned in on itself, outlawing homosexuality, refusing to name its practices in the press or see its presence in daily life, all the time creating "the homosexual" through the elaborate system of punishments and segregation—the very system that was meant to protect the naturalness of familial institutions.

2 The Homosexual Point of View

At the turn of the century, medical experts were clearly bewildered about the defining characteristics of the homosexual. Yet this confusion did not seem to conflict with the creation of precise descriptions of the supposedly typical homosexual. Confusion, rather than limiting representation, seemed to increase the need for distinct images of what an inverted man looked like. But what did homosexuals themselves think of the medical stereotypes? For the most part I have discussed the attitudes of those who presumably considered themselves outside the community of inverts. Given the authoritative tone of many medical writers on the subject, it is remarkable how little the experts knew of the day-to-day life of homosexuals. The recent biography of Havelock Ellis by Phyllis Grosskurth, for example, suggests that Ellis had very little firsthand experience with male homosexuals. He based his famous book *Sexual Inversion* mostly on case histories gathered by his collaborator, John Addington Symonds, with the help of Edward Carpenter.[1] This study, which became one of the standard references on the subject until the appearance of Kinsey's work in the 1940s, was initially based on only thirty-three case histories, with no attempt to ensure that they were a representative sampling. Freud's theories on sexual variations relied on even less direct experience—indeed, Freud repeatedly cited Ellis as an authority.[2]

In *The Intermediate Sex,* the famous defense of homosexuality written in 1908, Edward Carpenter warned of the danger of relying on information culled from the doctor's office: "It must never be forgotten that the medico-scientific enquirer is bound on the whole to meet with those cases that *are* of a morbid character, rather than with those that are healthy in their manifestation, since indeed it is the former that he lays himself out for."[3] One of the difficulties involved in writing the history of homosexuality is being forced to rely on this very kind of data—information drawn from the stories of people who considered themselves, and were believed to be, mentally ill. A patient who sought to cure his perversity through the help of a psychiatrist was a highly *unusual person* in the United States of the period between 1910 and 1940.

Fortunately, a few homosexual men wrote directly of their experiences and described the various subcultures built around homosexual lives. But in reading these documents we have to be equally cautious, always keeping in mind that, given the elaborate moral and legal restrictions on the frank discussion of sexuality, and particularly homosexuality, these works were also deeply peculiar. Often privately printed, or published in limited editions carefully restricted for the edification of medical and legal experts, they were extraordinary exceptions to the silence imposed on most gay men and women. By no means can they be taken as definitive views of the homosexual experience at the turn of the century.

Probably the most remarkable discussion of homosexual life to appear before World War I was *The Intersexes: A History of Similisexualism as a Problem in Social Life.* Written in 1908 by the obscure American novelist Edward Stevenson, under the pseudonym of Xavier Mayne, the book is an attempt at an exhaustive survey of contemporary male and female homosexual life in Europe and the United States. Although claiming scientific objectivity, *The Intersexes* is really a passionate defense of classes of men and women Stevenson considered to be third and fourth sexes. According to the author, "intersexes" were halfway between male and female. Stevenson's approach is pseudoscholarly, however, for although much of his material can be presumed to come from firsthand experience of homosexual life, he just as often relies on previous scientific texts. On occasion he quotes Krafft-Ebing's *Psychopathia Sexualis,* and his favorite terms were first coined by the sexologist Karl Ulrichs: "uranian" for male homosexuals and "uraniad" for females. His citations of late nineteenth-century scientific and psychiatric authorities are interspersed with excerpts from novels that Stevenson feels have "uranistic" themes, along with discussions of the work and lives of alleged homosexual geniuses of the past.

For Stevenson, the intersexes, practitioners of what he calls "similisexualism," are defined not by physical characteristics but by instincts, their psychic and sexual desire for those of the same sex. They are therefore hard to separate from the crowd: "These Intersexes are not physically obvious in the frank degree that we have foolishly expected such natural differences would be expressed. . . . They are the less perceived because their physical differences from the one or the other removed sex toward which they incline, but to which they do not attain, are not necessarily readily visible. Their subtle separation from their Over-sex [heterosexuals] begins at a deeper plane, on that alone, constantly—the psychological, not physical."[4] In stressing the psychological over the physical Stevenson is purposely countering the popular view of the male homosexual as obviously effeminate.

Probably Stevenson's emphasis on desire as opposed to physical attributes would have contradicted many of the assumptions made by members of his own homosexual community. For example, George Chauncey reports that gay men in Newport had an elaborate system for tagging their members. Descriptive names like "pogues," "straight," and "browned" were clearly based on sexual position and gender characteristics.[5] Earl Lind's *Autobiography of an Androgyne,* one of the few American sources besides Stevenson's written by a homosexual insider, has a classification scheme based on traditional concepts of masculinity and femininity. Lind goes along with Stevenson in claiming that there exists "no sharp dividing line between the sexes" and that the "two sexes gradually merge into each other"; but when he describes the transition from sex to sex in specific terms, a set of utterly traditional distinctions reasserts itself: "At the masculine pole stand the warrior, the blue-jacket, the pugilist, etc., and it was only such, the tremendously virile, who possess no gentle or feminine traits at all, to whom your author was ordinarily attracted. Further down the male side of the scale, after the man of adventure and sport, come, successively, the stevedore and his like, the manual laborer, and the merchant." Lind creates a hierarchy of masculinity in which the virility of men is rated according to their occupation and their social class. The more a man's livelihood is dependent on his hands, the more securely he represents the extreme masculine sex. Education, good grooming, and wealth are taken to be qualities of an ambiguous sexuality. The signs of an upper-class upbringing become confused with the signs of homosexuality. The scholar, for example, possesses "only a comparatively low degree of masculinity and virility."[6] Predictably, the closer a man's pursuit to the province of women, the more likely he is to be a true invert, as with the male dressmaker. For Lind, actual homosexual encounters do not affect masculinity. Having sex with a self-acknowledged "fairy" like Lind does not endanger the status of the truly virile man. Generally, a man's occupation and demeanor are more important than his sexual experience in determining his sexuality.

Even Stevenson ends up contradicting his assertion that inverts are no different physically from heterosexuals. He catalogues what he calls "minor bodily peculiarities," which are typical of uranians: "They include delicacy of the osseous structure: breadth of buttocks and pelvis: conical thighs; and a general roundness and softness of the corporeal outlines. Grace rather than strength is noticeable. The breast tends to curve, after the feminine mould: there is often a decided contour to the bosom suggesting female breasts."[7] Despite Stevenson's insistence that homosexuality is a matter of a deeply rooted sexual drive and not a result of the form of the body, the powerful stereotype that all inverts are physically effeminate permeates his description of the typical homosexual.

Again we have opposing opinions—this time in the same document—as to the possibility of detecting the homosexual merely from physical characteristics. Perhaps Stevenson ends up negating his own assertion that the invert appears and acts no differently from anyone else because he accepts from the outset the category "homosexual." After all, if the homosexual type is not in some way distinctive, he will be invisible not only to those who share his sexual tastes but to the author as well. He must therefore fall back on the idea that the experts, in this case other similisexualists, can recognize fellow travelers by their walks and their gazes.

The Signs of Homosexuality

How are we to recognize the presence of homosexuality in works of art if homosexuals themselves were unable to agree on the signs of their sexuality? The job is further complicated by the fact that one of the prevalent modes of being homosexual in America between the wars was to appear *not* to be a homosexual. For a homosexual artist to make a painting about the experience of his subculture was to risk public exposure. Certain artists took that risk, but just as often the representation of homosexuality in American painting followed the model of society at large—that is, it was veiled. Paintings about homosexuality made use of certain disguises that were meant to be uncovered only by a particular audience.

Of course, in images like Demuth's *Three Sailors on the Beach* the homosexual content is not disguised at all. Homosexuality is expressed in the most direct way possible: by showing men having sex with each other. Hiding here was a matter of keeping the watercolor from the public. The questions a picture like this raises —How did it come to be painted? What is its relationship to other works in the artist's oeuvre? What did it mean to the artist? How does it connect to aspects of homosexual life in the 1930s?—are distinct from the question of whether the picture represents some sort of homosexual practice. In this sense, the most obvious sign for homosexuality is the depiction of a homosexual act. Yet relatively few of Demuth's watercolors that concern homosexuality are as blatant as *Three Sailors on the Beach.* Whereas the poses in this painting allow for no confusion about content, in Demuth's earlier series depicting a Turkish bath the viewer frequently has to decode the sexual message inscribed in the images. No doubt in the most famous of the works, the *Turkish Bath Scene with Self-Portrait* of 1918 (fig. 4), the erotic content is fairly explicit. Any ambiguity about the nature of the encounter in this peculiar self-portrait has to do with the nature of the institution in which the men are meeting. Bathhouses and public showers were plentiful in major urban centers during a period when many people could not afford private washing facilities. Although they were not, by and large, the gay sexual institutions of the pre-AIDS 1970s and 1980s, a few baths in New York City were notorious as meeting places for sex. According to one source, just such a place, the Lafayette Baths (not to be confused with the Lafayette Hotel), was the location of Demuth's Turkish bath series.[8]

Kermit Champa, in his 1974 article "Charlie Was Like That," finds Demuth's watercolors from the 1910s sexual but not "distinctly homosexual."[9] Indeed, it was not unheard of for artists of Demuth's time to depict images of men bathing. Advocating the building of public institutions at a time when the urban poor were often

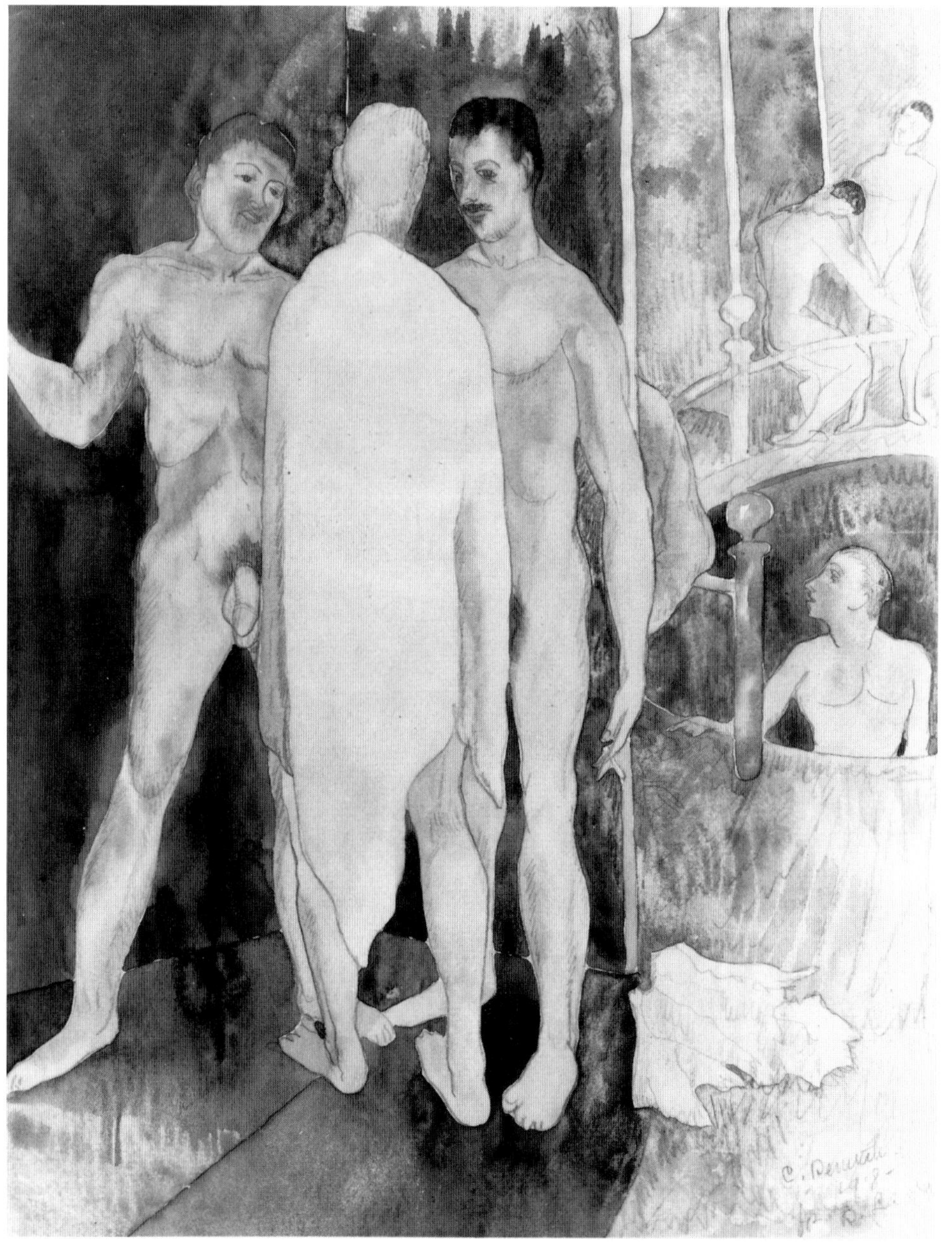

4. Charles Demuth, *Turkish Bath Scene with Self-Portrait,* watercolor and pencil on paper, $10\frac{15}{16} \times 8\frac{9}{16}$ in., 1918. Private collection.

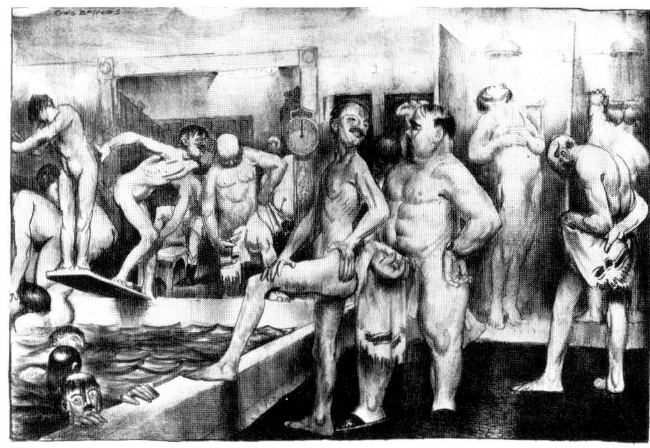

5. George Bellows, *Shower Bath* (first state), lithograph, 16 1/16 × 23 7/8 in., 1917. Amon Carter Museum, Fort Worth, Tex.

without the benefit of decent plumbing was a major part of the philanthropic movement of the turn of the century. This same movement resulted in the building of YMCAs in most of the cities of the United States, providing even more public spaces where men of different backgrounds might find themselves swimming and showering together. George Bellows, who frequently scanned the American scene for opportunities to paint nudes in realistic, practical situations that justified a lack of clothing, thought indoor public bathing interesting enough to merit a lithograph, *Shower Bath* (fig. 5). Milton Brown suggests that Bellows was popular because he was not a "sickly, sensitive, philandering bohemian, incompetent and outside the pale of normal society"—that is, he was not homosexual.[10] And Brown is right: *The Shower Bath* is determined to have nothing to do with clandestine sexuality but instead to report on the increasing democratization of American life at the beginning of the twentieth century.

The very suspicion that a given image of a public bath may have something to do with homosexuality derives from "insider" information on the viewer's part; and in various cases—Bellows's print, for example—the information may not be known, or if it is, may not be applied. It may well be that in 1918 few people besides homosexuals and members of law enforcement agencies knew that certain bathhouses provided the opportunity for gay men to have sexual liaisons. Stevenson wrote in *The Intersexes* that almost every major urban center in Europe and America had at least one such bathhouse. He described an institution located somewhere in Central Europe in great detail:

> On entrance, the first detail of striking suggestiveness, is the huge piscina full of tepid water. On special days of the week, such as Sundays and holidays, it is also full of a most mixed multitude of homosexuals, all naked (the ironical towel being made into an equation of nothing) and all immersed in the water up to their shoulders—decorously enough. All are promenading together, in a sort of friendly *cotillion;* their hands kept under water, not for swimming, but for—mutual investigations, which are to be expected when one enters the pool.[11]

According to Stevenson, in most of Europe and in the United States, homosexual bathhouses were more often places to make sexual contacts rather than to perform sexual acts: "In Paris, are at least a dozen baths that are homosexual rendezvous. Five or six are of wide popularity. In London, is a small group well-recognized. New York has several. But these, as most others, cannot be utilized, then and there, for homosexual practices. They are merely establishments for—anatomic inspections; for making appointments to meet elsewhere—some near hotels, for example."[12] However, Stevenson's assertion that men did not actually have sex in New York City baths may not hold true. In 1929, a German visitor was unlucky enough to be at the Lafayette Baths when the police staged a raid. He wrote about having sex in a room: "At about ten-thirty I go up to the dormitory and looked for a bed. Chance brings me together with a young, racy Sicilian. Unfortunately, we hadn't noticed that there were eight detectives among the customers of the baths. . . . Now it's midnight, and I'm already asleep, my friend at my side."[13] Demuth's painting is dated 1918—midway between Stevenson's observation and the German tourist's report—so we cannot be certain what activities were actually taking place at the Lafayette Baths at the time. Relying to a larger degree on Stevenson's claim that actual sexual encounters did not occur in New York baths, Koskovich feels that the viewer of Demuth's *Turkish Bath Scene with Self-Portrait* would not necessarily jump to the conclusion that what was being shown was a sexual encounter. He sees Demuth's image as purposely ambiguous and in effect conceives it as speaking to two separate audiences—heterosexuals, who would simply see a scene of naked men preparing to bathe, and homosexuals, who would suspect other possibilities. Although I agree that an image of the baths does not necessarily have to be about homosexuality, when faced with Demuth's *Turkish Bath Scene with Self-Portrait,* the viewer in 1918 would have had to shut his or her eyes tightly to miss many of the telltale signs of sexual liaison.

When we compare Bellows's lithograph with Demuth's watercolor, the point becomes clear. Whereas Bellows's middle-aged figures stand around drying themselves with little sense of self-consciousness, uninterested in their nakedness, the three central characters in Demuth's painting are turned in upon one another as if for some secret purpose. The central figure, completely wrapped in a towel—itself a sign of covering up—is placed so that we cannot tell whether his two companions are actually fondling each other. Yet if we look at the floor we can see that the feet of all three men touch or just barely touch. Although the peculiar unwritten rules of heterosexual male bonding allow for a whole range of physical contacts—a hand on the shoulder, even in certain circumstances a good-natured slap on the behind—the touching of bare feet is not among the acceptable intimacies of straight American men. Furthermore, in stark contrast to Bellows's *Shower Bath,* where the genitals of the men are all discreetly hidden by various, seemingly random poses, the penis of the redheaded figure on the left is emphasized beyond the bounds of propriety, while the towel dropped at the feet may suggest that his mustached companion (the self-portrait) has just exposed himself to the man with his back to us. In the lithograph by Bellows we can account for the actions of all the central characters: two are about to jump into the pool; one dries his body; several are in the pool or taking showers. At the center of the crowded gym a couple converses as if they do not care who hears. How are we to explain the figures in the background of Demuth's watercolor? In the far right corner, on the other side of the pool, a naked man almost kneels before his standing companion in a pose that can only be construed as fellatio. In the middle ground a fellow stares up from the water at the buttocks of a bending figure. Finally, there are the extraordinary red washes Demuth uses to color the central figures, which give their bodies an unnatural, almost sinister cast. It is clear that we are faced not with an innocent encounter but with the performance or planning of an act that is forbidden by the prevailing legal and moral standards of the society.

For all of Bellows's supposed realism—his honesty in depicting the sagging flesh of the bodies of the middle-aged men who frequented the Y—his image is still in the tradition of the male nude. The bent figure on the diving board is a direct quotation of the *Diskobolus,* and the assembly as a whole is surely meant to recall Michelangelo's *Battle of Cascina.* Indeed, the humor of his *Shower Bath* depends on the absurdity of such pedestrian bodies inadvertently taking classical poses. Bellows's iconoclasm is still dependent on icons of Western art. But Demuth's naked men do not take up the provided poses of action, rest, pain, and exhaustion drawn from the realm of battle, sport, or mythological erotic play. The refusal of the classical makes the figures of *Turkish Bath Scene with Self-Portrait* seem stiff and ungainly, but they also seem new. Demuth tentatively finds his way toward a male eroticism that is not manufactured out of the ideal but is instead based on watching the way a particular subculture interacts.

A final indication of the overt homosexual content in the bath series was Demuth's decision not to exhibit *Turkish Bath Scene with Self-Portrait,* even though it was highly finished and, as studies for the central figures suggest, Demuth took considerable care working out its composition.[14] Indeed, long after Demuth's death, the picture was thought to be scandalous. Darell Larsen, a Lancaster stage director and teacher who obtained the work directly from Demuth, supposedly kept the picture in a closet because he felt its subject was too explicit for mixed company.[15]

Encoding Ambiguity

Apart from Bellows's lithograph, the works we have looked at so far have all shown men in various states of nudity involved in some kind of sexual relationship. But is it possible to represent homosexuality without showing men having or about to have sex? Three other works by Demuth illustrate the problem. The *Eight O'Clock* series focuses on the interactions of a group of men in the city. Presumably the first of the set is *Eight O'Clock (Evening)* (fig. 6), now in the Wadsworth Atheneum. It depicts two men being served tea by a butler, while a third man

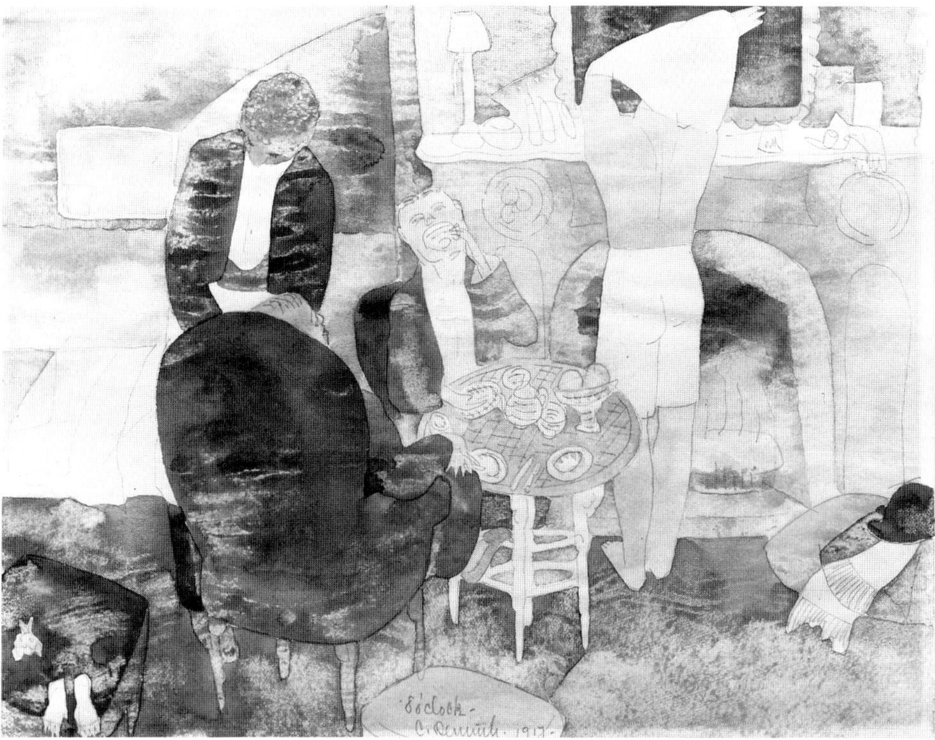

6. Charles Demuth, *Eight O'Clock (Evening),* watercolor and pencil on paper, 8 × 10⅜ in., 1917. Wadsworth Atheneum, Hartford, Conn.; gift of George J. Dyer.

in boxer shorts is either putting on or taking off his undershirt. The subject of this genre piece would appear to be friends in a hotel room or an apartment preparing for a night on the town. When the work is compared with the other two watercolors in the series, its meaning is less clear. In *Eight O'Clock (Morning #1)* (fig. 7, pl. 3), now in the Lobell collection, a man in a light pink suit or pajamas sits on a bed with his head in his hands while his companion, again in boxer shorts and undershirt, holds out his hands as if for money. In the background a nude man washes himself at a sink. The sense of despair on the face of the man on the bed and the demanding ges-

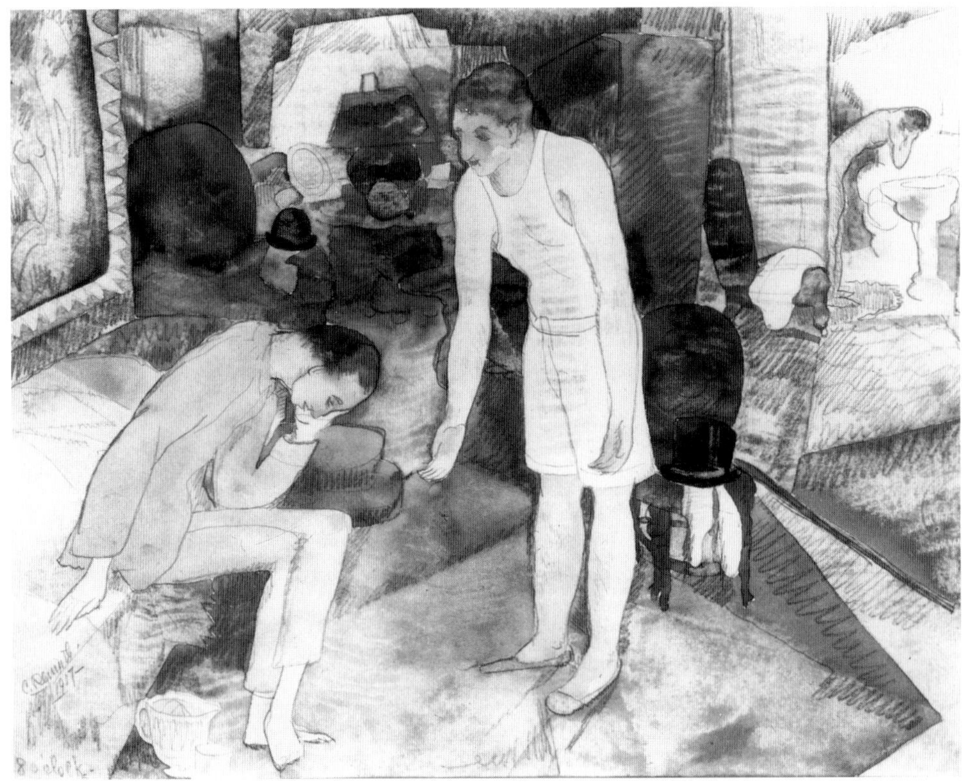

7. Charles Demuth, *Eight O'Clock (Morning #1),* watercolor and pencil on paper, 8 × 10¼ in., 1917. Collection of Mr. and Mrs. Carl D. Lobell.

ture of the semiclothed standing figure suggest a settling of accounts between a male prostitute and his client. A different version—*Eight O'Clock (Morning #2)* (fig. 8), in the Wadsworth Atheneum—focuses on a man in the process of dressing. His boxer shorts and undershirt suggest that he may be the possible male prostitute of the Lobell version. Also, as in the previous version, there is a naked figure washing, this time in a bath, again in the background.

A constant between the morning and evening drawings is the assorted men's furnishing placed about the room. In all three watercolors, a black bowler and a scarf are lying on a chair. Both versions of *Eight O'Clock (Morning)* add a top hat and a cane. In contrast to the elegant tea of the *Eight O'Clock (Evening),* the watercolors of the morning show the room to be in great disarray. Although the bowler, scarf, and gloves are neatly placed at night, in the morning, clothes are strewn about the apartment. The series is about a process of disrobing—from the mostly clothed gentlemen of the evening to the mostly naked figures of the morning. Whatever happened between 8 P.M. and 8 A.M., Demuth's *Morning* watercolors are surely meant to be about a morning after.

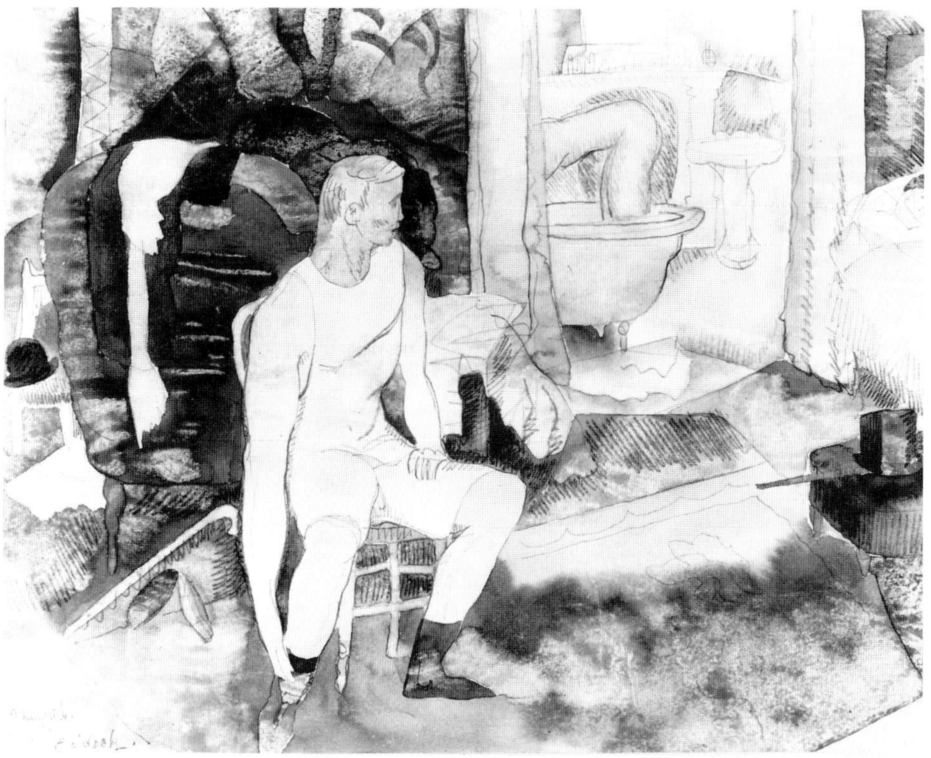

8. Charles Demuth, *Eight O'Clock (Morning #2),* watercolor and pencil on paper, 7⅞ × 10³⁄₁₆ in., 1917. Wadsworth Atheneum, Hartford, Ct.; Philip L. Goodwin Collection.

In a sense the *Eight O'Clock* series implies a narrative while purposely withholding the necessary clues to understanding the story completely. The continuity of title and characters asks us to find possible explanations for the relationships described in the watercolors, but those relationships remain ambiguous. If the work is about some kind of homosexual encounter, that homosexuality is somewhat masked by a possible alternative scenario that seems to offer the figures' states of undress as no more than the allowable intimacies of heterosexual men bedding down in close quarters. Of course, ignoring the possible homosexual content involves desexualizing the comparison of clothed and unclothed bodies that is at the center of Demuth's odd paintings. I suspect that such a desexualization would be impossible if Demuth's image were of women. In fact, a work like *Eight O'Clock (Morning #2),* with its men in the process of disrobing or watching others disrobe, is clearly related to works by Degas in which women, presumably prostitutes, are attending to their toilette (in particular, the background figure bent over in a tub in *Eight O'Clock [Morning #2]* is derived from Degas's bather series). Degas's nudes have been considered in terms of how they reproduce (and perhaps subvert) the gaze of the client over the seductive domain of the boudoir.[16] Whether Degas identifies with or despises his subject has been the subject of much argument (why not both?). Yet few critics deny that Degas's depictions of women undressing are images of sexual desire.

Paradoxically, the very homosexuality of Demuth's *Eight O'Clock* series was perhaps obscured in its time by its all-male cast. Given the heightened awareness of homosexuality in recent years, it may seem difficult to see the relationships described in Demuth's work as ambiguous. Barbara Haskell, for example, takes it for granted that the painting implies "homoerotic activity about to happen or having already occurred."[17] But most Americans in 1917 would not have seen in male-to-male intimacy even the possibility of a sexual relationship. By exhibiting *Eight O'Clock (Morning #2),* Demuth counted on the average American's inability to read homosexuality into men's interactions. The seeming innocence of the series was confirmed when *Eight O'Clock (Morning #1)* was purchased by such a respectable collector as Mrs. John D. Rockefeller.[18]

Making an image about homosexuality without showing obvious homosexual acts is clearly problematic in a culture that normally looks for sexuality only in terms of male and female coupling. Whether the standing figure in *Eight O'Clock (Morn-*

ing #1) is reaching out his hand for payment of sexual services rendered or for repayment of a gambling debt depends more on the expectations of its audience than on the information contained in the painting. It is probable that the paintings would have a different meaning for homosexuals than it would for those unfamiliar with the way certain young men in New York or Paris spend their nights. In fact, the very invisibility of the homosexual content for the majority of its viewers allowed the clandestine subject matter to be seen by an intended few without fear of repercussions.

Ambiguity functions in the *Eight O'Clock* paintings and, to a lesser degree, in the Turkish bath series as a kind of filter, allowing the initiated into a world of forbidden pleasures, while locking out those who know nothing about such practices. By initiated, I do not mean simply other homosexuals but, rather, those who shared some of the same spaces with the various homosexual subcultures—the motley group of intellectuals, artists, eccentric patrons, and hangers-on that made up the community of avant-garde life in such places as New York, Provincetown, and expatriate Paris.

Homosexual Love without Sex

If we agree that the *Eight O'Clock* series is about homosexuality, then it joins the Turkish bath series in signifying sexual acts about to happen or just finished. To the degree that these works can be taken to represent homosexuality, they do so by conveying the potentiality of sex. But is it possible to represent homosexuality without depicting sexual relationships or their imminence?

Marsden Hartley's *Christ Held by Half-Naked Men* (fig. 9, pl. 5), painted at the end of his career, is a rare work in which the love of men for men is expressed without representing specific sexual acts. Hartley's painting is an all-male pietà. At the center, Christ lies cradled in the arms of a bare-chested lobsterman. Christ's small bearded head is grossly out of scale with his muscular body and with the powerful frame of the man who holds him. In the background are seven more lobstermen, all without shirts. They wear the distinctive hat of the Nova Scotia fishermen among whom Hartley lived in his last years. Even the dying Christ holds one of these hats in his limp hand.

This recasting of Christian iconography is one of a series painted by Hart-

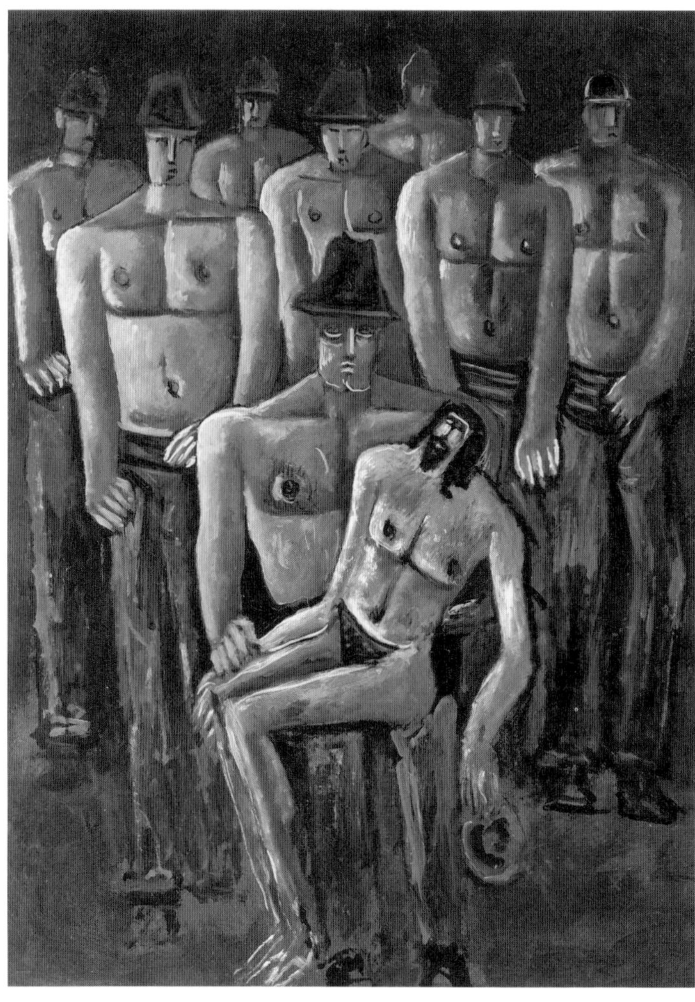

9. Marsden Hartley, *Christ Held by Half-Naked Men,* oil on fiberboard, 40 × 30 in., 1940–41. Hirshhorn Museum and Sculpture Garden, Smithsonian Institution, Washington, D.C.

ley between 1937 and 1944 to memorialize the death of two members of the Mason family, with whom he lived as a boarder in Nova Scotia. Hartley became particularly infatuated with one of their grown sons, Alty, whose tragic death at sea became the central subject of his late paintings and poetry. Yet the details of Hartley's love for Alty, which I shall discuss at length later, are not necessary to unravel the homosexual content of *Christ Held by Half-Naked Men*. Hartley's painting is an extreme example of the reversal of gender to express homosexuality. We have already seen in Demuth's *Eight O'Clock* paintings how such reversals can have different meanings depending on the viewer's expectations. In *Christ Held by Half-Naked Men* the transformation of Mary into a rugged fisherman removes much of the ambiguity. No doubt there are plenty of situations in which the absence of women registers as no more than an acceptable variant, but a pietà is not one of them: here absence reads strongly as displacement, not to say exclusion. Although critics have suggested that the modern all-male cast is an allusion to the twelve apostles, it is significant that Hartley has painted only seven figures in the background.[19] Furthermore, readings that focus only on the spiritual aspects of the painting miss Hartley's emphasis on the male body. Hartley certainly wanted to draw a connection between the modern fishermen whom he had come to know in Nova Scotia and the fisher of souls in the New Testament, but he also wanted to acknowledge his attraction to the male body. The exposed chests of the fishermen with their exaggerated musculature, seemingly so inappropriate to a pietà, combined with the conscious removal of females, focuses the meaning of the painting on the kind of physical relationships usually excluded from Christian dogma. The recasting of this iconic theme in such an original fashion is in itself a breach of acceptable norms, approaching the blasphemous and the parodic.

In the overt expression of homosexual love in *Christ Held by Half-Naked Men,* Hartley seems to have departed completely from the complex coding of the *Portrait of a German Officer* touched on earlier. Marsden Hartley's 1914 painting can be taken as an attempt to express his love for another man while precluding any sense of contact between two male bodies. (In a literal, "biographical" sense, death had already eliminated the possibility of such contact in Hartley's *Portrait of a German Officer* because the officer in question, Karl von Freyburg, had already been killed.)

Whereas *Christ Held by Half-Naked Men* is the work of an artist in old age, seemingly no longer worried about offending his audience, *Portrait of a German Officer* is a perfect example of homosexuality appearing and not appearing in a work of art. Its system of coding—the initials K.v.F. for Freyburg's name, the number 24 for Freyburg's age at death, the epaulet shaped like an E for Marsden Hartley's given name—mirrors to some degree the obligation homosexuals felt to devise elaborate masks to hide their sexuality and feelings in most daily interchanges. Whereas Demuth's *Eight O'Clock* watercolors rely on society's general willingness to desexualize male relationships, Hartley hides the homosexual subtheme of this work from most viewers through private symbolic language and abstract style. It is probable that in 1914 only a handful of Hartley's close friends would have guessed at the significance of the symbols in the painting. Of course, to some extent the radical form of the painting obscured all meanings—at least to American eyes. In its synthesis of cubist space and German-expressionist paint handling, Hartley's *Portrait of a German Officer* was the most advanced painting (by modernist standards) by an American up until that time. As I shall argue later, it may be no coincidence that Hartley's work reaches its most abstract stage when he attempts to express his love for another man and his fascination with German uniforms. The very modernism of the work hides the potential explosive effects of its subject matter. Indeed, largely because of their radical abstractness the military portraits were mostly ignored in the New York art world, and Hartley, rather than continue to risk denunciation for glorifying German aggression after America joined World War I, moved on to less controversial themes.

The Red Tie

Finding the homosexual content in Hartley's paintings from 1913 to 1915 is a matter of deciphering a code, the key to which is provided only by private sources—letters by Hartley and his friends and his unpublished writings. Over the past hundred years, when members of the homosexual community have come together in an environment free from the threat of prosecution, they have often used particular phrases or modes of speech that serve to underscore and even celebrate their difference from the larger society. Referring to one another as "she" or as "Mary," for example, is a method of dealing with the dominant culture's tag of femininity pinned on homosexual men. The conscious adoption and exaggeration of these otherwise derisive terms neutralize the stigmas, transferring their possession from the dominant culture to the subculture itself. Grossly mimicking a stereotype becomes a temporary means of liberation from that stereotype—temporary in that it functions only in selected environments whose boundaries are carefully policed by the stereotyping society.

Such insider slang is related to the codes that arose to declare homosexuality in a potentially hostile environment. At various times gay men have used particular articles of clothing, or have peppered their speech with certain phrases, in order to clue potential sexual partners when in mixed company. Unlike Hartley's private set of symbols for his dead lover, the success of such a code depends on its common parlance. At the turn of the century, for instance, one of the most popular articles of clothing used to signal the wearer's homosexuality was a red tie. When the famous crusader Dr. Charles Parkhurst wanted to take a trip into the lowest depths of the New York underworld in the 1880s, he hired a detective whose first act was to dress the saintly doctor and his assistant, Erving, in the clothing of a degenerate: "I searched around until I found a red necktie. It was an enormous one of puffed satin, and after I had stuck a brass shirt stud in it, and Erving had put it on, I carefully examined my companions. I was dressed 'tough' enough for any one, but they looked ten times harder. 'I say,' I remarked, as I led the way out of the house; 'your red neckties are a passport into any place we are to visit to-night. Come on.' " The red tie assured the investigators' entrance into the Golden Rule Pleasure Club, a male brothel where the sight of boys made up with rouge sent the naive doctor into the street screaming, "Why, I wouldn't stay in that house . . . for all the money in the world."[20] In Parkhurst's day the red tie seemed to have been a kind of universal sign of immorality, a subset of which was the homosexual world. On the other hand, Havelock Ellis, writing about the late 1890s, suggests the red tie was an exclusive sign of homosexuality: "It is notable that of recent years there has been a fashion for a red tie to be adopted by inverts as their badge. This is especially marked among the 'fairies' (as a fellator is there termed) in New York. 'It is red,' writes an American correspondent, himself inverted, 'that has become almost a synonym for sexual inversion, not only in the minds of inverts themselves, but in the popular mind.' "

In the ability of the code to connect diverse members of the subculture also lay its danger. The more people who understood the code, the less likely it was to be private and thus protect the wearer. Ellis continues: "To wear a red necktie on the street is to invite remarks from newsboys and others—remarks that have the practices of inverts for their theme. A friend told me once that when a group of street boys caught sight of the red necktie he was wearing they sucked their fingers in imitation of *fellatio*."[21] By and large, neither Hartley or Demuth used such obvious signs of homosexuality in their public works, perhaps because such signs were too easily detected or too prone to change. Unlike secret societies that build up a tradition of ceremonies and costumes written down in bylaws, the homosexual underground could not afford to maintain a set of signs that were immutable and therefore too easily recognized by the law. As I shall show, Hartley, in particular, wanted to avoid the kinds of stereotypes usually associated with such codes, as in the case of the red tie's being identified with flamboyantly feminine attire.

Paul Cadmus's notorious *The Fleet's In!* (fig. 10) breaks with Hartley's and Demuth's work by purposely using such a code—the dangerous red tie, in fact—to signal the homosexuality of its wearer. Though the consciously antimodernist style of the painting in a sense places it outside my subject, it is worth discussing at length because of the enormous public reaction it aroused. *The Fleet's In!* is one of the few painted depictions of homosexuality from this period for which we have a large body of written responses that can be tested. Were its signs of homosexuality—most notably the presence of a homosexual man in the painting—noted by the press? Did they contribute to the uproar that encircled the work?

Cadmus's *The Fleet's In!* depicts a group of sailors carousing with various locals along a wall that borders Riverside Park. Rather than focus attention on any single group in his composition, the artist has arranged the figures in an interlocking frieze with three major sections of action. Almost all the men in the scene are visibly drunk. The two gobs on the right are so unsteady that they have to lean on each other as they flirt with three high-heeled women. Liquor has presumably made another sailor so brazen that his lewd advances have to be met with the playful slaps of his female companion. The other young women in the picture seem more intent on getting a sailor than on fending one off. Whether these women are prostitutes, as

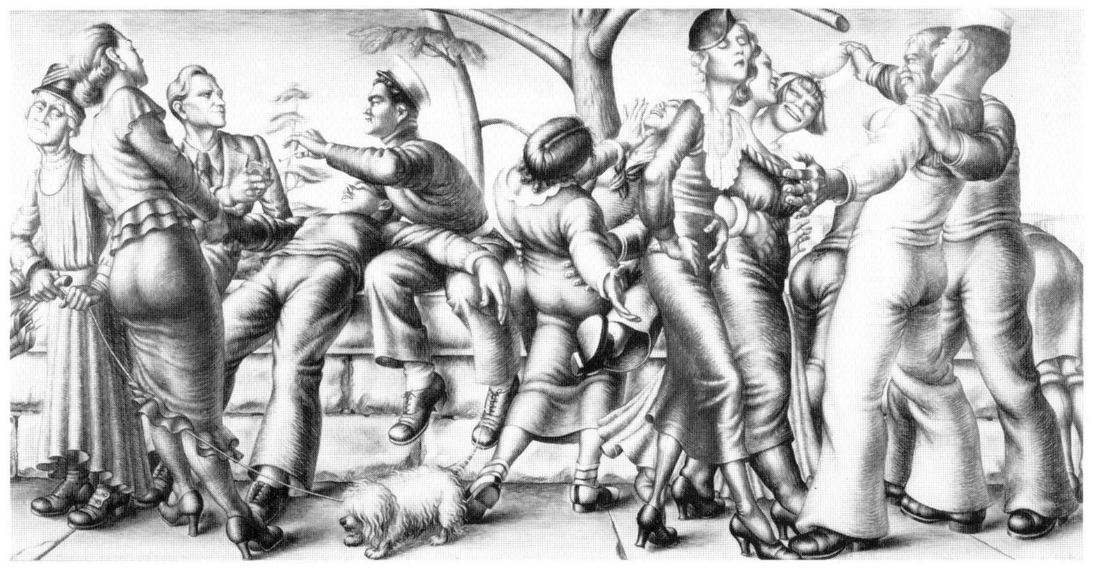

10. Paul Cadmus, *The Fleet's In!* oil on canvas, 30 × 60 in., 1934. Naval Historical Center, Washington, D.C.; photograph courtesy of Midtown Payson Galleries, New York.

contemporary critics suggested, or just women out for a good time, their clothes—brightly colored, tightly fitted, and cut short—suggest that they possess "loose morals," according to the standards of the day.

Ostensibly the painting appears to be about the antics of sailors and their female companions, but Cadmus has not limited his scenario to heterosexual encounters. To the left, slightly downstage, an elegantly dressed gentleman offers a cigarette to a smiling seaman. His carefully combed blond hair, stylish outfit, and contrapposto pose—so different in character from the rough-and-tumble stances of the sailors—are so many suggestions that this man is homosexual. The suspicion is confirmed by his bright red tie. The offering of a cigarette is perhaps only the beginning of another kind of offering, an exchange of sexual favors for money and perhaps a place to spend the night. It is significant that the two carry on their conversation over the prone body of a second drunken sailor. As if to save that fellow from

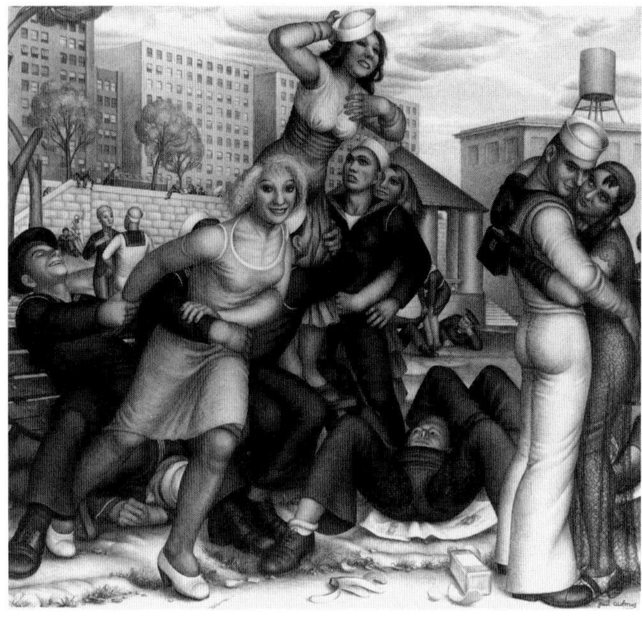

11. Paul Cadmus, *Shore Leave,* oil on canvas, 33 × 36 in., 1933. Whitney Museum of American Art, New York; gift of Malcolm S. Forbes.

a possible homosexual adventure, a woman dressed in a tight pleated skirt grabs one of his arms with both of her hands and tries to pull him up, while his other arm falls across the lap of the man reaching for the cigarette.

Lest the color of the gentleman's tie be taken as coincidental, I should point to Cadmus's use of the same device in his navy painting of the previous year, *Shore Leave* (fig. 11). A wittier and more outrageous work than *The Fleet's In!, Shore Leave* shows sailors and women in a kind of sexual tussle mimicking the poses of the *Laocoön.* In the background of this revelry, which also takes place in Riverside Park, is a pretty blond youth talking to a uniformed sailor. The boy has one hand on the sailor's shoulder and the other on the red necktie he is wearing. The marked separation of this couple from the heterosexual action going on in the rest of the picture reinforces the message of the red tie. Perhaps more surprising is the sailor lying on newspapers in the foreground. He seems rather uninterested in the women playing with his friends. His legs are spread wide in exhibitionist fashion, and an empty bottle lies on the ground, seemingly aimed at his anus. Such details, with their unsubtle sexual allusions, combine with the threatening grotesqueness of Cadmus's females to undercut—or at least to qualify—the painting's superficial heterosexual theme.

The Fleet's In! came to the attention of the navy and the press when it was initially included in a 1934 exhibit of paintings commissioned by the Civil Works Administration (CWA) at the Corcoran Gallery. During press previews the picture was singled out by reporters and critics for its humor and racy theme. Such attention brought the president's cousin, Henry Roosevelt, assistant secretary of the navy, to the exhibition. Horrified, he demanded that the painting be taken down immediately and put in his possession so that no more photographs could be taken. The CWA officials, worried about the ramifications of thwarting one of the president's relatives, let Henry Roosevelt take the painting to his office in spite of his having no jurisdiction over the exhibition. It was in Roosevelt's office that his boss, Secretary of the Navy Claude A. Swanson, came to the conclusion that the picture be permanently removed from the exhibition. Although Swanson felt that "it was right artistic," it was "not true to the navy."[22]

By April 19, the story of the removal of *The Fleet's In!,* along with photographs of the painting, had appeared on the front pages of the nation's leading newspapers. Editorials and letters quickly followed. None of the attacks that Cadmus's painting elicited mentions homosexuality—in fact, from reading the many newspaper descriptions of the picture one would not even know the work includes a male civilian. The criticism of the picture simply characterized the work as portraying the navy in an unflattering light. A letter of April 6 from Retired Admiral Hugh Rodman, commander in chief of the American battleship fleet operating in Europe in World War I, to Secretary Swanson provided the chief defense of the navy's position. In the letter, which was released to the press and published in the *New York Times,* Rodman claimed that the picture "represents a most disgraceful, sordid, disreputable, drunken brawl, wherein apparently a number of enlisted men are consorting with a party of streetwalkers and denizens of the red-light district." For Rodman, such a picture could only have "originated in the sordid, depraved imagination of someone who has no conception of actual conditions in our service."[23]

Despite the fact that Rodman does not mention homosexuality explicitly, the navy's rash and unauthorized removal of *The Fleet's In!* may in itself be an indication that such a subtext was perceived in Cadmus's picture. It is not, after all, self-evident that the heterosexual comedy on the surface of the picture would have been, on its own, a trigger to scandal and suppression. Philip Eliasoph, who was the first to reconstruct all the events of the *cause célèbre* surrounding *The Fleet's In!,* notes with reason that Cadmus's picture is only an exaggeration of other contemporary movie and stage depictions of sailors.[24] The point could be pursued further. The Chrysler Museum's 1983 survey of images of sailors, "The Sailor: 1930–1945," included many popular images of off-duty seamen enjoying their freedom with female companions.[25] Indeed, when in 1944 the establishment-sanctioned artist Norman Rockwell created his famous picture of the seaman, *Tattoo Artist,* he did so without worrying that references to the promiscuity of the sailor's life would bring down the wrath of the United States Navy. Rockwell's sailor is having the name of his girlfriend put on his arm. But "Betty" is on the bottom of a long list of scratched-out names. As Thomas Sokolowski suggests in the catalogue for the Chrysler Museum show, the sexual prowess of sailors, accentuated by their tight-fitting clothing, was an important aspect of their appeal to the popular imagination. But as he also claims, the sailor's sexual misadventures do not impinge on his fundamental aura of innocence. As the inheritors of a long tradition of myths about seamen, from Homer to Melville, sailors had the reputation for being both sexually active and somehow morally untouched by their promiscuity. In this view, the excesses of shore leave were the necessary correctives to the imagined chaste lives of sailors, far from land, with only other men for companions.

Perhaps the scandal of Cadmus's painting was that it gave too many details about the sailor's promiscuity for the myth of innocence to hold. Cadmus's seamen do not have the sweetness of the heroes of Broadway and Hollywood fantasies. As Cadmus himself pointed out, his sailors and their companions were not "particularly attractive."[26] But more particularly, the sailor flirting with the homosexual in *The Fleet's In!* portrayed an aspect of shore leave that did not tally with the vision of innocent boys out having a good time.

The navy was understandably worried about the issue of homosexuality.

Only some ten years earlier, it had been embroiled in a national scandal that involved exactly the kind of solicitation between civilians and sailors that Cadmus illustrates in his painting. What began as a naval vice probe centering on Newport, Rhode Island, turned into a major political uproar. To the horror of a Senate subcommittee, the navy had recruited sailors to participate in sexually illegal acts as part of a vice investigation under the assumption that allowing fellatio to be performed on the recruits would not make them homosexuals. Indeed, the Senate testimony makes clear that those sailors who had regularly accepted favors from civilians in return for sex were not considered homosexual by the navy. The discourse surrounding the scandal underlined the fact that the nomenclature *queer* does not refer to specific acts but to persons with a particular role in the sexual encounter. That role was defined by a "feminine" manner of dress and speech, by adopting a so-called passive position in sexual intercourse, and by exchanging money for sex. As long as the sailor was not in the sexual position usually attributed to females, his sexuality was considered normal, although there might be doubts about his virtue.[27]

Given this scenario, we should not be surprised that homosexuality goes largely unmentioned by the navy in their charges against Cadmus's *The Fleet's In!* Henry Roosevelt, aware of the role his cousin, the president, had played in the Newport scandal while holding the very same position, would certainly not want to raise that issue again. Yet there is an indication that certain reporters were aware of the homosexual subtheme. One article mentions a call Cadmus got from a stranger who asked "if he had ever been to Sands Street, near the Brooklyn Navy Yard."[28] The significance of this question is not explained in the article, but it is mysteriously repeated in *Newsweek*'s coverage of the incident, again without explanation.[29] Sands Street was a notorious homosexual cruising ground (it is the location of Charles Demuth's *On "That" Street,* which shows a gentleman picking up two sailors). Such a peculiar phone conversation inserted in a short article without explanation was a tip to the sophisticated reader about the kind of man Cadmus probably was.

Cadmus himself suggested that he could have made *The Fleet's In!* more scandalous and still have been true to the reality of navy life. The *New York World-Telegram* quoted Cadmus: "Why, any casual observer can see more in one hour than I've put in my paintings. I've seen sailors doing lots of things I couldn't dare paint. On

Riverside Dr. especially. It's always impressed me as a—well, a very sordid place." As with the reference to Sands Street in the same article, it is impossible to determine what Cadmus meant or what the reader would understand from comments like "lots of things" or "sordid." But these seemingly superfluous details gave clues to the artist's sexual orientation. The anonymous writer adds that Cadmus lolls on a couch with his face propped on an elbow, that he makes his own breakfast (which includes tea), and that he had just been playing Beethoven on the piano. In other words, Cadmus was the very opposite of the "virile" men he portrayed.[30]

In 1937, Lewis Mumford provided a sophisticated allusion to the homosexual content of Cadmus's paintings of the period, remarking that the result "is not so much satire as inverted sentimentalism; his hand lingers too lovingly on the flesh he would chastise." Mumford is far too clever a wordsmith (and too knowledgeable about the homosexual circle Cadmus moved in) to use the word *inverted* unconsciously. "Inverted sentimentalism" archly suggests the mawkish cliché of Cadmus's satire while providing those in the know with a reference to the artist's homosexuality. Such an interpretation might explain the vehemence of Mumford's outcry against the young artist's first one-man exhibit: "Instead of hating the subject the painting holds up to scorn, one comes pretty near to hating the artist himself for giving one such an unpalatable mouthful."[31]

Although there are these cryptic signs that a few viewers noticed the homosexual theme, the majority ignored the significance of the man with the red tie. The *Daily News* defended Cadmus's view of navy life with an editorial entitled "Should Sailors Be Sissies?" which asked rhetorically: "Should the United States Navy be a floating YMCA, a glorified Boy Scout camp on the sea; or should it be an organization made up of fighting men accustomed to doing any and all of the things that fighting men traditionally do?" For the *Daily News, The Fleet's In!* was a painting that depicted the modern sailor as virile, the very opposite of the popular image of the homosexual: "If most of our sailors have come to the point where they hurry alone to the Public Library or the museums on shore leave, instead of finding themselves some girl friends and doing a little drinking, dancing and the rest of the things that he-men do when they want to relax, then it's too bad for us and our Navy. The shore-leave activities so vividly pictured by Mr. Cadmus go with the fighting man's trade."[32]

The reaction of the *Daily News* seems flatly to contradict my conjecture that *The Fleet's In!* includes a homosexual seduction. But we have to remember that homosexuals who did not conform to the popular stereotype of effeminacy were largely invisible to the general public. Whereas the man with the red tie might be taken as a "fairy," the manliness of his naval companion was probably not suspect. For the editors of the *Daily News,* the attraction of the "sissy" for a man in uniform, if noticed at all, would be just another sign of the comparative virility of sailors. However, the naval command, with its detailed knowledge about the prevalence of male prostitution and other homosexual activity among the rank and file, would have been far less comfortable about what Cadmus's painting had to say.

Just as there is enormous confusion in society about the determining characteristics of homosexuality, there are no absolute rules for identifying homosexuality as the subject of works of art. If by an iconography of homosexuality we mean a set of signs for which a culture has built up prescribed meanings, then there is no real iconography of homosexuality. As we have seen, the codes used to convey sexual difference were necessarily unstable even among homosexuals. The various methods of clueing in possible companions had to be continually changing to protect the initiates from reprisals. Once introduced, given signs were often misinterpreted or became known by too many people. A commonplace of homosexual memoirs of the period is the harsh reprisal of a heterosexual man who accidentally gave out the wrong signal and then found himself the object of an unwanted advance.

Sometimes it was not the specific words so much as the particular emphasis or intonation given to them in the conversation—perhaps just a raised eyebrow or a significant glance. The inanimateness of paintings therefore makes the job of identifying the homosexual subject more difficult: it cannot be done merely by pointing to the portrayal of certain sexual acts, locations, ways of dressing, or articles of clothing. One may need to be attentive to modes of emphasis that are just as subtle and ephemeral as those used in the subculture—the repetition of certain themes, the exaggeration of particular details, or the placement of seemingly neutral elements in a context that gives them a peculiar quality. Yet inevitably, finding what we might call a gay text cannot be done simply by a close reading of the work of art. It depends on reconstructing issues that lie outside the frame.

But which issues count? I have already established that we need to understand the meanings homosexuality had for American society between the wars. Being aware of different audiences is crucial for understanding why a work of art may seem to be about homosexuality yet not be about homosexuality. Is biography a necessary component to this process of interpretation? One of the points of this chapter is to demonstrate the range of issues raised in works about homosexuality that are separate from the biographical. We do not need to know with whom Demuth or Cadmus slept to unravel the complicated issues their images raise about the situation of the homosexual in American society. Yet biography is a useful, if not essential, component. Although I do not believe it is necessary or desirable to reconstruct all the intimate details of an artist's sex life to comprehend his work, biography has a role in verifying interpretation. Often the question of intention is put aside in art historical analysis. But here the reconstruction of the artist's project is necessary to determine which audiences are being addressed. Because the artist himself is an audience (some would argue the most important audience), figuring out some sense of his sexual identification is crucial, particularly in light of the fact that many of the works under discussion were never shown in public during the artists' lifetime. In the case of Hartley's war motif series, it would be impossible to understand the symbolism of the paintings without biography, though this is not true of most other works discussed here.

Finally, biography is essential on a political level. It is significant that certain artists took the risk of exposure to create records of homosexuality. In any case, the history of how paintings about homosexuality came to be made cannot be easily separated from the question of what the paintings mean. Many of the works we shall look at in detail are not only artifacts of a generalized social struggle, or objects produced for pure aesthetic appreciation (if such a thing were possible), but attempts at expressing forbidden feelings. To leave out biography is to read out the role of art as both a form of self-revelation and a means of liberation from the prohibitions society places around those it deems abnormal.

3

Charles Demuth and "Some Unknown Thing"

In 1930, near his hometown of Lancaster, Pennsylvania, Charles Demuth painted a coat of arms on the wall of a farmhouse to commemorate the names of Lancaster's neighboring communities (fig. 12).[1] Executed as part of the owners' July Fourth picnic festivities, the shield is divided into thirds and depicts a plow for the town of Fertility, a small bird in a palm of a hand for Bird-in-Hand, and a man's hat and woman's bonnet tossed on the ground for Intercourse (perhaps the most joked-about town in Pennsylvania). Flanking the shield are a stag for Bucks County and a unicorn for the town of that name. The emblem is topped with a blue globe—a symbol not of the earth but of Blue Ball, yet another Lancaster County town with an unfortunate name. As if daring the viewer to read more into the emblem than merely the names of the proud towns, Demuth inscribes the words "Schlectheit seht alles schlecht," a German play on "Honi soit qui mal y pense," the motto of the Knights of the Holy Garter. Instead of "Evil be to him who evil thinks," Demuth fashions "Evil sees everything evil."

"Evil sees everything evil," with its shifting of moral responsibility for representation from the artist to the viewer, might be the perfect epigraph for the critical reception of Charles Demuth's art through the years. Demuth wrote very little about his own work, and when he did, it was only to express the impossibility of translating the experience of painting into words: "Across a Greco, across a Blake, across a Rubens, across a Watteau, across a Beardsley is written in larger letters

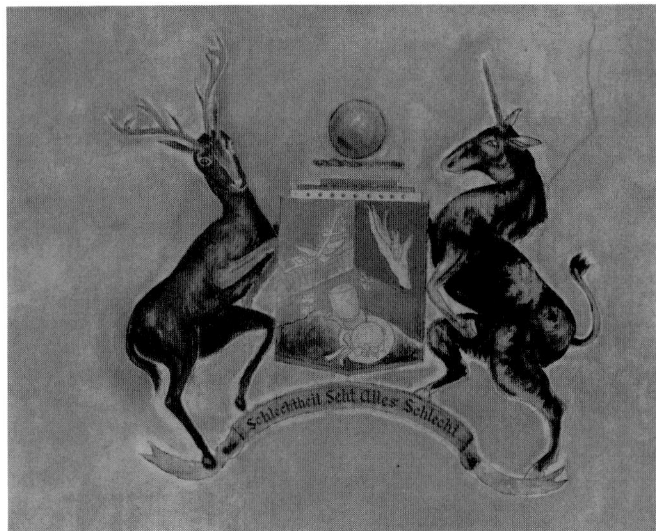

12. Charles Demuth, *Coat of Arms,* mural, 1930. Private collection.

than any printed page will ever dare to hold, or Broadway facade or roof support what its creator had to say about it. To translate these painted sentences, whatever they may be, into words—well try it. With the best of luck the 'sea change' will be great. Or, granting a translation of this kind were successful what would you have but what was there already, and as readable—and perhaps, on repetition, a trifle boring."[2] Instead he left it to his critics to ferret out those "vast implications of the little secrets of life" that his close friend Marsden Hartley felt were so important to Demuth's work.[3]

Since Demuth's death in 1935, his sexuality has hardly been a secret. Although there is no record of his discussing it directly, he hints at it in an unfinished story called "The Voyage Was Almost Over," which was found among his manuscripts following his death. The story is about a lone man on a cross-Atlantic passage. During a costume ball, he goes out on deck to look at the sea under a moonlit sky. At first glance he thinks he is by himself, but "if one looked . . . into the shadows cast by stacks and funnels, you would discover vague outlines. Outlines of forms which stood or sat but always in pairs."

The ocean triggers a catalogue of associations: "All the pauses in his wanderings around and around the deck and the wandering, too, were full of these ideas; how like the ocean is to that and how like the golden moon in her turquoise sky is to this." But of the lovers that line the deck he writes:

> Vague lines of forgotten looks half-awakened in his memory as he glanced into the shadows which held a pair. But, somehow, he could not say of these, they are like this or that, as he could of the sea or night or of the moon. . . .
>
> "Why, why was everything wonderfully made, perfectly made, and I given the power, above many, to appreciate this wonder and perfection? And yet denied the one thing which would perfect me, truly? If only a little white hand would beckon from without one of those mysterious shadows—then —well, then, to hell with these borrowed ideas. Then the sea would be no silly purple fish or blue flower but only a mighty living thing which somewhere beats against mightier existing coast. I would know?"
>
> And hate against some unknown Thing filled his soul.[4]

Demuth evokes the modern artist, the voyeur, watching from the shadows everyday life, jealous of the average person's lack of self-consciousness. Like Baudelaire's *flâneur,* he is in the crowd but not of the crowd. The artist's heightened perceptions always place him or her on life's margins. But Demuth's description is particularized by its mysterious "unknown Thing," which somehow bars him from the possibility of ever finding a relationship and joining the other couples on deck. It is assumed that Demuth's story is autobiographical, written sometime after his return from Paris in 1921, a year after he had been diagnosed with diabetes. Pamela Edwards Allara suggests that the "Thing" is the artist's illness, writing that this story is one of the few times Demuth ever expresses "the underlying fear and resentment he felt toward his illness."[5] Yet even though Demuth might have felt ostracized both by the lameness he endured from early childhood and by his recent development of diabetes, I am not convinced that any physical state alone merits the portentousness and mysteriousness of his capital T. I take Demuth's "Thing" to be his homosexuality.

Several of his friends, including George Biddle, William Carlos Williams, Stuart Davis, and Marcel Duchamp, have alluded to Demuth's homosexuality in discussions with his first biographer, Emily Farnham. Farnham conducted personal interviews and sent out questionnaires to several people who knew the artist. Some of her questions seem designed to elicit answers about Demuth's sexuality. After asking about Demuth's method of working and his personal tastes, Farnham followed with the vague questions "Was Demuth a moody person, and, if so, did his moods change easily? Was he a happy, well-adjusted person, or were his smiling personality and wittiness only a mask?"[6] Only George Biddle took the bait, writing flatly in response to the question about Demuth's likes and dislikes "He was a homosexual, 'fin de siècle.' "[7] In subsequent personal interviews Demuth's friends were more willing to discuss his sexual preference, perhaps at the unrecorded prompting of Farnham.

William Carlos Williams, a close friend since Demuth's art school days in Philadelphia, indicated that Demuth, while in Paris, tried to arrange a meeting with Marcel Proust "both because of his reputation as a writer and also as a perverted sort of person." Although Williams did not say that Demuth was a homosexual, he obviously thinks that the Proust anecdote amounts to such a declaration (following the guilt-by-association formula). He immediately added, "I don't know why it is, but several of my old friends, it appears now, were homosexual."[8] Stuart Davis was more direct. When he mentioned that Demuth had a "queer kind of feeling" for a woman in Provincetown, Farnham comments that she thought it sounded as if Davis were implying Demuth was a homosexual (the transcript does not mention what must have been Davis's emphasis on the word "queer"). Davis shot back, "Well, if he wasn't, I don't know what he was."[9]

The man usually discussed in the biographies as a possible lover of Demuth is Robert Locher, who was born and raised in Lancaster. The two became friends in 1909 and remained close until Demuth's death. Their affection is indicated by Demuth's will: Locher inherited all of the artist's unsold watercolors and the family house at the death of Demuth's mother (I assume that Augusta Demuth, in leaving her house to Locher, was following her son's instructions).[10] Shortly before World War I, Locher married Beatrice Howard, and although this was supposedly a marriage of convenience, the couple lived together and traveled widely. Locher divorced Howard sometime in the early 1930s and then became involved with Richard Weyand, with whom he lived the rest of his life.[11]

Barbara Haskell mentions that around the time Locher and Weyand's relationship began, Demuth wrote Alfred Stieglitz that he was not well and that "something else happened to me which almost finished me in another direction."[12] Yet she says elsewhere that there is no evidence that Demuth had consummated a relationship with Locher. We can only wonder what such evidence would be like; in an age of concealment and careful covering of traces, its existence seems highly unlikely.

How did Demuth present himself? Most of his friends agree that he was extraordinarily discreet about private matters. His letters to Stieglitz—the only extensive Demuth correspondence that we have—are mostly short and free of gossip. The most personal remarks amount to vague generalizations about his moods and the rocky state of his health. But just because he did not share intimate details with his friends does not mean that he was a retiring person—at least not until diabetes forced him to live most of the year in Lancaster. Duchamp spoke of his trips with Demuth to Harlem nightclubs. And in "Farewell Charles" Hartley frequently alludes to Demuth's forays into the nightlife of New York and Paris. Demuth went out of his way to dress so that he was noticeable. Indeed, rather than try to "pass," the evidence suggests that Demuth adopted several of the prevalent stereotypes of homosexuality. According to Hartley, because of his lameness he adopted "a special sort of ambling walk." His dealer, Charles Daniel, noted his taste in neckties: "Ah, Demuth. He was a rare one. I can tell you this right now—he wore the most beautiful neckties in New York. He must have the tie that he liked, and he liked the best. That was Demuth. It came out of his sensitivity. It had to be good. He was very vain; and wore unusual colors. His hands were the most extraordinary hands that I have ever seen. They were alive. Yet he was never affected; was without any pose."[13]

Another friend, Susan Watts Street, told Farnham: "Demuth was extremely vain and dressed extremely well. I remember for instance, that he had a Donegal Tweed jacket that was perfectly handsome. And at Provincetown when everybody else was looking sloppy, Demuth would appear wearing a black shirt, white slacks, a plum-colored scarf tied around his waist, and black laced shoes, highly polished. . . . He had a high, squeaky voice and a high giggle that sounded like the whinny of a horse."[14]

Much was made of Demuth's hands, which were considered unusually elegant and expressive. They served as a sign of his genius but also of his homosexuality. Stieglitz photographed them. Hartley wrote that they were "patrician hands . . . the fingers long and slender."[15] And Street writes that "he had very beautiful hands. I remember that he often sat with one hand drooping from the wrist and held in front of him like this (striking the pose), his elbow resting on the arm of a chair." Whether or not these memories of Demuth are colored by their authors' prejudice about how homosexuals act, dress, or speak—it would be hard to think of a more clichéd description of the limp wrist of a gay man than Street's—it seems clear Demuth did not worry about being tagged a homosexual.

In a sense, Demuth contributed to the assessment of his personality and work as typically decadent (a label he probably would not have minded) by acting out the part of the jaded dandy. When asked in an interview what he looked forward to, he gave the Wildean answer "the past."[16] Hartley wrote of his friend's manner: "It wasn't long before Charles made us particularly aware of him by a quaint, incisive sort of wit with an ultra sophisticated, post eighteen-ninety touch to it, for I always felt that Charles's special personal tone had been formed from that period, the murmur of imagined deaths of superior trifles clinging to his very sensitive hands, and a wistful comprehension of what many a too tender soul has called infectious sin, alas how harmless and sentimental it all was."[17] Although the term "infectious sin," in combination with "eighteen-ninety touch," is a convenient way to hint at homosexuality, Hartley's description of Demuth's sensibility as belonging to the 1890s undoubtedly comes out of a reaction to real aspects of his friend's character. It is often the nature of stereotypes to be based in part on perceived qualities. Was Demuth's pose as a decadent representative of his complete commitment in art and life to a late nineteenth-century aesthetic, or was it a means of acting out difference?

Critics often mention Demuth's admiration of Oscar Wilde's work and a recommendation to a friend to read Joris-Karl Huysmans's *A rebours*. Kermit Champa, for example, devotes much of his article " 'Charlie Was Like That' " to the parallels between the sensibility of the satiated hero of *A rebours,* des Esseintes, and Demuth. Champa notes des Esseintes's sexual hedonism and particularly his fascination with circus acts, comparing this to Demuth's vaudeville watercolors. He neglects to mention all the other artists who shared this interest with Demuth—artists like Degas, Picasso, and even the American Walt Kuhn—none of whom we would automatically place in the decadent camp. Demuth seems to have considered his passion for vaudeville not in terms of the aesthete's fascination with the bizarre but as an especially modern-American pursuit. In the play fragment *"You Must Come Over," A Painting: A Play,* Demuth has one of the characters say, "Couldn't we talk about American musical shows, revues,—the people who act in them (—have acted in them), and dance: they really are our 'stuff.' They are our time."[18]

I think Demuth spoke loudest through his taste in fiction, not so much in his suggestions to friends on "good reads" as in his choice of books to illustrate. Significantly, Demuth did not illustrate *A rebours*—or any of Wilde's work, for that matter. In recommending the work of Huysmans and Wilde (and in attempting to visit Proust), Demuth showed that he was not afraid of the scandalous. He was willing to express an active interest in novels that depict homosexuality and other forms of deviant behavior. But this does not mean that all Demuth's paintings are colored by a decadent sensibility or that his art never fully entered the twentieth century. One of the problems with much of the criticism of Demuth's work is that critics make no distinction between late nineteenth-century decadence in the manner of Oscar Wilde and Aubrey Beardsley and the later use of sexual imagery in the art of the early twentieth century (part of this confusion, I suspect, has to do with an automatic equation between decadence and homosexuality).[19] Demuth certainly enjoyed shocking middle-class morality, but, as I try to show, in ways that were linked less to the consciously refined gestures of the late nineteenth-century aesthetes than to the avant-garde strategies of his friends in New York and Paris.

Different Modes

The greatest danger of the label decadent is that it has given art historians the permission to find clandestine subject matter in all aspects of

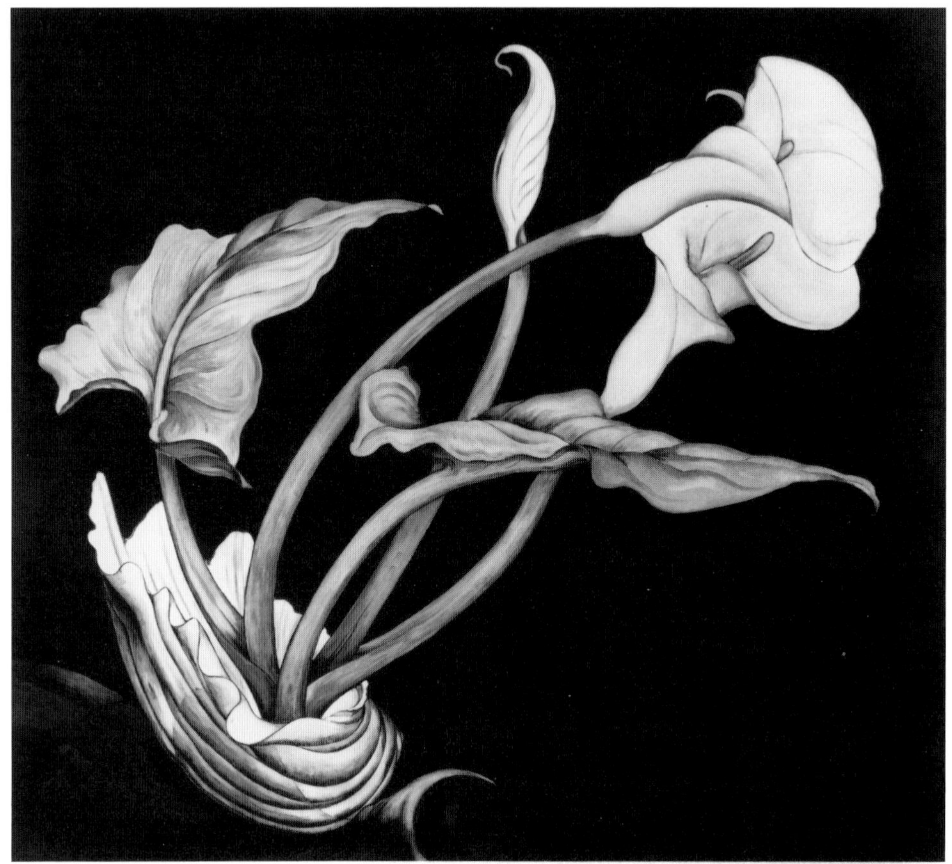

13. Charles Demuth, *Calla Lilies (Bert Savoy),* oil on board, 42⅛ × 48 in., 1926. Carl van Vechten Gallery of Fine Arts, Fisk University, Nashville, Tenn.; from the Alfred Stieglitz Collection; gift of Georgia O'Keeffe.

Demuth's diverse work, from the still lifes to the paintings of smokestacks. Champa defends his discussion of Demuth's sexuality on the grounds that "to avoid it means to overlook so much contained in so many images that there remains too little left to see."[20] Discussion of Demuth's sexuality comes only at the cost of leaving the impression that virtually all of Demuth's works are somehow expressions of his deviance.

Demuth's flower paintings have been especially scrutinized for this. Critics have exaggerated the phallic quality of his flowers, suggesting that they are *fleurs du mal*. I personally do not see anything particularly evil or, for that matter, homosexual in the majority of Demuth's watercolors of zinnias, gladiolus, daisies, and iris. When Demuth intended a flower to be read sexually, he was not subtle. *Calla Lilies (Bert Savoy)* (fig. 13) is an homage to the famous female impersonator whose career ended dramatically when he was struck by lightning. Barbara Haskell writes that the painting suggests Savoy's cross-dressing by exaggerating aspects of both genders in the painting.[21] The long stem and stamen of the flower suggest the male genitals, and the opening of the clamshell vase the female. Completely detached from any landscape, Demuth's brash lily has a brittle, artificial quality as if it were made of wax. Its aggressiveness—the lily seems to almost lunge out at us like a man-eating plant from a science fiction novel—is the very opposite of Demuth's intricate interweave of stems and translucent foliage of *Yellow Calla Lily Leaves* (fig. 14). In spite of the similar subject, the watercolor is about being with rather than "against nature."

The large number of flower studies in Demuth's work may have affected critics' judgments of his status, if only unconsciously. Whereas flowers were thought to be an appropriate subject for a female artist such as Georgia O'Keeffe, there is a suggestion that it was not masculine to be so enamored with blossoms. For Paul Rosenfeld, Demuth's flowers are "tender and pungent." In comparison Rosenfeld finds that John Marin's watercolors of the Maine coast or New York City have a "granite American crudeness. So strong and rough has Marin water-colour become, that the elders complain he has transcended the natural limits of his medium." According to Rosenfeld Demuth's talent is "limited" because "there is always the suspicion of an almost feminine refinement in his wash."[22] The very sensitivity that allows Demuth to be so attuned to the complexity of even the smallest bud seems to undermine his artistic reputation. When Hartley wrote that Demuth "never could abide the vulgarities in the world of flower painting produced by a powerful painter like Courbet," it was with the assumption that such artistic power was dependent on not being in sync with precisely the feminine flowers that were Demuth's forte.[23]

Demuth's love of flowers is just another bit of evidence for those critics who find homosexuality spilling uncontrollably into all aspects of his art—flower studies

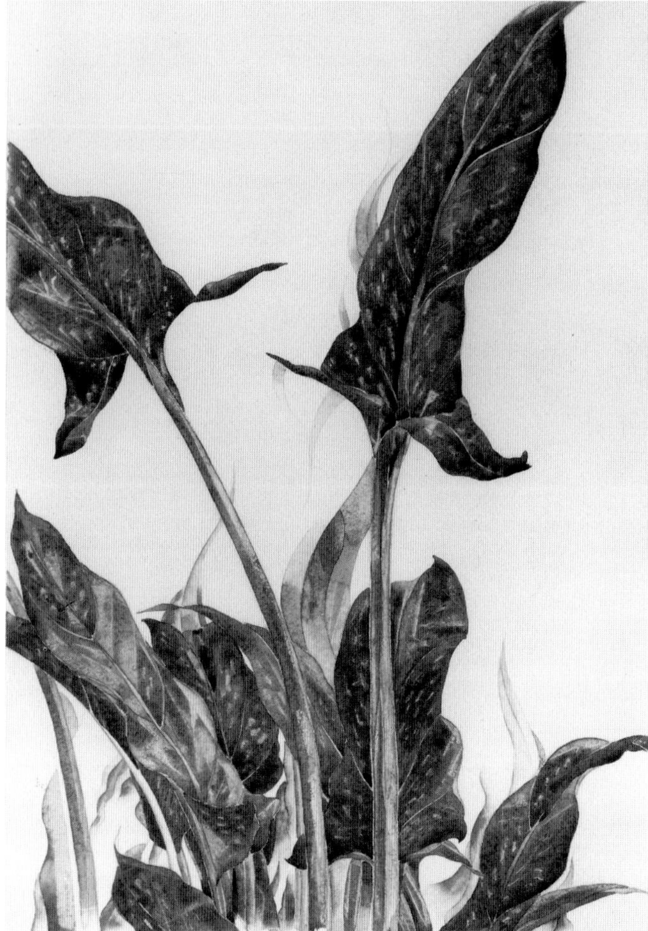

14. Charles Demuth, *Yellow Calla Lily Leaves,* watercolor and pencil on paper, 19⅞ × 13⅞ in., ca. 1922. Yale University Art Gallery; The Philip L. Goodwin Collection, B.A. 1907.

are termed "fleurs du mal," paintings of smokestacks are phallic, and his illustrations "reveal a deep unbalance in his nature." Besides reducing Demuth's carefully observed still lifes into minor studies in Wildean corruption, this view ignores evidence suggesting that Demuth carefully chose the subjects in which he represented sexuality. Or, alternatively, it assumes a Demuth—and indeed, a notion of representation in general—in which such choices are ultimately irrelevant, given the pervasive power of "some unknown Thing" beyond the artist's conscious control.

The idea that Demuth's art is "randomly sexual," to borrow Champa's phrase, was dispelled by the 1987 Whitney retrospective. This was the first museum exhibition to put the artist's overt homosexual images—watercolors of sailors in various states of undress and mutual admiration—alongside his flower studies, poster portraits, and cityscapes. One of the surprising aspects of the show was its revelation of how carefully Demuth segregated the subjects of his art. Indeed, it is hard to think of another American artist who purposely pursued such separate subjects and styles of painting simultaneously. Basically, Demuth made three kinds of pictures: figurative images (including illustrations, erotica, and vaudeville studies drawn in a loose calligraphic line, then colored in Rodinesque watercolor washes); still lifes (also executed in watercolor but with a greater sense of exactitude and volume); and larger, more heraldic semiabstract pictures, quasi-cubist cityscapes, and poster portraits executed in oil or tempera.

As Demuth's art matured, his different modes were honed to address specific audiences. His popular flower paintings and still lifes sold well and provided the artist (who, though well-off, was not rich) with a steady income that gave him a necessary sense of independence from his mother (whom he lived with, when he was not traveling). The very popularity of Demuth's still life watercolors, however, made them suspect in the eyes of the avant-garde circle around Stieglitz, a group that never fully accepted Demuth's art until after his death. In contrast to his still lifes, Demuth's so-called precisionist cityscapes, and in particular his semiabstract poster portraits, were attempts to speak a modernist language that would be understood by Stieglitz's stable of artists. Significantly, the poster portraits—emblematic, graphically powerful representations of character through a collagelike joining of words and telling details from his subjects' lives—are not of Lancaster friends, but almost exclusively of members of Stieglitz's circle: Arthur Dove, Georgia O'Keeffe, John Marin, and William Carlos Williams.

Demuth's figurative mode reached its maturity at the time of World War I. In scale and subject matter, it was more private than either his highly finished still lifes or the bold poster portraits. Although Demuth's images of nightclubs, circuses, and vaudeville performances were publicly exhibited, his paintings of bathhouses from the 1910s and his series of seminude sailors from the 1930s were never shown and were probably done to please himself or, at the most, a select group of friends.

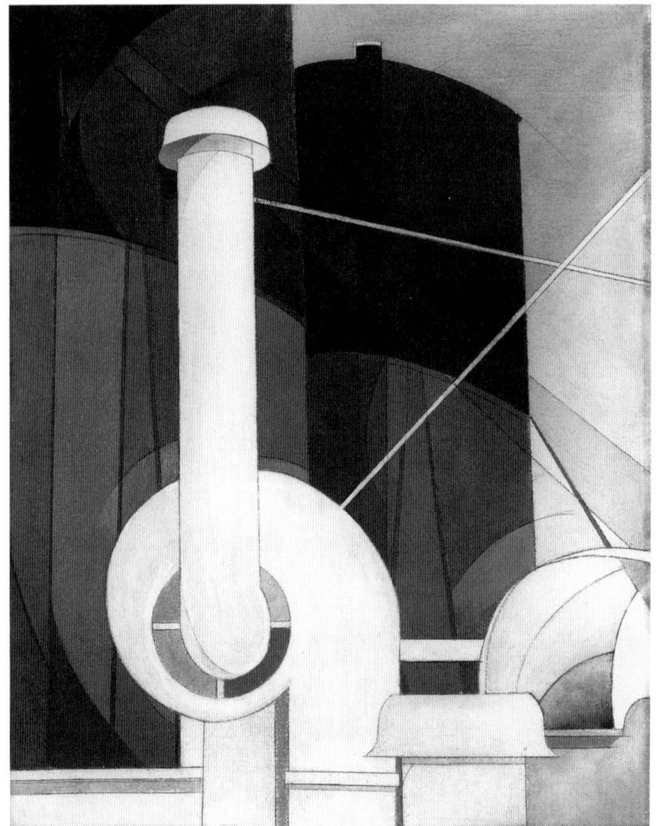

15. Charles Demuth, *Paquebot "Paris,"* oil on canvas, 25 × 20 in., 1921–22. Columbus Museum of Art, Columbus, Ohio; gift of Ferdinand Howald.

For all the discussion of phallic imagery in Demuth's art, this awareness of audience—the consciousness of what is permitted and not permitted depending on certain settings and viewers—is probably more telling of Demuth's homosexuality than his occasional punning on male genitalia. When Champa alludes to the sexual randomness of Demuth's art, he invariably has in mind pictures like *Paquebot "Paris"* (fig. 15), with its tall funnel that is curved at the top, or *In Vaudeville, Bicycle Rider* (fig. 16) in which the handle of the bicycle is suggestively placed at the rider's crotch. But such sexual joking was standard fare among the American avant-garde. The aggressive sexuality of the funnel in *Paquebot "Paris"* cannot be separated from similar gestures by other artists, for example, Morton Schamberg's sculpture of *God* (fig. 17) or Marcel Duchamp's *Fountain,* which Demuth defended in print.[24]

There is nothing necessarily homosexual about phallic imagery, yet to be a homosexual in America before World War II was to be intensely aware of different modes of presenting the self. Although Demuth might have felt comfortable with his sexuality among other homosexuals or with certain members of the avant-garde in New York or Paris, the open expression of same-sex love was not deemed appropriate to most daily interactions. Even in the freewheeling atmosphere of a speakeasy, where gay men often went to meet their friends or make new contacts,

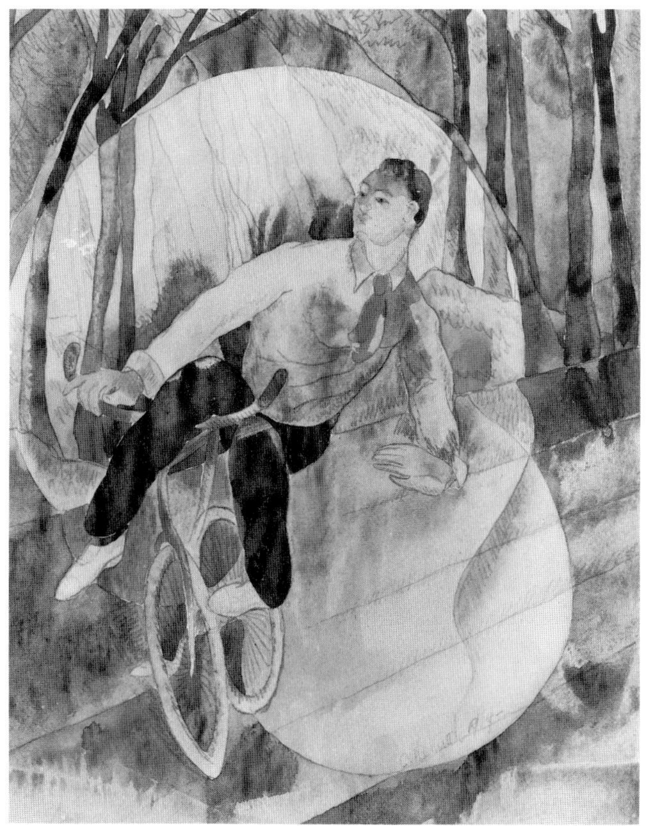

16. Charles Demuth, *In Vaudeville, Bicycle Rider,* watercolor and pencil on paper, 11 × 8⅝ in., 1919. Corcoran Gallery of Art, Washington, D.C.; gift of the Honorable and Mrs. Francis Biddle.

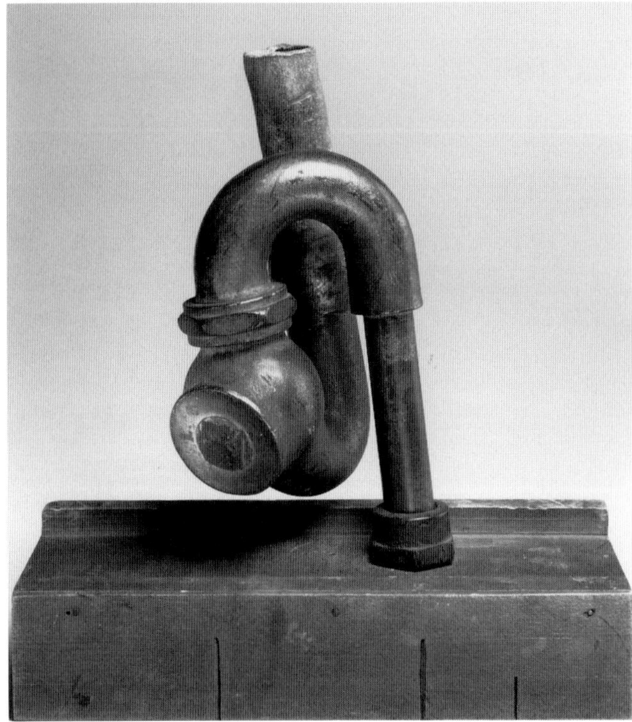

17. Morton Schamberg, *God,* wooden miter box and cast-iron plumbing trap, 10½ in. high, ca. 1918. Philadelphia Museum of Art, Philadelphia; Louise and Walter Arensberg Collection.

Demuth would have had to be on his guard. The attractive hustler might easily be a blackmailer; or the policeman on the take drinking at the bar might return the next day leading a morals raid. Blackmail was an ever-present peril for the homosexual in pre–World War II America. Various well-publicized cases of famous men destroyed by scandal—the ruin of Oscar Wilde, the suicides of munitions magnate Friedrich Krupp and the highly placed Austrian intelligence officer Alfred Redl—reinforced the idea that public exposure of homosexuality amounted to the ending of career and life. All these cases, which were well known in the United States, involved the accused denying the charges of sexual misconduct, in spite of the virtual certainty of their homosexuality.[25] As André Gide suggested in his famous defense of sexual difference, *Corydon* (published in 1911 in a limited edition of twelve copies), homosexuality had many victims but few martyrs willing to admit and defend their sexual orientation. Gide went on to say that exposure threatened not only the homosexual's status and his livelihood but the mental and financial health of his entire family—often including a wife and children.[26]

Blackmail was particularly frightening in that the homosexual could do little to strike back at his persecutor. The designation homosexual placed a person outside the protection of the law—the blackmailer and his victim were both considered criminals, because no one knew if the "crime against nature" was any less a crime than extortion. It is no surprise, then, that the police showed almost no interest in defending from harassment those they considered to be sexual offenders. Stevenson writes: "The blackmailer is often right, in spite of all the law's judiciousness, when he warns his writhing victim that even if he, the blackmailer, will be punished as an offender—or co-offender—so will the victim be punished. The law cannot always distinguish. Sometimes it will not do so—whether failing intolerantly or stupidly."[27]

Even if the courts were sympathetic, few homosexuals were willing to expose their sexuality in a legal case. In an interview, Stuart Davis told of an incident in which Demuth was threatened in what should have been hospitable surroundings: "Once Demuth and I happened to go together to a speakeasy in New York. It was about midnight. Demuth was sick, and nervous. In the speakeasy there were a lot of cops—their gun belts, guns in them, hanging on the coat-racks. A cop came over to our table and loaded his gun right in Demuth's face."[28] Davis does not explicitly state that the policeman was reacting to the perception that Demuth was homosexual, but he implies it. Demuth's elegant attire, his cane, his brightly colored accessories, like the red tie of Cadmus's *The Fleet's In!,* would have tagged him as a "pansy" in the types of speakeasies and clubs the New York avant-garde frequented. During a period in which homosexual men were harassed for merely appearing to be effeminate, we can imagine Demuth's fear before the policeman's loaded gun.

Although the man in uniform in Davis's story represents oppression, he nonetheless appears as a central character in several of Demuth's images of homosexual desire. An early work in the Hirshhorn Museum (fig. 18) shows a policeman in conversation with a sailor and a soldier on the street. They are turned inward as if they are talking about something the viewer should not overhear. This same composition is echoed exactly in the late *On "That" Street* (fig. 19, pl. 4) in which the policeman

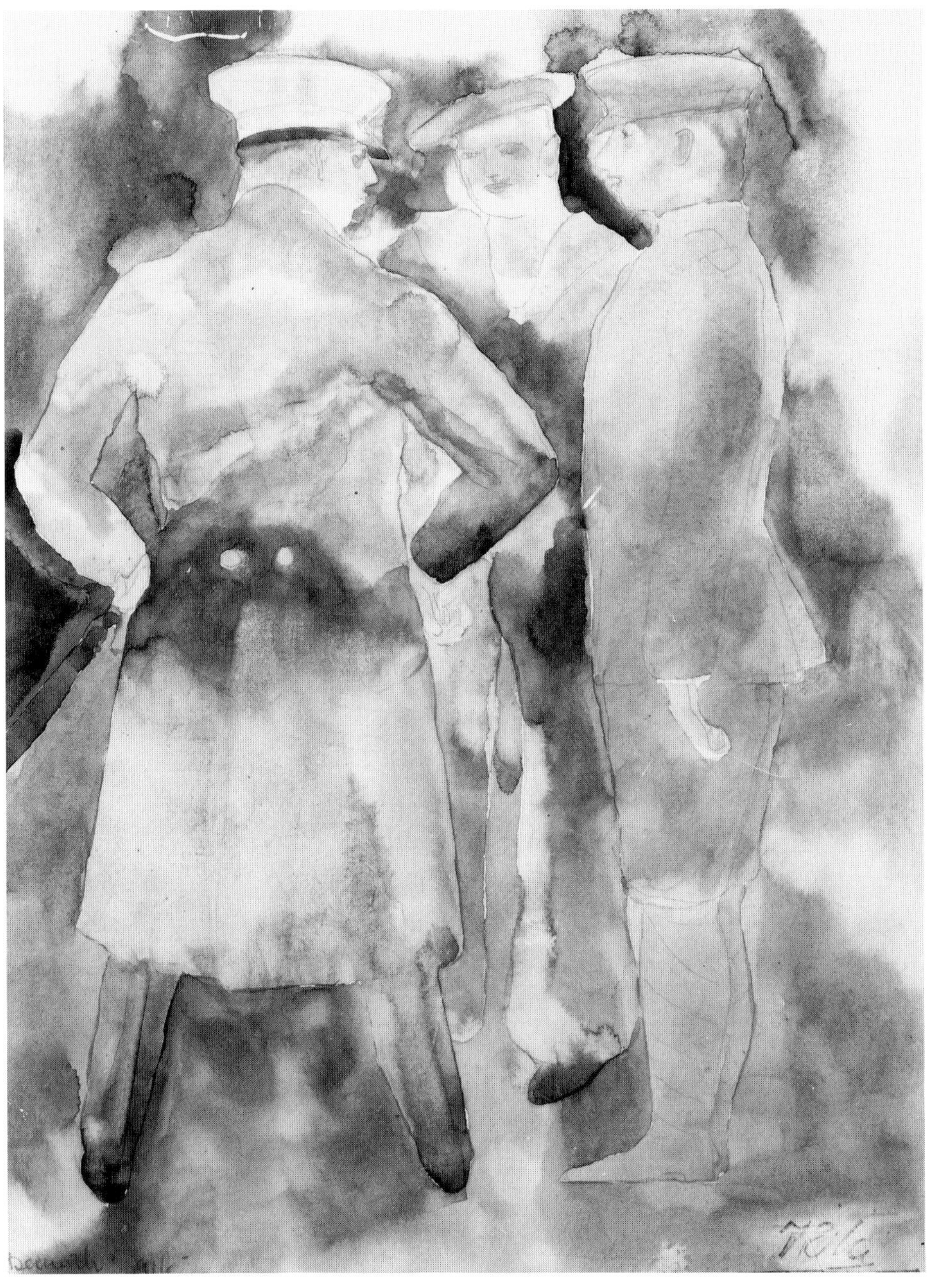

18. Charles Demuth, *Sailor, Soldier and Policeman,* watercolor and pencil on paper, 10½ × 8 in., 1916. Hirshhorn Museum and Sculpture Garden, Smithsonian Institution, Washington, D.C.

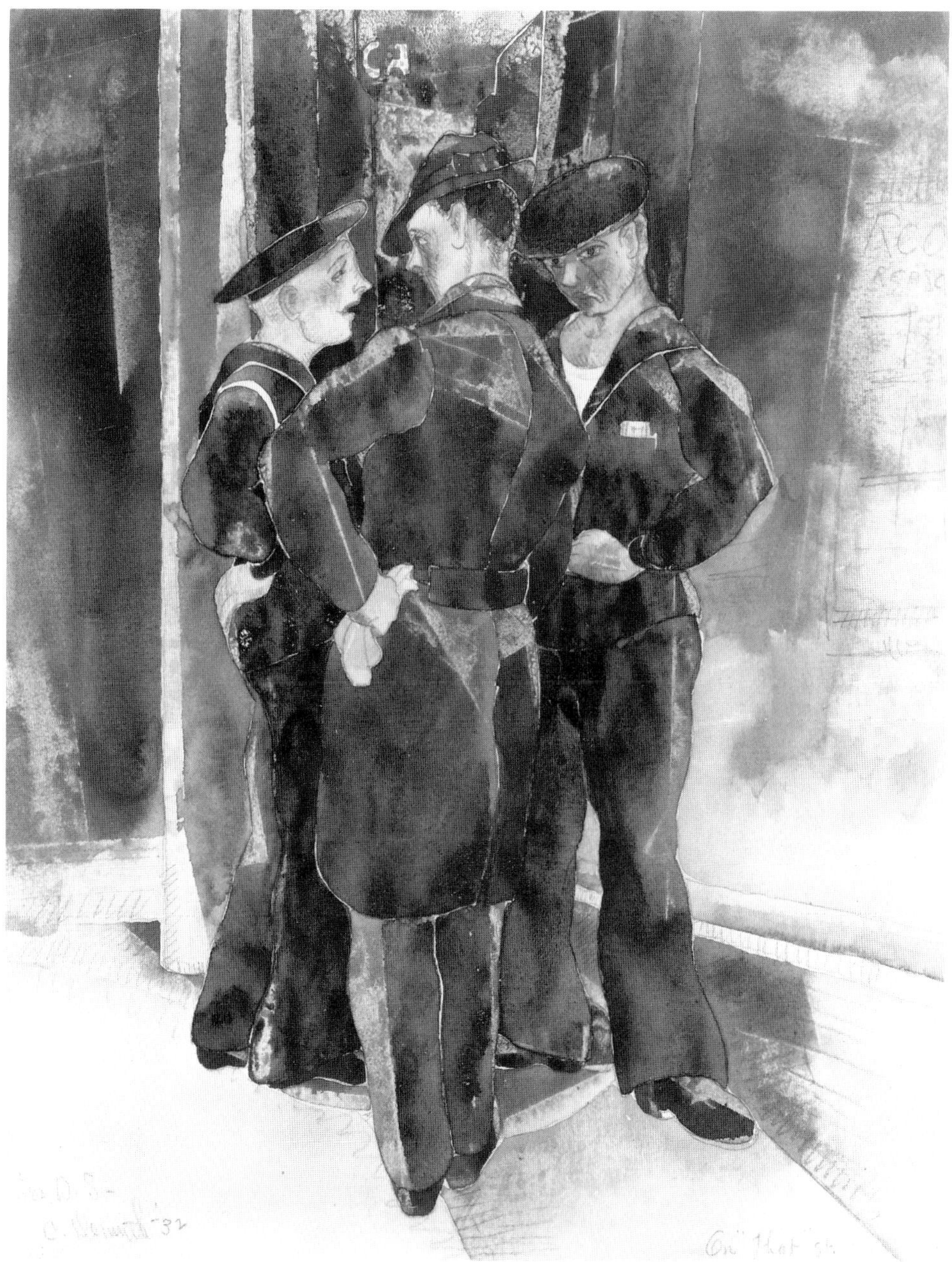

19. Charles Demuth, *On "That" Street,* watercolor and pencil on paper, $10^{15}/_{16} \times 8\frac{1}{2}$ in., 1932. Art Institute of Chicago, Chicago.

has been replaced by a gentleman with a cane who quite obviously is propositioning two sailors. Something of the mixture of sexual exhibitionism and aggression that characterizes the act of Davis's drunken policeman reappears in Demuth's late erotic watercolors. The policeman's pistol-phallus becomes an actual penis in *Three Sailors on the Beach*. Here another kind of men in uniform display their "guns" in lewd gestures that are both seductive and threatening.

Undoubtedly the pleasure of sexual contact with sailors, soldiers, and policemen was heightened by the danger of arrest or violence. But because certain homosexuals took such chances does not mean that the fear of violence, blackmail, or arrest was not real. This is one of the reasons *Three Sailors on A Beach* is so remarkable. If homosexual men traveled to the waterfront in search of sexual liaisons, they rarely made records of the fact, which could be used against them later. Yet Demuth's initials tattooed into the arm of one of the figures are a sign that he was, at least in spirit, engaging in an illegal activity. Had Demuth's erotic paintings been seen by the wrong audience, they would have permanently ruined his reputation and his family name.

4

Illustrating Difference

Demuth did not risk doing blatantly erotic work until the early 1930s. He was then in his fifties and in such ill health that perhaps the danger of scandal no longer seemed so frightening. The late sailor watercolors are a return in style to the figurative mode he worked out between 1916 and 1919, when his art reached its maturity. Thematically they are also connected to the works of the 1910s. Close analysis of the series of illustrations that Demuth did during World War I suggests a conscious effort to explore the points in which sexual definition comes under pressure in society.

Although the sexual content of Demuth's illustrations in no way equals the explicitness of his late sailor watercolors, he chose subjects that by and large would have been considered shocking to most Americans during World War I. Henry McBride claimed that one had to view Demuth's illustrations for Emile Zola's *Nana* in the back room of Charles Daniel's gallery so as not to offend the public. "There are some watercolors of Mr. Demuth that have not been hung upon the wall. The subjects were selected by a reading of Zola's 'Nana.' They are kept hidden in a portfolio and are only shown to museum directors and proved lovers of modern art upon presentation of visiting cards. They are quite advanced in style."[1]

In general the stories Demuth chose to illustrate are remarkably consistent in their insistence on the centrality of sex in human affairs. Invariably they focused on the margins of society, the places where the moralizing systems of a culture seem most in danger. A recurring theme is the confusion of traditional masculine and feminine roles—sexual identification and the signs of gender always seem to be in the process of breaking up. If the stories do not directly depict male homosexual relationships (although female homosexuality is almost always present), their characters either share with the homosexual of Demuth's period the edges of the city—the so-called demimonde, where forbidden entertainments flourish—or struggle with a dangerous and essential secret, the homosexual's typical burden. In this way, Demuth can be taken to be constantly alluding to a homosexual experience that is, as it were, just outside the picture.

Although Demuth dwells on a clandestine world where sexual deviants are common, his art is not a plea for sexual liberation. All the works Demuth illustrated—*Nana,* "The Girl with the Golden Eyes," the *Lulu Plays,* "The Turn of the Screw," "The Beast in the Jungle," "The Masque of the Red Death," and "Distinguished Air"—show human relationships, sexual or otherwise, as invariably unhealthy or incomplete. Either desire is brazenly destructive, taking the form of an aggressively seductive female (Nana as Venus, before an adoring crowd, or Lulu as an act in a circus show), or it lurks as some hidden danger, something that may, or may not, come (the ghosts in "The Turn of the Screw" or the Beast in "The Beast in the Jungle"). Demuth's view of sex, heterosexual or homosexual, is bleak. His characters are as trapped when they push against the boundaries of permissible behavior as they would be if they never questioned the rules.

Why did he do illustrations? The question is complicated by Demuth's peculiar choice of works to illustrate. Instead of choosing works with sparse descriptions (fairy tales, myths, and Bible stories have proven the perfect texts for illustration because they rarely include detailed descriptions of what people and places looked like), Demuth chose to work with writings that were particularly rich in descriptive language and, perhaps more problematically, in psychological complexity of character. In fact, one of his favorite authors, Henry James, directly attacked the idea of having his stories illustrated, arguing that his words had already done the illustrator's work: "Anything that relieves responsible prose of the duty of being, while placed before us, good enough, interesting enough and, if the question be of picture, pictorial enough, above all *in itself,* does it the worst of services."[2]

Of course, Demuth's watercolors were never meant to be published with the books they illustrate and so do not wreak havoc with the author's intentions. But it is in the nature of Demuth's chosen medium that we are forced back to the other artist's words, ideas, and narrative if we are to find an explanation for these paintings. For Demuth, at this early stage in his artistic development, the danger that his pictures would be redundant or superfluous when compared to the words of James, Balzac, Poe, Pater, and Zola did not outweigh the benefits gained in tying his painting to major works of art that grappled with crucial issues of modern life. The viewer's association of words and images would transform small figurative watercolors by a provincial artist into complex meditations on sexual experience—or so it was hoped.

By 1915, when he began his illustrations, Demuth had already been to Europe three times, including a sixteen-month sojourn from 1912 through 1914. In Paris, at Gertrude Stein's, he saw some of the best examples of cubist and fauvist painting. In New York, during the same period, he would have seen the work of Picasso and Matisse at Stieglitz's gallery. But Demuth was slow to take in the example of modern painting. Although he eventually confronted the influence of cubism in the Bermuda series of 1917, his initial reaction to Picasso's and Braque's experiments was to leave them out of his art. Unable, or unwilling, to take up their formal inventions immediately, Demuth instead found in illustration an indirect way to explore one great assumption of much contemporary art and theory: the primacy of sex in human relationships. Heretofore Demuth had yet to do major work. The ploy of illustrating unillustratable texts allowed Demuth to make a leap to significance and centrality. At the same time he found a way to investigate safely parallels to his own sexuality: through illustration, moral responsibility seemed to shift to an absent author.

Nana

The prologue to his earliest set of illustrations, known as the Nana series, is sometimes called *Nana's Awakening* (fig. 20). In the center of the image Demuth places a lamp with a brazenly phallic stem before a religious icon. This juxtaposition is a kind of signature of the artist's interest in sex as a center of fascination, worship, and contention. The scene, though it features Nana, is actually not part of the novel. Instead it illustrates an incident in Nana's childhood, from Zola's earlier novel *L'assommoir.* High up behind a transom Nana looks down on her mother and her lover. On their way to the bedroom, the amorous couple is oblivi-

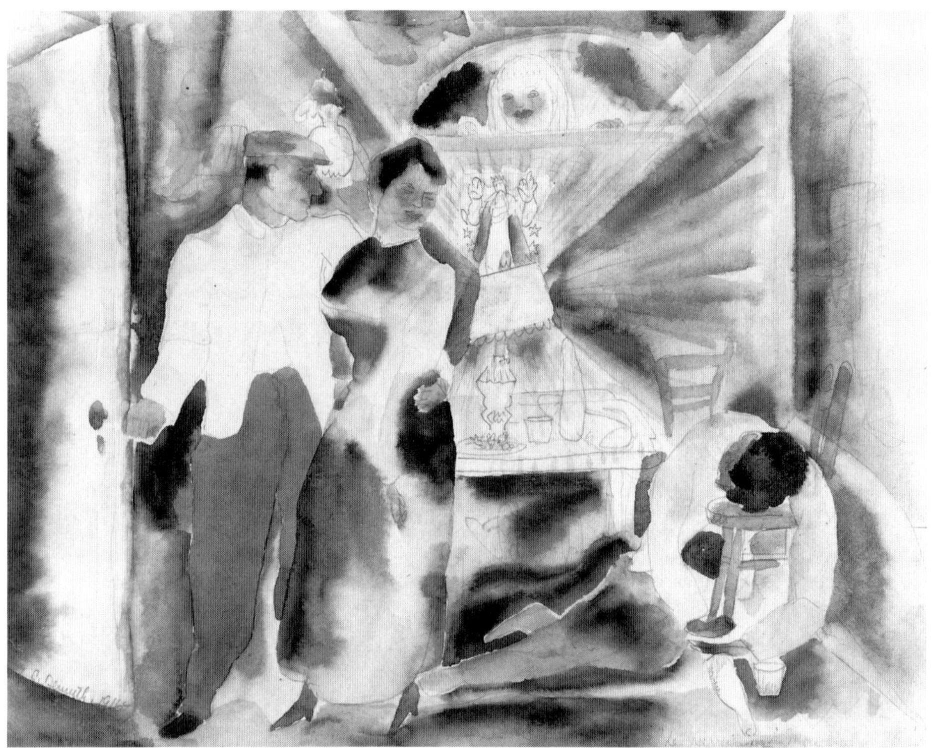

20. Charles Demuth, *Nana's Awakening* or *Gervaise and Lantier Find Corpeau Drunk,* watercolor and pencil on paper, 8 × 10½ in., 1916. Illustration for *L'assommoir,* by Emile Zola. Philadelphia Museum of Art, Philadelphia; A. E. Gallatin Collection.

ous to the child, and unconcerned with Nana's drunken father, who has passed out on the floor before them: "Nana appeared at the glass door of the little room, behind one of the panes. The child had just woke up, and she got up softly in her night-dress, pale with sleep. She saw her father wallowing in his vomit; then, with her face against the glass, she stood there waiting until her mother's petticoat had disappeared into the other man's room opposite. She stood there very seriously. She opened her eyes wide, vicious young eyes, lit now with a sensual curiosity."[3]

In the lower right-hand corner Demuth wrote and then erased the words "Le

Début."[4] The watercolor was probably painted at the end of the series, but it functions in relation to the other images drawn from Zola's *Nana* as a commencement, an introduction to Nana's career. It is a kind of primal scene with the father, sick and impotent, replaced by the lover of Nana's mother. In *L'assommoir,* Zola suggests that Nana not only watches her mother go into her lover's bedroom but continues to listen to their lovemaking. Nana's grandmother gossips the next day: "The most shocking part of it is, that Nana must have been able to hear it too. . . . She was restless all night, she who usually sleeps so sound; she tossed and turned as if she had live coals in her bed."[5]

If *Nana's Awakening* is the prologue to the *Nana* suite, it is also the epilogue. It functions as an explanation for Nana's history, and so it has the quality of a memory. The title, referring both to Nana's being disturbed from sleep by her mother's entrance and to her new-found knowledge of the world, is specially ironic given the dreamlike quality of the image. The mottled spread of washes undermines the solidity of the objects Demuth draws. Color spills over the edges of his figures, giving them a soft, diaphanous quality. Demuth departs from the text slightly. Whereas Zola had Nana stand at a glass door, Demuth instead raises her off the ground to a glass transom above the scene. From this vantage point she floats over the drama, her face flushed. She is no longer an innocent child. Her new-found knowledge raises her above the rest of her family—it gives her power. This power is symbolized by the very obvious penis Demuth works into the lamp stem directly at the center of the painting, directly below Nana.

Adding Demuth's lone illustration from *L'assommoir* to the other Nana illustrations alters Zola's narrative. Zola's Nana is inconsistent at best—she comes off more as a conglomeration of what Zola took to be female characteristics than as a real woman with a past and a coherent personality. The illustration suggests that Demuth was interested in the origins of Nana's sexual exploits. Closely associated as he was with other artists in Provincetown and New York, all of them steeped in the latest psychoanalytic theory, Demuth may have been acknowledging the idea that an adult's later sexual responses and character are largely determined by childhood experience. His representation of Nana as a child individualizes her, makes her less Zola's symbol of all women and more of a particular case history. It suggests that Demuth was drawn to *Nana* for reasons that go beyond its catalogue of perversions and sexual degeneracies. At the same time, Demuth's prominently placed phallus seems to undermine the seriousness of Zola's text. Instead of a description of the final decay of a working-class woman's life and its inevitable poisoning of her daughter's moral fiber, we get a bawdy farce. The vulgarity of Demuth's joke, its irreverent connecting of sexual organs with religious worship, seems an attempt to distance the proceedings or give them a comic form. But by placing a phallus right under Nana, where her body would be if we could see through the back wall, it is as if Nana has been endowed with male genitals, and so can more fully become a surrogate for the artist himself.[6] The Baudelairian artist Demuth described in his own "The Voyage Was Almost Over" is also that wide-eyed child voyeuristically watching what her parents do at night. Here are the seeds of the future courtesan, and also of the flâneur.

In Demuth's illustrations as a whole, Nana's monstrousness is this ability to take for herself the forms of masculine power, even going so far as to keep her own courtesan. In *Count Muffat's First View of Nana at the Theatre* (fig. 21), the entire image is the peephole through which Muffat sees Nana in her transparent costume as Venus. Although it can be argued that looking at any depiction of a naked body is inherently voyeuristic, throughout the Nana series Demuth exaggerates the voyeuristic stance of the viewer. In *Count Muffat's First View of Nana* ours is specifically the passive view of someone who watches the forbidden object from a hidden location—the role that Nana played in *L'assommoir,* which she here exchanges to become the object of watching eyes. We see Nana standing absolutely erect, her buttocks turned toward us, so that her vagina and breasts—the signs of her sex—are hidden. Her back is arched and muscular. At the moment when her body is most exposed to view, she appears most androgynous, with the power and allure of both sexes. Despite her seductive nudity, she is almost masculine; but she is equally capable of becoming a beautiful, if terrible, mother. Later, in *Nana and Her Men* (fig. 22), Nana occupies a huge chair. Her body is enormous, softened, and rounded by the armchair. She is purposely out of scale in relation to the now-tiny Count, who is like a child at her feet. She occupies a similar chair and position in *Scene after Georges Stabs Himself with the Scissors* (fig. 23). Rather than show the violence of Georges's suicide,

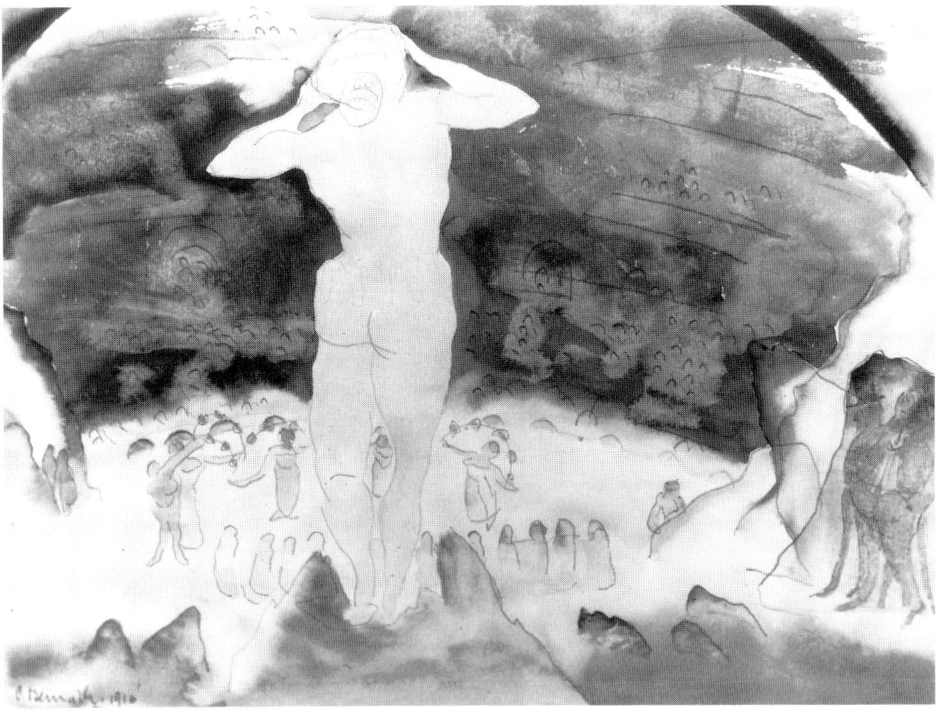

21. Charles Demuth, *Count Muffat's First View of Nana at the Theatre,* watercolor and pencil on paper, 8½ × 10¾ in., 1915–16. Illustration for *Nana,* by Emile Zola. Barnes Foundation, Merion, Pa. Photograph © 1993 by the Barnes Foundation.

Demuth focuses on the aftermath. While Nana sits in her chair contemplating the disaster, her maid is busy scrubbing Georges's blood out of the carpet:[7] "That was all. In her stupefaction Nana had sat down, still wearing her hat and gloves. The house relapsed into a heavy silence; the carriage had just driven away; and she sat motionless, not knowing what to think, her head buzzing after all that had happened." Zola coldly writes: "For the last few minutes the maid, who had brought a towel and bowl of water out of the dressing-room, had been rubbing the carpet to remove the blood-stain before it dried."[8]

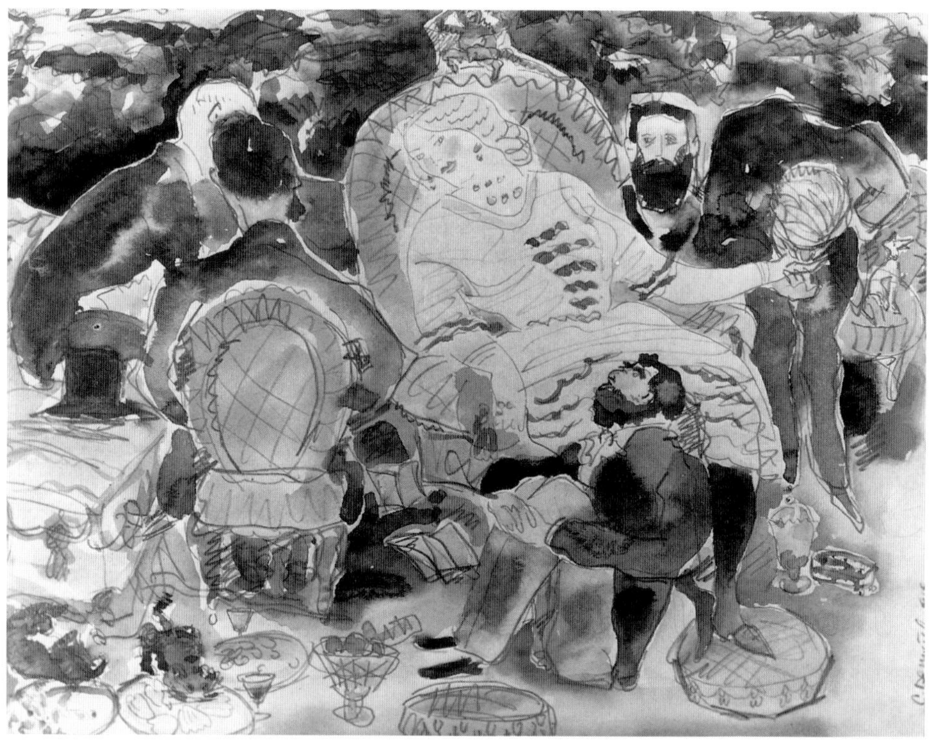

22. Charles Demuth, *Nana and Her Men,* watercolor and pencil on paper, $8\frac{1}{2} \times 10\frac{3}{4}$ in., 1915–16. Illustration for *Nana,* by Emile Zola. Barnes Foundation, Merion, Pa. Photograph © 1993 by the Barnes Foundation.

In Demuth's illustration, Nana holds Georges's suicide weapon, the implication being that though she did not kill her child-lover, she is responsible for his death. Holding the bloody scissors, Nana symbolically takes the genitals that were conferred on her by Demuth in her "Début." Although all of the Nana illustrations are painted in broad washes that blur and confuse the edges of objects, in the Barnes version of this subject the forms are particularly unsteady.[9] The rigidity of Nana's figure seems to drain out of her body like the blood from Georges's wound, leaving the scissors dangling from her hand, about to drop.

The image of Georges's suicide is just one of the illustrations in which death and sexuality are linked. In *Nana before the Mirror,* Demuth repeats the pose of Nana standing with her back to the viewer, which first seduced the count, but instead of performing she is admiring herself in the mirror.[10] Muffat cowers on his knees with his hands covering his eyes. He has looked at Nana's reflection and seen a skull. The pencil drawing that provides the armature of the watercolor is crude. Demuth put aside the delicate line that he used for most of the pictures of this period and pressed down heavily with what seems to be a blunted point or the side of the pencil. Nana's body is outlined several times, and Demuth applies black paint under her left arm

23. Charles Demuth, *Scene after Georges Stabs Himself with the Scissors (Second Version),* watercolor and pencil on paper, 7⅞ × 11¾ in., 1915–16. Illustration for *Nana,* by Emile Zola. Museum of Fine Arts, Boston; Charles Henry Hayden Fund.

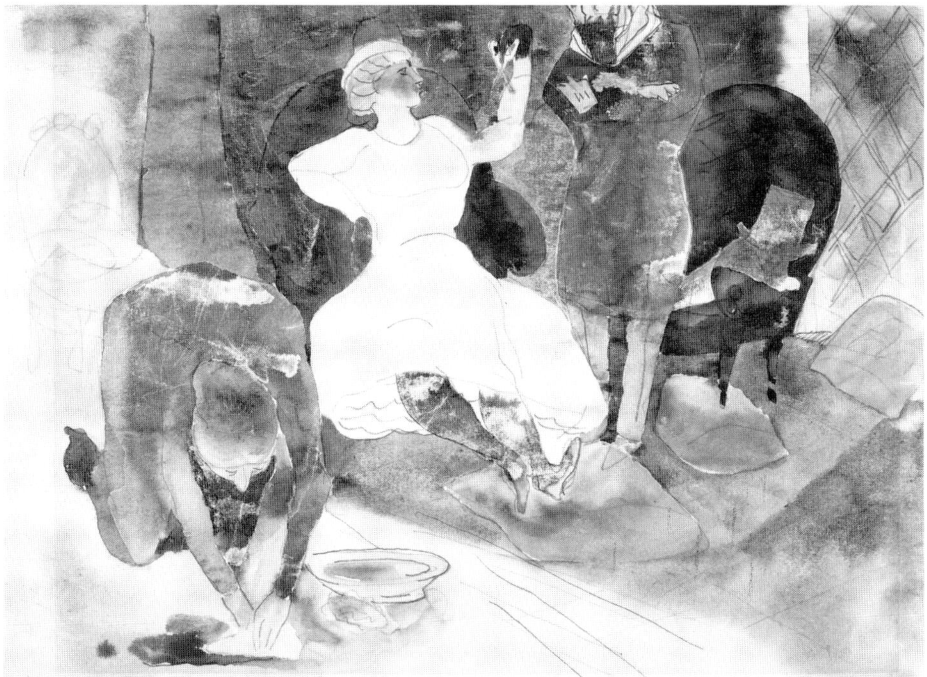

to increase the contrast between her pink body and the jumbled background of scattered furniture and clothing. The background is further diffused by Demuth's impatient scribbles. Nana's nude figure is emphatically contained by Demuth's dark line, but the line of Muffat's form trembles and breaks—the anatomically incorrect drawing expressing his terror as he imagines her death in the mirror.

The mirror of *Nana before the Mirror* predicts *Nana*'s finale. The bedroom is the site of seduction for most of the novel but in *The Death of Nana* (fig. 24) it is given over to disease. Nana is laid out on the bed: "Nana was left alone, her face upturned

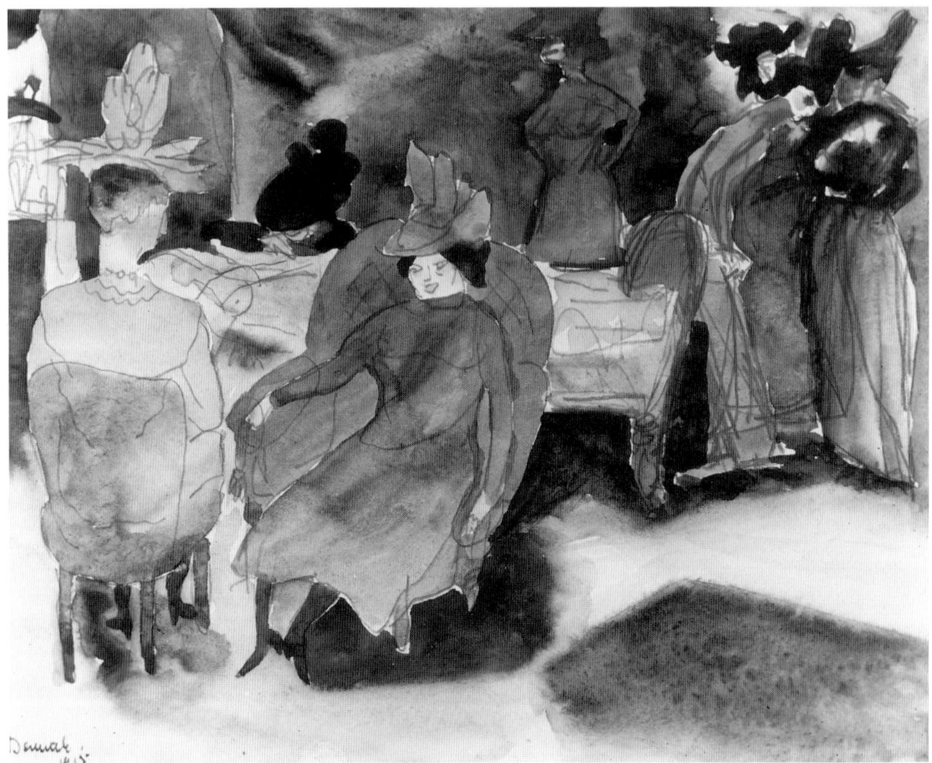

24. Charles Demuth, *The Death of Nana,* watercolor and pencil on paper, 8½ × 10¾ in., 1915. Illustration for *Nana,* by Emile Zola. Barnes Foundation, Merion, Pa. Photograph © 1993 by the Barnes Foundation.

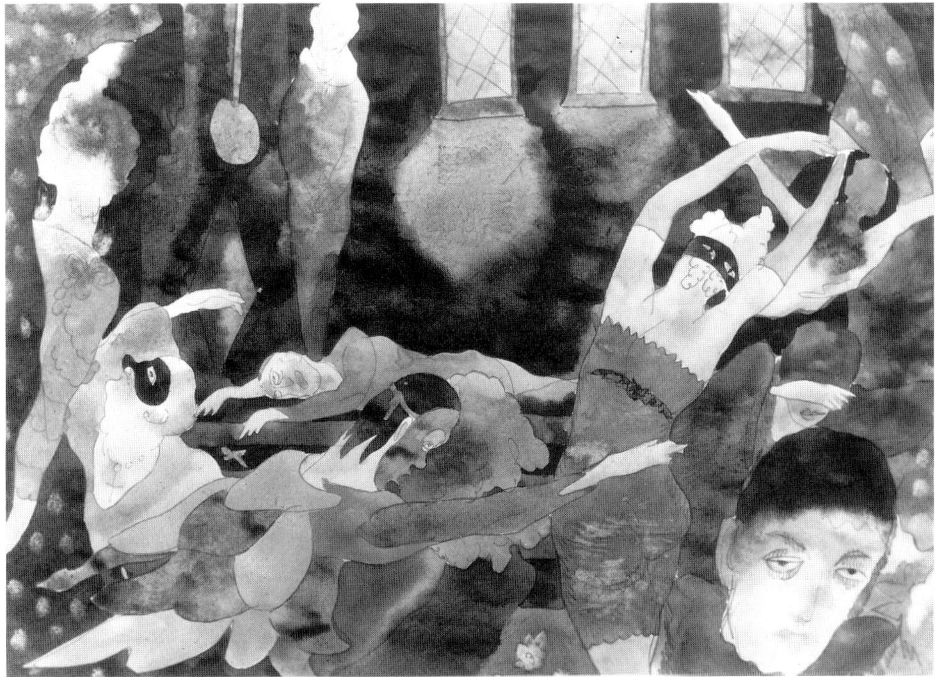

25. Charles Demuth, *The Triumph of the Red Death,* watercolor and pencil on paper, 8½ × 10¾ in., 1918. Illustration for "The Masque of the Red Death," by Edgar Allan Poe. Barnes Foundation, Merion, Pa. Photograph © 1993 by the Barnes Foundation.

in the light from the candle. What lay on the pillow was a charnel-house, a heap of pus and blood, a shovelful of putrid flesh. . . . A large reddish crust starting on one of the cheeks was invading the mouth, twisting it into a terrible grin. And around this grotesque and horrible mask of death, the hair, the beautiful hair, still blazed like sunlight and flowed in a stream of gold. Venus was decomposing."[11] Demuth does not give us Zola's close-up but instead shows the scene as a social occasion. The body itself is in the background.

That restaging of Zola's Grand Guignol finale seems characteristic of Demuth's art as a whole. When he chose to illustrate the terrible face of the plague from Poe's *The Triumph of the Red Death* (fig. 25), he took care to place the face itself

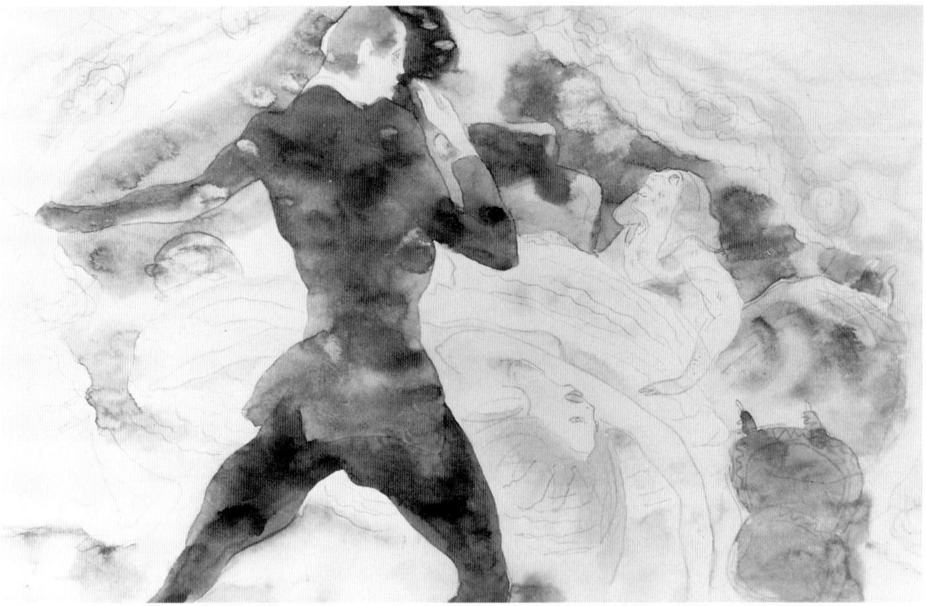

26. Charles Demuth, *The Girl with the Golden Eyes,* watercolor and pencil on paper, 8½ × 10¾ in., 1915. Illustration for "The Girl with the Golden Eyes," by Honoré de Balzac. Barnes Foundation, Merion, Pa. Photograph © 1993 by the Barnes Foundation.

far in the background. Demuth is not an artist whose eroticism is laced with delight in suffering or desire for extinction. Eros may indeed lead inevitably toward death; that does not make death itself erotic. Of all the writers Demuth chose to illustrate Poe is the only one whose work was firmly part of the decadent canon; and even with Poe he chose not to pull out all the horrific stops. Death is a vague, red-pocked figure in the distance; or the undefinable crisscrossing of lines, over there, on Nana's syphilitic corpse.

Demuth maintains the same sense of emotional and erotic distance even when he is illustrating as violent and bizarre a story as Balzac's "The Girl with the Golden Eyes" (fig. 26). In the single illustration he did for the story, he focuses on the final scene, in which Henri de Marsay bursts in on his beloved Paquita to find that she has been butchered by the Marquise de San Réal: "De Marsay lightly scaled the stairs, with which he was familiar, and recognized the passage leading to the boudoir. When he opened the door he experienced the involuntary shudder which the sight of bloodshed gives in the most determined of men. The spectacle which was offered to his view was, moreover, in more than one respect astonishing to him. The Marquise was a woman." Henri's horror is caused not just because the girl with the golden eyes had "expired in a bath of blood" but because his rival for her love has turned out to be a woman with whom he shares the same physical features.[12] De Marsay suddenly realizes that the marquise is his twin, separated from him since childhood.

In Demuth's image, de Marsay's back dominates the composition, hiding the worst from our view.[13] The girl's body is thrown back in the manner of the figure in Henry Fuseli's *Nightmare,* and brother and sister stand on either side of the bloody body. De Marsay looks at his sister, as if in a mirror. They are, in a sense, meant to be opposite sides of the same destructive and manipulative personality. The interchangeability of their genders had already been acted out in an earlier stage of the short story when Paquita had forced de Marsay to dress in a woman's costume as if making the brother and sister one. Demuth's composition creates a similar mixing of genders. By placing the two across from each other on either side of the dead Paquita, Demuth links them again through her butchered body. As with Nana's posture in *Count Muffat's First View of Nana at the Theatre,* Demuth has put an extraordinary emphasis on de Marsay's buttocks. They are pushed out and carefully delineated by tightly fitting (and historically inappropriate) clothing. Marsay's sinuous body, painted boldly in a sweeping black wash, is much more fully realized than Paquita's limp body. Significantly, Paquita's vagina is hidden by de Marsay's anus—one genital has been exchanged with another, and the feminine and the masculine are visually merged.

The fascination of "The Girl with the Golden Eyes" for Demuth is not merely the chance to project aggression toward women—though this element is undoubtedly there, as it is in Balzac's text. As with his illustration of *The Death of Nana,* he is far more tactful than the texts he is using in describing death. It is important that "The Girl with the Golden Eyes" joins *Nana* (and *Lulu*) in including lesbian relationships of great intensity. Margarita's passion for Paquita is far more powerful than Henri's. Although he contemplates killing Paquita out of jealousy throughout the story, his sister beats him to it. Continuing the confusion of genders, Margarita's weapon is characteristically phallic—a dagger that she thrusts repeatedly into Paquita's body. In Demuth's illustration, Henri's ineffectual arms, one raised to his mouth with horror, the other dangling, suggest impotence in the presence of this terrible struggle that has covered both women with blood. It is true that lesbianism was almost a staple of French literature by 1915—often functioning as a vehicle of male fantasy uninterrupted by the intrusion of male players. Yet although

27. Charles Demuth, *Nana Visiting Her Friend Satin,* watercolor and pencil on paper, 8½ × 10¾ in., 1915. Illustration for *Nana,* by Emile Zola. Barnes Foundation, Merion, Pa. Photograph © 1993 by the Barnes Foundation.

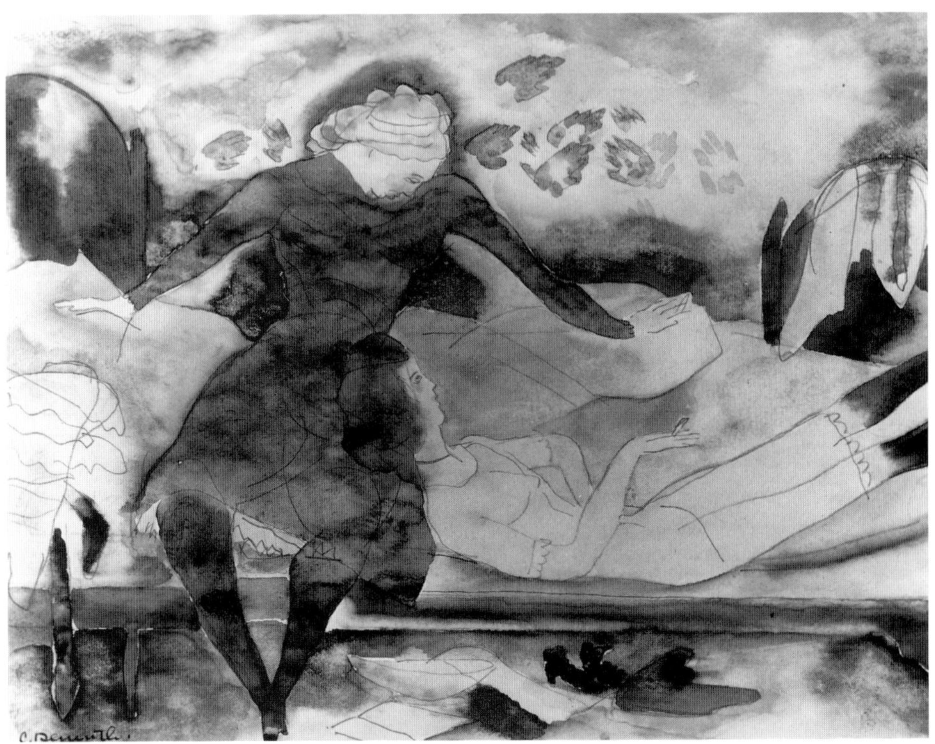

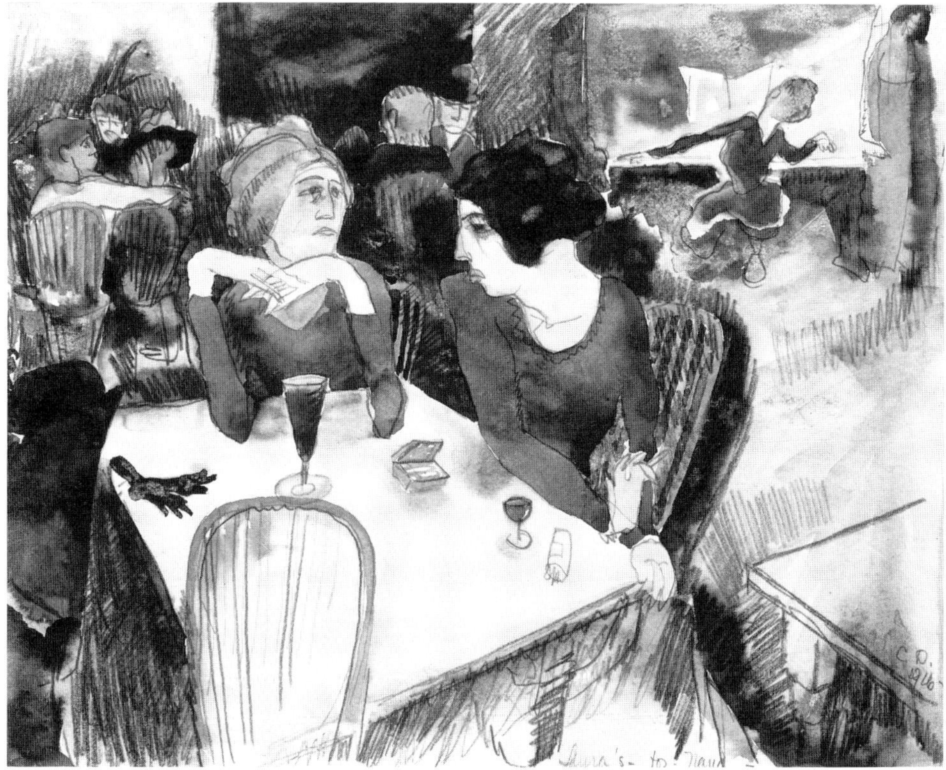

28. Charles Demuth, *Nana, Seated Left, and Satin at Laure's Restaurant,* watercolor and pencil on paper, $8\frac{1}{2} \times 11$ in., 1916. Illustration for *Nana,* by Emile Zola. Museum of Modern Art, New York; gift of Abby Aldrich Rockefeller.

Demuth acknowledges the lesbian content of his texts, he does not show moments of high eroticism. Paquita's death, her body covered with red marks (not unlike the plague marks in the Poe illustration), her vagina hidden by Henri's torso, is hardly a typically erotic scene. Nana and Satin are not having sex in *Nana Visiting Her Friend Satin* (fig. 27); they are talking, Nana recounting the beatings she has received from her lover. Demuth also gives us the pair at the lesbian restaurant, Laure's (fig. 28). The image lacks drama and seems determined not to be titillating. It is a scene of

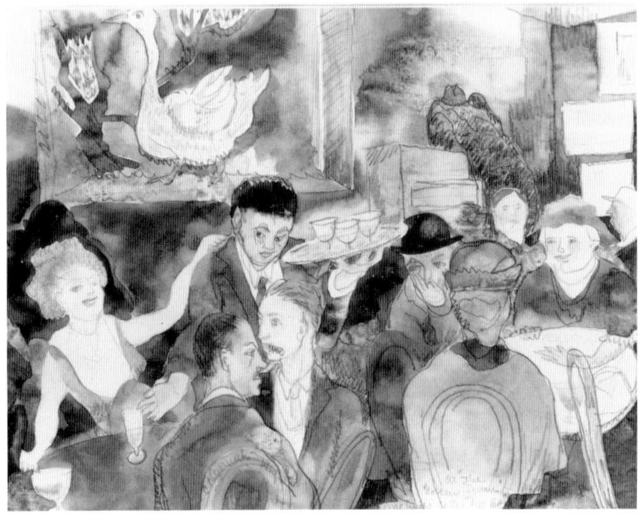

29. Charles Demuth, *At the Golden Swan,* watercolor and pencil on paper, 8 × 10½ in., 1919. Collection of Irwin Goldstein. Photo: Kurt Muller.

two women conversing, surrounded by other women, some in dresses, others in male drag. Its presence in the series may point to Demuth's desire to find equivalent scenes for the types of speakeasies and cafés, often frequented by homosexuals, that he liked to visit in Harlem and Greenwich Village (Nana and Satin's conversation at a café is similar to the discussion between the artist and Marcel Duchamp that occupies the foreground of the slightly later *At the Golden Swan* [fig. 29]). No doubt depicting lesbians was a way for Demuth to represent the world of same-sex relationships in comparative safety. All the same, Demuth does not exclude the lesbian world from the unhappiness and violence of the heterosexual; same-sex love, like that between men and women, ends in disease or murder.

There is a story about Charles Demuth that traces his lifelong bachelorhood to the ending of an affair with the divorcée Emmasita Register. Register had refused Demuth's proposal because, having contracted syphilis, she was "ruined" and could "never honorably become any man's wife." When she informed Demuth, he was so panicked that he tried at once to leave her house undetected. As he was attempting to pull himself through a back window, he heard her cry, "What an end! What an end!"[14] Given the psychological bent of so much of the writing on Demuth, it is remarkable that scholars have not made more of this story. Built into the episode is an initial attraction: the dream, reaffirmed in Demuth's story "The Voyage Was Almost Over," of the possibility of a normal heterosexual life—a dream destroyed by syphilis. According to the original account, Demuth only alluded to Register's disease; and so, as in the "Voyage," the possibility of a happy married life is destroyed by some "unknown Thing."

What is essential about the cruelty of the incident is Demuth's moving toward and away from the woman he supposedly loved; the pattern of attraction and avoidance, which I have suggested is built into Demuth's use of the form of illustration itself, also appears in his life. Demuth comes to Register to ask her for her hand, only to end up escaping out of a window like a child who has done something terribly wrong. Demuth's illustration for the finale of James's "The Turn of the Screw," *Miles and the Governess* (fig. 30), reproduces this relationship between threatening woman and child-man. In the picture the governess wraps her arms around Miles. Miles's pose is one of complete ambivalence. One of his hands is on her shoulder, but his body is rigid and pushed back away from her embrace. Even as his head is turned away, out of the corner of his eyes he looks back at her face. Demuth gives us the moment when the governess asks Miles what he did at school that caused him to be expelled: "Did you take letters?—or other things?"[15] In typical James fashion, those other things remain elusive or, as the initial narrator puts it, "the story *won't* tell." All we know is that these "things" are connected to the influence of the "Ghost" Quint, who before his death "had strange passages and perils, secret disorders, vices more than suspected." Whether or not James had homosexuality in mind, I would speculate that a homosexual reader of the story would most likely infer—particularly in light of the close relationship of Quint and Miles, that these vices included homosexuality. The governess's intention is to shield the children from the ghosts and the unknown vices by means of her own virtue. But that shielding itself becomes physical—almost sexual: "I held him [Miles]—it may be imagined with what a passion; but at the end of a minute I began to feel what it truly was that I held. We were alone with the quiet day, and his little heart had stopped."[16]

The governess's embrace is passionate and finally deadly, the child succumbing

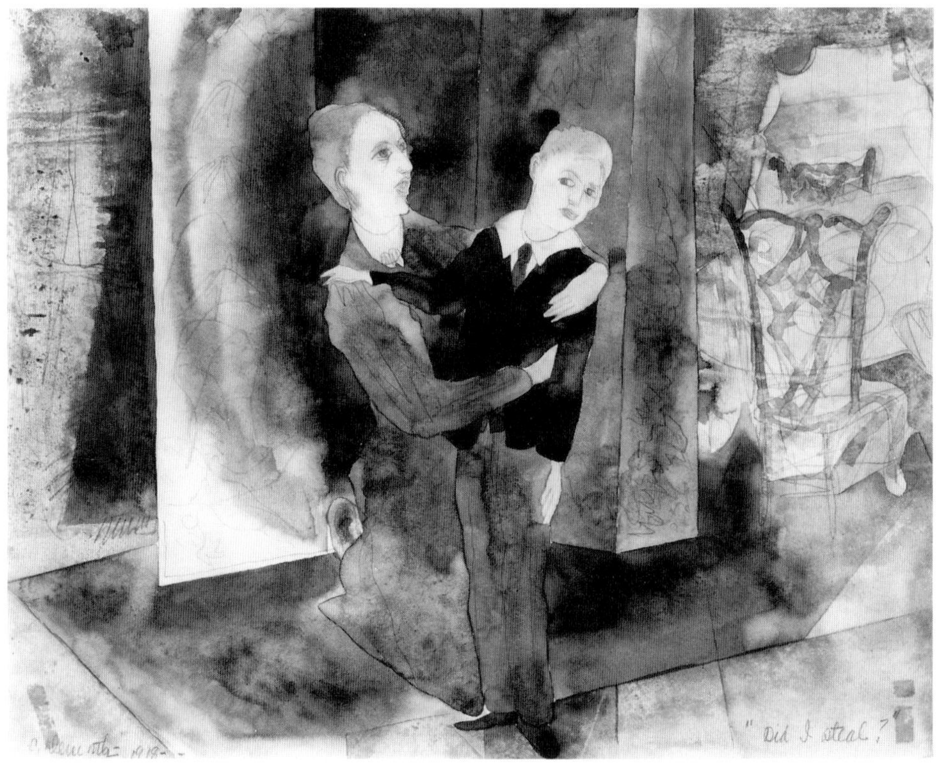

30. Charles Demuth, *Miles and the Governess,* watercolor and pencil on paper, 8 × 10⅜ in., 1918. Illustration for "The Turn of the Screw," by Henry James. Philadelphia Museum of Art, Philadelphia; given by Frank and Alice Osborn.

to the terrible touch of an engulfing woman. It has been suggested that the operating force in these paintings, as well the *Nana* and *Lulu* series, is Demuth's supposed misogyny. In her dissertation devoted to Demuth's illustrations, Pamela Edwards Allara flatly states that Demuth's recurring theme of a femme fatale "who destroyed every man with whom she came in touch would have confirmed Demuth's own homosexual view of women." She supports her view with a quote from Demuth's dealer, Charles Daniel, who said of his *Nana* series, "Underneath his admiration for *Nana* lay a desire to believe all women worthless."[17] There is little doubt that

Demuth's illustrations express a deep ambivalence toward women, yet in my view his attitudes are more complex than Allara will allow. They incorporate both identification and attraction.

We still have to confront the classic psychoanalytic account that underlies Allara's equation of misogyny and homosexuality—the rooting of homosexuality in a pathological child-mother relationship. In such a view the illustration of the relationship between the governess and Miles, or those endowing Nana with a phallus and illustrating her subsequent castration of Georges, plays out the homosexual's terror before the phallic mother.[18] It is difficult to unveil Demuth's unconscious drives with so little basic information about his relationship with his mother, other women, and men. Whether Demuth's view of women is a result of the dynamics of familial relationships or an internalization of society's disapproval of and violence toward homosexuality cannot be determined. But we can wonder about the artist's conscious intentions in choosing stories in which sexual difference and violence play such a large and obvious part. Is Demuth's work, as Champa suggested, compulsively sexual, or is its sexual content carefully exploited to articulate his own sexuality? In the case of "The Turn of the Screw" illustrations, although we cannot ignore the implications of Demuth's imaging of an overly protective woman, equally important is the fact that the governess's killing of Miles is rooted in those "other things," whether imagined or real, that he did with Quint or at school. Demuth's ostensible focus on a smothering feminine embrace, while representing fears about the other sex—fears that both heterosexual and homosexual men may share—is also a means of alluding to other sexualities outside male-female relationships.

Any interpretation of Demuth's supposed ambivalence toward women has to take account of the degree to which Demuth himself consciously draws attention to it. The most glaring example is the opening of the Lulu series, *The Animal Tamer Presents Lulu,* which shows a parted curtain and a small circus ring.[19] The tamer holds his whip, and out of his mouth come the words "Hop, Charlie, march." Lulu, dressed in a clown suit that looks more like bloomers, says, "Your bride is here!" Wedekind's verse seems to reaffirm the message that it is women who bring disease:

She was created to incite to sin
To lure, seduce, corrupt, drop poison in,—
To murder, without being once suspected.
Your bride is here?
Hop, Charlie, march! Carry her to her cage.[20]

Between the bodies of the tamer and Lulu we can just make out the head of a young man, whose expression suggests that if Lulu is his fate, he is not entirely pleased by the fact. Here are all the symbols for Charlie's misogyny, and his alleged near miss with syphilis, spelled out for us by the artist himself, to the point that he includes lines that contain his own name, identifying Lulu as his prospective bride. Yet it would be a mistake to take Wedekind's plays or Demuth's illustrations at face value. The Lulu plays are not, to put it mildly, naturalistic. They move between modes of farce and horror, and it is difficult to determine how many of the observations about women are meant to be satirical comments on a hypocritical society.

Demuth's awareness of the antinaturalistic quality of these plays, and of their moments of absurdist humor, is indicated by his highly conscious incorporation of artifice in the *Lulu* pictures. In every watercolor of the series he includes a red curtain, usually on either side, to indicate that we are seeing a play. Dialogue is indicated within balloons, creating an allusion to the humor of cartoons and caricatures. This is not to say that these comic devices distance the artist completely from the events he depicts. Demuth signifies this by placing his own name in the tamer's balloon—he too becomes the brunt of the satire. Demuth's high degree of self-awareness is missing from the view that sees his art as a kind of sublimation of misplaced sexual drives.

"The Beast in the Jungle"

Demuth's insistent expression of an aversion to women and to the institution of marriage points us to those men who are *not* heterosexual. Both "The Voyage Was Almost Over" and Demuth's episode with Emmasita Register function as explanations for his failure to marry or finally to be heterosexual. Supposedly the artist would have married but for Register's disease—he would have taken the beckoning hand but for some "unknown Thing" that stopped him. Indeed, until very recently, male homosexuality was considered as much a drive away from women as a move toward men. This viewpoint pervades Demuth's attitude toward his own sexuality. Perhaps Demuth conceived of homosexuality not as an alternative form of romantic love but as the absence of love. Such a conception of his own sexuality might explain Demuth's attraction to James's "The Beast in the Jungle," the subject of his final series of illustrations of the 1915–19 period.

A mysterious excuse is at the very center of James's story and Demuth's illustrations. In James's novella, the hero, Marcher, spends his whole life waiting for some unknown event or revelation to happen to him. He is never sure what it is, but he knows it makes him different, cuts him off from those around him. In describing it to May Bartram, he can only say that though it may be unnatural to everyone else, to him it will seem natural "and of course, above all, unmistakable. I think of it simply as *the* thing. *The* thing will of itself appear natural."[21] Demuth's Thing from "The Voyage Was Almost Over" is much like Marcher's Beast. Allara has noted Demuth's seemingly close association with the character of Marcher in the final image of his "The Beast in the Jungle" illustration.[22] In *Marcher Receives His Revelation at May Bartram's Tomb* (fig. 31), Marcher prostrates himself before May's grave. At his side is a cane, which is not called for in the James story but which Demuth always carried. As if to make the connection even clearer, Demuth has put his signature into the hat that has fallen from Marcher's head.

Demuth's capitalization of *Thing* in "The Voyage Was Almost Over" works like the italicized *the* of James's text. They are both attempts to wrest the words from their ordinary usage, to give their ordinariness an extraordinary quality. In both James's and Demuth's texts we sense that what is being striven for is a state not easily described. The point of "The Beast in the Jungle" is that the "Beast" resists being named by Marcher, either because it does not exist or because it is so terrible (or wonderful) it cannot be imagined. Both James's and Demuth's "thing" interfere with their characters' having a traditional heterosexual attachment. Marcher's "conviction, his apprehension, his obsession, in short, wasn't a privilege he could invite a woman to share: and that consequence of it was precisely what was the matter with him."[23] In Demuth's story we sense that it is not because of the character's physical traits that the white hand never beckons from the couples on the deck. The hand is never offered because the hero is incapable or unwilling to take it.

In her essay on James, Eve Kosofsky Sedgwick has explored the connections

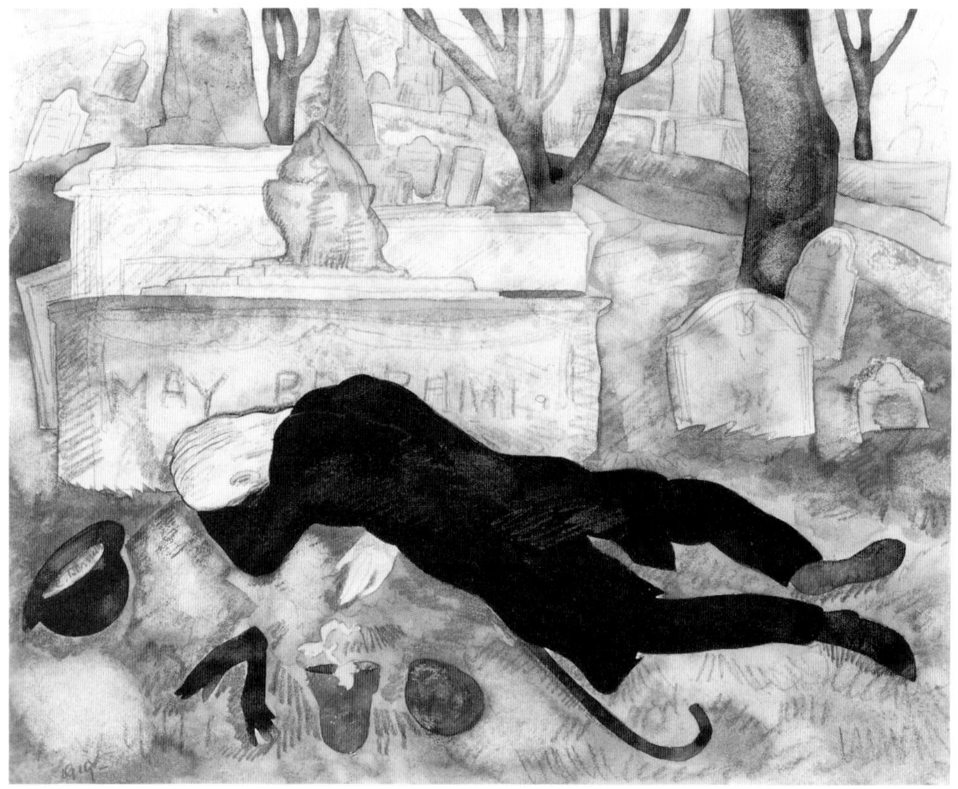

31. Charles Demuth, *Marcher Receives His Revelation at May Bartram's Tomb,* watercolor and pencil on paper, 8 × 10⅛ in., 1919. Illustration for "The Beast in the Jungle," by Henry James. Philadelphia Museum of Art, Philadelphia; given by Frank and Alice Osborn.

between the Beast and homosexuality. James's insistence on the unnameable quality of Marcher's Beast gives it the preferred non-nomenclature of late nineteenth-century society for the "love that dare not speak its name." But Sedgwick is careful to state that although Marcher is not a homosexual man, "Marcher lives as one who is *in the closet.*"[24] Evidence that Demuth read the Beast to be homosexuality is suggested by the first illustration for "The Beast in the Jungle," called *The Boat Ride from Sorrento* (fig. 32). The scene is actually a flashback in the novel. May reminds Marcher that he first told her about his secret during a boat ride in Naples:

> "You know you told me something that I've never forgotten and that again and again has made me think of you since; it was that tremendously hot day when we went to Sorrento, across the bay, for the breeze. What I allude to was what you said to me, on the way back as we sat, under the awning of the boat, enjoying the cool. Have you forgotten?"
>
> He had forgotten.[25]

Instead of placing the two in shade as the text would suggest, Demuth shows them on the boat in bright sunlight. Perhaps recalling the composition of Mary Cassatt's *The Boating Party* (fig. 33), Demuth creates the most geometrically dynamic of his illustrations. As in Cassatt's famous painting, the boat is radically foreshortened, but instead of moving away it moves directly toward us. Cassatt's rower is prominent but anonymous, as we see only his back. In Demuth's boating scene, the rower faces forward at the center of the composition. Demuth's oarsman is an interloper on the intimate conversation between Marcher and May. His oars create a line that cuts across the edge of the paper, both slowing the movement of the eye into the picture and creating a boundary that the eye has to cross. We see Marcher and May only by looking across the oarsman's athletic body. Marcher does not even look at May as he talks. In the background there is a smoking volcano, a sign of the Italian locale and a symbol of the Beast within Marcher. But the placement of the oarsman so prominently between the couple seems to interfere with the possibility that Marcher and May could share passion of any sort—beastly, volcanic, or otherwise.

At the end of the novella Marcher realizes that he should have returned May's love. This knowledge comes only after she is dead, when there is nothing he can do about it. "The escape would have been to love her; then, *then* he would have lived."[26] Loving a woman would have been his chance to evade the Beast, yet the Beast was the very reason he could not love a woman. Originally perceived as something that was supposed to happen to Marcher, something that Marcher longed for, the Beast becomes instead a fate that he wants to escape.

Significantly, the moment of revelation Demuth illustrates, when Marcher collapses before the tomb, is brought about through an encounter with another man who has been grieving at the cemetery. Sedgwick notes that Marcher's despair is

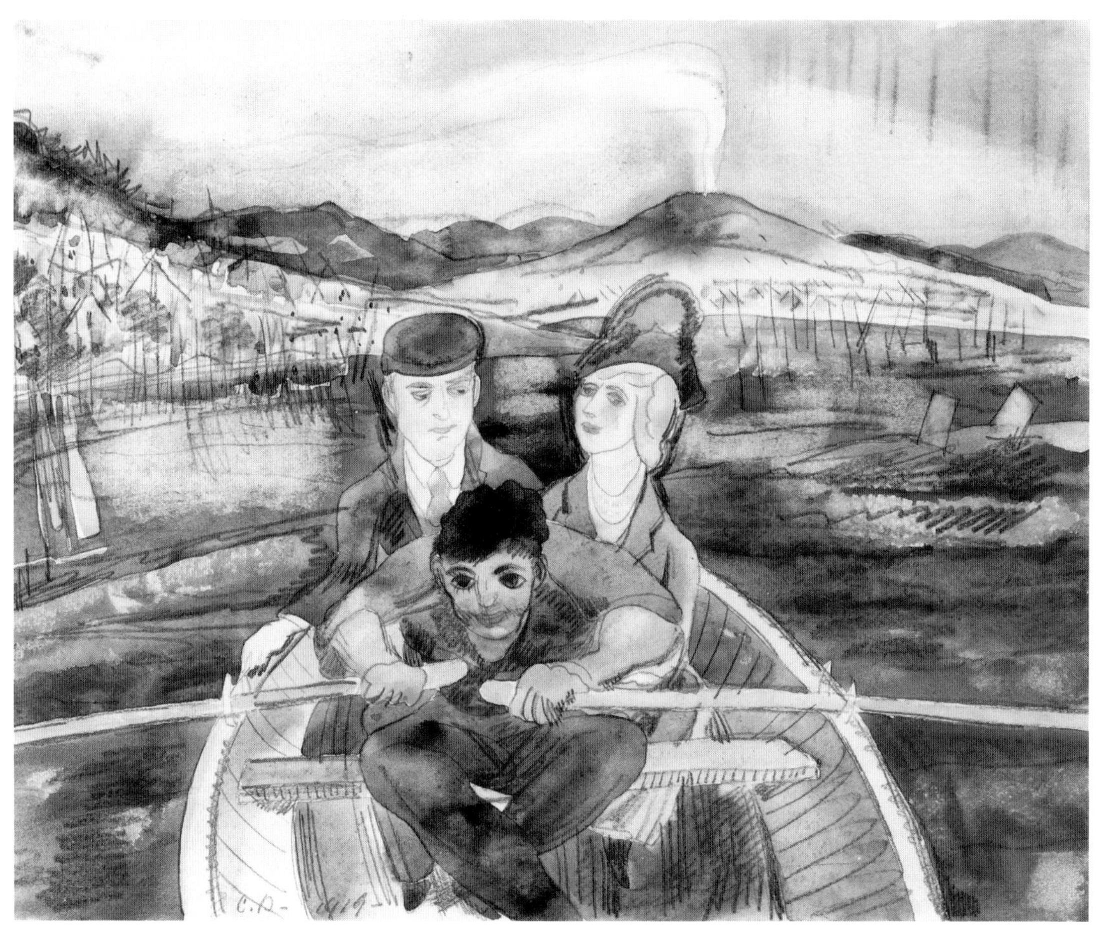

32. Charles Demuth, *The Boat Ride from Sorrento,* watercolor and pencil on paper, 8 × 10⅛ in., 1919. Illustration for "The Beast in the Jungle," by Henry James. Philadelphia Museum of Art, Philadelphia; given by Frank and Alice Osborn.

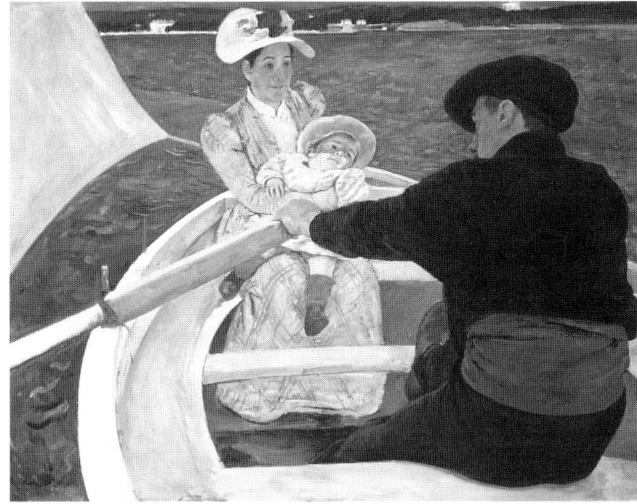

33. Mary Cassatt, *The Boating Party,* oil on canvas, 35½ × 46⅛ in., 1893–94. National Gallery of Art, Washington, D.C.; Chester Dale Collection.

mediated through the passion of this mysterious stranger. James's description of Marcher's reaction to the stranger's mourning is highly erotic: "He felt it, that is, so deep down that he winced at the steady thrust."[27] The depth of emotion that this man feels for some unknown loved one stands for the relationship that Marcher never had with May. Another male's passion, voyeuristically experienced, is as close as Marcher can get to emotions he should have felt at the death of his female friend. Viewing the painting, we too assume Marcher's relationship with that unknown man as we feel only through Marcher's emotions.

Another illustration assumed to have direct autobiographical implications for Demuth is *A Prince of Court Painters* (fig. 34, pl. 8). It is ostensibly a portrait of Antoine Watteau as seen through the eyes of Walter Pater, but the telltale cane that leans up against a chair—as in *Marcher Receives His Revelation at May Bartram's Tomb*—might suggest that we are looking at another alter ego for the illustrator. Demuth shared many qualities with the Watteau of Pater's *Imaginary Portraits.* Like Pater's Watteau, Demuth is sickly. Born in a provincial town, he is drawn to the city for the career opportunities it offers and for its glittering entertainments. Yet he needs his

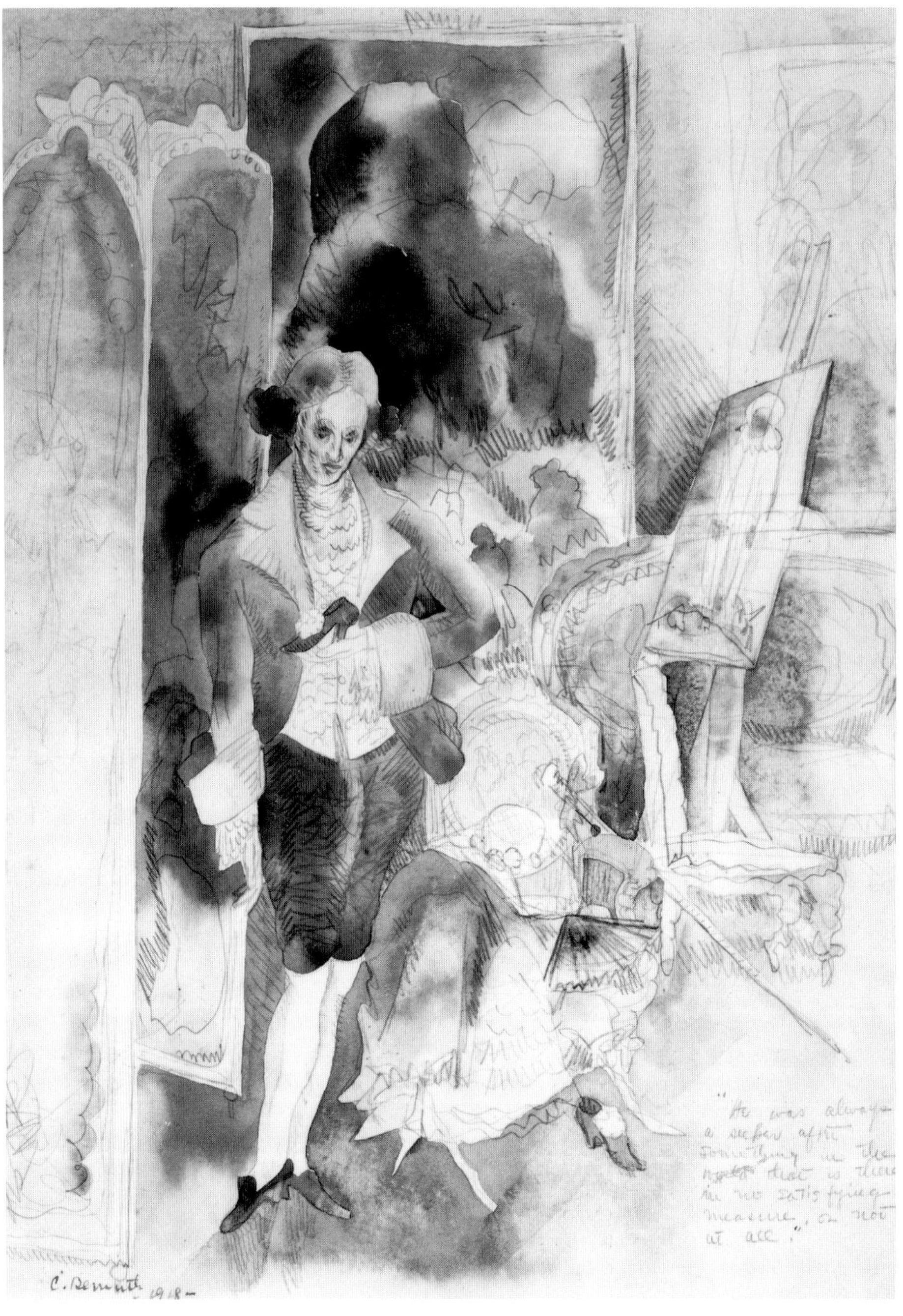
"He was always
a seeker after
something in the
that is there
in no satisfying
measure, or not
at all."
C. Demuth 1918

home as a kind of anchor. He is ambivalent about the wealthy society he frequents and paints.

> Antony Watteau paints that delicate life of Paris so excellently, with so much spirit, partly because, after all, he looks down upon it or despises it. To persuade myself of that, is my womanly satisfaction for his preference—his apparent preference—for a world so different from mine. Those coquetries, those vain and perishable graces, can be rendered so perfectly, only through an intimate understanding of them. For him to understand must be to despise them; while (I think I know why) he yet undergoes their fascination. Hence that discontent with himself, which keeps pace with his fame.[28]

As we shall see, Demuth shares this ambivalence about his own social milieu. He is drawn to the avant-garde society of the art centers yet firmly anchored in a provincial town. In the 1920s, his combination of attraction and disgust for Lancaster provides the impetus for his precisionist cityscapes.

Pater's "A Prince of Court Painters" tells a story similar to "The Beast in the Jungle." Pater's fictionalized biography of Watteau is in the form of a diary kept by the sister of one of Watteau's pupils. She is quite clearly in love with Watteau, but her love is never reciprocated. Instead of Marcher, waiting for the Beast that never springs, the narrator of "A Prince of Court Painters" waits for an impossible love: "I have a fancy always that I may meet Antony Watteau there again, any time; just as, when a child, having found one day a tiny box in the shape of a silver coin, for long afterwards I used to try every piece of money that came into my hands, expecting it to open."[29] Just as Pater's biography of Watteau is simultaneously a short story about unfulfilled love, Demuth's illustration is not merely a portrait of Wat-

34. Charles Demuth, *A Prince of Court Painters,* watercolor, 8 × 10 in., 1918. Illustration for "A Prince of Court Painters," by Walter Pater. Private collection.

teau but suggests elements of a romantic narrative. A woman's clothing is visible on the chair behind the artist, and Watteau holds a woman's shoe in one hand. The narrator mentions that she posed for the artist but that Watteau never could bring the work to completion. She also suggests that Watteau had an affair with Mademoiselle Rosalba, a female painter who is also consumptive, "like Antony himself."[30] Whether the woman's clothing belongs to the narrator, to Rosalba, or to an anonymous model of Demuth's invention, Watteau's contemplation of a woman's shoe suggests a peculiar relationship. Barbara Haskell assumes the narrator is the model: "The absent gaze that Watteau directs toward the model's shoe suggests the psychological distance that he retained between himself and the adoring narrator."[31] Pamela Allara also sees the contemplation of the woman's shoe as a sign of distancing from a sexual relationship. She writes, "Demuth was illustrating his own impotence as well as Watteau's in this work."[32] The act of gazing at the shoe, however, does not desexualize Watteau's relationship to women but displaces it onto an inanimate thing; the shoe is a classic fetish object.[33] What both Allara and Haskell ignore is the significance of a male's fascination with an article of woman's clothing. A mingling of genders, after all, is at the root of Pater's story. The narrator describes Watteau at work as "restless and disquieting, meager, like a woman with some nervous malady."[34] And Pater himself chooses to write his portrait through the eyes of a woman.

Through the shoe Demuth both creates a sense of Watteau's sexual ambiguity and reproduces something of Pater's dominant tone of longing. The shoe suggests absence—perhaps the female narrator who cannot fully make it into Watteau's life—but it also converts the image into a kind of *vanitas*. Watteau is contemplating a piece of woman's finery in much the way hermits are shown looking at skulls. The difference is that Watteau is thinking not so much of death as of desire. The central theme of Pater's essay is the inability of life to fulfill human emotional need. Demuth added to the corner of the watercolor Pater's closing words: "He has been a sick man all his life. He was always a seeker after something in the world that is there in no satisfying measure, or not at all."[35]

5

Demuth's Erotic Watercolors

Walter Pater's "something" points us back once again to Henry James's "*the* thing" and Demuth's "unknown Thing." All three stories are united by their heroes' failure to establish a heterosexual relationship. Demuth's final illustration for "The Beast in the Jungle," showing Marcher prostrate before the tomb, the artist's signature inscribed in Marcher's hat, is like Demuth's cry against the unknown Thing. It amounts to a mourning for a nonrelationship, the lack of a sexual relationship with a woman. Although in "The Turn of the Screw" James alludes to unspeakable evils, in "The Beast in the Jungle" he never fixes responsibility for the absence of a heterosexual drive in his character. We never know why Marcher is driven to imagine the Beast. Pater's Watteau is alone because his art will allow him no other companions. But in Demuth's case, there is evidence that the absence of heterosexuality was equated with an attraction toward other men. That Demuth thought of homosexuality as an alternative to heterosexuality is suggested by the series of erotic watercolors he created at the same time he was making his illustrations. Demuth began to work on his Turkish bath series in 1915, the same year as the *Nana* project. Although his pictures of the Turkish baths are not as numerous as his illustrations, we should keep in mind the likelihood that many of his erotic watercolors, both early and late, were destroyed.

Who made up the audience for these pictures? As I mentioned earlier, it is assumed that Demuth made the erotic watercolors for his own pleasure, because, unlike the illustrations, they were never publicly exhibited in his lifetime. But Hartley's memoirs provide a clue that these works were not hidden from everyone. Hartley mentions that while Demuth was making his illustrations he was also at work on a series of watercolors of "sailors in wild pursuit," along with pictures of acrobats and "ladies in quest of submarine favors."[1] It is unclear which pictures Hartley had in mind. None of the figures in the Turkish bath paintings is obviously a sailor. Hartley may have been thinking of Demuth's two watercolors of sailors dancing, or of one called *Sailors on Leave,* but none of these works fits the description wild. Could it be that Demuth did drawings of sailors during the period of the illustrations—between 1915 and 1919—comparable to his late erotic watercolors, but that those works have been lost or destroyed? Just as likely Hartley assumed that the later explicit pictures of sailors from the 1930s were actually painted in the 1910s, the time of the majority of Demuth's figurative work. In any case, the phrase "sailors in wild pursuit" suggests that Demuth's erotic work was not secret from everyone. And we know that in the early 1930s Demuth made a gift to his friend Darell Larsen of the most famous of the series, *Turkish Bath Scene with Self-Portrait.*

Among Demuth's early work are a number of figure studies and even a couple of studies of male bathers, but nothing to prepare us for the overt homosexual themes of his figurative work of 1915 through 1918. What accounts for Demuth's comparative brazenness? My guess is that it was his repeated contact with Europe. At the outset of World War I, Demuth returned from an extended stay in Paris, where even the most conservative art practice was comfortable with the study of both the male and female body (in sharp contrast to the Philadelphia Academy, where Eakins had to fight to work from nude female models). The society in which the Paris avant-garde and the American expatriates gathered was far more tolerant toward homosexuality and familiar with its reversal of gender roles. In his memoir of Demuth, Hartley recalled the fanciful characters who frequented the restaurant Thomas in Montparnasse, where the two first met.

> Charles will recall . . . two figures that came to life with a sort of Beardsleyesque persistence . . . one of them ostensibly a man, disturbingly stylized if you cared that way, a kind of Fleurs du Mal silhouette, with his velvet jacket, black of course, and his white lace cuffs falling over long white hands to which many

> untouchable thoughts of night seemed to be clinging, and a cascade of immaculate silk edged with lace down the front of the shirt, velvet coat flaring at the waist, large dark ring on forefinger with a black cane of Empire style to complete the drawing—evidence of much powder about the face, hours spent doubtless at manicure, and was there not even a light touch of rouge upon the lips. . . .
>
> Accompanying this Phocas figure known to us as Stuart Hill of Edinburgh, another extreme came into view, and the opposite of course, of masculine virility, the very manly George Banks, whose fate was to look so singularly like the author of the Ballad of Reading Gaol, that she was soon to be impeded with his name, and titled Oscar Wilde la Seconde.[2]

In Paris, Demuth visited the salon of Gertrude Stein and Alice B. Toklas. Although the effect of the works by Picasso, Matisse, and Cézanne on their walls was crucial to Demuth's later artistic development, perhaps equally important psychically was the introduction to two women who lived openly as a lesbian couple.[3] In 1913 Demuth also traveled briefly to Berlin to visit Marsden Hartley's friend Arnold Rönnebeck; there, Demuth would have found an even more active homosexual community than in Paris.

Of course, the sexual freedom of Paris and Berlin in the 1910s is easily exaggerated. Boundaries of social control were enforced on both sides of the Atlantic. Hartley mentions the stares and whispers that Stuart Hill, with his made-up face, elicited from the bourgeoisie along the boulevard. A more profound analysis of prejudice against homosexuals in France and a plea for tolerance is André Gide's *Corydon.*[4] Blackmail and police prosecution were a constant fear among homosexuals in Germany, particularly after the Friedrich Krupp scandal. Nonetheless, Paris and Berlin were environments far more conducive to difference than were New York or Philadelphia.

I mentioned that Richard Weyand had suggested that *Turkish Bath Scene with Self-Portrait* was a picture of the Lafayette Baths in New York City, but the locale of

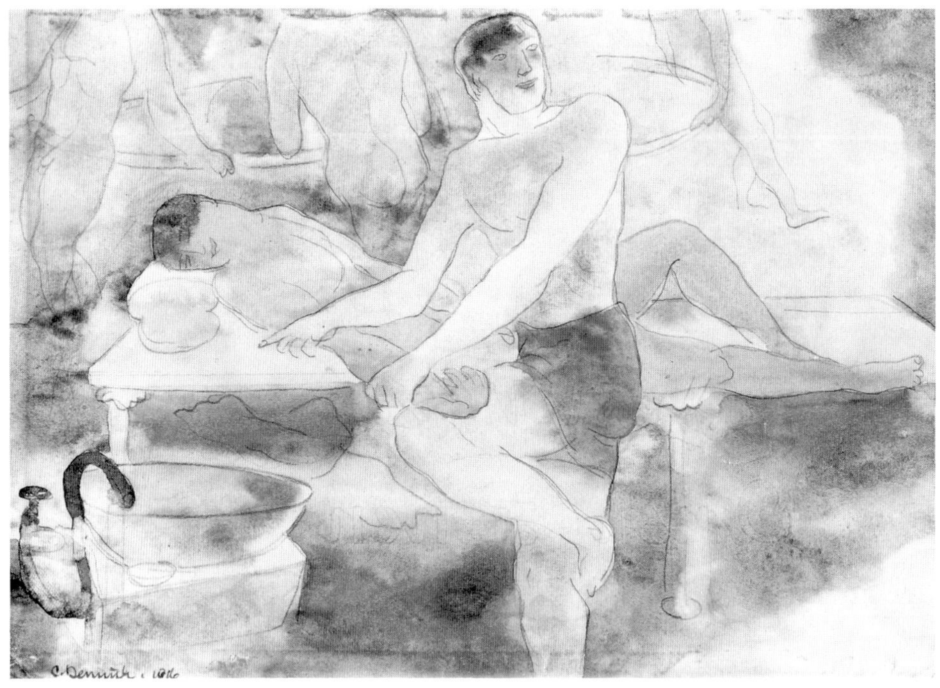

35. Charles Demuth, *Turkish Bath,* watercolor and pencil on paper, 7⅝ × 11 in., 1916. Fogg Art Museum, Harvard University; anonymous loan.

the baths in the series could easily be Berlin or Paris. Indeed, *Turkish Bath* (fig. 35) depicts a facility like one that was photographed in Berlin (fig. 36). Both photograph and watercolor share a joke in the conspicuous positioning of a faucet in the left corner. Demuth particularly exaggerates the spigot to mimic a penis, thus compensating for the genitals that are hidden by the men's towels.

The joke of the faucet is an old one: in fact, it ties Demuth's *Turkish Bath* to Albrecht Dürer's *The Bath House* (fig. 37) of 1496. Dürer's woodcut depicts a group of seminude men who seem less interested in cleaning themselves than in looking at one another. It has been suggested that the image is an allegory of the five senses or the four temperaments,[5] but Erwin Panofsky rejects "any cryptic allegorical meaning," calling Dürer's characters simply "fun-loving men."[6] Panofsky does not give any details, but the musicians who serenade the bathers, in particular the prominent flute player—a favorite Renaissance symbol of sexual play—suggest that the "fun" Dürer had in mind is homosexual. The flute is not the only pun for the male genitals. A bearded gentleman leans on a fountain as he gazes longingly at the handsome flute player who returns his glance. The fountain's spout is placed at exactly the point of the bearded man's crotch. An ornamental bird—one of the oldest symbols for the penis—perches on the faucet, making the joke even more explicit.

At first glance, Demuth's *Turkish Bath* in the Fogg appears innocent, particularly in comparison to Dürer's blatant print. Ostensibly, the only physical contact in Demuth's picture is that between masseur and client in the foreground. But the figure in the left corner, leaning on the rail that circles the central pool of the establishment, has an erection. His sexual excitement is a sign that if the men are not gathered to have sex on the spot, they are, as Edward Stevenson suggested in *The*

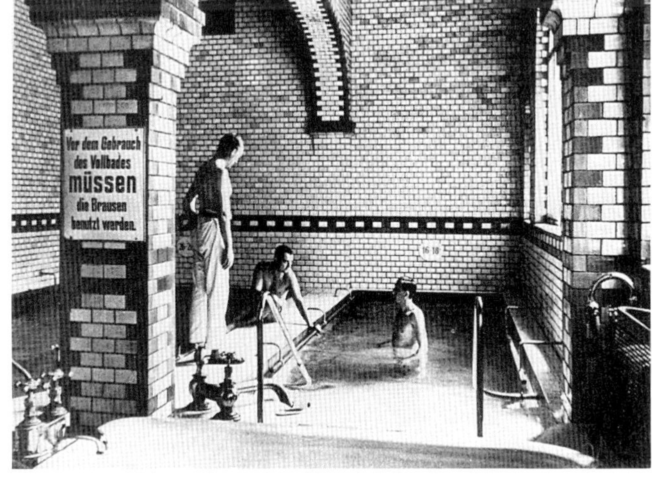

36. *Russian-Rumanian Bath for Men in Potsdamer Platz, Berlin.* Date unknown. Landesbildstelle, Berlin.

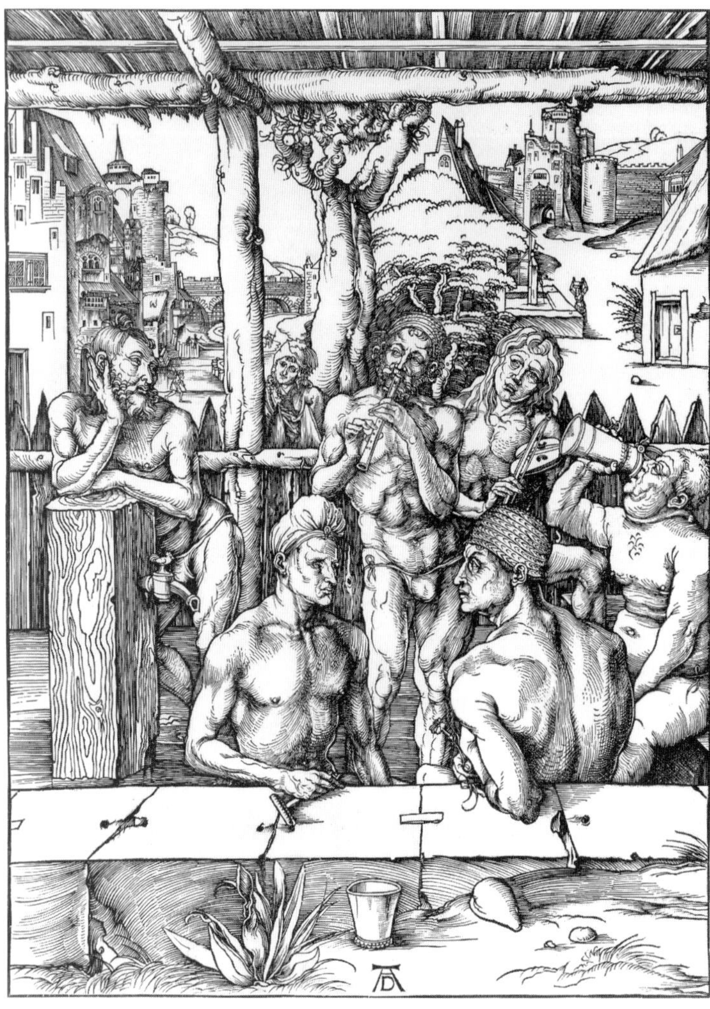

37. Albrecht Dürer, *The Bath House,* woodcut, 15⅜ × 11⅛ in., ca. 1496. Yale University Art Gallery; Everett V. Meeks Fund.

Intersexes, involved in "anatomic inspections" that may lead to later rendezvous. More discreet is the *Turkish Bath* of 1915 (fig. 38, pl. 7), perhaps the earliest in the series. The central character is a masseur seen from behind. Wearing nothing but a scanty loin cloth, he massages the back of a client who lies on his stomach. In the background a short, fat attendant is drying off another visitor to the establishment. The customer has his arms spread, allowing the attendant to wrap the towel around his stomach. In the right background another fellow lies on his stomach, perhaps waiting for a massage.

Compositionally, the *Turkish Bath* of 1915 is remarkably similar to Demuth's illustration for the *Girl with the Golden Eyes.* As with the marquis, the masseur's back

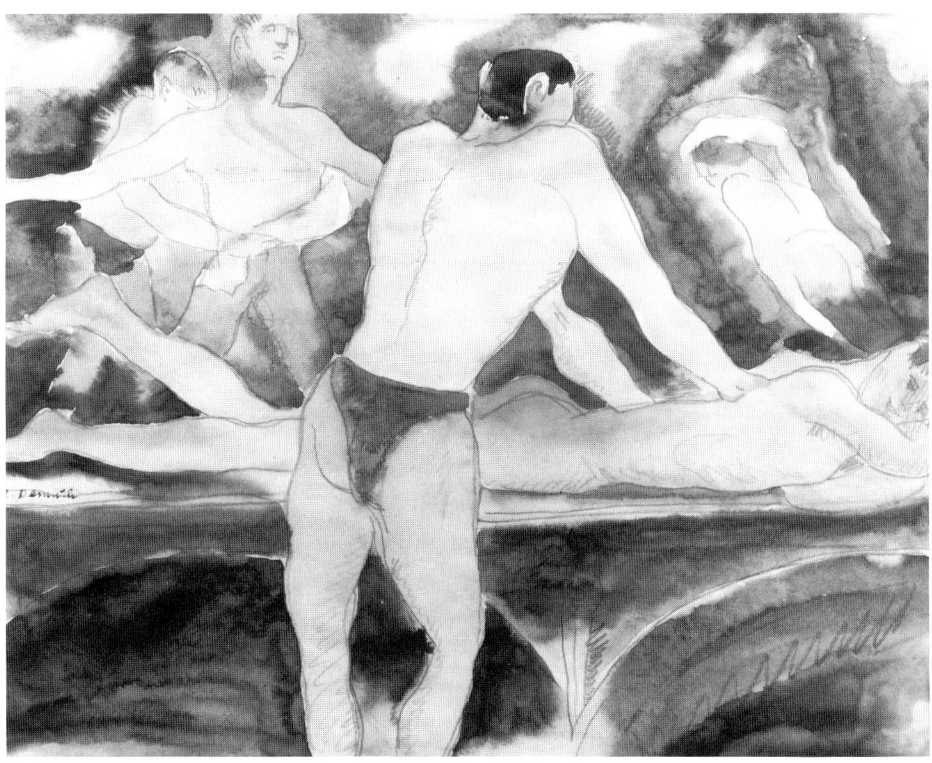

38. Charles Demuth, *Turkish Bath,* watercolor and pencil on paper, 8 × 10½ in., 1915. Private collection. Courtesy Owen Gallery, New York.

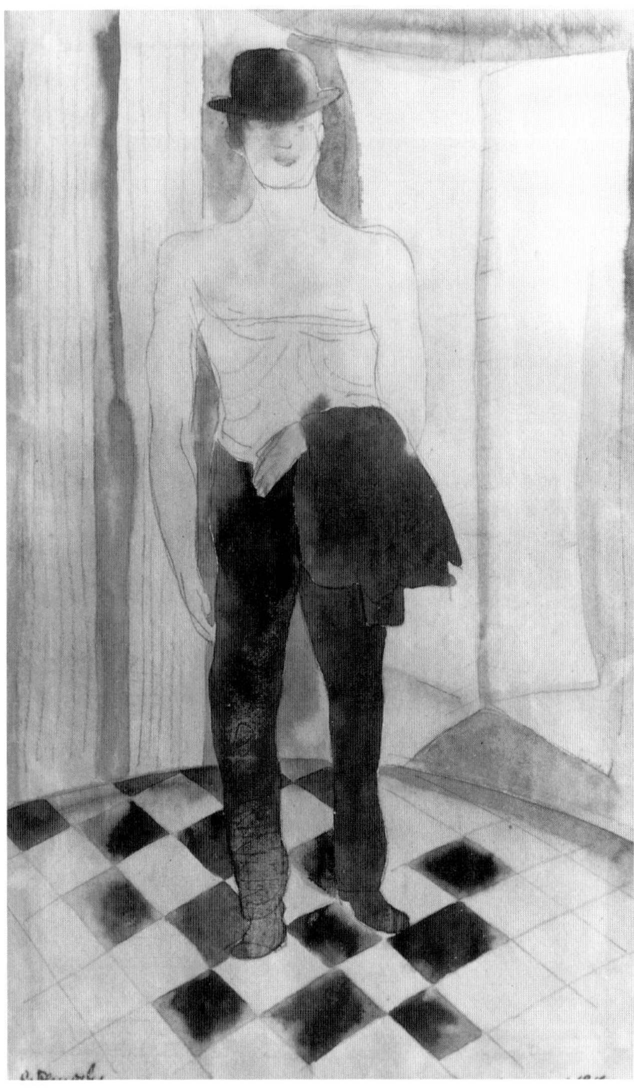

39. Charles Demuth, *Turkish Bath: Male Figure,* watercolor and pencil on paper, 12⅜ × 7⅝ in., 1916. Collection of Michael De Lisio.

dominates the painting. Although Demuth includes frontal nudity in the man being dried by the attendant in the background, the major sexual focus of the work is on the buttocks of the central two figures. Whereas in the *Girl with the Golden Eyes* Demuth substituted the marquis's anus for the vagina of Paquita, here the masseur does not cover up his client's body. Instead, we sense the closeness of the masseur's muscular body to the patron's behind, which Demuth has emphasized with a bright red wash. The almost silly smile on the man's face suggests his abandonment to the pleasures of the massage.

Three of the watercolors of the Turkish bath series do not depict sexual contact per se but instead focus on the male body as an object of sexual desire. *Two Figures: Turkish Bath* features two men in a shower room, one of whom sits on a bench, while the other stands.[7] Both wear towels around their waists. As the standing figure turns a faucet, he looks down toward the crotch of his companion. This same composition is repeated in the later and more elaborate *Two Men in a Shower Bath.*[8] In this version, Demuth makes the bodies of his subjects more muscular, and the tattoo—of hearts and a star—on the arm of the seated figure suggests that he is of the working class. But the erotic connection between the standing man's hand on the faucet and his desiring stare at the other fellow is even more explicit here.

Turkish Bath: Male Figure (fig. 39) is the only one in the series to concentrate on a single figure. A shirtless young man, holding a jacket and wearing a bowler hat, stands facing the viewer. The hat works like the famous shoes on the otherwise naked Olympia of Manet—it forces us to think about the character's state of undress, to wonder why he wears a hat but not a shirt. We could say that the picture is about dressing and undressing, but doing so with such impatience that the normal order for putting on or taking off clothes is disrupted. Whether or not that impatience is caused by lust or the heat of the bathhouse is left for the viewer to decide.

The *Turkish Bath* of 1915 depicts a situation—a massage—in which men are allowed to be physical with each other in public. At the same time Demuth was making the Turkish bath paintings, he made two watercolors of sailors dancing, one of which is now in the Museum of Modern Art (fig. 40) and one in the Cleveland Museum of Art (fig. 41). At the center of each of the paintings—which are almost identical—two sailors dance with each other, flanked by two heterosexual couples. This display of affection between men may appear shocking for that period. Yet as

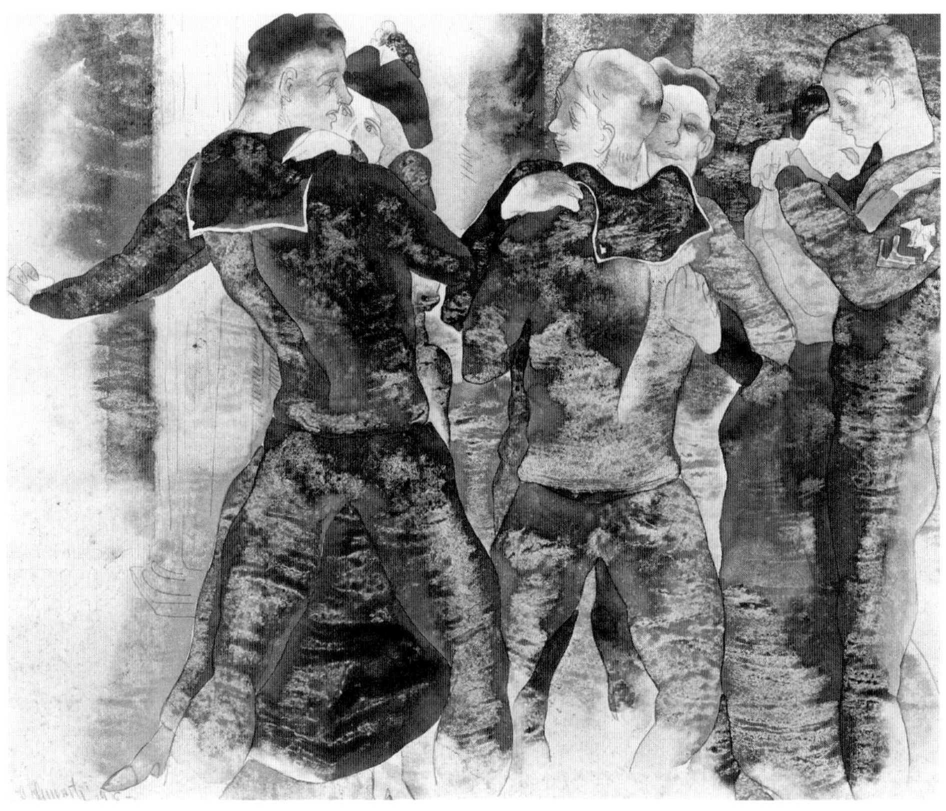

40. Charles Demuth, *Dancing Sailors,* watercolor and pencil on paper, 7⅞ × 9⅞ in., 1918. Museum of Modern Art, New York; Abby Aldrich Rockefeller Fund.

Alvord L. Eiseman points out in his discussion of the Cleveland Museum's *Dancing Sailors* from 1917, it was not unusual for sailors to dance with each other in the absence of women: "There were no such places as USOs during World War I. Also it was not considered 'nice' for a young girl to go out with members of the armed forces during this time except under very special conditions. It is noteworthy that none of the 'couples' seems to find anything unusual with two men dancing together."[9] That dancing among sailors was acceptable in the eyes of the American public probably explains Demuth's willingness to exhibit the painting at the Museum of Modern Art in 1929.[10] Yet, as with several of the Turkish bath pictures, Demuth builds into the dance several signs that the relationship of the men goes beyond simple friendship. Instead of showing a fast dance in which there is little close contact—the kind that sailors were perhaps more likely to do with a male partner—Demuth focuses on slow, sultry moves. The men hold each other very closely, their bodies and faces touching. Eiseman implies that this intimacy elicits little attention from the other couples. Not from the women, it is true; but the sailor on the left seems to stare

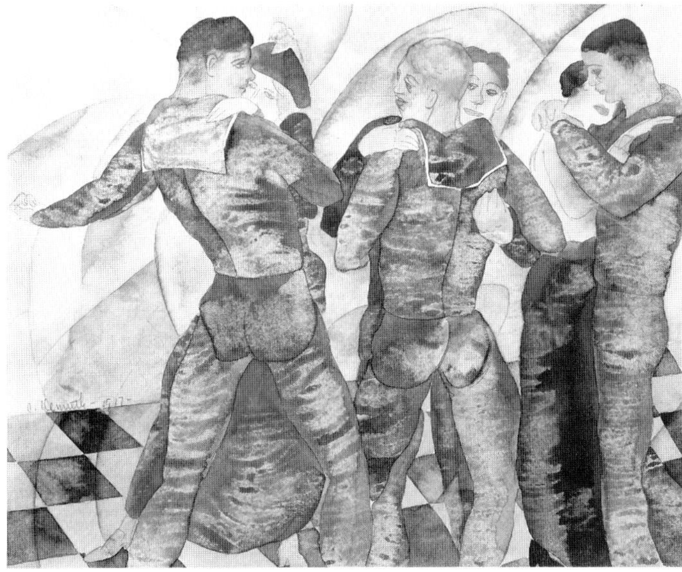

41. Charles Demuth, *Dancing Sailors,* watercolor and pencil on paper, 8 × 10 in., 1917. Cleveland Museum of Art, Cleveland; Mr. and Mrs. William H. Marlatt Fund.

past his clinging partner and to exchange glances with the male to his left. The legs of the two adjacent male dancers appear to brush against each other as the couples dance on the floor. The central focus of the composition is not on the bodies of the women, which are mostly covered by their long loosely fitted dresses and the backs of their male partners, but on the muscular bodies of the sailors—particularly their buttocks. Finally, the explanation that the two fellows are dancing with each other because of the absence of women is contradicted by the painting's own inclusion of two women.

The tension in *Dancing Sailors* and the Turkish bath series is generated by the suspicion that even though what is pictured may still be just within the range of acceptable behavior, the men are in danger of stepping over the line of what is permissible. In *Turkish Bath* (1915) the scanty clothing of the masseur, his client locked in the triangle of his arms, suggests an eroticism that is supposedly not present in the locker room. The two males in *Dancing Sailors* are seemingly too closely entwined to be dancing simply for the pleasure of dancing. But the boundary of permissible behavior just barely maintained in these watercolors appears to be completely violated in *Turkish Bath Scene with Self-Portrait,* the most finished and ambitious of the series. The importance of the picture for Demuth is suggested by the full-sized study he made (fig. 42, pl. 6) and, of course, by the fact that he seems to have included a self-portrait in the figure with the moustache.

Turkish Bath Scene with Self-Portrait is different from the other works in the series in several respects. Not only does Demuth put his characters in far more explicit sexual relation to one another, but he realizes their bodies more completely. Whereas the figures in the early paintings are rather flatly painted, Demuth here has carefully blotted the paper to provide shadowing, creating a greater sense of three-dimensionality. The earlier faces were all but featureless; here there is enough detail for the mustached man to be considered, rightly or wrongly, a self-portrait. Perhaps most shocking from the standpoint of an audience in 1918 is Demuth's careful modeling of the penis of the red-haired man. The picture's most explicitly erotic features—its frontal nudity and the figures in the background at the right—are missing from the full-scale study in the Fitch Collection. As Demuth worked on the series, he became noticeably bolder. And the overall tone of the picture changed as Demuth

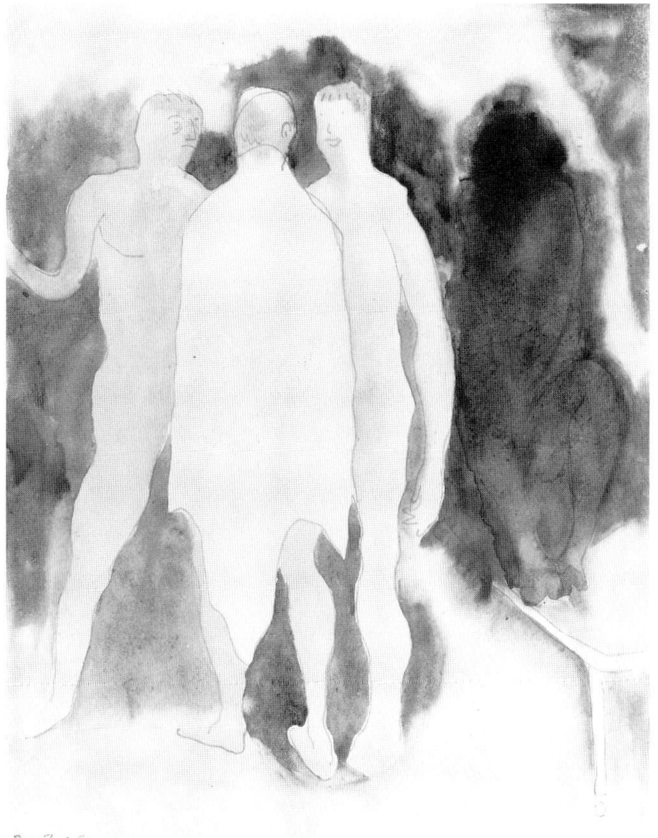

42. Charles Demuth, *Turkish Bath,* watercolor and pencil on paper, 10⅞ × 8 7/16 in., ca. 1915. Yale University Art Gallery; gift of George Hopper Fitch.

inserted more detailed and potentially dangerous information. The silly grin of the man getting a massage in the *Turkish Bath* of 1915 is replaced by the somber and intense look of the self-portrait. Demuth's likeness stares into a tight group, which we are not allowed to penetrate. The towel of the man with his back to us is draped not around his waist, as it is in all the other works in the series, but over his shoulders. It is so large that it entirely hides what is going on among the three figures. The towel stands for hiding and for the risk these men are taking in meeting at the baths. The towel also makes of the central figure a kind of apparition. We saw that

Demuth's illustrations focused on the destructive consequences of sexual relationships between men and women. Sex and death are linked throughout the stories. But the *Turkish Bath Scene with Self-Portrait* suggests that Demuth's fears extend beyond heterosexual relationships. The ghostly man shrouded in a towel may be a representation of illicit desire, but he is also a figure of death. And at a time when homosexual acts with strangers might lead to blackmail, disgrace, physical violence, or (just as with heterosexual intercourse before the discovery of penicillin) a potentially terminal disease in the form of syphilis or gonorrhea, it is hardly surprising that Demuth would image homosexuality in such spectral terms.

I have noted the closeness of the men's bodies in *Turkish Bath Scene with Self-Portrait* and, in particular, how their feet touch or almost touch. The coming together portrayed here is as much confrontational as it is intimate. If Demuth is showing us the beginnings of a sexual encounter, the participants are not lovers but strangers meeting anonymously, sizing up each other's physical qualities. When Demuth returns to homosexual themes in the 1930s, sizing up is literally the meaning of the even more explicit *Two Sailors Urinating* (fig. 43), in which two men stand in a lavatory of a café or bar and compare each other's sexual endowments. This same quality of competition is built into the triumphant boxer pose of the man taking off his shirt in *Three Sailors on the Beach*. Or sex becomes a matter of negotiation. In *On "That" Street,* the poses of *Turkish Bath Scene with Self-Portrait* are converted into what seems to be a bargain between two sailors hustling a john for money and perhaps accommodation for the night. Indeed, the clichéd heart and arrow etched on the sailor's biceps in *Three Sailors on the Beach* is as close as we get to a hint of love in Demuth's erotic world, where affection of any kind is rarely expressed.

The absence of love in Demuth's erotic painting seems to tally with the unhappiness of "The Voyage Was Almost Over." Only heterosexuality in the guise of the "little white hand" appears to be able to offer Demuth long-term love. The melancholy tone of the story, with its intimations of death in the title, suggests that

43. Charles Demuth, *Two Sailors Urinating,* watercolor and pencil on paper, 9½ × 13¼ in., 1930. Location unknown.

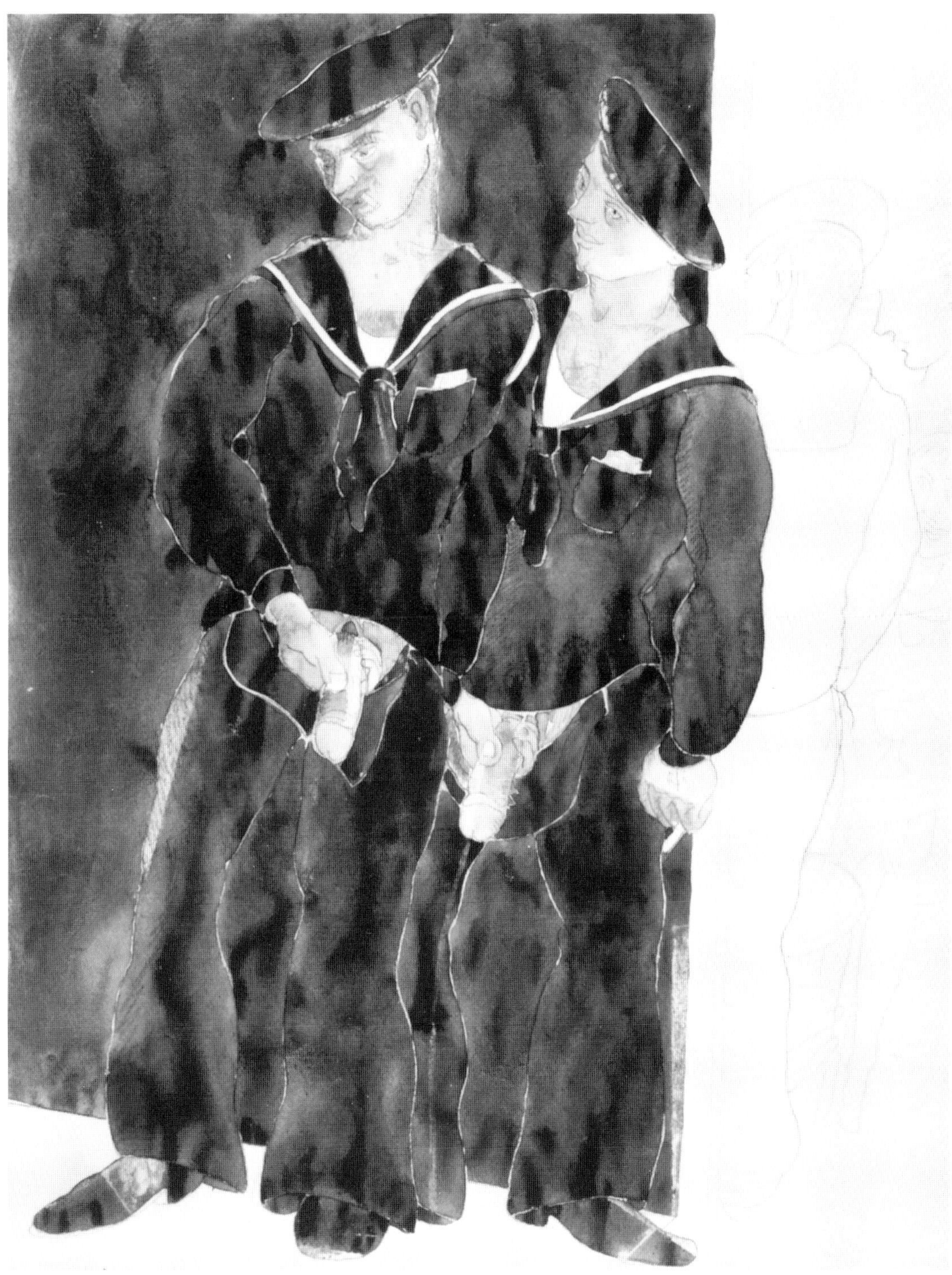

societal prohibitions on same-sex relationships may have been too great in Demuth's time for him even to imagine a fully evolved homosexual relationship that would be the equivalent of the love of the couple on deck. Instead, when he represents homosexuality directly, it is in terms of anonymous encounters between men in search of sexual satisfaction.

It is tempting to focus on the absence of love in Demuth's erotic art in exclusively tragic terms, particularly after reading "The Voyage Was Almost Over" or dwelling on his struggle with diabetes. Yet if his art appears to be pessimistic about the viability of long-term relationships, it also reveals a marvelous sense of humor as it rejects monogamy and the middle-class respectability that goes with it. Demuth's erotic watercolors become funnier as they become less inhibited—all inhibitions having completely fallen away in the late watercolors. Except for the *Turkish Bath Scene with Self-Portrait,* Demuth focused exclusively on the buttocks of his subject. One of his favorite compositions is a group of figures speaking in a circle with their backs to us. He uses this trope in *Sailor, Soldier and Policeman* (1916) in the Hirshhorn Museum, *Three Bathers* (1917) in the Brooklyn Museum, and *Turkish Bath Scene with Self-Portrait* (1918). It reappears in the late *Man and Sailors (Sands Street Brooklyn, New York)* and *On "That" Street,* of circa 1930 and 1932, respectively. This grouping of figures not only centers desire on the buttocks of the subjects but also suggests clandestine conversations or acts. But in *Two Sailors Urinating* Demuth turns the men around and we see that the hand of the left-hand figure is on the penis of his companion. There is now little mystery to their relationship. In place of the supposed sexual ambiguity of his earlier work is a blatant display of sexual play in a setting that cannot be described among polite company.

Most of Demuth's erotic watercolors do not easily fit any category for representing the public nude. In *Three Sailors Urinating* (fig. 44) Demuth places the men in much the same position as the three goddesses in Rubens's *The Judgement of Paris* (fig. 45). Each of the three sailors is essentially the same type, viewed from a different angle. This opportunity to suggest the three-dimensionality of the erotic object in two-dimensional terms was at the heart of the appeal of the motif of the Three Graces and the Judgement of Paris. Although the act of urination places Demuth's image in the realm of the "obscene," it is not simply this earthbound act that violates the original arrangement; Demuth also transposes the classically endorsed female poses to an all-male world of lower-class sailors. The change of gender and the specificity of social class detach the picture from its sanctified sources. If Demuth had depicted three plump nude goddesses relieving themselves, we could not help but think of the image as a gross spoof of Rubens's *Judgement of Paris*. The history of art contains many examples of women attending to their toilet—the classic image is Rembrandt's *Susanna and the Elders* with its leering old men watching a beautiful woman wash her body. In art, peering at the naked female body is an encouraged transgression. Rembrandt's *Susanna* or Titian's *Diana and Actaeon* provide the viewer with precisely the forbidden experience that their painted male protagonists are punished for. The prestige of classical or biblical texts eliminates moral responsibility; art allows us to see what we are normally not permitted to see. It seems, however, as if the aesthetic does not easily contain an equivalent display of masculine privacy and vulnerability. Because Demuth's gaze is homosexual, it falls outside the mediating force of those erotic conventions that most readily absolve the viewer of collusion. If the artist is suspect for making a watercolor of such material, what of the audience that looks at it? To watch unobserved beautiful women tending to their bodies is to be a connoisseur; to look with the same interest on the private functions of men is to be a pervert.

Three Sailors on the Beach is "pornographic" by most standard definitions of the term. To cite two representative examples: the British Committee on Obscenity and Pornography defines a pornographic work as one that "has a certain function or intention, to arouse its audience sexually, and also a certain content, explicit representations of sexual material (organs, postures, activity, etc.)";[11] and David Copp in his introduction to *Pornography and Censorship* declares that pornography "consists in obscene sexual depictions, and . . . that the obscenity of a sexual depiction is determined in relation to a canon or standard of propriety or appropriateness that governs sexual depictions."[12] Copp's definition shifts the problem of pornography away from reconstructing the intentions of a potential pornographer to the issue of the cultural standards concerning the proper representation of sex. In the end, the question of whether these particular erotic works are pornographic seems to turn not on their technical quality as drawings (they are not throwaway sketches and they

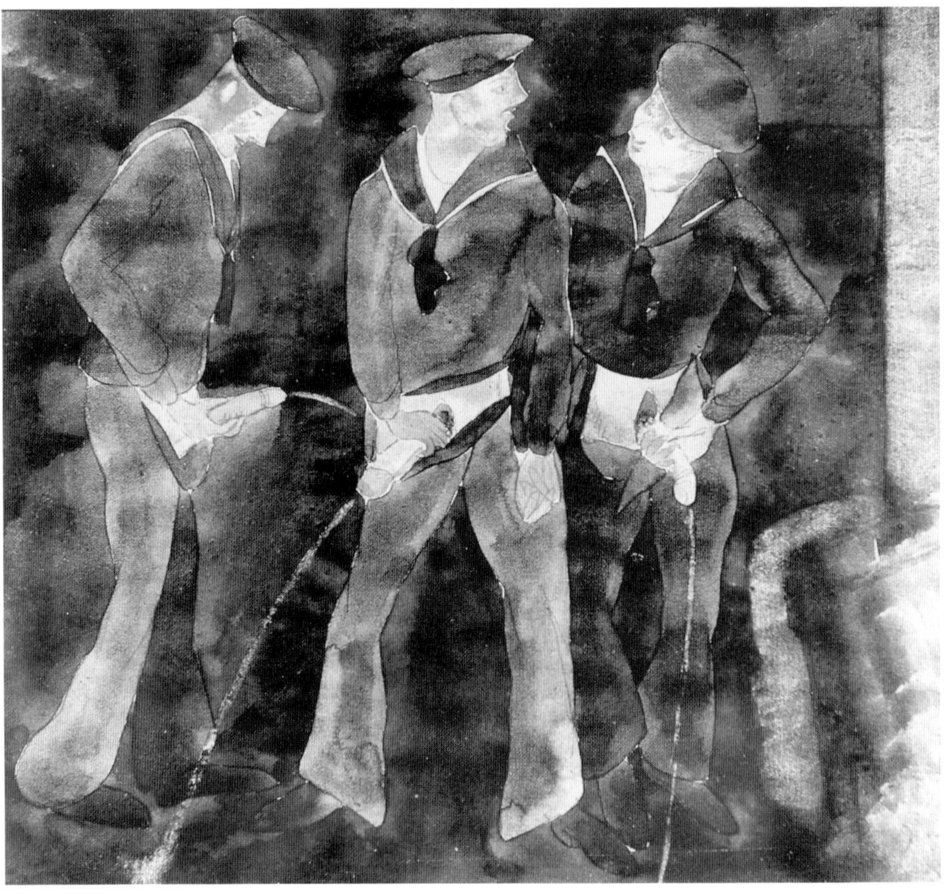

44. Charles Demuth, *Three Sailors Urinating,* watercolor and pencil on paper, 9½ × 13¼ in., 1930. Private collection.

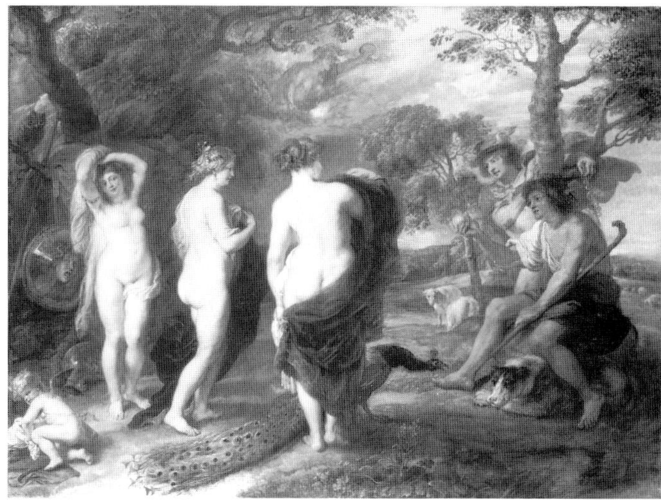

45. Peter Paul Rubens, *The Judgement of Paris,* oil on canvas, 47 × 63½ in., ca. 1634. National Gallery, London.

exhibit a strong command of anatomy and a mastery of technique) nor even on their sexual content—many of the most-admired works of the Western tradition contain sexual subject matter. Rather the question has to do with the complicated decorum of eroticism: what the canon permits or forbids at any given time. At the deepest level, that canon is less a catalogue of particular acts than a whole, specific economy of sexual *attitudes*—an economy, above all, of modes of activity and passivity, of dominance and submission. No doubt society has depicted the female body in an extraordinary variety of states; but from Titian's *Rape of Europa* to Delacroix's *Abduction of Rebecca,* the preferred female response to the often-violent advances of male seduction is the semiconscious sigh of acquiescence. Although painters of the Renaissance and baroque periods occasionally produced paintings of Ganymede—works in which the victim of divine rape is a boy instead of a woman—by the seventeenth century, erotic etiquette did not allow the male to be both obviously sexually excited *and* a passive love object. We think nothing of images of females in various states of undress admiring each other's beauty, but a drawing of men in the same state of vulnerability and mutual admiration is not part of society's repertoire of aestheticized erotic subject matter. In this sense, the root pornographic element of Demuth's pictures—in Copp's terms, their break with acceptable visual practice—is not that they represent an illegal activity (rape, after all, was similarly illegal) but that their representation of homosexual acts involved assigning men passive sexual roles usually given to women. The threat posed by homosexuality to the social order is complex, undermining both the moral codes of society and its stereotypes of gender on many levels. Unlike the graphic depiction of heterosexual intercourse, which only makes explicit what is already intimated in so many of the central images of art, the overt representations of homosexual acts are multiply obscene, multiply other.

Of course Demuth's images of men urinating do more to outrage middle-class sensibilities than just show homosexual encounters—they combine homosexuality with urolagnia (the clinical term for a fascination with urine). In *Two Sailors Urinating* one of Demuth's sailors actually holds his buddy's penis as they both urinate, while in *Three Sailors Urinating* two of the men hold hands as they relieve themselves. In both works urine is being aimed in the direction of the viewer. The perspective of *Two Sailors Urinating* is significant. Demuth draws the sailors as if from a crouching position. The viewpoint could be compared to that of the man with the erection who looks up at his friend's crotch in *Three Sailors on the Beach.* The sense of thrusting the audience's eyes into the scene is increased by the shallow background and the tight cropping that pushes the sailors' bodies forward. Demuth's use of color on only the left side of the picture further centers the audience's eye on the action of the two sailors.

Despite the explicitness of the late erotic watercolors with their emphatic exhibitionism, they were obviously not made for public viewing in Demuth's lifetime. And so when we speak of the viewer in reference to these works, we are speaking of a peculiar construct, made up of the artist, intimate friends, and those who were meant to discover the work after Demuth's death. In this sense, the late pictures of sailors urinating have the quality of intimate confessions or of a memoir discovered long after its author has passed away. They could almost be illustrations for the kind of sexual tales told to the sexologist in strictest confidence, which made up such an important part of my discussion of the status of homosexuality in America in chapter 1. The characters and peculiar perspective of *Two Sailors Urinating* form a scene that parallels a fantasy recorded in Havelock Ellis's *Sexual Inversion.* The hero of one of Ellis's case histories claimed that when he was a child he "became subject to curious half-waking dreams. In these he imagined himself the servant of several adult naked sailors; he crouched between their thighs and called himself their dirty pig, and by their orders he performed services for their genitals and buttocks, which he contemplated and handled with relish."[13]

It turns out that this case history belonged to none other than Ellis's collaborator on *Sexual Inversion,* John Addington Symonds. Symonds includes a variation of the same story in his memoirs, which were published posthumously.[14] Although Symonds was clearly attracted to the kind of sailors Demuth painted, he did not seem especially interested in bathroom functions. However, the subject of another of Ellis's case histories in *Sexual Inversion* insisted that his sexual enjoyment consisted of imagining undergoing "physical humiliation and submission to the caprice of [his] male captors, and the central fact became the discharge of urine from [his] lover over [his] body and limbs." One of his earliest memories is of watching farmhands urinating:

> On two or three occasions when I accompanied farm laborers to their occupations I saw them pause by the way to relieve nature. My extreme shyness as regards such matter in my own person made this performance in my presence like an outrage on my modesty; it had about it the suggestion of an indecent solicitation to one whose inclination was to headlong and delirious surrender. I stood rooted and flushing with downcast eyes till the act was over and was conscious for a considerable time of stammering speech and bewildered faculties. . . . My mind secretly embraced the fearful sweetness of the newly discovered sensation, surrounding the performance of the function with all sorts of atrocious and bizarre inventions.[15]

Demuth's erotic watercolors visualize what the scientific studies on sexology only describe. As in Ellis's work, the exploration of one form of sexual abnormality leads to other perversions, requiring other clinical terms. One could argue that in showing homosexuals fascinated by urine Demuth was providing more evidence for the experts' fear that one form of sexual degeneracy leads to another. But one could counter that the revelation of Demuth's watercolors is the truth that the entire body is sexual and that all aspects of the love object may be desirable. Ellis attempted such an apologia for urolagnia in a later volume of the *Studies in the Psychology of Sex* and, more famously, in his autobiography, *My Life*. Ellis went so far as to attribute his first interest in medicine to a childhood fascination with the comparative abundance and strength of his schoolmates' urination: "I observed the differences in vesical energy among my schoolfellows, my own being below the average, and began to measure it exactly as private opportunities offered. Many years afterwards I continued these observations and published the results in a paper on 'The Bladder as a Dynamometer' in the *American Journal of Dermatology*, May, 1902."[16]

Readers of Ellis's autobiography, published in 1939 after his death, were shocked to find that this childhood fascination with urination became part of his relations with women. Yet any reader of Ellis's *Erotic Symbolism* of 1906 should not have been surprised. In the chapter on urolagnia Ellis fashioned an elaborate defense of the sexual practice. Just as Symonds and Carpenter had defended homosexuality by insisting that men of artistic genius were particularly prone to inversion, Ellis wrote in *Erotic Symbolism* that "there is ample evidence to show that, either as a habitual or more usually an occasional act, the impulse to bestow a symbolic value on the act of urination in a beloved person, is not extremely uncommon; it has been noted of men of high intellectual distinction; it occurs in women as well as men; when existing in only a slight degree, it must be regarded as within the normal limits of variation of sexual emotion."[17] Ellis based his defense on the idea that desire is focused not just on the love object's face or even genitals but on all aspects of the body, including its productions. Since urine and feces both come from the genitals—the site of intercourse—they are particularly prone to be fetishized. In his autobiography he claimed that urination was actually beautiful: "It was never to me a vulgar interest, but rather an ideal interest, a part of the yet unrecognized loveliness of the world, which we already recognize in fountains."[18] Of more pertinence to Demuth's images of sailors urinating is Ellis's claim that excretory acts are symbolic of the act of intercourse itself: "It is, indeed, in the muscular release of accumulated pressures and tensions, involved by the act of liberating the stored-up excretion, that we have the closest simulation of the tumescence and detumescence of the sexual process."[19] Built into Demuth's *Two Sailors Urinating* is precisely this sense of release. Demuth's characters are releasing urine, but the artist's exaggeration of his subjects' penises and their lewd expressions is a *release* from the more-veiled representation of homosexuality in the earlier Turkish bath series and in the illustrations. Demuth's erotic world may not include the monogamous relationship represented by the little white hand that never beckons, but it is still a world of pleasure.

Yet it is fleeting pleasure. If the sailors are taking liberties with each other, we sense that it is only for the moment and that the relationships described will not last the morning after. Rather than see this transience as necessarily symptomatic of Demuth's psychic lack—his inability to love or be loved—we could take it as representative of much of gay life from 1910 through 1940. The settings of Demuth's homosexual watercolors—bathhouses, streets along the docks, bathrooms, and beaches—are a fairly extensive catalogue of the places gay men were able to meet. Unfortunately, the law was most likely to arrest homosexuals at such public places. Given the rules of evidence, and the private nature of most sexual liaisons, it was often difficult to catch a sodomite in the act. Mayor Fiorello LaGuardia's Committee for the Study of Sex Offenses in New York City published a detailed report that provides statistics on court cases involving sodomy between 1930 and 1939. The unsurprising findings of the committee, though confined to the last ten years of the period I am discussing, were probably valid for the first part of the twentieth century. We can be confident that between 1910 and 1940 only a tiny fraction of the countless numbers of sexual acts forbidden by the sodomy law were prosecuted in court. The report comments: "It is well known that homosexual practices among men are fairly common, particularly in certain vocational and social circles. It is evident from the above figures as to the ages of victims of sex crimes that cases of sodomy in which the sodomistic partner was an adult rarely come into our courts. Of the 404 male victims of sex crime 35 or 8.6% were 18 years of age or over. Sodomy between adults therefore rarely receives any police attention. Only when children or young adolescents are involved in sodomistic acts does the case come into the court."[20] As a result homosexuals tended not to be arrested for committing sodomy, but for solicitation, loitering, public indecency or, in rarer cases, conspiracy to commit sodomy.[21]

Why did homosexuals use public places for sex? Why did they risk being caught by the police? The answer is complex. In smaller cities and towns there was not much of a homosexual community to provide relatively safe places for gay men to meet. In big cities the issue undoubtedly had to do with the ostensibly undifferentiated nature of public spaces. Many men who used bathrooms for public sex did not necessarily consider themselves homosexual.[22] A man who frequented a notorious saloon or fraternized with known "fairies" was in danger of being tagged, but "normal" men used public bathrooms or walked along the street. At the same time, socializing with homosexuals in the comparative safety of private parties was more likely to impact the person's sense of self-definition. Of course, once such places are associated with homosexuality they may cease to be just convenient locations for sex and become the centers of fantasy. For some the danger of punishment may have heightened the pleasure. But there was also a different kind of danger in such spaces, the danger to society itself. The homosexual "tearoom" or the bathhouse-gymnasium was not necessarily differentiated from heterosexual institutions—indeed there was always the possibility that straights might stumble in on the proceedings. Public bathrooms or the YMCA showers, which provided ample opportunities to see the genitalia of other men, were the kind of sites in which deviance might not quite hold its place. The use of such places by homosexuals means that they are not just inhabiting exotic red-light districts or ghettos of marginalized peoples but are in fact sharing spaces with straights. Homosexuals and heterosexuals may find themselves together in precisely that state of transition that Mary Douglas felt was so dangerous to society's sense of the sanctity of its institutions.

Regardless of the reason for their appeal to homosexuals, sexual encounters in such environments were carried out under the constant fear of discovery and were therefore necessarily performed quickly, often with little or no conversation between the participants. Michel Foucault, reflecting on the possible existence of a homosexual sensibility, touched on the effect that forcing homosexual acts underground had on gay men's concept of love and desire. Foucault claimed that although the literature of heterosexuality has for the most part dealt with what he calls the "panel of amorous courtship," resulting in a "poverty" of "appreciation of the sexual act as such," the "modern homosexual experience has no relation at all to courtship." He states: "Homosexuals were not allowed to elaborate a system of courtship because the cultural expression necessary for such an elaboration was denied them. The wink on the street, the split-second decision to get it on, the speed with which homosexual relations are consummated: all these are products of an interdiction. So when a homosexual culture and literature began to develop it was natural for it to focus on the most ardent and heated aspect of homosexual relations." Although I am worried by Foucault's mode of generalizing for all homosexuals, his description of the role memory plays in the pleasure of anonymous contacts seems particularly applicable to Demuth's erotic paintings:

> For a homosexual, the best moment of love is likely to be when the lover leaves in the taxi. It is when the act is over and the boy is gone that one begins to dream about the warmth of his body, the quality of his smile, the tone of his voice. It is the recollection rather than the anticipation of the act that assumes a primary importance in homosexual relations. This is why the great homosexual writers of our culture (Cocteau, Genet, Burroughs) can write so elegantly about the sexual act itself, because the homosexual imagination is for the most part concerned with reminiscing about the act rather than anticipating it. And, as I said earlier, this is all due to very concrete and practical considerations and says nothing about the intrinsic nature of homosexuality.[23]

Demuth's late erotic watercolors in particular have this quality of memory. Barbara Haskell speculates that by 1930 Demuth may have been impotent from diabetes. His return at this time to erotic figuration after a ten-year lapse may have come when he needed to remember sexual encounters to continue to think of himself as a sexual being. But all the erotic pictures, early and late, share a quality of making permanent brief moments of desire and pleasure. In fact, Demuth's paintings are not seductive in the mode of much erotic art. They seem made less with the intention of eliciting desire in the spectator than with the intention of recording feelings and encounters. If for Demuth they served the purpose of recapturing the memory of sexual escapades lived or dreamed, for us they provide rare visual evidence of how many homosexuals found intimacy during the period between the wars. The illicit sexual meetings that made up so much of gay life were designed to be invisible. Demuth's paintings upset that design.

6 Numbering the Dead

He had perhaps not had more losses than most men, but he had counted his losses more; he had not seen death more closely, but he had, in a manner, felt it more deeply. He had formed little by little the habit of numbering the Dead.

—Henry James, "Altar of the Dead"

He is a new sensation today for those with eyes who will see here another, broader and deeper prescience, full of late courage and passion, of a sort of love that's not easy to kill or to understand either for that matter—lying at the base and under a shaken but unmoved world.

—William Carlos Williams, *A Recognizable Image*

In my discussion of Charles Demuth, I frequently quoted from Marsden Hartley's prose portrait "Farewell Charles," which he wrote just after Demuth's death. From 1913 to 1917 Hartley and Demuth were frequent companions in New York, Paris, and Provincetown. They shared a house in Provincetown and traveled together to Bermuda. Demuth never wrote an extended description of Hartley, but he did sketch in pencil a "poster portrait" of his friend (fig. 46, pl. 9). The sketch is in the same mode as Demuth's famous *The Figure 5 in Gold* (fig. 47), though it depicts a more three-dimensional space. Demuth's poster-portrait format combines objects and words significant to the person portrayed. In the case of *The Figure 5 in Gold,* Demuth fashioned a painting of his friend William Carlos Williams by illustrating a poem by Williams that describes a speeding fire truck.

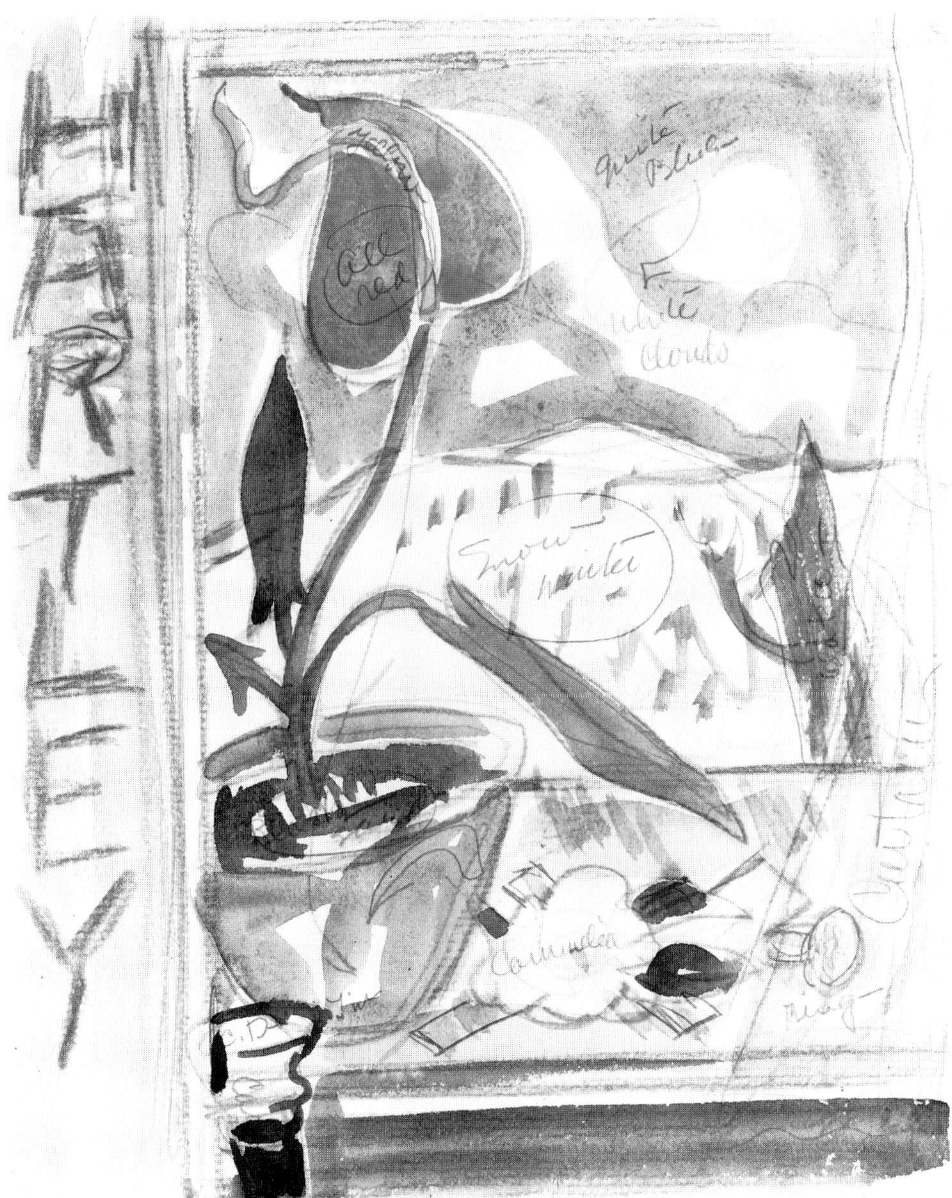

46. Charles Demuth, *Study for Poster Portrait: Marsden Hartley,* watercolor and graphite on paper, 10⅛ × 8⅛ in., 1924. Yale University Art Gallery; Stephen Carlton Clark Fund and Everett V. Meeks Fund.

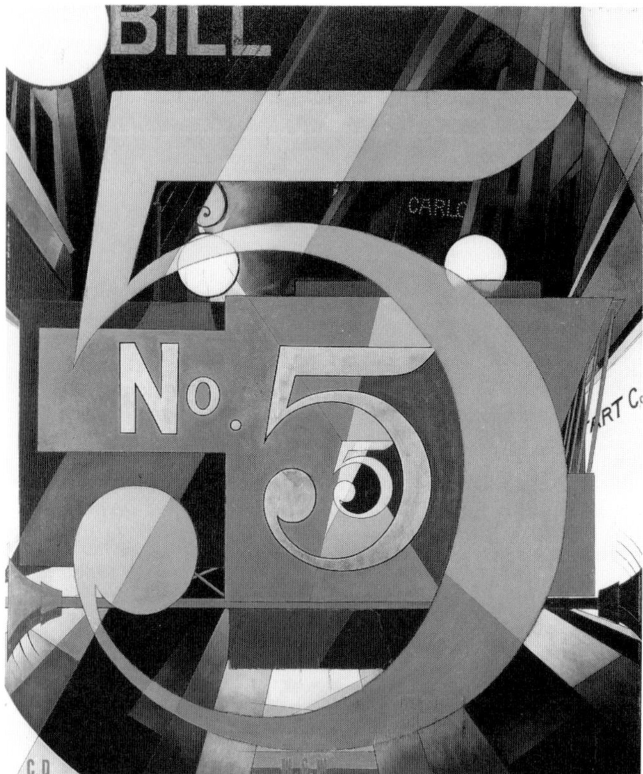

47. Charles Demuth, *The Figure 5 in Gold,* oil on composition board, 36 × 29¾ in., 1928. Metropolitan Museum of Art, New York; Alfred Stieglitz Collection, 1949.

At first glance it is hard to connect the elements of the portrait of Hartley with the subject's life or art. Demuth's sketch consists of a windowsill upon which is a potted anthurium with one large phallic blossom.[1] At the base of the plant are a camellia and a ring. In the background one can make out a severed tree and a large mountain. HARTLEY is written in big block letters along the left side of the drawing. The sketch has several notations describing intended colors and objects for a painting Demuth never made. For example, the ring is labeled "ring," the single petal of the anthurium blossom is marked "red," and the long snaking stamen is "yellow." Across the landscape are the words "snow" and "winter," and on the sky, "quite blue" and "white clouds."

What do these elements have to do with Marsden Hartley? Just as he borrowed from Williams's poems to symbolize the poet, Demuth culled images from Hartley's paintings to symbolize the artist. The anthurium and the camellia appear to be taken from Hartley's *Still-Life with an Eel* (fig. 48), which was probably painted during or just after the trip Hartley and Demuth made to Bermuda in 1917. (Another indication of the personal significance of the painting is that their mutual friend Williams owned it.) In both Demuth's sketch and Hartley's painting, the stamen of the flower is purposely elongated so that its sexual quality is exaggerated. Hartley curved the stamen to echo the serpentine movement of the eel in the background; the stem of the camellia is crossed by another snakelike form. On the table is something that looks like a pointed hat. The meaning of Hartley's still life is ambiguous, but the picture is certainly charged—maybe overloaded—with phallic connotations.[2]

The background of Demuth's sketch appears to be taken from one of Hartley's early *Dark Mountain* landscapes that Stieglitz included in his "Younger American Painters" exhibition of 1910, perhaps *The Dark Mountain No. 1* (fig. 49). This painting shares with the Demuth sketch a winter landscape and a prominent tree stump, behind which we see a mountain. Ronald Paulson has described the Maine landscapes of this period as having the effect of an "oppressive yet protective shape bearing down on tiny traces of life."[3] Whether *The Dark Mountain No. 1* and other paintings in the series evoke Hartley's loss of his mother when he was a child or some more recent sorrow, the dark brooding landscapes, with their small farmhouses surrounded by hostile nature, are surely expressive of loss and death. Indeed, Stieglitz claimed that Hartley was considering suicide during the time he painted the *Dark Mountain* canvases.[4]

Demuth's portrait, then, is made up of a juxtaposition of two kinds of Hartley paintings—the sexually charged still lifes of 1917 and the dark landscapes of 1909–10. But Demuth did not simply combine these two motifs into a whole. As Robin Frank has noted, the head of a cane leans against the windowsill. In signing the drawing "C.D." on the head, the cane becomes Demuth's surrogate.[5] Also, the odd arrangement of two flowers and a ring does not appear in any single Hartley painting. Although the phallic anthurium, the vaginal or anal camellia, and the ring suggest tokens of a relationship, the precise details of that relationship are left

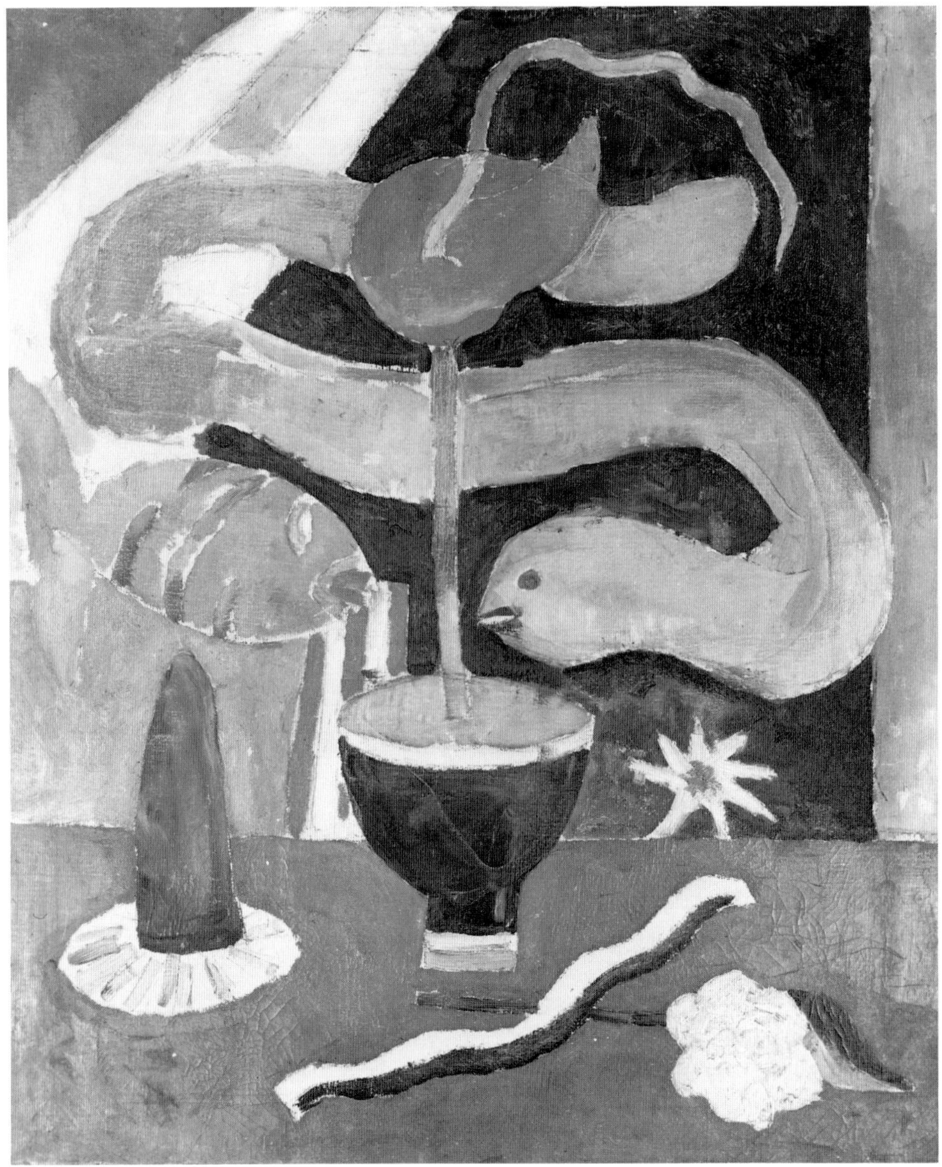

48. Marsden Hartley, *Still-Life with an Eel,* oil on canvas, 30½ × 25 in., 1917. Museum of American Art, Ogunquit, Maine; gift of Mrs. William Carlos Williams.

49. Marsden Hartley, *The Dark Mountain No. 1,* oil on composition board, 14 × 12 in., 1909. Metropolitan Museum of Art, New York; Alfred Stieglitz Collection, 1949.

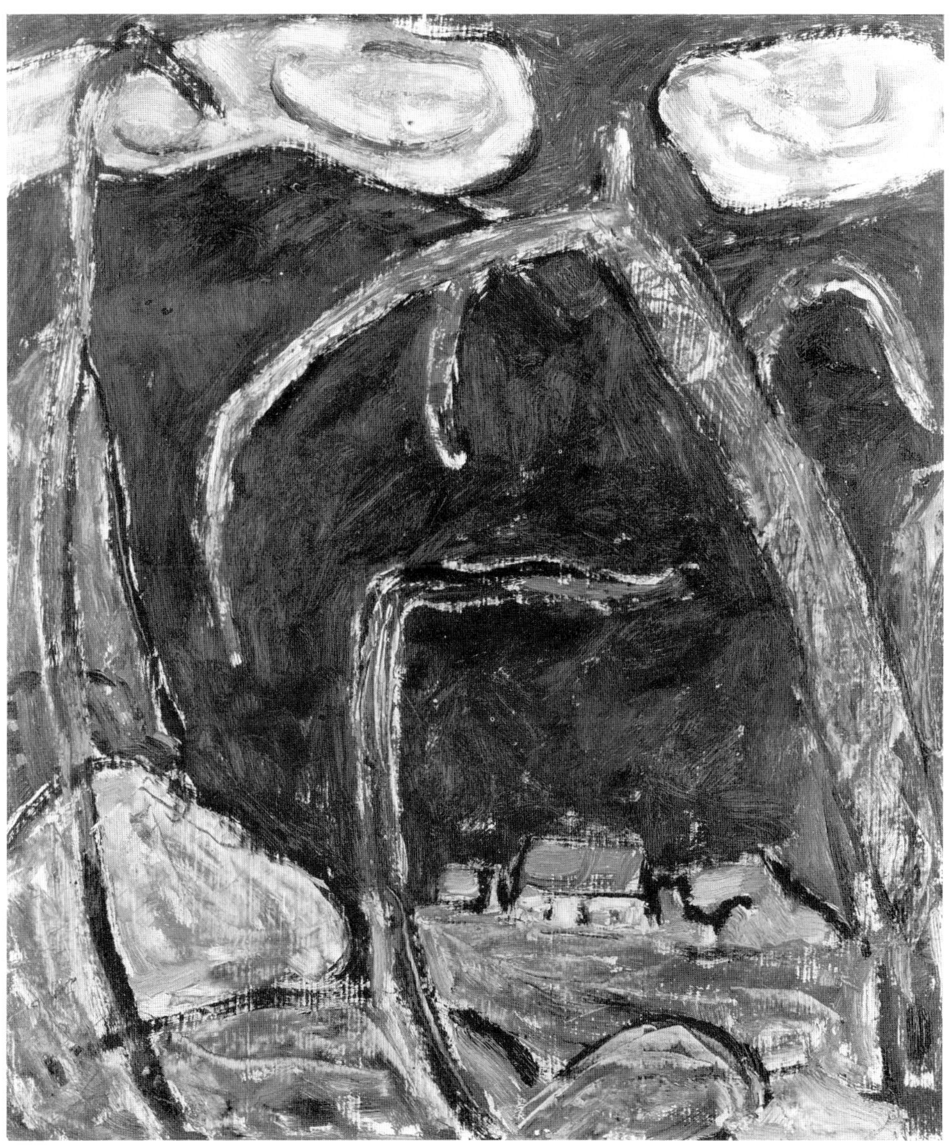

to our imagination. (Could the flowers symbolize Hartley and Demuth's friendship?) The suggestive quality of the anthurium seems to invite a sexual reading of the image. Yet that sexuality is seen against a bleak winter landscape that speaks of death and within a broken tree that speaks, perhaps, of impotence. With a minimum of means—juxtaposing and condensing elements from Hartley's own painting—Demuth suggested what I think is one of the central characteristics of Hartley's art: his habitual presentation of desire in a context that included death.

A large portion of Hartley's vast body of writing—both published and unpublished—is about death. His favorite vehicle in the 1930s was the obituary. Along with the essay on the death of Charles Demuth, he wrote several memorials to Hart Crane and a series of remembrances entitled *Letters Never Sent,* dedicated mostly to dead artists and friends (Hartley's original title for the series was *Letters to the Dead*).[6] "Farewell Charles" begins with a discussion of Hartley's frequent losses: "No one wants to see death stalking in the wake of his friends as persistently as I have been obliged to do of late. I don't recover from these episodes as quickly as some are inclined to do, accepting them as plain facts of life, and I am still wanting the vibrant companionship of those who have brought either richness or fun, or both, into my life."[7]

Although written in 1935, these paragraphs could apply to any time in Hartley's life. His mother died when he was eight, and he was raised alternately by his father and his sister, shuttling back and forth between Cleveland and Maine.[8] An implied resentment toward his father appears in his unpublished autobiographical fragment "Somehow a Past," in which he suggests that his mother's death left him parentless: "At the age of eight left alone on the doorstep of the world I sat me down on the cold stones to learn what it was all about." And a few pages later, "I was left alone as the dreaming child to forage for myself and make cloth out of rainbow spun for the naked spirit."[9] Referring to his status as an early orphan, Hartley makes the claim that his life was "99 percent what I made it, since due to the circumstances of early childhood, there was no one to tell me what it was." Oddly, Hartley does not describe his mother or her funeral in his memories of his childhood.[10] Instead he attributes the course of his later art to the death of a kitten:

> The foundation of all that was to come after was a strong love of flowers, as it was later on to be mountains, then the sea, delicacy, strength, moving forms, and the death of a white kitten over which my youngest sister and myself cried. . . .
>
> The kitten was carried in the salt box to the Franklin pastures . . . and on the east side of it was a brick yard and on the west side, a stream of clean water running sort of tumbling through a glade, where [there are] trilliums, dogtooth violets, Jack in the pulpits, and of course white and blue violets, and it was among the latter in a little knoll surrounded by new boxberry leaves that the early symbol was buried.[11]

Clearly the kitten seems to be an early symbol for Hartley's mother. The kitten's funeral becomes a way for Hartley to place his mother in a natural paradise, her body becoming one with the earth and the flowers that he painted throughout his career. Perhaps this passage is all the evidence needed to support those who see in Hartley's landscape art, particularly its repeated depiction of mountains, his desire to be reunited with his lost mother.

The instability of Hartley's childhood and his sense of repeated abandonment were played out when he matured—Hartley never stayed in one place for more than a year. He often found himself separated from family, lovers, and friends by untimely deaths, but just as often, he severed relationships through his own restlessness. He was always leaving town in hopes of finding a place that was more conducive to his art and life. Or he would create tension between himself and his closest friends by asking for something he knew they could not give. In his autobiography, William Carlos Williams described a visit to Hartley's room in New York City. The tiny room had been cut out of a larger apartment using a thin partition:

> On one side [of the partition] was the couch in which Marsden slept, a few inches [on the other side] was the bed of two lovers.
>
> "Yes they often entertain me at night," he [Hartley] said.
>
> I felt sorry for him, growing old. That was the moment he took for his approaches. I, too, had to reject him. Everyone

> rejected him. I was no better than the others. One of our finest painters. He told me I *would* have made one of the most charming whores of the city.[12]

Hartley was not unaware of his difficulty in getting along with other people and adapting to new places. After being thrown out of Mabel Dodge Luhan's house for fighting with her guests, Hartley wrote an apologetic letter: "I belong to a less specialized species, to commoner elements. I must never do more, at most, than walk in as graciously as possible, sit a little, and pass out again for there is always the quality of wonder in being really not quite anywhere at all times."[13] The voice is not far removed from Charles Demuth's lonely young man who walks the ship deck in "The Voyage Was Almost Over." Once again we are confronted with the flâneur who watches and records a world of which he never feels fully a part. Like Demuth's hero, Hartley feels cut off from the kind of loving relationships others take for granted. Furthermore, both Hartley and Demuth allied the artist's sense of alienation from his subject with the homosexual's position of estrangement from society. Whereas Demuth suggests homosexuality in his refined distance from the heterosexual lovemaking that goes on around him, Hartley's allusion to his homosexuality is somewhat derogatory in the passing reference to commoner elements.

Hartley was ambivalent about his sexuality. As Williams's odd story suggests, Hartley made no secret of his homosexuality, at least not with his close friends. But Hartley was not at ease writing about homosexuality. Although he wrote of his enormous capacity for friendship with certain men, even using the word *love,* rarely did he feel comfortable discussing men as objects of sexual attraction. The writer and publisher Robert McAlmon received a few explicit letters from Hartley. Although McAlmon's letters to Hartley are not available, it is clear from Hartley's contribution that the correspondence included descriptions of erotic adventures by both writers. Hartley writes of how much he enjoyed McAlmon's description of a sex shop: "I was so amused with your picture of things in the shop, people asking for rubber hardons, etc.—I had the 'great privilege' of seeing one in Berlin, so I know what they look like, and according to report, the balls can be filled with lukewarm water, and squeezed by the wearer to simulate the thing itself, but I didn't know that sort of thing would be in use over here, but one never can tell."[14] Another letter concludes with Hartley asking McAlmon to "give somebody a careful look and say its from me, and I mean to get down that way and do it all for myself eventually, but there will be N.Y. again in January, and that is something—my god in June and July before I left, all the navies in white duck, and the thighs and arses something to tell mother about—simply wonderful."[15]

During World War II, sailors and soldiers were very much on Hartley's mind, as the East Coast, and New York in particular, was flooded with conscripts:

> I got such thrills out of Broadway last winter, of course with all the Army and Navy, it was simply incredible and if there is a better looking bunch of kids anywhere in the world, I'd like to see them, and are all so fine physically, and so well mannered as of course they come from the better and best families now. As for some that are in the Army and Navy, well how in the world did they ever let 'em in and keep 'em after they got in, but I guess the rigidity of the whole thing scared the piss out of the softies, and they found that even they can act like men.

He tells McAlmon of a near encounter:

> To my consternation one evening on Fifth going home, a soldier tried to pick me up, doing the usual fagged out stunt of turning up a side street. I wish now I had followed just to see how it talked, but on the other hand these days it doesn't do, and there is never a bat of an eyelash either from the Army or the Navy on Broadway, so they must have had a course in that too, and I think someone said they have severe rules on that subject, etc.[16]

The letter suggests some of Hartley's feelings about his homosexuality. Even though he is writing to someone who shares his sexual tastes, he feels constrained in naming homosexuality—referring to "that subject" and to a homosexual soldier as "it." Hartley makes it clear that he is attracted to men, but he distances himself from effeminate homosexuals. He discussed the exclusion of more-flagrant homosexuals from the armed forces in the same letter: "They have psychological analysis when they are called up and if they are too far gone over on the girly side, they tell 'em so and discard them—as one examiner said to one of them in N.Y.—you would do more harm than good, and dismissed #her# [*sic*] respectfully."

Hartley's disparaging remarks about effeminacy are ironic given the various reports that describe Hartley himself as fitting this stereotype. In the 1910s he seems to have dressed flamboyantly. Alfred Kreymborg described Hartley's appearance around the time of World War I: "When Spring came, if he could afford nothing else, Marsden managed to buy a gardenia for his buttonhole. The others thought him a snob. His ways were superior. . . . His exquisite tastes, the exotic longing he had for warm, precious stones, aggravated the impression. These predilections and starved, mystical obsessions tended to give him a place apart. And he wrapped his coat like a toga about his spare form, held his nose in the air, used his aristocratic cough as a warning not to come too close."[17] Hartley's fastidious dress and affected manner (as well as his sexual proclivities, I suspect) made him the brunt of a joke in the avant-garde journal *New York Dada,* which did a spoof of a society column. Under the headline "Marsden Hartley May Make a Couple—Coming Out Party Next Friday" ran this description: "Master Marsden will be attired in a neat but not gaudy set of tight-fitting gloves and will have a V-back in front and on both sides. He will wear very short skirts gathered at the waist with a nickel's worth of live leather belting. His slippers will be heavily jewelled with brass eyelets, and a luxurious pair of dime laces will be woven in and out of the hooks. He may or may not wear socks. He has always been known as a daring dresser."[18] Out of context, the column might seem like a vicious satire of Hartley's mannerisms and sexuality, but it was probably meant to be both knowing and friendly. We must remember that the magazine's editor, Marcel Duchamp, proudly stepped out in drag. Still, the choice of Hartley for this joke was hardly coincidental. In fact, the passage almost predicts Hartley's costume at a ball in Berlin a year later.

In 1922, Hartley described this ball in a letter to Madelaine Rice. The letter brings into high relief the contradictions in Hartley's attitude toward men who appeared "effeminate." He describes a transvestite he had seen at "one of the, if not the nicest private affairs" he had ever been to in Berlin: " 'She' sat in a swing under palms between two doors under soft glowing light, for the chandeliers were covered with pink roses—and received her friends in this graceful picture. It is as complete a case of transferred psychology as is to be found probably—and one found no embarrassment whatever. The others there were all somehow or other—'otherwise' and the pictures to be seen were most engaging." The euphemism *otherwise* for homosexual is significant. For Hartley, homosexuality was clearly other. As if worried that Rice would get the wrong idea about his tastes, he prefaced this description by saying that such displays usually "distress" him "excessively" and that he dislikes "all or most all feminine aspects in men." Yet in spite of this disclaimer, in the very same letter, he tells Rice of a magnificent costume he had just worn to a party in Berlin:

> I myself had as fine a costume as [anyone?]—and I was often told so both evenings. I was a kind of thousand and one nights magnificent creature in a . . . coat with silver cloth sleeves & trousers and a turban like hat of silver—buried in small and large spangles of silver-hemlock blue and flaming ruby—and all over the coat were glittering spangles of mirror gems—my face painted Indian-red. . . . I was the object of much polite comment and not infrequent conscious or subconscious love-making from enamored young men who seemed bewitched with the effect I made on them—one nice young fellow said—if I were a girl I'd make love to you at once.[19]

In the last sentence Hartley seems to get his pronouns confused. Does he unconsciously wish he or the "nice young man" were a girl? Still he appears delighted with the idea of being an object of male desire, perhaps even being confused with a beautiful woman. But he makes sure that Rice knows that he dislikes "most all feminine aspects in men," even as he seems jealous of the transvestite's ability to be comfortable in public with "no embarrassment whatever." Like many other homosexuals of his generation, Hartley's defense mechanism against the prejudices of the dominant society was to distance himself through sarcasm from gay men who appeared "girlish." This sarcasm was at least unconsciously directed against his own mannerisms and desires.

Hartley's worry about effeminacy spills over into his aesthetic judgments.

He seems to have held typically patriarchal views about gender differences. He frequently drew sharp divisions between the masculine and the feminine—almost always finding that the feminine was the lesser sphere. He wrote in an essay on literary theory that the new poetry calls "for an arm. We need not be afraid of muscularity or even of 'brutality.'" He noted proudly that "painting has become definitely masculine at last," but added a qualification: "Delicacy and frankness are not necessarily feminine. Nor are strength and vigor necessarily masculine."[20] Hartley habitually cast the masculine as the natural, while relegating the female to the civilizing realm of the domestic and the routine. He also suggested that only men are capable of truly transcendent art. Writing Stieglitz in 1914 about a recent issue of *Camera Work,* he claimed that the works by women ran to "hyperbole and sentiment and the male phase to indefiniteness and mysticity [*sic.*]"[21] He makes it clear which work he prefers by adding that a "woman is never mystical of course—or I mean a woman is never a mystic." Hartley often used the word *mystical* in connection with his own art. It was a way for him to suggest spirituality without specific religious connotations. In excluding women from the mystical, he was excluding them from the kind of art he valued most.

What were Hartley's relationships with women? Was he exclusively homosexual? Hartley had several friendships with women. Late in life he maintained close contact with the artist Adelaide Kuntz and with his niece, Norma Berger. And he counted among the great losses of his life the premature death of Alice Miriam, fiancée of Arnold Rönnebeck. Yet women represented entanglement to Hartley. In his letters he frequently suggested that he was attracted to women but did not want to get married. In 1912, he wrote Stieglitz that he was about to go out to lunch with a friend: "I expect her in a little while to take lunch with me. Unless one has a mistress or a wife here one misses company for everyone sort of pairs off here and so there are groups of lone men all around—some through preference and some through necessity. I could have had one of the most fascinating girls in all Paris—but I told her to be sensible and stick to the man who has money. . . . But the English girl and I are very good pals and so I can enjoy her companionship without the encumbrances and without complications." He was clearly threatened by women who were intelligent and talented. He wrote that he liked Greta Williams because she was "adorably fascinating" and "clever without knowing too much," adding, "I hate them when they know too much and it is almost as bad when they are such idiots as some."[22]

According to Andrew Field's biography of Djuna Barnes, Hartley and Barnes were lovers: "The seduction began with Marsden drawn up before Djuna coolly detailing for her like a patient salesman of celestial goods the superior dimensions of his sexual equipment and endowment."[23] The evidence for Hartley's affair with Barnes, however, is sketchy at best, and Field provides no proof of such a liaison.[24] In a letter to Leon Tebbetts, Hartley suggested that sex with women inevitably conflicted with developing a close relationship: "Men often know men better than women (me anyhow[)]—and I have experienced that frequently because with women sex interferes and with men it does not—it becomes a higher kind of thing—and if I do say it myself, I have a real gift for friendship and it is my best talent."[25] Here, Hartley's wording is typically ambiguous. Is he saying that sex does not interfere with male relationships because men commonly do not have sex with each other, or is it that homosexuality does not involve men in complicated entanglements? Whatever the interpretation, male companionship is idealized. If Hartley did have an occasional affair with the opposite sex, for the most part he avoided women's sexual advances because, he claimed, women required commitment. He wrote Stieglitz that he was against "fixed conditions. . . . I can't see myself into it—I know now that I shall be a wanderer taking what I can take in the way I can take it and ask nothing more—I know the masculine nature so thoroughly—I know the feminine well—and yet I still have to wonder at a woman—abstractly we all know they are lovely—intimately I don't know if anyone knows anything and I hate intimacy—I myself am too mystically composed I am certain ever to let any one person walk wholly into my domain."[26] Hartley claims to understand the masculine character, but women are mysterious; they make demands of intimacy that he cannot provide. Significantly, Hartley's unwillingness to make a commitment to women is an aspect of his mysticism. Those who refused women's advances were wanderers. In 1915, Hartley did not yet see in homosexual relationships an alternative to heterosexual domesticity.

Toward the end of his life, Hartley worried about his sexual orientation being made public. In 1936, Hartley wrote to Arnold Rönnebeck of his concern when he heard that McAlmon had written a memoir: "I heard of it in N.Y. last winter and trembled a little for myself as I do not want to figure too vividly in aspects of recollection that have their right to their own privacy." The recollections that Hartley refers to are characteristically left ambiguous, but it is clear from the following that he means some kind of homosexual adventures in Europe:

> I miss all that—and I wish it would be returned or some sort of equivalent. I forego much now that I want—chances in which to be "free" in such small communities like this—as it doesn't do to destroy our better side by reverse pictures—but the chances here are on every hand and could be had for the taking and nothing would be thought—but that is the way I always have felt about living intimate in such places. I have not wanted to disturb the picture by being conspicuous in it—for *such* reasons. In large cities one need care less but even there, at least in our U.S., people are cheap and I found it even expedient to give up certain friendships because they were not fine and true enough. As for the rest you know, how one can go out and be common in cities and no one need know—it wouldn't matter if they do but there is no reason why they should.[27]

The passage summarizes Hartley's method for dealing with his homosexuality. Hartley was afraid to "live intimate" when he was in the small communities where he often went to paint, preferring to have sex in the more anonymous realm of the city. But the letter also suggests that sexual experiences he had in cities were usually casual. When sexual friendships became too serious, they had to end because the companions were "not fine and true enough." Yet the word "expedient" suggests that long-term intimacy actually was avoided out of a desire not to be conspicuous. In any case, Hartley implies that the quality of male friendship may be undermined by sex, a practice that he refers to derogatorily as being common.[28] Perhaps the most interesting element of this passage is the use of painterly terms to refer to the effects of homosexuality. Having sex with men in a small community results in a "reverse picture." Being overt threatens to "disturb the picture."

The Example of Leonardo da Vinci

In the end, Hartley was to make a positive aesthetic value out of this ability to avoid emotional commitment. The argument is clearest in an essay left unpublished at his death, "The Element of Absolutism in Leonardo's Drawings." Bombastic and confused as the essay may be, it is, I believe, the key document for understanding Hartley's feelings on the relation between art and everyday life.

Great art, says Hartley, comes about when the artist is able to divorce himself from emotion: "Passion for its own sake is not worth troubling about, and all in all, a cheap form of entertainment." For all the "voluptuous tendencies" of the Renaissance period, "when sex lusts were at their height," Leonardo "did not indulge in debaucheries of the body or the heart, he used his eye as the sextant by which he determined all directions, all latitudes and longitudes of sense and sensibility, he was the see-er supreme." According to Hartley, Leonardo was a loner, who was "socially difficult" because of his superior knowledge, which was not just scientific. Leonardo "was preeminently a psychologist, he never confounded male and female sensibility . . . and he knew that feminine beauty is often found in alien countries of the human concept." Hartley does not mention Leonardo's homosexuality, but it is implied in his ability to find "feminine" beauty outside of women. Hartley adds that "if his own feminine sensibility was now and then in evidence he knew how to counteract it by some other phase of knowledge and so, because he knew, he was never weak in knowledge." Typically, in Hartley's view of gender, knowledge is opposed to femininity. The homosexual, in danger of being overwhelmed by his "feminine sensibility," must counteract that tendency with a "masculine" mind. He compares Leonardo's art to Bach's partitas, which are "loftily impersonal as all great art is, no weeping for confused love as in the case of Tchaikovsky." Tchaikovsky's "confused love" is again a veiled reference to a pedestrian form of homosexuality—a homosexuality undermined by "femininity."[29]

Hartley credited Paul Valéry's essay "Introduction to the Method of Leonardo" for the idea of the absolutism and universality of Leonardo's art.[30] But Valéry has practically nothing to say about Leonardo's life or "femininity." The style of Hartley's description of Leonardo walking along the Arno is closer to Walter Pater's famous essay "Leonardo da Vinci, Homo Minister et Interpres Naturae." Hartley mentions reading Pater's essays as early as 1906.[31] It also seems likely that Hartley had read Sigmund Freud's *Leonardo da Vinci and a Memory of His Childhood,* in which Freud devotes an extensive discussion to Leonardo's sexuality.[32] But given Hartley's fear of having his homosexuality revealed in public, it is no surprise that he does not refer to Freud directly in his essay, since *Leonardo da Vinci and a Memory of His Childhood* contains one of Freud's most extensive and clear discussions of the origins of homosexuality. Freud locates Leonardo's insatiable need to investigate the natural world in the artist's childhood experience. He gives great weight to evidence that Leonardo was raised by two mothers. According to the biographical material available to Freud, Leonardo was born to an unwed mother. When he was five, his father took him away from his mother to be brought up in the paternal household under the guidance of his father's wife. According to Freud, the absence of Leonardo's father during his first five years contributed to the formation of Leonardo's homosexuality. In the course of this initial stage, the "boy found himself left entirely under feminine influence." Freud continued: "The child's love for his mother cannot continue to develop consciously any further; it succumbs to repression. The boy represses his love for his mother: he puts himself in her place, identifies himself with her, and takes his own person as a model in whose likeness he chooses the new objects of his love. In this way he has become a homosexual."[33] When Leonardo matured, he sublimated homosexual desire into his search for knowledge: "The core of his nature, and the secret of it, would appear to be that after his curiosity had been activated in infancy in the service of sexual interests he succeeded in sublimating the greater part of his libido into an urge for research." Even though Leonardo sublimated his sexuality, traces of homosexual desire remain in his nurturing relationship toward his pupils. For Freud, therefore, Leonardo must be "reckoned as a homosexual."[34]

There are some surprising parallels between Hartley's life and Freud's version of Leonardo's biography. Like Freud's Leonardo, Hartley seems to have been raised by two mothers and to have suffered from the abandonment of his father. As I mentioned above, in his autobiographical fragment, Hartley tells almost nothing about his parents. Yet the tone of "Somehow a Past," with its condensation of his mother's death into the memory of a kitten's funeral, suggests that he felt a closeness to his mother that he did not share with his father. His insistence that his mother's death left him "alone on the doorstep of the world" implies that he was estranged from his father. Again, we know nothing about Hartley's relationship to his stepmother except for the curious fact that when he decided to change his given name, Edmund, in 1907, he chose his stepmother's maiden name, Marsden. Hartley wrote that he chose his stepmother's family name for "sentimental reasons" because she had "endeared herself to us by sharing her life with my father."[35] Barbara Haskell guesses that the choice may have been an attempt to "reconcile himself with his father and to draw closer to his stepmother."[36]

Hartley's adoption of his stepmother's name is intriguing, given Freud's interpretation of Leonardo's *Madonna and Child with St. Anne*. Freud describes the peculiar pose of the full-grown Mary on the lap of her mother: "One is inclined to say that they are fused with each other like badly condensed dream-figures, so that in some places it is hard to say where Anne ends and where Mary begins." But according to Freud, the peculiarity of the painting is "vindicated in the eyes of analysis by reference to its secret meaning. It seems that for the artist the two mothers of his childhood were melted into a single form." He added that the London cartoon, which Hartley concentrates on, represents a more extreme condensation, since the Christ child is held by Mary, who in turn sits on Anne's lap.[37] Remarkably, Hartley's description of the cartoon creates its own form of condensation: "That amazing face of St. Anne . . . shaming the Giaconda into dullness for the great revelation of that most inexplicable of all human demonstrations, namely the smile. Look at the first smile of an infant and then ponder upon the smile of a face from which all the rest of life has departed, and you know what I mean, that most pathetic of all compliments, to smile in memory at what has past [*sic*] and to face the unknowable with the same delicate weapon."[38]

In Hartley's reverie, St. Anne's smile is appreciated only after looking first at the smile of an infant, and so the baby and the grandmother oddly merge. Hartley's reference to Anne's smile as a delicate weapon is a reworking of Pater's description of the *Mona Lisa*'s smile as having something "sinister in it."[39] But it also must be dependent on Freud's analysis, which sees St. Anne as a depiction of Leonardo's real mother and her smile as a disturbing symbol of "his destiny and the privations that were in store for him."

I do not raise the issue of the supposed etiology of Leonardo's homosexuality with the purpose of explaining the origins of Hartley's; rather, I think Hartley was drawn to Leonardo not just because of Leonardo's genius but because Leonardo's life legitimized Hartley's relationships with men. Hartley wrote his essay on Leonardo when he was in his sixties. The evidence suggests that although Hartley was sexually active (or liked to hint he was), he had yet to have a long-term sexual relationship with a man or a woman (he was never in one place long enough). Freud makes a virtue out of Leonardo's inability to find satisfying erotic commitments. Hartley's description of Leonardo walking the river bank alone, scorned by his society, corresponds to Hartley's description of himself as a lonely wanderer. Finally, Hartley shared Leonardo's refusal to limit his talents to painting. At the end of his life he was spending as much time writing as he was making pictures.[40] Leonardo was therefore a model for Hartley, both as an artist-scholar and, more important, as a man who desired but distanced homosexual love.

"Dead in Love"

In *Troubadour,* Arthur Kreymborg ends his description of Marsden Hartley with this observation: "Among them all he was easily the loneliest. . . . Whenever he could manage it, Marsden Hartley stole away from town and, whenever he couldn't help it, stole back again. None of the young men ever froze so bitterly, or looked as frozen as the eagle from the state of Maine."[41] We have seen how this quality of attraction and avoidance characterized most of Hartley's relationships with people and places. Hartley's admiration for Leonardo hinges not only on the probability that Leonardo was homosexual but also on his avoidance of passionate entanglements. It is little surprise, then, that desire and distance—and if we take these two qualities in their most extreme forms, love and death—are themes repeated in almost all the paintings Hartley made that deal to some degree with his homosexuality.

Since the publication of Michael Lynch's essay "A Gay World After All" in 1977 and of Barbara Haskell's catalogue for the 1980 Hartley retrospective at the Whitney Museum of American Art, it has been acceptable to talk about Hartley's homosexuality. Lynch suggests, but does not fully explore, what for me is the most striking characteristic of several of Hartley's paintings—their expression of the love of men for men in the context of death. The colloquial phrase Hartley used to describe his feelings for Abraham Lincoln, "I am simply dead in love with that man," characterized all the great loves of Hartley's life (at least those we know about).[42] Dead in love—Hartley seemed capable of making art about love only when the lover was dead and the love could therefore no longer be returned.

In a sense, this theme begins with the earliest Hartley painting still extant, *Walt Whitman's House* (fig. 50).[43] The small picture is somber, colored in ochers and grays. Although the picture is modest in scale, not more than ten by six inches, its composition and tone predict Hartley's later war motif series.[44] Like *Portrait of a German Officer, Walt Whitman's House* is unusually flat. Hartley approaches his subject straight on, with little foreground mediation or spatial clues. He crops out the surrounding buildings, increasing the flatness of the facade. The window panes are black and impenetrable, and the door seems uncomfortably narrow, as if squeezed. On the lowest level, the cellar door is shut and small windows are painted black. Like the later war motif series, Hartley's subject almost seems to be superimposed over a black scrim. The effect is to express a sense of secrecy—a house that holds treasures but cannot be entered.

The small townhouse displayed no particular aesthetic qualities that might have made it a fit subject to paint. Hartley was drawn to the house because of its famous occupant. Years later he wrote that he "was all Whitmanic then."[45] Among his possessions at his death was a signed photograph of Whitman, given to him by William Sloan Kennedy, a Whitman follower.[46] Painting Whitman's house was a way to connect with the dead poet, whose work was important for Hartley, not just for its expression of homosexuality but for its attempt to make a marginalized experience central to the culture. Robert K. Martin, in *The Homosexual Tradition in American Poetry,* writes about the attempt of homosexual poets not only to express their sexu-

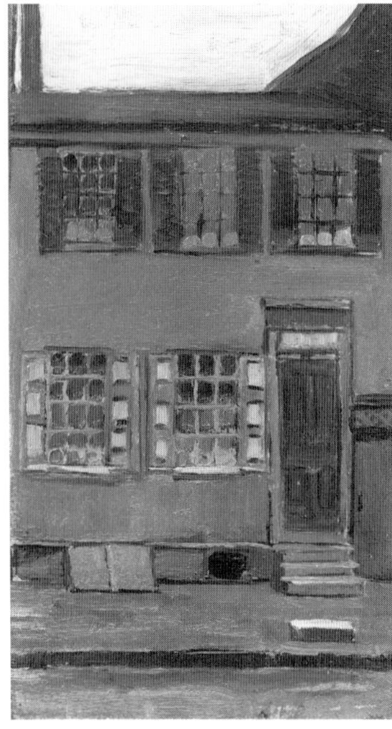

50. Marsden Hartley, *Walt Whitman's House, 328 Mickle Street, Camden, New Jersey,* oil on board, 9½ × 5½ in., 1905. Private collection.

ality but to establish a tradition of earlier gay writers: "I . . . argue that the sense of a shared sexuality has led many gay writers to develop a particular tradition, involving references to earlier gay writers. This tradition has been founded partly out of a need for communication (in which allusions can serve as code references) and partly out of a feeling of exclusion from the traditions of male heterosexual writing."[47] Significantly, Martin begins his study with Walt Whitman, who he believes is the central figure for gay poets of the twentieth century.

For many homosexuals at the turn of the century, coming to terms with Walt Whitman was part of a process of coming to terms with their sexuality. John

Addington Symonds attributed to Walt Whitman a crucial role in the "path of self-construction" necessary to accept his homosexuality: "He taught me, as no enthusiasm of humanity could do, the value of fraternizing with my fellows—for their own sakes, to love them, to learn from them, to teach them, to help and to be helped by them—not for any ulterior object upon either side."[48] Although in this passage Symonds emphasizes the platonic element of Whitman's love of man, elsewhere he made it clear that he located that love in homosexuality. In a lengthy correspondence, Symonds unsuccessfully tried to get Whitman to acknowledge the homosexual content of the *Calamus* poems.[49]

Hartley's *Walt Whitman's House* is an oddly noncommittal way to memorialize the poet. Instead of illustrating his poetry, or making a portrait of the poet himself, Hartley paints a small picture of the place where Whitman lived. The picture tells us nothing of Hartley's admiration for Whitman or what Whitman might represent to him. In a curious way it hides as much as it reveals about Hartley's affection for Whitman. What might Walt Whitman have represented to Marsden Hartley in 1905?

At around the time Hartley painted *Walt Whitman's House,* he became friendly with a group of Whitman followers, led by Horace Traubel. Traubel is probably most famous for his remembrances of his years as Whitman's private secretary, recounted in *With Whitman at Camden.* When Whitman died, Traubel devoted his career to promoting the work of the poet. He also became involved in the Ethical Culture Movement, a kind of religion without god, which stressed the search for moral and humanistic values rather than theological arguments. Traubel founded and edited the newspaper *The Conservator,* which was originally the organ of the Ethical Culture Society in Philadelphia, although he eventually broke with the society. During the time that Hartley was friends with Traubel, approximately 1905 through 1910, *The Conservator* was devoted to articles on Walt Whitman and to discussions of Traubel's particular brand of socialism.

The Conservator was committed to carrying out what Traubel thought was the message of Whitman's work: a call for a universal human fellowship. Inevitably, *The Conservator* had to grapple with the sexual component of Whitman's idea of comradeship. Traubel (who was married) and the other writers on the journal clearly wanted to promote Whitman's idea of adhesiveness—the love of men for other men—without crossing over into the realm of homosexuality. The issue was raised when Richard Burke published a volume containing Whitman's letters to his probable lover, Peter Doyle, a streetcar conductor. Hartley's old friend William Sloan Kennedy wrote a review of the book that was surprisingly frank—though he did not use the word *homosexuality*. Kennedy claimed that those who thought they knew Whitman would "find themselves readjusting their focus on reading the Peter Doyle letters," which give us a "concrete instance of his boundless and passionate love": "Let none such attempt to read them in detail, unless he or she is fond of the pretty nothings that lovers say to each other. The bard writes to his friend as one workman to another; he adapts his style and his matter to his lover's likes and level. His passionate longing for a constant return of his affection makes him ignore all that would set up estrangement between them." Kennedy warns that those who want to "divinize" Whitman may be "shocked by these letters, which show their poet in undress," but he implies that the shocking element is not the possible sexual component but Whitman's love for someone from the working classes.[50]

Hartley seemed to share with the writers of *The Conservator* a curiosity about Whitman's love life. But whereas Traubel seemed to want to normalize Whitman's sexual relationships, Hartley shared Symonds's need to know if comradeship was meant to include sex. He wrote years later that he had asked Traubel about Whitman's supposed affair in New Orleans: "I do recall being bold enough once to ask Horace about the 'Lady in New Orleans' and the 'children' supposed to be those of Walt Whitman—but I got nothing but a quiet smile out on that—and no one has ever heard anything on that subject from sources near to the matter—and I have always felt it to be a half-protective myth." Hartley met Peter Doyle but did not learn much from Whitman's old comrade: "What-ever he said was of no consequence—it was the glamour of Whitman about him that made him what he was—a good solid Irishman. No doubt there were plenty of things he could tell about Whitman and doubtless told many of them to Horace Traubel but to a man like that memories are precious and are not told to everyone and I guess there were few who ever heard the story of Whitman's love for him—or at least from Peter."[51]

Hartley's pilgrimage is significant, given the pattern of his later attachments with men. Like Whitman, Hartley was usually attached to men who were much younger than himself, often from the working class or in a profession that required a uniform. Doyle was, as Hartley put it, "solid"—intelligent and sensitive, but not sophisticated. Above all, unlike the typical artist, he was neither self-conscious nor riddled with doubts. These same qualities were to draw Hartley to the Mason family of Nova Scotia.

Traubel generally avoided specificity in the debate about Whitman's sexuality, consistently defining Whitman's love for his fellow men in the most general terms. Indeed, I would argue that the importance of Walt Whitman for Hartley, as well as for other homosexuals at the turn of the century, was his poetry's suggestion that same-sex love was part of a more universal love of humanity. In *Calamus,* Whitman wrote of being on the margins:

> In paths untrodden,
> In the growths by margins of pond-waters,

but he also claimed to

> proceed for all who are or have been young men,
> To tell the secret of my nights and days,
> To celebrate the need of comrades.[52]

In the *Calamus* series Whitman moves from intimate relations, "We two boys together clinging," to a national vision:[53]

> I believe the main purport of these States is to found a superb
> friendship, exalté previously unknown,
> Because I perceive it waits, and has been always waiting
> latent in all men.[54]

Whitman does not simply celebrate homosexual friendships, he puts male bonding at the center of what it is to be American.

Marsden Hartley came under the orbit of the Traubel group at a crucial time in his life. Before meeting Traubel and his friends, he had considered a religious vocation, perhaps hoping to sublimate his attraction to men in the good works of the ministry. Whitman's philosophy, as transmitted by Traubel and his followers, presented a model for making the love of men for men into something analogous to a religion. Indeed, Kennedy wrote of Whitman's love for Peter Doyle as being a "Christ-love."[55]

Although Traubel and his followers tried to keep Whitman's comradeship on an exalted plane, Hartley quickly seemed to want something more concrete and physical. By 1908 he was already writing the poet Shaemus O'Sheel about his friendship with Traubel as if it were more than platonic: "I've a bunch of beautiful love letters from Traubel sent during the past three years, and last summer. I saw so much of him at Green Acre where he came as often as possible to be with me."[56]

All his life Hartley had a tendency to exaggerate—to hint at sexual relationships without committing himself to any details. The "love" letters Hartley refers to have been saved and—as is rarely the case—we have both sides of the exchange. Although the letters do suggest that Hartley had a "crush" on the editor of *The Conservator,* Traubel's contribution to the correspondence is more constrained. Hartley's letter of 1907 is indicative:

> My love, all of it to you my dear Horace; I think much and often of you, see your maimed and bruised fingers and feel the throbbing of your pulses, but never a quaver in the song. I spread you round in my every chance and you do not pass unheard even here in the desert of factories and relinquished ambitions, where souls seem dead and bodies look famished and worn.[57]

A month later:

> I remember with joy those last moments with you on the train[,] your arm about me feeling the love throbs passing over me and the parting was so filled with beauty and promise. When I think of the days and years to come, getting nearer and nearer to you as love brings us together. It is enough to live.[58]

Traubel responds with words of love, but in more abstract terms:

> I am hard pushed & buried deep in accumulated work but I think I can still yell hello in a voice you may hear. Maine is not so far from Pennsylvania—when love claims the right of way. I visit you in body & spirit. You all belong to me whether you will or no. And I hope I belong to you. That is for you to say. Philadelphia is tropical. I go back to the shore today until Monday. Love!
>
> Horace[59]

The correspondence ended in 1911, perhaps because Hartley grew tired of the chasteness of Traubel's form of love for men. Hartley seems to have found his own Peter Doyle, though for only a brief period. In the last long letter in the collection (addressed, significantly, not to Traubel but to his wife), Hartley writes about a sailor named Wilson. He expresses delight that Wilson does not have to return to sea as he had originally thought: "This is why I am especially jubilant this sunny morning in Baltimore—and why Pleasant Street—on which I am stopping & where I write will for always be one of the pleasantest streets I know of—I feel as if I and the world had been given some wondrous sweet gift—to be sure only a man's soul & body—but somehow it seems enough to me. . . . I will send you his picture that you may look at the face of one who is inwardly lovely & loveable."[60] It does not seem coincidental that Hartley's correspondence with Traubel ended about the time Hartley had the prospect of a more concrete relationship with a man than his platonic crush on Traubel.

The influence of the Traubel circle on Hartley waned soon after he established himself in the New York art world. Hartley became a member of Alfred Stieglitz's circle in 1909. Yet Walt Whitman continued to be a major factor in the formation of Hartley's poetic and visual aesthetics and was crucial to Hartley's concept of homosexuality and masculinity. In 1913 he wrote the German expressionist Franz Marc that Whitman was "our greatest poet" and that his poetry was the "keynote of what the real modern art is to be."[61] Later, in 1923, Hartley testified to Whitman's importance to his art by pairing him with Cézanne in an essay in *Adventures in the Arts.*

"Whitman and Cézanne" is a somewhat strained attempt to link what he called the "two most notable innovators" in poetry and painting. In it Hartley endeavors to find the overlap between experimentation and expression in these two artistic mediums.[62] In the unpublished essay "The Business of Poetry," he wrote of Whitman's work in remarkably visual terms, as if Whitman *were* a painter: "One finds him presenting the picture. Yet the effect of Whitman on the 'sick soul,' as William James calls it, is essentially a brutal one. His simple frankness hurts. He removes the loin-cloth because it always hints at secrecy and cheap morality. He undresses the body we are forever dressing. He thinks it handsomest so. He is right. It is a poor body that doesn't look best without clothes. Nature is naked, and, not to speak tritely, quite unashamed. It has no moralistic attitude. It has no attitude at all. It is therefore natural."[63] For Hartley, Whitman presents "the picture." Significantly, Whitman's aesthetic is discussed in terms of the naked male body (we know the body is male because of the "loin-cloth" and the description handsomest, which is usually reserved for men). Whitman's "brutality" consists of removing the "loin-cloth" that "hints at secrecy and cheap morality." For Hartley, Whitman brings the love of the male body out from the margins. Whitman's celebration of the beauty of the naked male is the opposite of perversion; stripped of his confining clothes, Whitman's man is the very essence of the "natural."

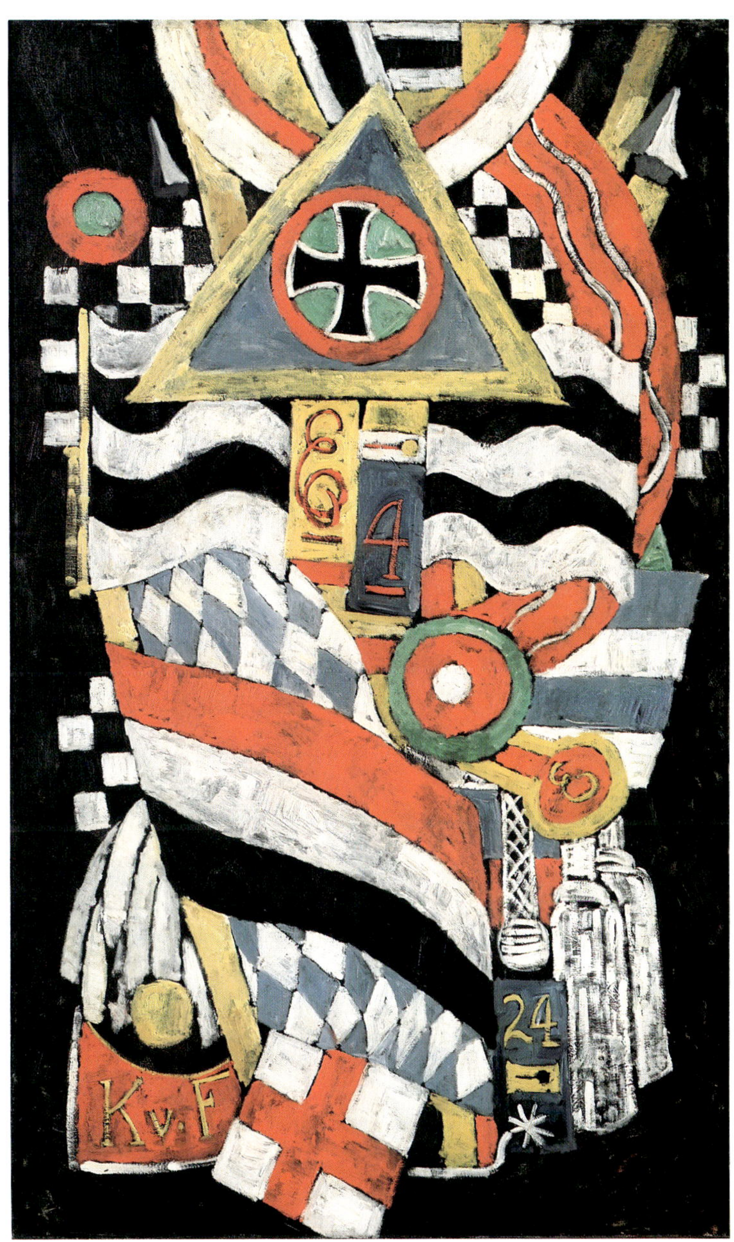

Plate 1. Marsden Hartley, *Portrait of a German Officer,* oil on canvas, 68¼ × 41⅜ in., 1914. Metropolitan Museum of Art, New York; The Alfred Stieglitz Collection, 1949.

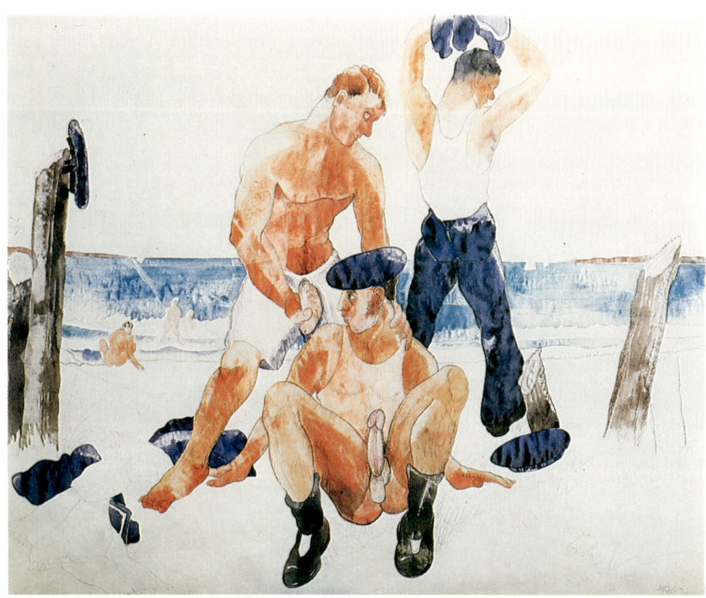

Plate 2. Charles Demuth, *Three Sailors on the Beach,* watercolor and pencil on paper, 13½ × 16½ in., 1930. Private collection. Courtesy Richard York Gallery, New York.

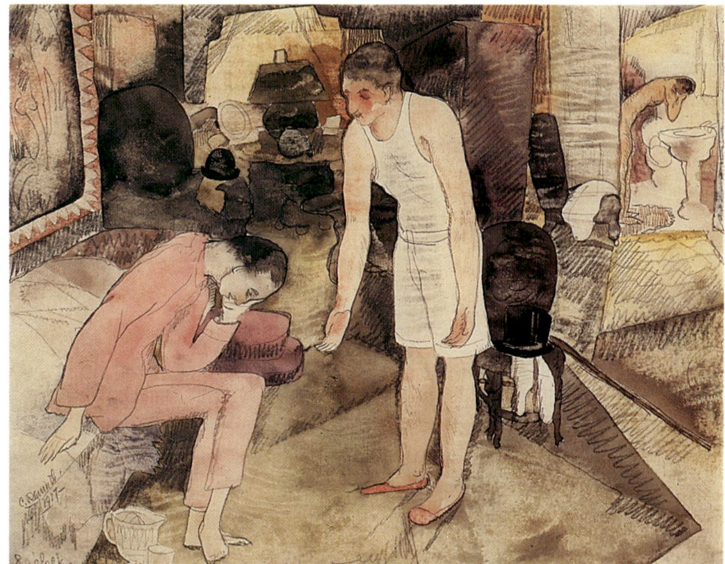

Plate 3. Charles Demuth, *Eight O'Clock (Morning #1),* watercolor and pencil on paper, 8 × 10¼ in., 1917. Collection of Mr. and Mrs. Carl D. Lobell.

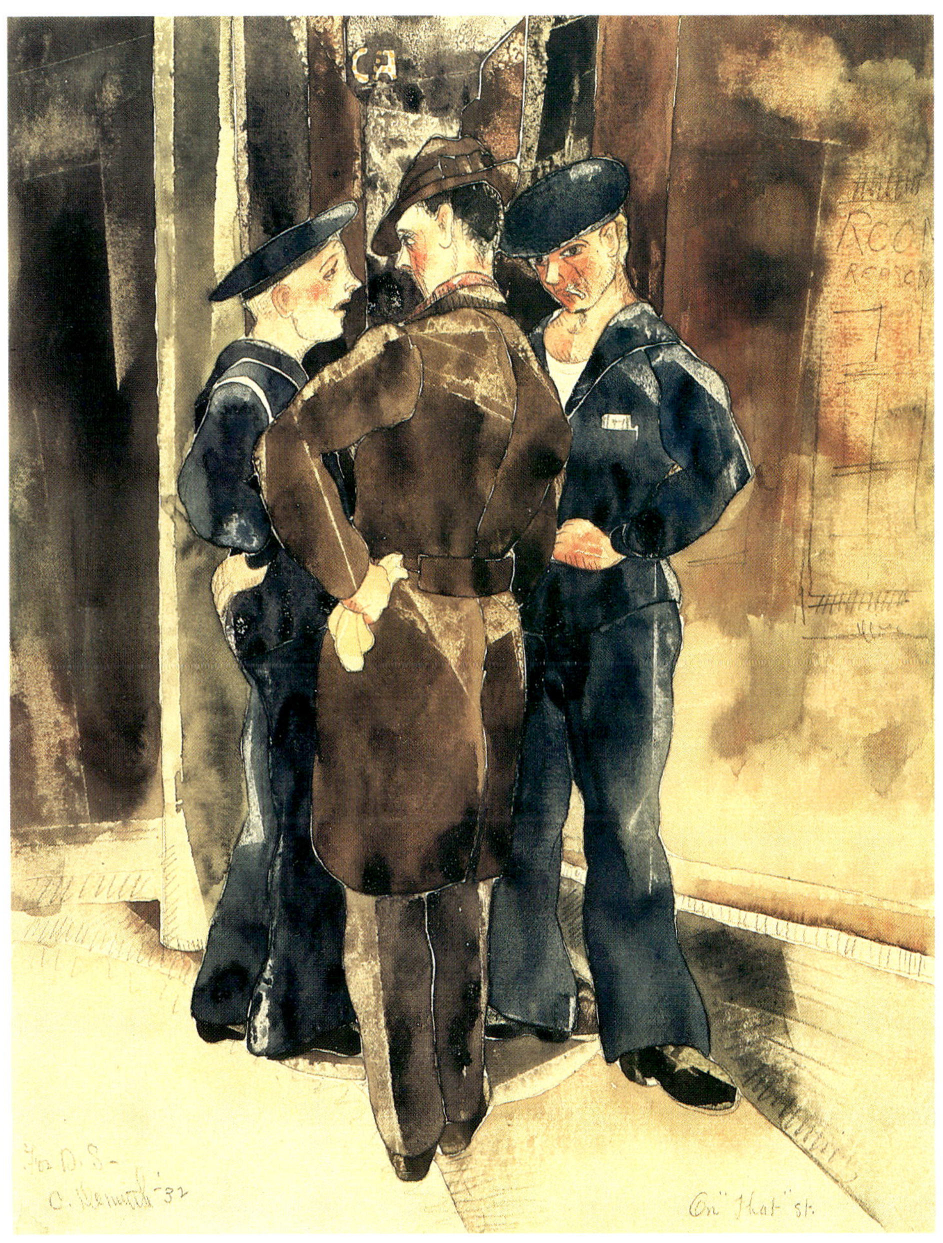

Plate 4. Charles Demuth, *On "That" Street,* watercolor and pencil on paper, 10 15/16 × 8½ in., 1932. Art Institute of Chicago, Chicago.

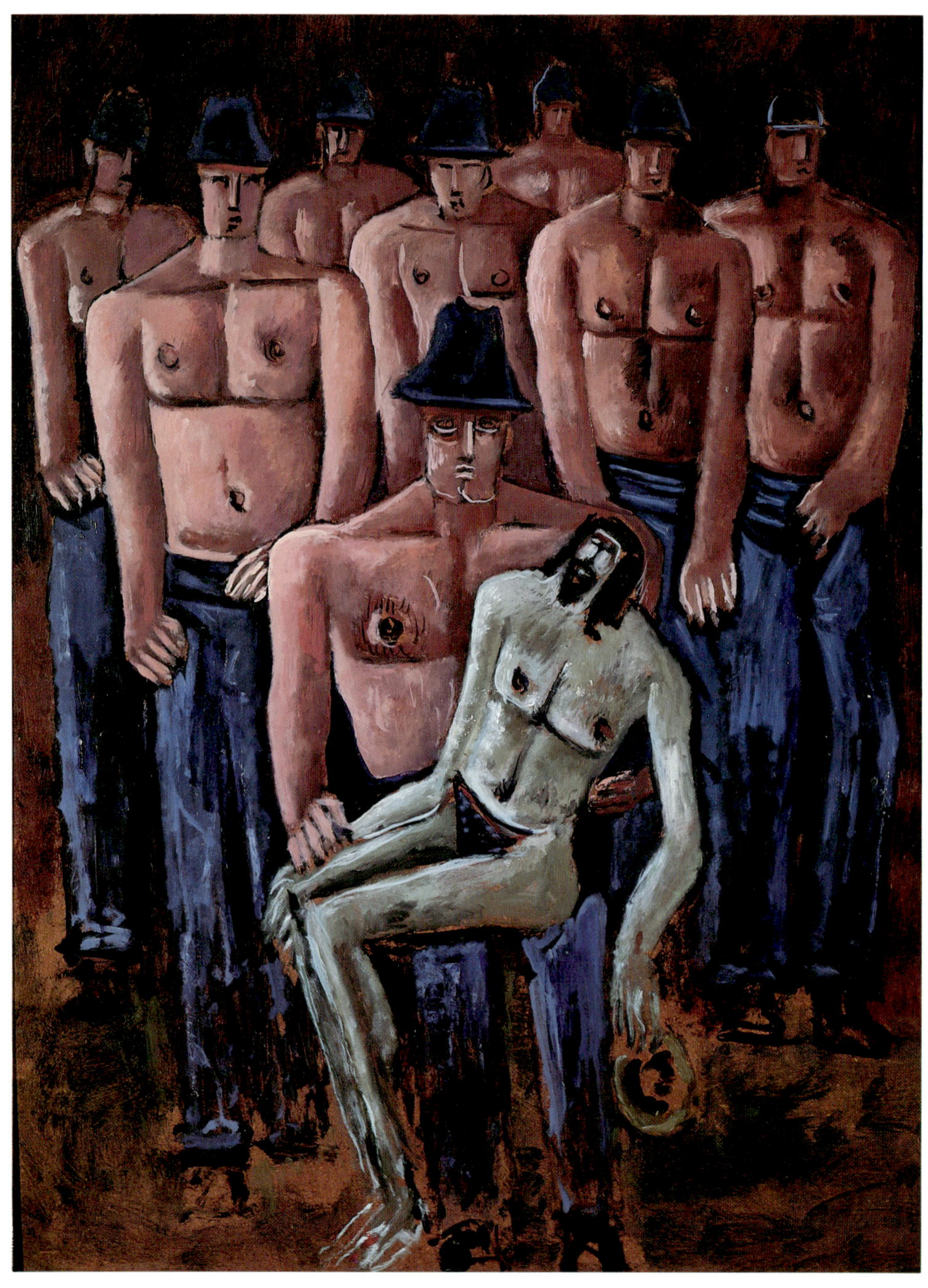

Plate 5. Marsden Hartley, *Christ Held by Half-Naked Men,* oil on fiberboard, 40 × 30 in., 1940–41. Hirshhorn Museum and Sculpture Garden, Smithsonian Institution, Washington, D.C.

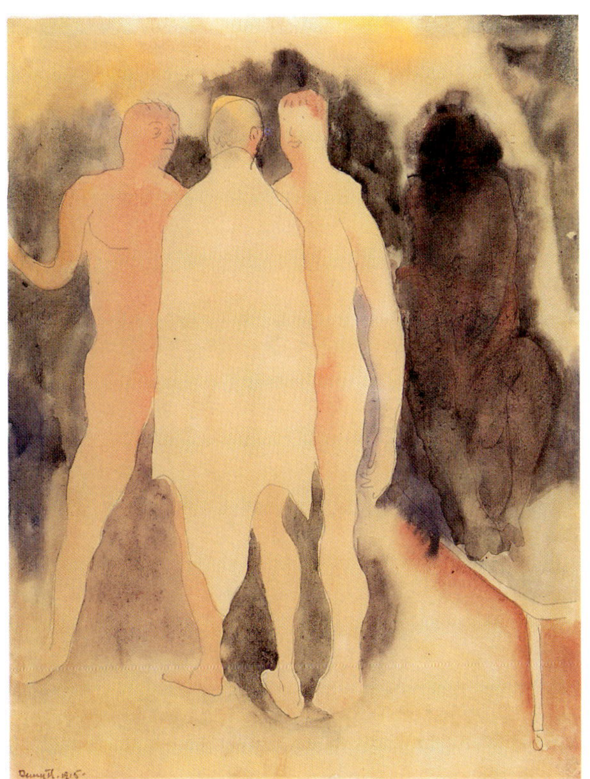

Plate 6. Charles Demuth, *Turkish Bath,* watercolor and pencil on paper, 10⅞ × 8 7/16 in., ca. 1915. Yale University Art Gallery; gift of George Hopper Fitch.

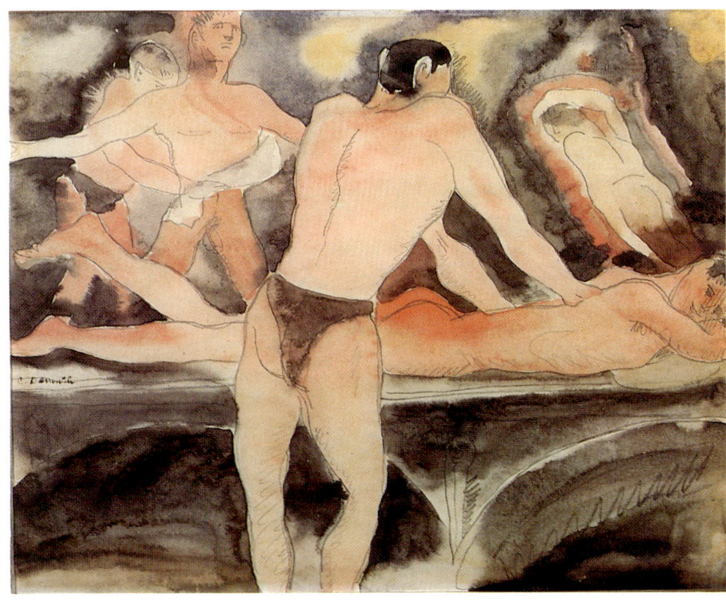

Plate 7. Charles Demuth, *Turkish Bath,* watercolor and pencil on paper, 8 × 10½ in., ca. 1915. Private collection. Courtesy Owen Gallery, New York.

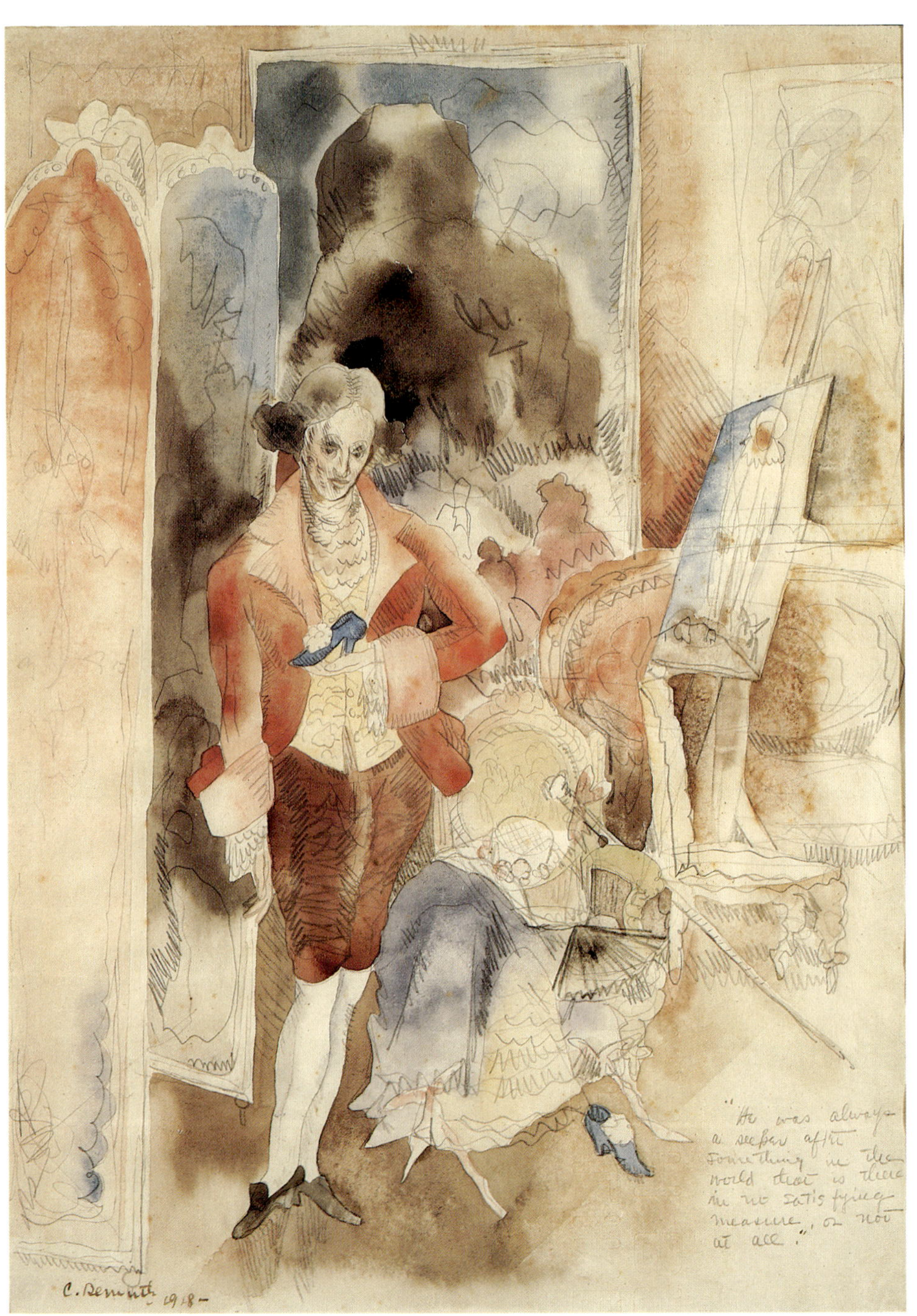

Plate 8. Charles Demuth, *A Prince of Court Painters,* watercolor, 8 × 10 in., 1918. Illustration for "A Prince of Court Painters," by Walter Pater. Private collection.

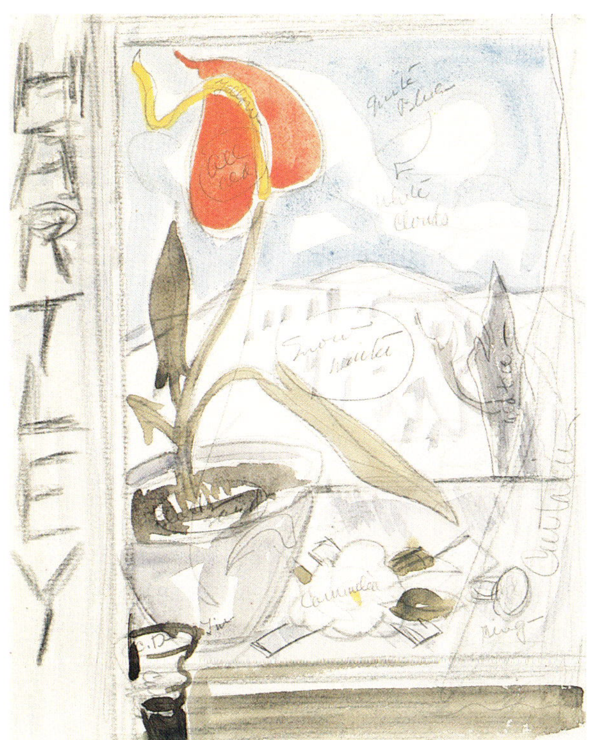

Plate 9. Charles Demuth, *Study for Poster Portrait: Marsden Hartley,* watercolor and graphite on paper, $10\frac{1}{8} \times 8\frac{1}{8}$ in., 1924. Yale University Art Gallery; Stephen Carlton Clark Fund and Everett V. Meeks Fund.

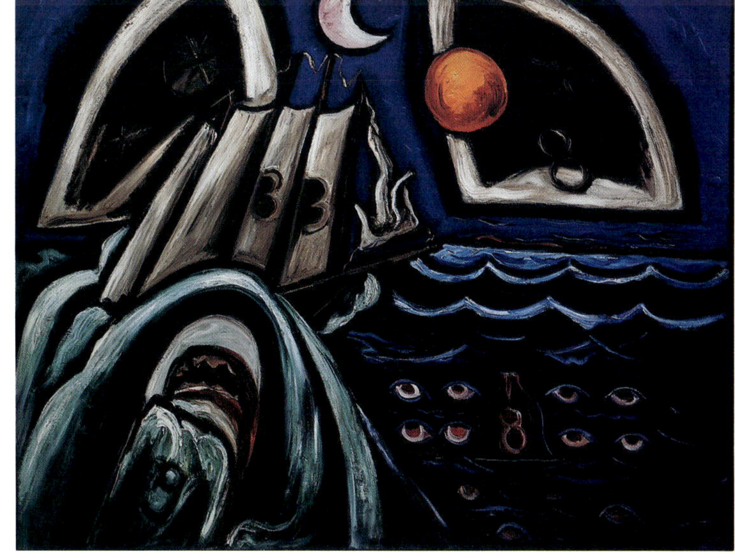

Plate 10. Marsden Hartley, *Eight Bells Folly, Memorial for Hart Crane,* oil on canvas, $30\frac{5}{8} \times 39\frac{3}{8}$ in., 1933. Frederick R. Weisman Museum of Art, University of Minnesota, Minneapolis; gift of Ione and Hudson Walker.

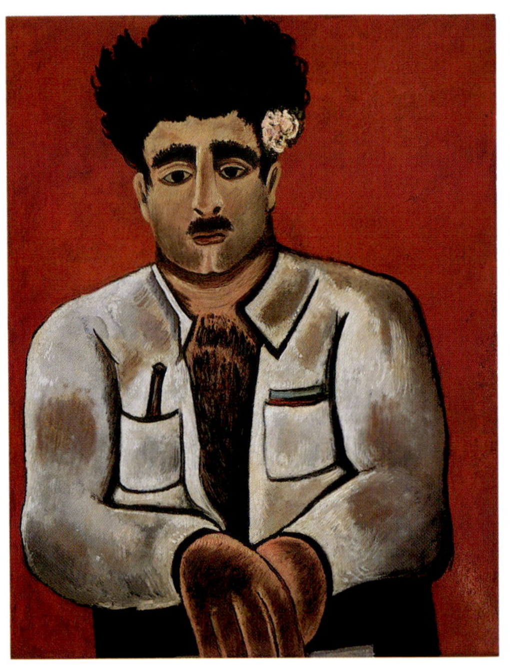

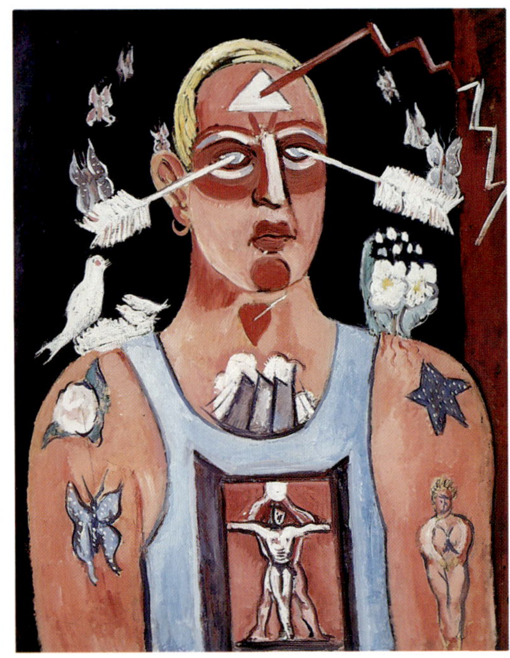

Plate 11. Marsden Hartley, *Adelard the Drowned, Master of the "Phantom,"* oil on academy board, 28 × 22 in., ca. 1938–39. Frederick R. Weisman Museum of Art, Minneapolis; bequest of Hudson Walker from the Ione and Hudson Walker Collection.

Plate 12. Marsden Hartley, *Sustained Comedy—Portrait of an Object,* oil on board, 28⅛ × 22 in., 1939. Carnegie Museum of Art, Pittsburgh, Pa.; gift of Mervin Jules in memory of Hudson Walker.

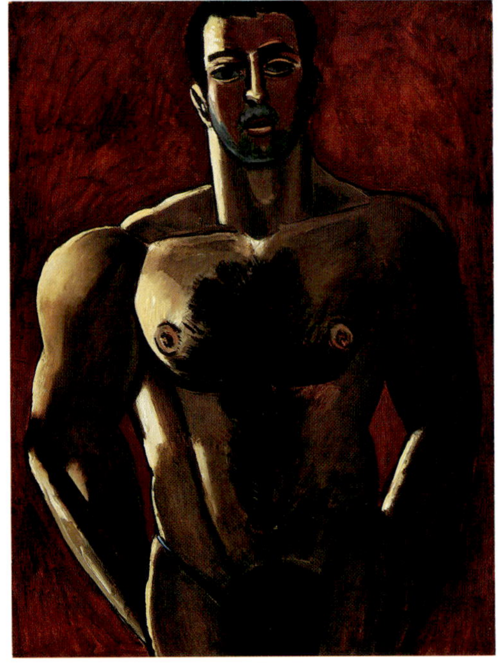

Plate 13. Marsden Hartley, *Madawaska—Acadian Light-Heavy (2nd Arrangement)*, oil on hardboard, 40 × 30 in., 1940. Art Institute of Chicago, Chicago; bequest of A. James Speyer.

7 German Warriors

Hartley's first trip to Europe in 1912 probably accelerated his shedding of the humanist philosophy of the Traubel circle, with its desexualization of Whitman's message of "adhesiveness." Stieglitz had made the trip possible by providing Hartley with money for an extended stay. Like Charles Demuth, whom he first met in Paris, Hartley found in Europe a culture that was more sympathetic to his art making and his way of living. Gertrude Stein's apartment at 27 rue de Fleurus was particularly stimulating. Her collection of paintings by Picasso, Cézanne, and Matisse made Hartley feel "sort of like a severed head living of itself by mystical excitation."[1] In addition to the cultural advantages of Paris, Hartley found a city where gay men and lesbians took risks by publicly displaying their difference, Gertrude Stein and Alice Toklas being perhaps the most notorious examples. And Hartley insisted that it was common in the Paris of the 1910s to see men dressed as women, and women dressed as men: "Life was like that then, and all seemed to be a part of the day's run, and brings up an amusing and funny Paris."[2] Yet for all the relative freedom of Parisian bohemia, Hartley never felt comfortable in Paris.

Unlike Demuth, who wanted to live permanently in France, Hartley was drawn to Germany. In 1914 he wrote Stieglitz (who was from a German-Jewish family and had been educated in Germany, though born in the United States) that "the conditions of Paris for living are about as bad as they could be." In thinking over his experiences, he observed, "It is with Germans I have always found myself both in New York and in Paris—and now it is in Germany that I find my creative conditions—and it is there that I must go."[3] Hartley first went to Germany around Christmas of 1912 for a three-week stay with Arnold Rönnebeck, whom he had met in Paris. He wrote of being "so overcome with the speed the brilliance and the spotlessness of the life and the city" of Berlin that he decided to move there later.[4] Hartley was especially flattered by the reception he received from German artists, whereas in Paris he had been just one of hundreds of expatriate painters and writers. Although he had been welcomed into Gertrude Stein's home, he was not fully accepted as an equal in the French art world. Hartley liked to make much of Stein's claim that his use of color was more advanced than Picasso's, but Stein was neither French nor a painter. The artists who were at the center of advanced painting in Paris—Picasso, Braque, Gris, Matisse—paid little attention to Hartley. In the same letter to Stieglitz in which he boasted about Stein's praise, he told about Picasso's reaction to his work: "*Picasso has seen the drawing there*—said to Gertrude that he could not understand it . . . pointed to it and said 'Where are the eyes and the nose' etc."[5] Hartley's reception in Germany, however, was very different. He quickly became friends with the Blau Reiter group assembled around Franz Marc, and he was introduced to Kandinsky, who praised his work. He wrote Stieglitz excitedly about how, in five days, he had found his "place in the art circles of Europe." One painter even told him that he "was famous in Munich."[6] Most important, he was asked to participate in future Blau Reiter exhibitions.

Besides the respect of the German expressionists, Hartley also found a family in Berlin. During his first few weeks and then on later visits to Germany, Hartley stayed with Arnold Rönnebeck's family. Rönnebeck remembered: "During the several years he lived in Berlin he insisted that it was his privilege to light my mother's cigarette after dinner just before the Sunday evening quartet started. In his last letter to me, shortly before his death, he speaks with deep emotion about the *home* he had found in Berlin, i.e. in the house of my parents."[7] And of course, Hartley fell in love with Rönnebeck's cousin, Karl von Freyburg.

Hartley was so happy with Germany that, during his second visit, he wrote Stieglitz that he thought he had found a permanent home. Even when war broke out in August 1914, he felt no compunction to leave. Only after the death of Freyburg and the growing breakdown of communications with the United States was Hartley forced to abandon Germany.

In Germany, Hartley found professional respect, friends, and perhaps even a lover, in addition to being drawn to the social life. Barbara Haskell has emphasized the relative freedom of Berlin's gay subculture as an explanation for Hartley's attraction to Germany.[8] Indeed, Berlin had an extensive underground network of private clubs, bathhouses, and brothels. James Steakley claims that the Berlin police were relatively tolerant of homosexuality and estimates that by 1914 there were approximately forty gay bars in the city.[9] Germany had the most advanced homosexual liberation movement in the world, led by the sexologist Magnus Hirschfeld. In 1898, Hirschfeld had worked to organize opposition to Paragraph 175, which outlawed "unnatural sexual acts," and was even able to enlist the support of the Social Democrats in his attempt to legalize homosexual relations. Yet though Hartley enjoyed Germany's gay institutions and probably knew of Hirschfeld's public crusade, it is doubtful that civil rights alone explains his extraordinary attraction to German culture. Paris, after all, offered similar opportunities to be common (as Hartley liked to put it). But Hartley claimed that "if you don't want the exotic kind of thing in Paris, there is nothing." I would argue that Germany's appeal for Hartley was not merely the size or the relative freedom of its gay subculture but the integration of homosexuality into the dominant German culture.

In general, art historians have treated Hartley's love for Germany delicately, particularly his fascination with its military. Several critics have discussed Hartley's use of military emblems in his war motif paintings, but they have had relatively little to say about why Hartley emphasizes the militarism of German culture. Specifically, there has been no discussion of the link between military and homosexual cultures in Germany during World War I. Hartley's memories of the period are characterized by a sexualization of military imagery. Remembering a military procession in honor of the marriage of the kaiser's daughter, he wrote: "It was of course the age of iron—of blood and iron. Every backbone in Germany was made of it—or had new iron poured into it—the whole scene was fairly bursting with organized energy and the tension was terrific and somehow most voluptuous in the feeling of power—a sexual immensity even in it, when passion rises to the full and something must happen to quiet it."[10] The prewar mood of Germany was contagious. In the *Autobiography of Alice B. Toklas,* for example, Stein claims that she had taken a great interest in Hartley's friend Rönnebeck when she first met him in 1912. But she and Toklas were

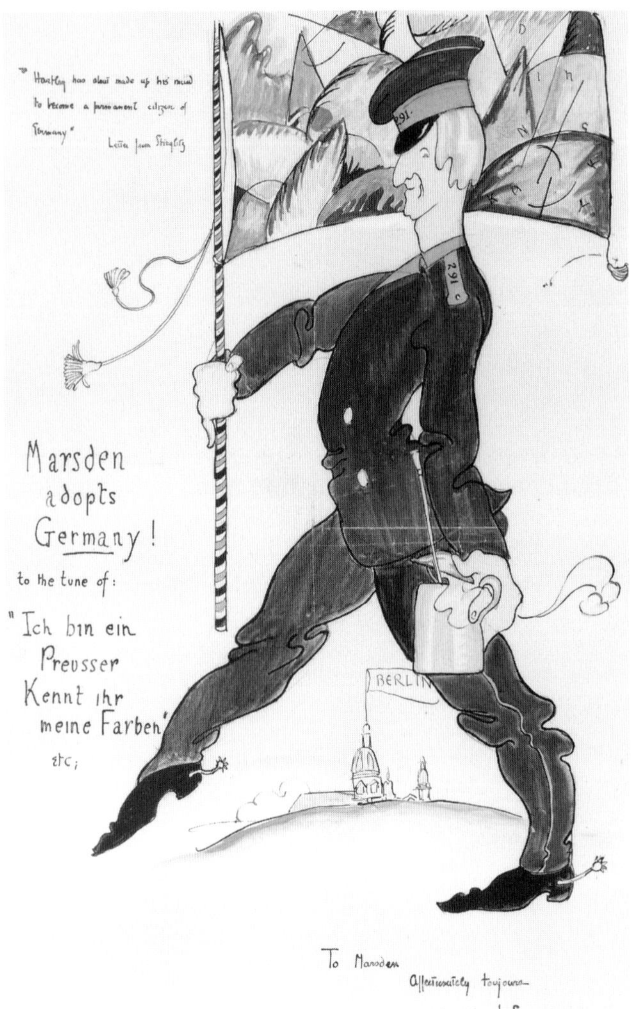

51. Lee Simonson, *Caricature of Marsden Hartley,* watercolor on paper, 17 × 11 in., 1913. Beinecke Library, Yale University.

dismayed when he visited them a year later and exhibited a newfound enthusiasm for everything military: "When we all came back that winter Rönnebeck was different. In the first place he came back with lots of photographs of ships of the German navy and insisted upon showing them to us. We were not interested. . . . He had photos of himself with all the counts and there was also one with the crown prince of Germany who was a great friend of the countess."[11] Lee Simonson seemed to notice a similar change in Hartley. He made a watercolor in which he parodied Hartley's enthusiasm for German culture (fig. 51).[12] In the caricature, Hartley proudly struts in the uniform of a Prussian soldier and carries an unfurled banner that displays an abstraction somewhat in the style of Kandinsky. On the flag can be made out the scattered letters of Kandinsky's name. Across the top corner is written, "Hartley has about made up his mind to become a permanent citizen of Germany." Although Simonson parodies what he considers to be the dangerous influence of Kandinsky on Hartley's art, the choice of German military regalia for Hartley is significant, suggesting that the German military exerted as powerful an influence on Hartley's art as did the expressionist movement.

One of the first paintings in which Hartley expressed his fascination with the regalia of war is *The Warriors* (fig. 52). The painting was probably also Hartley's first significant figurative effort. Hartley's oeuvre is unusual in that it contains few examples of early figure drawings and portraits. Presumably, the bulk of such immature work was destroyed. Up until 1914, Hartley's reputation had been based on landscape painting and still lifes. It is clearly significant that Hartley's first mature figurative painting was of soldiers. Perhaps the experience of military pageantry was so overwhelming that he had to use a new genre to express his attraction to it.

Yet *The Warriors* is a somewhat tentative attempt at figuration. Three horsemen are depicted in profile. They float on cloud forms that in turn hover over an orange half-circle. Behind the cavalry officers are pointed ovals, which look something like mountains. At their peak is a horseman, riding off with his back to us. These central forms are superimposed over a background made up of dozens of saluting cavalrymen. The repetition of horses' tails, unfurled banners, and plumes of the helmets creates a patterned effect—the flatness of the design resembles wallpaper. The horsemen look more like tin soldiers than full-blooded figures. The painting is quite flat and abstracted, a composite of still life, landscape, and figurative elements.

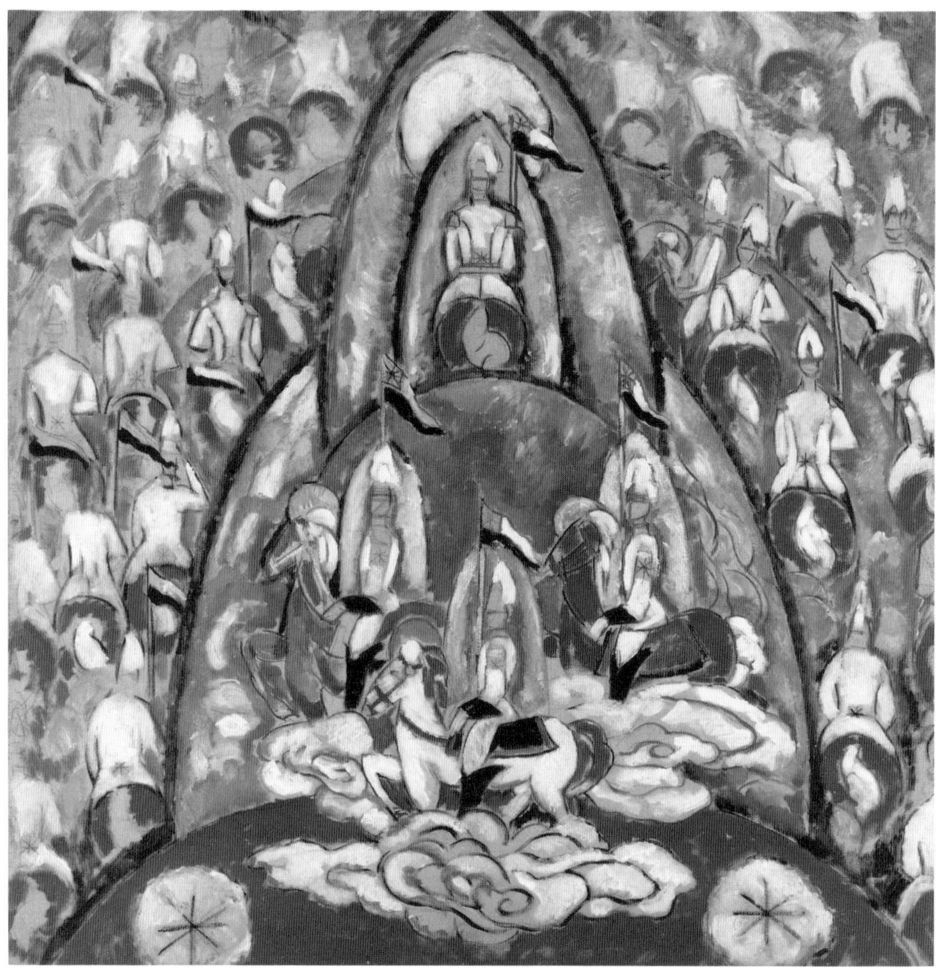

52. Marsden Hartley, *The Warriors,* oil on canvas, 47¾ × 47½ in., 1913. Regis Collection, Minneapolis.

In "Somehow a Past," Hartley described the event that inspired *The Warriors:*

> The Pariser Platz was packed, jammed to the stoops and windows with those huge cuirassiers of the Kaiser's special guard, all in white—white leather breeches skin tight, high plain enamel boots—those gleaming, blinding medieval breast plates of silver and brass—making the eye go black when the sun glanced like a spear as the bodies moved. There were the inspiring helmets with the imperial eagle, and the white manes hanging down. There was six foot of youth under all this garniture—everyone on a horse, and every horse white—that is how I got it, and it went into an abstract picture of soldiers riding into the sun—a fact to take place not so long after, for all of those went out into the sun and never came back.[13]

As if worried by the militarism and eroticism of this description, Hartley attributed his attraction to pageantry to his early love of the circus. Yet the painting is not simply an image of a state celebration. Hartley left out any traces of the civilians who must have watched along the parade route. Instead, he focused on soldiers with their skin-tight breeches. Rather than emphasizing the benign aspects of the day, the very title is a reminder that the pageant is a celebration of potential aggression.

There is an iconic quality to *The Warriors.* On either side of the clouds is an eight-pointed star—a mystical symbol for Hartley that he claimed to see everywhere in Berlin. Its symmetrical and hieratic structure almost give the picture the quality of an altarpiece for a militaristic cult. I previously mentioned Hartley's religious interest, which ranged from Christianity to Eastern mysticism. His admiration for Traubel was based on a desire to find some kind of spiritual grounding for his life, including his need to love men. In Germany he found a culture that was heavily male-oriented—it possessed what amounted to a cult of male beauty. Hartley wrote Rockwell Kent that it was masculinity that made the country so appealing to him: "Germany is essentially masculine with masculine ruggedness and vitality." Hartley claimed that in comparison to the Germans the French were "utterly feminine."[14] There was certainly militarism in the other Western nations; Hartley could have easily seen military marches in Paris or the United States. But to the degree that homosexuality was visible in Paris, it conformed to the decadent model—it was "other" from the virile display of masculinity. The cult of masculinity in Germany, however, incorporated—if only uneasily and for a short time—a homosexual component.

This is not to say that German society sanctioned homosexuality. As George Mosse suggests in *Nationalism and Sexuality,* Germany struggled more than any other European nation with the relationship of homosexuality to male bonding. The militarism of German society that so appealed to Hartley in 1913 was closely related to the German youth movement, begun in 1901. Mosse traces the danger that such a nationwide movement of exclusively male groupings presented to what he calls bourgeois respectability. Male bonding always risked turning into homosexuality. The adult leaders of the youth movement advocated a return to nature and to the genuine. They contrasted their ideal of masculinity—typically a youth clothed in a loin cloth—to the city-bound degenerate, "disfigured by disease, debauchery, a hypocritical way of life, and narrow professionalism."[15] The type of the *Wandervogel* youth was to fascinate Hartley for the rest of his life, reappearing in its most complete form in his love for the Mason sons. For Hartley, the German youth movement was another version of Whitman's love of simple working men or his contemplation of bathing youths. The values advocated by the movement—back to nature, the genuine, toughness, independence, physicality—were all qualities that Hartley strove for in his art and in the men to whom he was attracted.

There were several attempts to purge the youth clubs of homosexuality. Although the youth movement was supposed to encourage chastity, this was not always so in practice. Mosse discusses several scandals in which its leaders were denounced for homosexuality. He writes that one of the "frightening aspects" of the "rediscovery of the body of the youth movement" was that it "drew out implications which had been present all along . . . in the nudity of Greek statues, and in the virility of the national stereotype."[16] The Gemeinschaft der Eigenen (Community of the Special), a conservative club founded by Adolf Brand, Wilhelm Jansen, and Benedict Friedländer, actually advocated pederasty. From 1896 to 1931, the Community published a journal called *Der Eigene.* Although Brand, Jansen, and Friedländer shared Magnus Hirschfeld's call for sexual freedom, they were opposed to the liberal agenda of his Scientific-Humanitarian Committee. In particular, they objected to the medical model of homosexuality. Friedländer wrote: "Taken by itself, the very fact that the general public sees no one but doctors in the movement's leadership must further the erroneous notion that the movement is concerned with disease or at least some kind of sickness."[17] Rather than viewing homosexuality as an illness that required treatment, the Committee of the Special claimed that they themselves were an elite. Citing Greece as a model, the Committee encouraged relationships between boys and adult men: "The positive goal . . . is the revival of Hellenic chivalry . . . by chivalric love we mean in particular close friendship between youths and even more particularly the bonds between men of unequal ages."[18] The Greek model was used to back up the claim by Friedländer that homosexuals actually made better soldiers than heterosexuals.

A more crucial example for Hartley of the aesthetics of the youth movement was the circle around the poet Stefan George, probably the most famous German poet of that period. George had a group of young disciples whom Mosse claims were selected less for their talent than for their good looks. Although George's poetry is very different from Whitman's, the two writers shared a belief that the spiritual could be recognized in the beauty of the male body. According to Mosse, "Such beauty came alive for George in one young boy, Maximin, whom he presented to his followers almost as a living god; and after the boy's early death in 1905, the myth of Maximin became symbolic of heroic youth. . . . In his most famous cycle of poems, *Der Siebente Ring* (*The Seventh Ring*, 1907), he sounds a strongly eschatological note: salvation lies in that which is imminent, to be expounded by an élite under the leadership of the prophet." Mosse adds: "Many a volunteer carried it [*The Seventh Ring*] in the First World War as a font of hope and dedication."[19]

George's obsession with Maximin is similar to Hartley's placement of Karl von Freyburg at the center of his war motif series. Like George, Hartley idealized a young man for more than his intrinsic qualities: "You know what friendships are to me—how slowly I make them and whenever made how I almost worship them. I had every reason in this wide world to adore this fellow. . . . If there was ever a true representative of all that is lovely and splendid in the German soul and character it was this fellow at the age of 24 perfectly equipped for a life of joy and strength and beauty—most exceptionally handsome with that rarest accompaniment of soul and character which one finds so often lacking in great beauty."[20] Freyburg's spiritual qualities grew in Hartley's memories. Over twenty years after Freyburg's death, Hartley wrote in *Letters Never Sent* of a dream in which the officer is resurrected in a blaze of light:

> At my feet to the left of me, was a huge snake coiling and writhing and suddenly the lightning struck it, and I can still see its mouth springing open in agony, showing its flame illumined fangs, can still hear the sizzling of its flesh in the conflagration of its coils, even smell the odor of the burning flesh. . . .
>
> A singular white light arose out of the mangled heap of coils, up my entire right side—left facing myself as spectator—growing brighter and whiter to the point of striking incandescence, and then there appeared in the whiteness of the illumination a full length image of yourself [Freyburg] clad in full uniform but the uniform, purged of all military significance, was white.
>
> I looked at you as I turned my head toward this light, square in your incandescent face, and out of it you smiled and I in return smiled. It was the sublimation of our intended relation and was without blemish, and you were therefore in this dream, immortalized.[21]

The image of lovers united in a blaze of white appears in *Prayer I* of George's *Maximin:*

> I am yours, so take and keep me
> Fuse me with yourself and sweep me
> Through your white and inmost blaze![22]

And in *Incarnation* George writes how he becomes one with his young lover through a dream:

With your ichor I have stilled
My desire crouched to take,
With a breath that never slacks,
With your essence I am filled.

So that tears and ecstasy,
Clouded foam and light combine
To a fused and living sign:
Dream begot by you and me.[23]

Hartley wrote Stieglitz that he had met several members of George's circle and that they "had heard of the nature" of Hartley's work and "expressed great interest in seeing it."[24] And in an unpublished essay entitled "Notes on the Rilke-Jacobsen Relation," he wrote of the awe for George's work in Berlin just before World War I: "I soon began to hear the names of Rilke and of Stefan George . . . and there was a kind of religious glow over the place when their names were spoken." He adds: "The Siebente Ring (Seventh Ring) of Stefan George had about that time made its appearance—bound in papal purple with rich gold letters and looked decidedly liturgical. . . . No one knew just what either of these writers meant because it was cloaked in somber and untouchable occultism."[25] Later in the same essay he wrote that Rönnebeck often spoke of George, referring to him as "another 'heilige name.'"

The point is not that George directly influenced Hartley but rather that George's cult of male beauty was an extreme example of the German idealization of masculinity and youth. German culture increasingly invested male beauty with a quasi-religious status. More important, George and the Community of the Special represented a movement that questioned the view that homosexuality was restricted to the margins—to, as Mosse puts it, "a coterie of outsiders." War, which placed all-male groupings into life-and-death situations, only furthered this tendency.

The War Motif Series

Hartley's *Portrait of a German Officer* makes Freyburg a modern martyr. The symbolic structure of the painting has been decoded with the help of Arnold Rönnebeck. In a letter to Duncan Phillips, written just after Hartley's death, Rönnebeck claimed that he too was depicted in the portrait:

> There is a very personal and emotional connection between this picture and myself, because I am partly symbolized in it. I am one half of the Prussian officer. The other half is a cousin of mine. . . . Rather dominating is the Iron Cross. . . . He received the Iron Cross a day before his death. . . . In the lower left corner we distinguish the initials K.V.F. My cousin's name was Karl von Freyburg. The triangle symbolized the friendship and the understanding between 3 men. . . . During the winter of 1914/15 I was hospitalized, wounded and battered, in Berlin, but the Iron Cross had already been awarded to me. Hartley admired its beautiful shape, designed by the great German architect Schinkel in 1813 and asked me to leave it on his palette-table as something of a silent friend who had left us.[26]

Rönnebeck's insistence that the picture is really a double portrait is based largely on the assumption that the E of the epaulet stands for the patroness of his regiment, Queen Elisabeth of Greece. As I suggested earlier, I think it is more likely that the E is the first letter of Hartley's given name, Edmund, just as the letters K.V.F. are the initials of Freyburg. It seems to me that Hartley would have included Rönnebeck's initials if he had intended to make a painting that represented the triangle of their friendship. In his essay on Rilke, Hartley writes of doing "a full length portrait of an officer killed early in the war," which certainly must be *Portrait of a German Officer.*[27] In any case, Rönnebeck, though wounded, was not killed in World War I, and the black backdrop of the painting clearly makes the painting a memorial.

Missing in Rönnebeck's descriptions is how the black cross, flags, epaulets, numbers, and letters are loosely assembled along the vertical to suggest a body. This figural quality is more pronounced in *Painting No. 47, Berlin* (fig. 53). Again Hartley includes Freyburg's initials, but the tassels are at the top center, suggesting the decorations on a cavalryman's helmet, behind which are circles that create a halo effect. In a letter to Stieglitz written a month before Freyburg's death, Hartley actually calls the German soldiers modern martyrs:

> A real ecstasy for war is the only modern religious ecstasy—The only means of displaying the old time martyrdom—one

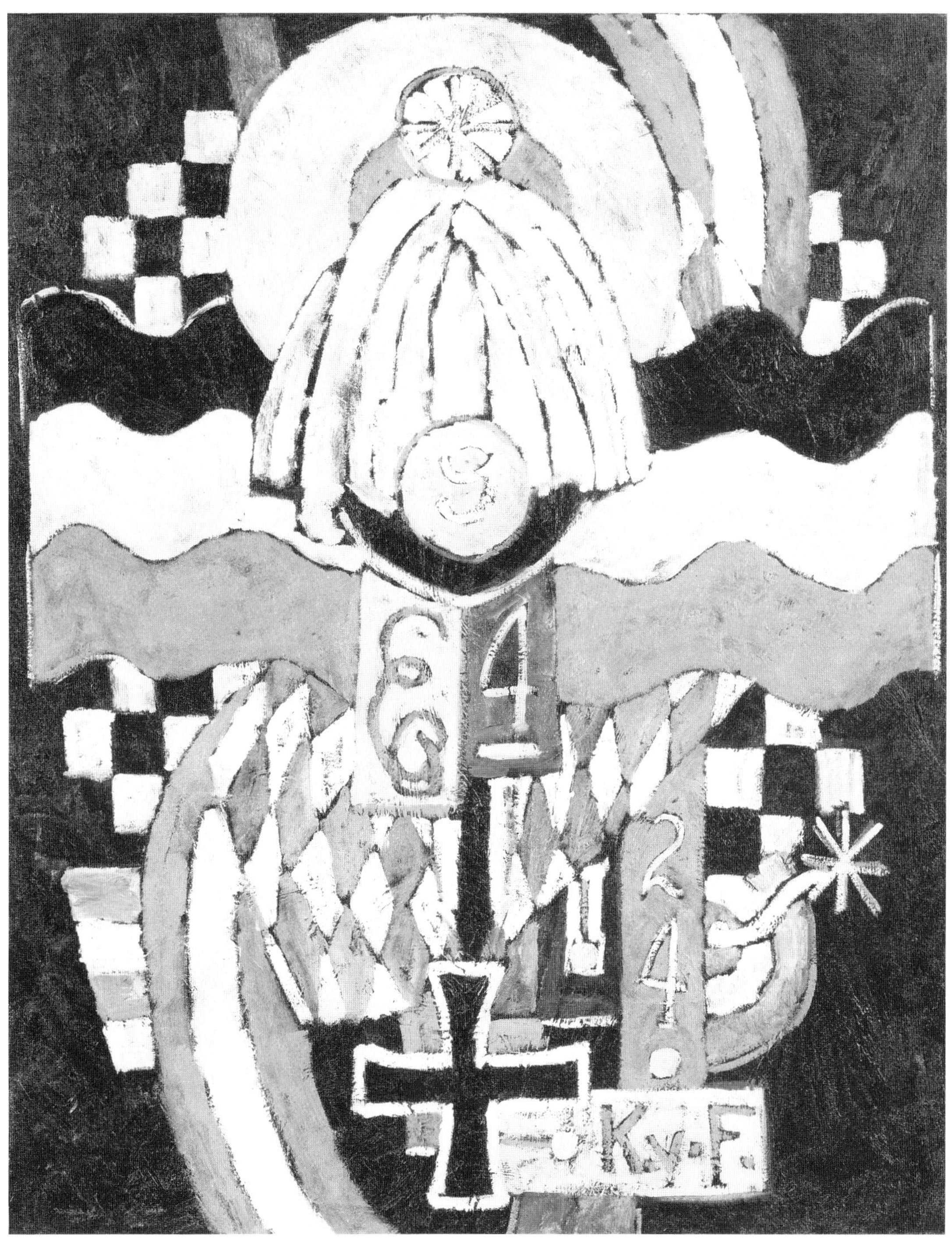

53. Marsden Hartley, *Painting No. 47, Berlin,* oil on canvas, 39½ × 31⅝ in., 1914–15. Hirshhorn Museum and Sculpture Garden, Smithsonian Institution, Washington, D.C.

> shall not forget their handsome smiling faces going by—waving hands throwing kisses and shouting auf Wiedersehen. Now already many are silent and will remain so forever—and many have arrived back broken wickedly—all this in our modern day! It is still not to conceive—But if there is a real heroism instinct—it is certainly prevalent here—and doubtless in other places too—though one must say the English are not showing themselves up to much as to bravery.[28]

The anti-English sentiment of this last line may come as a shock. As the war continued, Hartley often expressed his despair at the folly of war and at the egotism of nations. But for all his proclamations of neutrality, his comments about the English and French reveal that he was pro-German. In 1915, seemingly not realizing that he was contradicting his claim of neutrality, he wrote to Stieglitz: "I have achieved a nearness to the primal intention of things never before accomplished by me. The Germans have helped me to this—therefore I am loyal."[29]

I do not believe that Hartley was lying when he said he hated war. But by choosing to depict his subject through the paraphernalia of war—the bright colors of the German flag, the gold buttons and tassels of the officer's uniform, the powerful and simple forms of the iron crosses and eight-pointed stars—Hartley fails to suggest a sense of disillusionment with its deadly results. Hartley's *Portrait of a German Officer* does not represent the anonymous foot soldier dead in the trenches for no reason. Hartley's officer is a hero who is killed fighting for the fatherland, and Hartley's painting, for all its modernist form, is part of the tradition of military memorials.

Years later, Hartley seemed embarrassed by the militaristic quality of his attraction to Freyburg. In his account of the dream in which Freyburg appeared in a flash of light, he writes that Freyburg was in "full uniform" but that it was "purged of all military significance." (One wonders how one would know it was a full uniform if it was so purged.) In chapter 2, I discussed the importance of the soldier for the homosexual subcultures of Hartley's and Demuth's time. Earl Lind was no doubt voicing a common view when he claimed that the military man was the ultimate in masculinity. Perhaps it was not only physical beauty but the possibility of being accepted by their supposed opposite that made the man in uniform particularly appealing to certain homosexuals. In Freyburg's love, Hartley might find approval from the very type of man who was supposed to despise homosexuals most. The Germanic aspect of the war motif series actually reiterates this interpretation. Hartley's letters show his awareness that most Americans were unsympathetic to the German cause and that many thought war with Germany would be inevitable. Hartley's warriors and officers are therefore potential enemies of his own nation. His desire to become a German was another aspect of his need to be loved by men who were, as Hartley might put it, ultramasculine. Gaining the trust of those of another cultural background and experience was a way of ceasing to be "otherwise"—of overcoming difference. Hartley wrote, "It may be true, as an American friend once said long ago to me in the mountains—you are outwardly American and inwardly German."[30]

For all Hartley's bravado about eventually taking German culture by storm, he knew that his reputation and his income were dependent on how his art was received in New York. What was the reception of the war motif series when Hartley was forced to return home? Did anyone guess at the secret content of the paintings? Hartley first exhibited the series at Stieglitz's 291 Gallery in 1916, from April 4 to May 22. The first published American reaction to the paintings appeared in the *New York Times* from an anonymous reporter who had seen Hartley's exhibition in Berlin. The title of the review is "American Artist Astounds Germans: Marsden Hartley's Exhibition in Berlin Surprises, Pains, and Amuses." The tone of the article is satiric, as if the reviewer is a witness to some peculiar rites of a species of animal called artists. In the atmosphere of growing tension between the United States and Germany over supplying ammunition to the allies, the reporter seems somewhat surprised that an American would dare to exhibit in Germany. According to the reporter, Hartley is the "nerviest American . . . who with the eccentricity of genius thought that Berlin was a good place in which to give an exhibition of his master works, in optimistic defiance of the bad taste left behind by the submarine controversy and the very sore, ever present feeling about American ammunition." The writer suggests that *The Warriors,* painted in 1913, predicted the advent of World War I: "Mr. Hartley, with a prophetic intuition of coming events, had immortalized the Kaiser's own Cuirassier Guards going into war on canvas two months before war was declared. . . . You know they are going to war because the horses' noses are pointed to the west; only their tails are depicted, but these squarely face the American war correspondents." The *Times* follows with a detailed description of the war motif series itself and a discussion of Hartley's neutrality:

> In the second chamber you come to Mr. Hartley's real war pictures. . . . Here, for instance is a battle picture which may be more nearly the real thing than most correspondents know. A snarl of triangles, squares, rectangles, flags of all nations, in glaring solid, primitive colors, shuffled together, produces a picture puzzle that absolutely defies you to say that it isn't a battle. Most unneutrally, as some will think, the American artist has sprinkled the battle canvases with Iron Crosses, though German connoisseurs with whom I spoke stoutly protested that Mr. Hartley's paintings were pro-German. In fact, some of them apparently thought just the opposite. There was here and there just a suspicion that these critics thought German battles were being ridiculed.[31]

The article reports Hartley's unwillingness to explain the paintings and concludes with a brief synopsis of German reviews of the exhibition. Although the *Times* review has a humorous tone, it is generally supportive of Hartley's work. The reviewer seems to suspect Hartley's pro-German sympathies but is willing to entertain the possibility that Hartley is actually neutral or may even be satirizing the German war effort.

The *Times* quotes at length Hartley's insistence that the war motif series is essentially abstract: "Pictures that I exhibit are without titles and without description. They describe themselves." Hartley expands on this idea in the small catalogue for the 291 exhibition: "The Germanic group is but part of a series which I had contemplated of movements in various areas of war activity from which I was prevented, owing to the difficulties of travel. The forms are only those which I have observed casually from day to day. There is no symbolism whatsoever in them; there is no slight intention of that anywhere. . . . They are merely consultations of the eye—in no sense [*sic*] problem; my notion of the purely pictorial."[32] Given the very obvious symbolic elements in the paintings, Hartley's claim that his work contains no symbolism whatsoever has struck critics as strange. Gail Scott writes flatly that Hartley was trying to forestall an "interpretation of the works as pro-German or pro-war." Yet Hartley's own statement draws attention to the German military content. He calls the paintings a Germanic group and tells the viewer that the paintings arose out of a general plan to contemplate "various areas of war activity." It seems more likely that Hartley is deflecting attention from the personal symbolism of the paintings, their representation of homosexual love. Indeed, none of the reviewers missed the military content; what they lacked was the key to the code of the military paraphernalia. McBride, who was himself homosexual and privy to personal gossip about New York artists, is the only writer to hint at the possibility of a hidden content: "There are triangles which can be readily accepted as soldiers' tents, and there are swords and all the pomp and circumstance of war. So much even a Philadelphian could make out. But as to the exact episode or emotion that the artist portrays there will be less certainty."[33]

In a sense, Hartley's foreword to the exhibition catalogue is only one of many masks that hide the homosexual content of the war motif series. The very form of the paintings in the series is masklike. If Hartley's *Portrait of a German Officer* is a portrait at all, it is one in which the features of his subject are hidden.

At the beginning of the twentieth century, hiding was certainly one of the dominant strategies of existence for homosexuals in America. The various stigmas against sexual difference in American society, the fear of physical violence, blackmail, and ostracism, produced behavior that various homosexual men shared despite differences in class, character, and education—a mode Edward Stevenson calls the "Mask." Stevenson's Mask does not suggest any single way of acting—just the idea of hiding. The Mask itself might take on infinite forms; indeed, to be effective it could not be regularized, lest the wearer be easily found out. At the same time, if the homosexual male was to make contact with others like him, he had to find ways of letting the Mask down momentarily without putting himself in danger. Stevenson melodramatically describes the emotional toil of this way of life: "The Uranian must often 'go through' the most overwhelming, soul-prostrating of loves, finding his nerves and mind and body beaten down under the passion, his day and nights vivified or poisoned by it, all without his doing anything so persistently as to hide his sentiment forever from the object of it! Hide it he must. Accounted a diseased human thing, an outcast from men, a beast, if his secret be probed. . . . Ever the Mask, the shuddering concealment, the anguish of hidden passion that burns his life away!" Stevenson suggests that the ultimate effect of what we today would call living in the "closet" was to damage severely a potentially warm and generous personality: "What this 'masking' of his real self is to any Uranian temperament naturally expansive, emotional, unfriendly to checks, one can imagine. . . . It begets in the uranistic type that bitter humor, ironic wit, self-mockery, that are often so entertaining to those who do not know what is covered."[34]

Whether Hartley's personae fits Stevenson's description is not the issue, but certainly Hartley's ability in the war motif series to both hide and reveal a homosexual content to different audiences is analogous to the Mask Stevenson describes. Even the way Hartley overlaps flags, medals, epaulets, tassels, and helmet on a very narrow field, surrounded by black, suggests a mask. In *Painting No. 47,* the tassels actually seem to hide a face. Hartley once wrote Madelaine Rice that for costume parties he had devised a white mask of gold and blue spangles that gave him "the pleasure of a mask without the isolation of one."[35] That may be seen as the essential accomplishment of the war motif series: it finds a way of representing homosexuality without the danger of isolation that an overt display would certainly have caused.

A crucial element in the process of covering up is the abstract form of the paintings that combines overlapping geometric shapes reminiscent of cubist collage with the bold palette and paint handling of German expressionism. In 1913 Hartley experimented with styles closer to German abstraction, particularly those of Kandinsky and Marc. Yet the compositional structure of the war motif series is more dependent on Picasso. It may even be that *Portrait of a German Officer* is directly linked to Picasso's work of 1912. That year Hartley wrote Stieglitz that "Picasso's new things are not as interesting." But his description of Picasso's 1912 canvases anticipates the style of his own war motif canvases: "Just now he is doing things that have [recurring words?] and across these network designs—names of people and words like jolie or bien and numbers like 75."[36] He includes with the description a little thumbnail sketch of his memory of one of Picasso's paintings (fig. 54), probably *The Architect's Table* (fig. 55) in Gertrude Stein's collection.[37] Hartley's reinterpretation of Picasso is fascinating, because he exaggerates both the flatness of Picasso's cubist style and its reliance on words and numbers. Instead of utilizing the complex breaking up and reassembling of the visual world that was part of analytic cubism, Hartley seized immediately on the heraldic quality of Picasso's *Jolie* paintings. It has often been pointed out that Hartley's flattening of cubist forms in a fluid decorative surface is similar to Picasso's synthetic cubist style of 1914–15.[38] Yet Hartley probably did not know of Picasso's synthetic cubist paintings when he was in Berlin. Rather, in exaggerating one aspect of analytic cubist painting and collage, he seems to have paralleled Picasso's own progression.

In a sense, it was war and death that finally gave Hartley the opportunity to represent his love for Freyburg. The prewar Berlin paintings had celebrated military pageantry, and by extension masculine display, only in a very general way. Not until *Portrait of a German Officer* was Hartley's attraction located in affection for a particular man, though even then with the man's name carefully disguised. He could take this risk because death desexualized and normalized Hartley's relationship with the officer. At funerals it is proper for a man to talk of his love for another man—even to cry. Before August 1914, Hartley barely mentioned Freyburg in his letters to Stieglitz, but once Freyburg was dead, he repeatedly wrote of his adoration for the officer.

During World War I there was a profusion of poetry and prose by men mourning the death of young soldiers and celebrating the extraordinarily close relationships fostered by war. In *The Great War and Modern Memory,* Paul Fussell discusses the intersection of homosexuality, poetry, and World War I. He quotes W. H. Auden: "In times of war even the crudest kind of positive affection between persons seems extraordinarily beautiful, a noble symbol of the peace and forgiveness of which the whole world stands so desperately in need."[39] Fussell adds that "the gender of the beloved will not matter very much." War incites sexuality, he claims, and since women are not available, it promotes homosexuality. But he cautions: "Of the active, un-

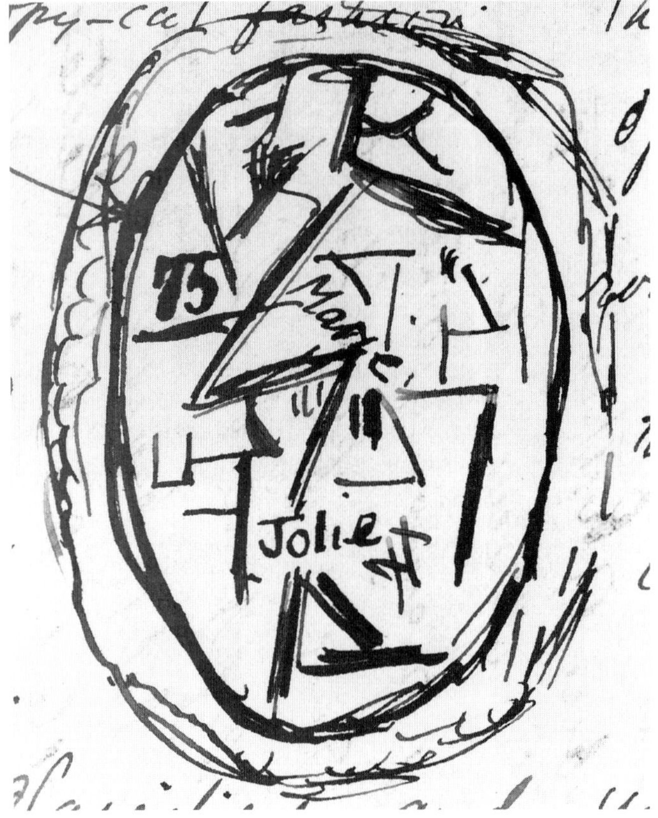

54. Marsden Hartley, sketch of Picasso's *The Architect's Table,* ink on paper in letter to Alfred Stieglitz, received 12 July 1912. Beinecke Library, Yale University.

sublimated kind there was very little at the front. What we find, rather, especially in the attitude of young officers to their men, is something more like the 'idealistic,' passionate but non-physical 'crushes' which most of the officers had experienced at public school." Fussell points to a "severe dichotomy": "On the one hand sanctioned public mass murder. On the other, unlawful secret individual love."[40] This dichotomy is built into Hartley's war motif series. What is more representative of "sanctioned public mass murder" than medals given for bravery or the shiny uniform of an officer? Yet these signs of "heroism" are merged with the initials of the forbidden lover who is himself killed by other acts of "heroism."

If death provided the occasion for Hartley to express his love for Freyburg, it also removed all the complications of a potential relationship. If *Portrait of a German Officer* is about homosexual desire, it is also about keeping desire at bay. I wrote in chapter 2 that the war motif series is notable for expressing the love of a man for another man without depicting a sexual act—or indeed a body at all. By focusing on the military aspects of Freyburg, emphasizing those qualities that were "masculine," Hartley also avoided the stereotype of homosexuality being less than manly. Just as Hartley avoids "femininity" in representing his lover, he also avoids what heterosexual relationships meant to him—commitment. Freyburg was no longer alive to force Hartley into a "fixed condition." The portrait is a visual equivalent of *Letters Never Sent,* the writing project about which Hartley began to think two years later.

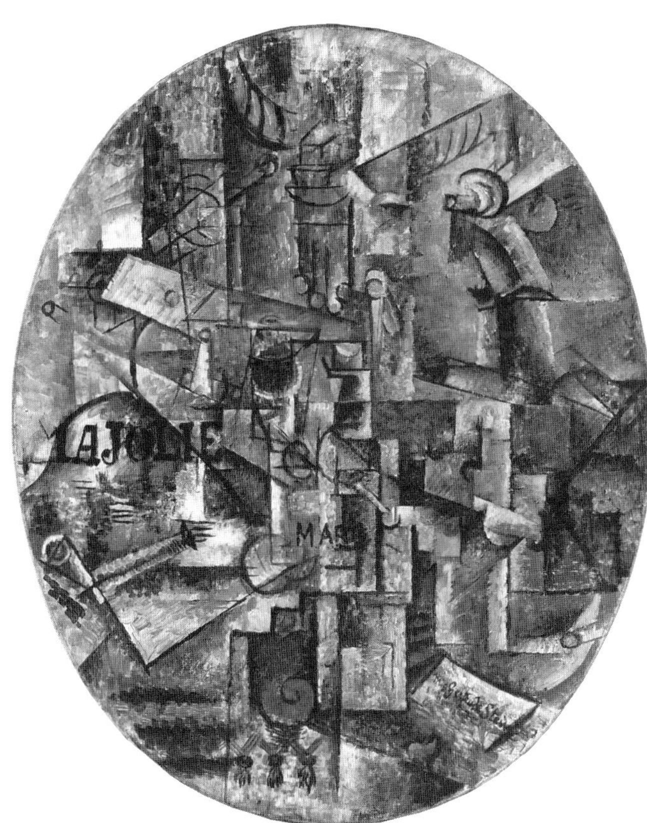

55. Pablo Picasso, *The Architect's Table,* oil on canvas mounted on (oval) panel, 28⅝ × 23½ in., 1912. Museum of Modern Art, New York; William S. Paley Collection.

The title perfectly suggests Hartley's attraction, his need to love (one of the letters is to Freyburg), but also an inability to make a connection (the letters are never sent). Hartley's method of abstraction in the war motif series parallels his habit of declaring love while at the same time distancing himself from the declaration. Whereas the earlier *Warriors* disperses tiny figures across the entire field, *Portrait of a German Officer* and *Painting No. 47* focus in on one man. Yet the subject is fragmented and flattened out. Instead of a three-dimensional body, we are given surface, the patterns of flags, and medals, as if the torso within has disappeared, leaving only the uniform. Hartley represents homosexual desire only to diffuse it through the multiple masks of literary obfuscation, abstract style, encoding, and death.

8 Hartley's Late Paintings

Prudently, Hartley retreated from German themes at about the time the United States entered World War I. Except for some pastels of muscular nudes from the early 1920s, homosexuality does not reemerge in his paintings until the 1930s. When it does, it is in the guise of another memorial "portrait": *Eight Bells Folly* (fig. 56, pl. 10), a homage to the poet Hart Crane. Crane committed suicide in the Gulf of Mexico in 1933; his death had an enormous effect on Hartley, but it is unclear how close the two poets were. Although they had met occasionally, it was only when they both received Guggenheim fellowships to work in Mexico that they saw each other regularly. Still, there is little indication in Hartley's letters that Crane meant much to him until after the poet's suicide. At that time Hartley felt compelled to find an adequate means to remember Crane. He not only painted *Eight Bells Folly* but drafted two versions of a memorial essay and a long poem.

If Hartley and Crane were ever close, it was during the few months before Crane threw himself off a boat in the Gulf of Mexico. Crane's poetry was more sophisticated and original than Hartley's—his work used the kind of complex literary allusions that Hartley avoided. Yet the two poets shared certain aesthetic interests. They were both fascinated by native American cultures. Robert Martin has written about the similarity between Hartley's and Crane's views of the native American cultures of the Southwest as being "a source of natural virtue and spiritual depth."[1] Both artists admired the work of Walt Whitman—indeed, Whitman's influence was essential for each man's poetry. Finally, both were ambivalent about

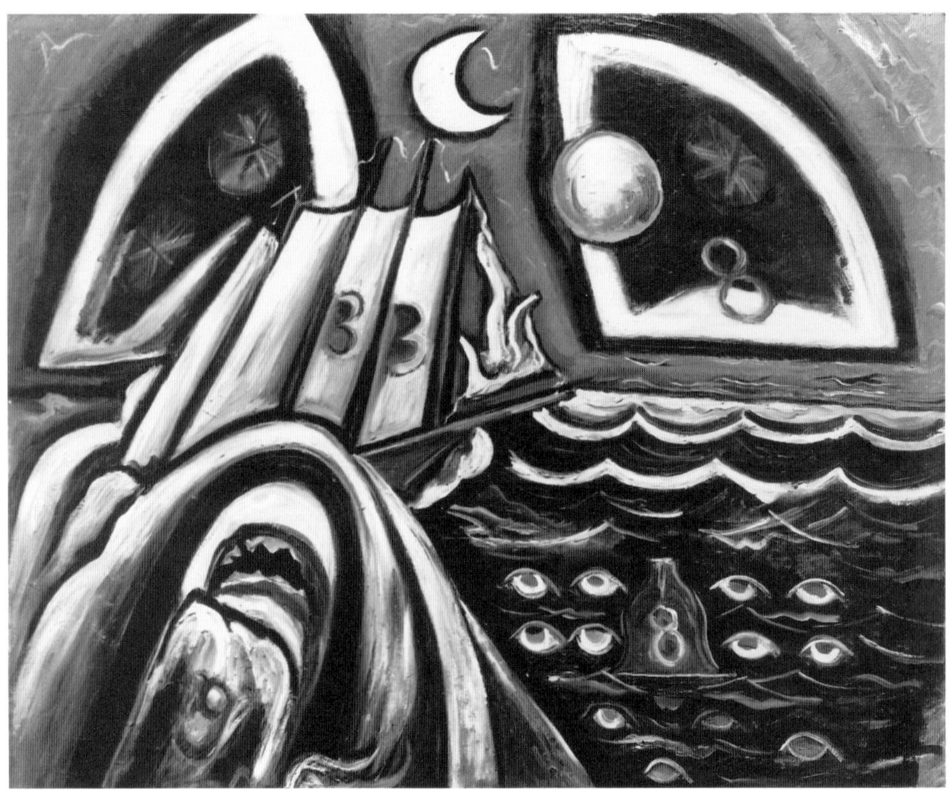

56. Marsden Hartley, *Eight Bells Folly, Memorial for Hart Crane,* oil on canvas, 30⅝ × 39⅜ in., 1933. Frederick R. Weisman Museum of Art, University of Minnesota, Minneapolis; gift of Ione and Hudson Walker.

their sexuality, though they expressed their ambivalence differently. As we have seen, Hartley hid his homosexuality from all but his closest friends, even writing disparagingly about homosexuals, as though he were not one of them. Whereas Hartley was relatively circumspect, Crane was often indiscreet. He once wrote his good friend Gorham Munson for counsel on how to deal with the question of his homosexuality: "I am all-too free with my tongue . . . and doubtless always shall be—but I'm going to ask you to advise [me] and work [to make] me better with a more discreet behavior."[2] Yet despite this request for help, Crane was never able to hide his sexual interests. To his friends' embarrassment, he often talked frankly about his experiences of trying to pick up sailors. One of Crane's letters describes, almost proudly, an incident in California in which he was beaten up. It began with a waterfront bar:

> Speakeasy joint with booths. Many bottles of dubious gin and whiskey . . . flashing a fat pay roll—and treating three or four still more dubious 'merry andrews' who had invited themselves to our noisy nook. It being midnight, all ordered out. . . .
>
> A street, or rather several streets. Our 'guests' very insistent on taking a hotel room in which to finish the fire water. ----- and I both reeling but refractory. I finally noticed ----- being spirited away by three of them, while it was evident that I, who had been more emphatic in my wishes, was being guarded by two others. I broke away—and had just caught up to ----- who was being put around a dark corner—when all five started slugging us.[3]

Given the makeup of the population along the waterfront—sailors, dockworkers, hustlers, some welcoming the advances of homosexuals, others impervious to their interest, still others selecting them as victims for theft—it was extraordinarily dangerous for Crane to be, as he writes, "more emphatic in my wishes."

Hartley suggested the difference between himself and Crane in one of his unpublished memoirs of the poet: "Hart belonged to the species opposite to me mentally speaking—there being two kinds of people—one for whom something must 'act' constantly . . . the other is the type that does nothing about anything much, and life simply presents itself."[4] In a letter to Adelaide Kuntz, Hartley was more direct about Crane's self-destructive character: "He couldn't help disturbing the peace of others, not maliciously ever—but he seemed to demand succor from those he admired and much endurance. Hart was never mean—but some people are born that way and seem to have to make friends pay for their love and affection—they don't mean it but life swamps in on them and they aren't ever master of it. . . . They want order and continuance but they seem impelled to destroy it in the wild disordered craving for the color of life—and color is no good unless it has a basis of form." Hartley told Kuntz that he had "learned the basic principle of Hart's life." The "skeleton in the closet" was Hart's relationship to his mother, who repeatedly threatened suicide, but it was Hart who "had said he would sooner or later do it—and it was done." Hartley attributed Crane's altercations with the police to an "inordinate lust for masochism—mainly to force dramatic excitement—or what he liked to call the quiver of life."[5]

Given their basic differences, why did Crane's death have such a strong effect on Hartley? Like Freyburg, Crane was another martyr ("poor dear loveable Hart"), but instead of being a soldier, he was an artist—the kind of artist Hartley was afraid of becoming. Crane had told Hartley that "he had nothing more to say." The specter of a burned-out homosexual artist must have disturbed Hartley, since he, too, had experienced his own doubts about subject matter and reputation. When Hartley went to Mexico, he was arguably at one of the low points of his career. The critical reception to his paintings of the past five years had been decidedly negative. His longtime dealer, Stieglitz, was exasperated with Hartley's 1927–28 series of Mt. St. Victoire, in which he painted the mountain Cézanne made famous. Stieglitz had little sympathy for Hartley's attempt to revitalize his art by immersing himself in Cézanne's motif and what Stieglitz deemed were European influences.[6] Hartley returned to the United States to find his relationship with Stieglitz degenerating. In 1931, in desperate need of new and stable subject matter, Hartley went to Gloucester, Massachusetts, where, at Dogtown Commons, he found the first examples of the rough New England landscapes that dominated his late style. Before leaving for Gloucester, he learned he had won a Guggenheim travel grant for the following year. Ironically, winning the Guggenheim interrupted Hartley's discovery of a native subject, because the fellowship required him to leave the United States. Like Hart Crane, Hartley chose Mexico, in part because it was as close to the United States as possible. Hartley ended up hating Mexico; he claimed that it "devitalized" his "energies" and that it was the one place that was "wrong" for him.[7]

When Hart Crane died, Hartley was frustrated with his own career. At the age of fifty-five, he was virtually broke and continued to suffer from bouts of loneliness and depression. Suicide was the one terrible solution to the money problems, loss of inspiration, and sexual unhappiness that the two artists shared. As I mentioned above, Hartley may have already considered taking his life in 1909–10 at the age of thirty-three, the age at which Crane committed suicide. Hartley's memorials were ways of coming to terms with Crane's suicide and his own self-destructive impulses. Because Hartley believed Crane's choice was ultimately the wrong one, his memorials heroize Crane at the same time as they undervalue him.

As Robert Burlingame points out, Hartley's memorial painting for Hart Crane is a return to the symbolic structure of the war motif series. As in *Portrait of a German Officer,* Hartley used numbers to represent the subject. Whereas he was unwilling to explain the symbolism of *Portrait of a German Officer,* he wrote Adelaide Kuntz a detailed interpretation of *Eight Bells Folly* even before it was complete: "It has a very mad look as I wish it to have—there is a ship foundering—a sun, a moon, two triangular clouds—a bell with "8" on it—symbolizing eight bells—or Noon when he jumped off—and around the bell are a lot of men's eyes—that look up from below to see who the new lodger is to be—on one cloud will be the number 33—Hart's age—and according to some occult beliefs is the dangerous age of a man—for if he survives 33—he lives on—Christ was supposed to be 33."[8] In the final painting he moved the number 33 from the clouds to the sails of the ship, but the work maintained its mad look. As with the various symbolic portraits of Freyburg, the subject is given a religious aura. The idea of Hart as a martyr is reinforced by the allusion to Christ. And the war motif series and *Eight Bells Folly* share the eight-pointed stars that Hartley had seen "everywhere—on the foreheads of hundreds of people. . . . The Kaiser wears it always—Frederick the Great did also—on the breast—the occult say it has a deep symbolism."[9]

In *Eight Bells Folly,* Hartley includes allusions to Crane's poetry, particularly his most important work, *The Bridge.* Supposedly, Crane discussed the form of the poem with Hartley when the two accidentally met in Marseilles in 1927.[10] The imagery of drowning figures prominently in *The Bridge,* but especially in the "Cutty Sark" section, the title of which refers to both the famous ship and the whisky, which perhaps hints at Crane's alcoholism. Hartley's boat is closer to a nineteenth-century clipper ship than to the modern one upon which Crane made his last voyage. The poem begins in a bar and, according to Crane, is meant to be a drunken reverie. Just as Hartley said his painting had a mad look, Crane called the form of his poem "erratic," for "it is meant to present the hallucinations incident to rum-drinking in a South Street dive, as well as the lurch of the boat in heavy seas etc."[11] Hartley's boat also seems to lurch as it plows through the waves. In the foreground of *Eight Bells Folly* is the mouth of an enormous shark, which presumably devoured Crane's body. At the same time, the shark suggests the man in the bar who introduces "Cutty Sark":

> I met a man in South Street, tall—
> a nervous shark tooth swung on his chain.[12]

The most striking elements of Hartley's painting are the eyes that stare up from the ocean, perhaps representing the submerged eyes that are a recurring motif in *The Bridge.* The water flows "Like one whose eyes were buried long ago" in "The River";[13] and the line "Sea eyes and tidal, undenying, bright with myth!" appears in "Cape Hatteras."[14] Hartley probably was drawn to "Cape Hatteras" because it is an ode to Walt Whitman.

Hartley echoed Crane's image of sea eyes in his poem "Un Recuerdo—Hermano—Hart Crane R.I.P.":

> And What is the iron purpose of it all,
> to be pall-bearer and parson at one's own funeral?
> And none but sea-eyes peering ghoulishly in
> through the slapping, trapping wave-din
> windowed to excess, and no wall to stop
> and give a neighbor-lover hope.[15]

The sea eyes of Crane's poem recall the "pearls that were his eyes" of Shakespeare's *The Tempest,* the hope being that the blindness of drowning can be converted into poetic vision.[16] But Hartley's ghoulish sea-eyes are a repudiation of this hope and an implicit criticism of Crane.

The Bridge is a notoriously difficult poem, and it is unlikely that Hartley fully appreciated it. Hartley's prose assessment of Crane was typical of Crane's readers in the 1930s. Hartley wrote that Allen Tate's criticism had done "as full justice as anyone" to Crane's work.[17] Tate encouraged Crane's talent, but he felt that Crane had still to find his subject matter.[18] But when Hartley wrote, "For the kind of true poet Hart was—he needed the gift of restraint," he echoes Yvor Winters. In the patronizing essay "The Progress of Hart Crane," Winters grudgingly recognized Crane's talent but claimed that his flaws were so great they "were almost of the nature of a public catastrophe." Ironically, Winters's essay ended by referring to the "wreckage" of Crane's struggle with Whitman's influence.[19]

Many of the criticisms leveled against Crane in the 1930s might be seen as more appropriate to Hartley's writings and paintings. Hartley's poetry and prose are characterized by a lack of restraint, formlessness and overindulgence; he was not given to careful editing. His painting of the 1920s seemed to suffer from the lack of "a suitable theme," as Tate said of Crane's work. Perhaps this weakness in his own work made it even more crucial for Hartley to protect himself from what he deemed Crane's failed practice. Hartley included his favorite eight-pointed stars in *Eight Bells Folly* perhaps as a symbol of an afterlife. But the stars share the sky with the sun and moon; *Eight Bells Folly* is meant as a doomed, apocalyptic vision. Hartley wrote: "The story is told now and the sea has silenced all of it far too early—for Hart had not done his work." He concluded with characteristically clumsy harshness: "Hart extinguished his own light forfeiting his right to its fine burning."[20] For all Hartley's sympathy and admiration, the message of his various memorials to Crane—both painted and written—is that Crane's poetic vision is finally *not* redemptive.

Eight Bells Folly is best seen, I think, as yet another painting in which Hartley puts the love object at a distance. As he put it in his poem to Crane, there is "no wall to stop and give a neighbor-lover hope." But remarkably, in using the memorial form to define Crane's self-destructiveness, Hartley found himself. *Eight Bells Folly* marks a shift in Hartley's art. The subject of the painting—the death of a young

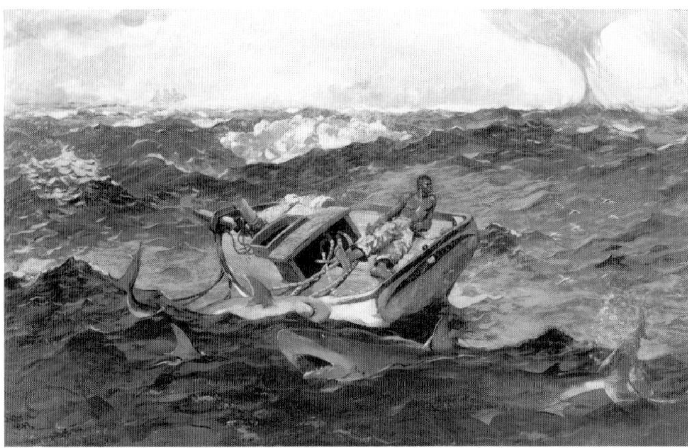

57. Winslow Homer, *Gulf Stream,* oil on canvas, $28\frac{1}{8} \times 49\frac{1}{8}$ in., 1899. Metropolitan Museum of Art, New York; Wolfe Fund, 1906; Catherine Lorillard Wolfe Collection.

man in the Gulf of Mexico, drowned or eaten by the menacing shark in the foreground—links the painting to Winslow Homer's *Gulf Stream* (fig. 57). Probably unconsciously, Hartley connected Crane's death with an image that directly centers on a beautiful male body—but a male body that is about to be destroyed. It is crucial, too, that Homer's hero is an African-American—another outsider in American society who, unlike the homosexual, could not disguise his difference, or "pass."

Hartley's allusion to Homer was significant for more than the iconography of *Eight Bells Folly.* Not too long after this time, in the mid-1930s, Hartley made the conscious decision to declare himself the painter of Maine, his home state, and thus tried to supplant Winslow Homer's traditional position. Homer, who lived his last days in Maine, was the perfect model for Hartley in his old age. He had never married and had lived in relative seclusion on the edge of the sea, as Hartley was to do for much of the rest of his life. More important, Homer's stance as an outsider—his estrangement from society—had been taken as a sign of both his supposed masculinity and his Americanness.

Hartley's published discussions of Homer reveal a certain ambivalence about Homer's work. Unlike Albert Ryder, whose art of New England Hartley unreservedly embraced, Homer's painting was not in favor with the New York avant-garde.

In *Adventures in the Arts,* Hartley signals his awareness that Homer was not sufficiently modernist by writing that "narrative . . . was first and last with Homer, and the only creative aspect of his pictures is concealed in the technique." He follows with the modernist's most damning insult, that "he was an illustrator." But as the essay continues, Hartley seems to warm to Homer's work: "Homer typifies a certain sturdiness in the American temper at least, and sends the lighter men away with his roughness, as doubtless he sent the curious away from his cliffs with the acidity of truth he poured upon them. . . . He was filled with Yankee tenacity and Yankee courage." He concludes that Homer "was intense, vigorous, and masculine" and admits that although Homer's "mind was too local," the specificity of his art becomes its strength. Homer comes to stand for an aspect of the "American temper." Like the theme of the margin of his other heroes—Whitman, Thoreau, and Ryder—Homer's theme, that of the lonely coast, is taken to be peculiarly American.[21]

A Nova Scotian Family

In spite of Hartley's attempted usurpation of Homer's popular title as painter of Maine, it was not Maine so much as Nova Scotia that provided Hartley with the last great themes of his career and the works in which homosexuality is most overtly represented. "The most elevating experience" of Hartley's life proved to be the two summers he spent with the Mason family south of Halifax, Nova Scotia, during which time he developed a familial friendship that ended abruptly when their two sons, Alty and Donny, were drowned.[22] Some three years after their deaths, Hartley completed a series of paintings and a long prose poem, *Cleophas and His Own,* based on his experience there. In the poem and in the titles of his paintings he gave the members of the Mason family fictional, almost mythical names. Francis, the father, is named Cleophas; Martha, the mother, is Marie Sainte Esprit; the two sons, Alty and Donny, are called Adelard and Etienne; and the daughters, Alice and Ruby, are Felice and Marthe. Yet in spite of the fictional names, the poem is faithful to the details of the drowning given in Hartley's letters.

In *Cleophas and His Own* and in various letters, Hartley claims that his discovery of the fishing community outside of Lunenburg, Nova Scotia, was almost accidental. But I do not think it a matter of chance that the community in which Hartley came to feel at home was made up of German Canadians. Almost from the moment he arrived in Nova Scotia, he met with Germanic types. He was surprised to find that the people of Lunenburg had the "most German names ever imaginable—Zwick, Zwicker, Knickle, Knaulbach, Eisner, etc., and none of em speak German or know a word of it & yet so many of them have thick, low German accents—not a word of German do they understand."[23] Hartley was saved from the provincial vulgarity of the town by the suggestion of a taxi driver—"a man of strong build, pink complexion and smiling face, very Germanic in appearance"—who introduced him to the nearby village of Blue Rock.[24] Initially he stayed there with Libby and Leander Knickle, but he soon met the Mason family and asked if he could pay for room and board in their home on East Point Island.

East Point is a small community south of Halifax. Hartley wrote Kuntz that there was no plumbing and that "it is a salt of the earth country & so good to get down to earth and its true values again—very primitive of course."[25] But even in the remoteness of East Point, Hartley had not left Germany. He made a journal entry: "I have but barely settled down on these Nova Scotia shores for the summer, the 'Hindenburg' had flown over the [horizon] at seven this morning. I have not yet got out of the whirl of the city into the marches of the lonesome sea."[26] Above all, he was delighted to learn that the Masons were half German and wrote his old friend Rönnebeck about his first summer with them: "The special family I lived with are half German and half French—though they spoke neither French nor German but have all the qualities of both—two sons—Giants—a sister—father and mother—all saints—and simply heavenly."[27]

I have discussed in detail Hartley's pro-German stance during World War I and its ramifications for his art. But what was Hartley's attitude toward Nazi Germany?[28] Hartley's adoration for Germany continued in the early 1930s. He made his last trip to Germany in 1933 and found it much changed from his visit during the Weimar period. He no longer had friends in Hamburg and spent much of his time like a hermit.[29] Although he repeatedly wrote Adelaide Kuntz that he did not follow politics, he could not help commenting on the new Germany: "I can't talk of political realities—I know little or nothing of them—only that Hitlerism does nothing to the surface of life as far as I can make out. I hear the good things he has done and they are good—outside of the Jewish question which is of course tragic."[30] Once again he comments on the cleanliness of Germans: "I don't know how they do it. Of course all Germans are an excessively clean people and they shine their very hide so it glistens. Such an edifying contrast to the filthy Mexicans."

He clearly admires Hitler:

> They all believe in Hitler for natural reasons—he is their only savior. He saved them from internal revolution less than six months ago whatever his faults are, and heroes always are full of faults. So they can only believe in him. The outcome seems promising then for everyone but Jews and it must be sad for them for to be a member of the new party is to be anti-semitic instantly. As far as I know or have heard they are not abusing them in any other way. They have their shops open of course and do what business they can. They are out of all the banks I hear. Well it's a problem they must settle for themselves and its pretty dreadful.[31]

His ambivalence about Hitler was expressed in another letter to Kuntz, in which he wrote of vacillating about going to a rally in Munich. As it turned out, he arrived late and missed Hitler: "So I didn't see Hitler and wish I had done, for he won't be coming down this way again for a long time." Later he heard Hitler's speech on the radio: "He has an incredible fine voice and fine style, with all the rapture and ecstasy in it of an imbued person, mounting at times to nothing less of course than religious fervor. There is at least no bluff about him no matter what his faults are, he puts on no cheap rhetoric whatever, for he is of course a plain person himself, and having but one object in heart and mind, the restoration of the people to their rightful place, he cannot help but inspire every individual to thinking he is important and inevitably necessary in the new scheme which of course he is."[32] He wrote later that he was trying to arrange a meeting with Hitler because he thought it "would even have value in New York among Germans I would meet. . . . The man is really quite remarkable."[33]

It is doubtful whether Hartley completely understood Hitler's platform. He seems somewhat disturbed by the persecution of the Jews, perhaps seeing it as the bad side of a good thing. For Hartley, the chief appeal of Hitler was the prospect that he might restore Germany to its earlier imperial vigor and pageantry. And, for a brief while, Hartley seemed to see in the new Germany some of the spirit of his beloved prewar Berlin: "It takes one's breath really to see the young here all marching and marching of course as usual. One gets the feeling Germany is always marching—but O such health and vigour and physical rightness they possess." But he adds chillingly, "They are soon to sterilize 400,000 persons here early in the year—to kill out defectives—imagine—but it is really an all right idea abstractly. There is no use having defectives to support. I saw a woman yesterday pushing a man of forty on a sled by the house—great hulk of a body and an idiots face—sad really—and she of most obvious excellent family. No one should be born who can't meet life somehow decently."[34] It is ironic and sad to read of Hartley acquiescing to a policy that would sterilize deviants—a policy so similar to the castration of homosexuals during the late nineteenth century. But Hartley's admiration for Hitler is only an extreme version of his need to gain acceptance from the "enemy."[35] His eroticization of Germans and Germany even allowed him to believe in the rightness of eliminating those who did not fit an ideal of physical and mental perfection. Yet Hartley himself—aging, effeminate, the protégé of a Jewish art dealer—would hardly have passed muster in the new Germany he wished to admire.

Hartley left Germany in 1934 without meeting Hitler. He was unable to return because of the war, and in a few years he took back his kind words about Hitler. His later discussions of his favorite foreign country were sprinkled with the appropriate horror of the Nazis and a lament for the destruction of Germany. But I think the search for what Germany represented to him—masculinity, youth, and cleanliness, intertwined with an element of erotic exhibitionism—continued in his adoration for the Mason family.

Of the five members of the family—a seventy-year-old fisherman, his wife, their daughter, and two sons—Hartley was drawn most to the males. Gail Scott, Gerald Ferguson, and Ronald Paulson discuss Hartley's relationship to the Masons in great detail in *Marsden Hartley and Nova Scotia,* the catalogue for his 1987 exhibition. Although the authors do not ignore the issue of homosexuality, the general tendency is to minimize its role in Hartley's attraction to the Masons and in the art he made about the family. The catalogue contains Hartley's letters to Adelaide Kuntz, for example, but not his more explicit letters to Arnold Rönnebeck. The introduction by Gerald Ferguson, curator of the show, emphasizes Hartley's relationship to Francis Mason more than his feelings for Mason's two sons. And that friendship with Francis Mason is described in exclusively spiritual terms, as if he were no more than a father figure for Hartley, despite only a ten-year difference in age. Hartley's description of Francis Mason in the guise of Cleophas in *Cleophas and His Own* is similar to Horace Traubel's description of Walt Whitman's last years. Both Whitman and Mason seem to have been wise men full of sensuous vitality even in old age. Francis Mason may have been like a father to Hartley, but he also was a man of great sexual attraction. Hartley had a tendency to eroticize all his relationships with men. Hartley describes Francis/Cleophas as he was in the period before the death of his sons:

> His body is as hard as the rocks and his hands being huge look as if they could take trees in twos and twist them together like rope.
>
> I look at him as we walk among the pyrites glistening in the iron bound shale on one shore of the island, that which he digs out with his fingers, dislocates them with the press of his strong digits, see him break out of what seems to be like stolen sleep of thought into articulation and a boy's smile, feeling the translucence of his spirit covering me, I feeling myself growing bigger. I can't help this, neither of us can, we are two human beings together who have learned much in the university of the imagination, he from the sea—I from the little things on the edge of the sea, intricately enfolding, binding us together and I know it is a case of true unspoken love.[36]

As in Whitman's *Leaves of Grass,* the spiritual and the sexual are fused. Phallic imagery—"his strong digits," "I feeling myself growing bigger"—suggests sexual excitement *and* inspiration. An even more erotic passage follows. Cleophas picks a rose and then begins to eat its petals:

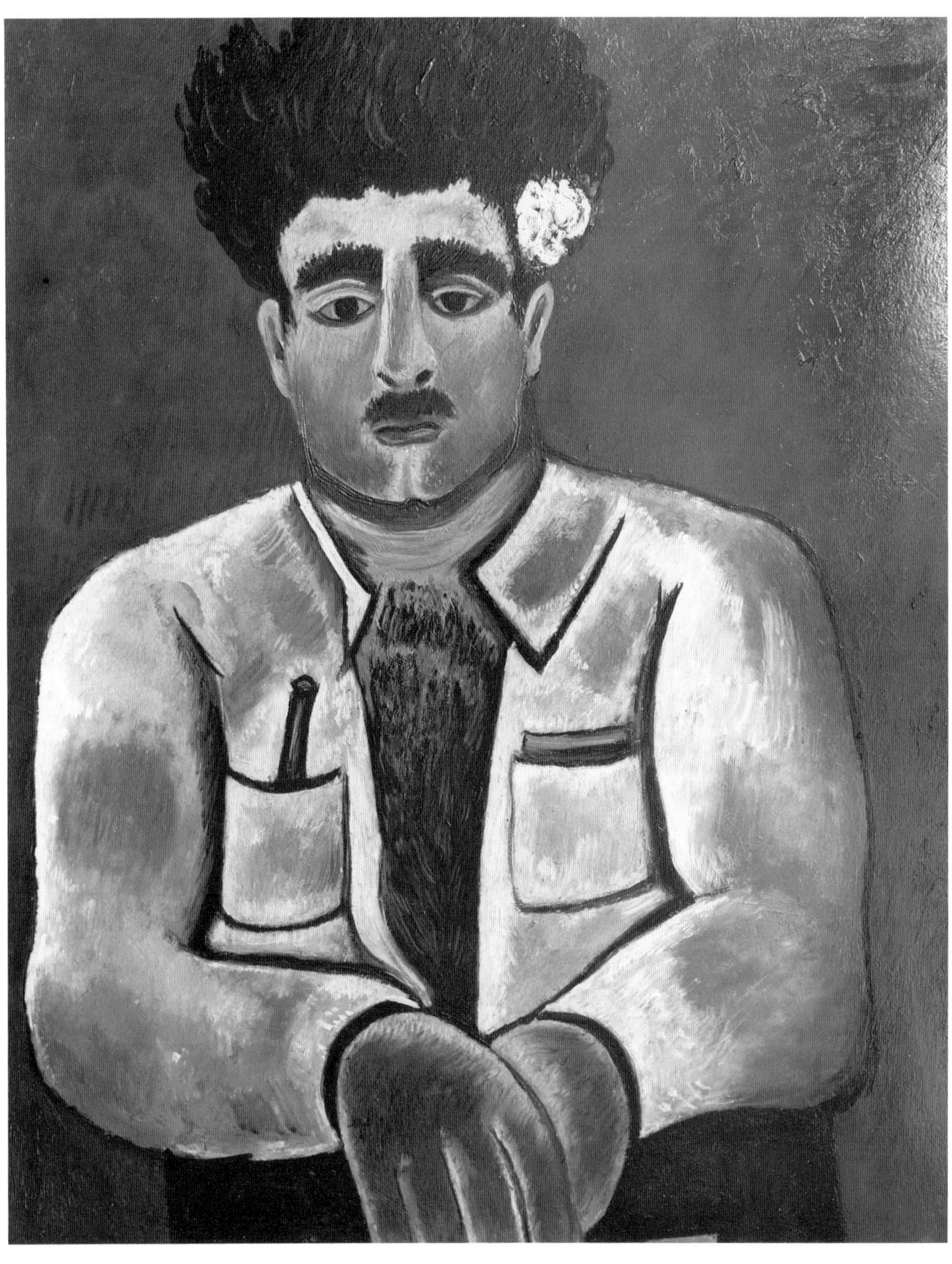

> . . . it was as if a little red flame, the first flick of the fine large morning was burning in the middle of his seventy year old face. He grew radiant with what was best that had remained with him all his life—"handsome, isn't it," he said.
> I saw the petals of the new-born rose disappear between his teeth, and he seemed suddenly to glow within—then he twisted the calyx and the left leaves together casting them among the cucumber vines over the little hill in the garden, over beyond the light.[37]

Again Hartley merges the sexual with the spiritual. The taking of the rose petals into his mouth fills Cleophas with a kind of divine light. A catalogue entry in *Marsden Hartley and Nova Scotia* claims that the rose is the "symbol so intimately associated with the Masons."[38] But I think the rose is also symbolic of Hartley—his last painting, left unfinished at his death, was of a bouquet of roses.[39] And in Hartley's painting *Adelard the Drowned* (fig. 58, pl. 11), Alty wears a white rose in his hair, as if the flower were from a lover.

The narrative form of Hartley's prose poem allows him to describe the Mason parents both before and after the death of their sons. In *Cleophas, Master of the Gilda Gray* (fig. 59) Hartley fuses both times in a single portrait of Francis, whose boat was the *Gilda Gray*. Cleophas's strength and desirability are suggested by making Francis seem young. One would never guess from Hartley's painting that Francis was seventy years old—he could easily be the same age as Alty. Yet, where Hartley's portrait of Alty, *Adelard the Drowned,* emphasizes the sensuousness of the son by showing his open shirt and hairy chest, the body of the father is stiff and compacted. Cleophas's shirt is buttoned up, his arms are crossed in front of him, and his eyes stare fixedly ahead.

58. Marsden Hartley, *Adelard the Drowned, Master of the "Phantom,"* oil on academy board, 28 × 22 in., ca. 1938–39. Frederick R. Weisman Museum of Art, University of Minnesota, Minneapolis; bequest of Hudson Walker from the Ione and Hudson Walker Collection.

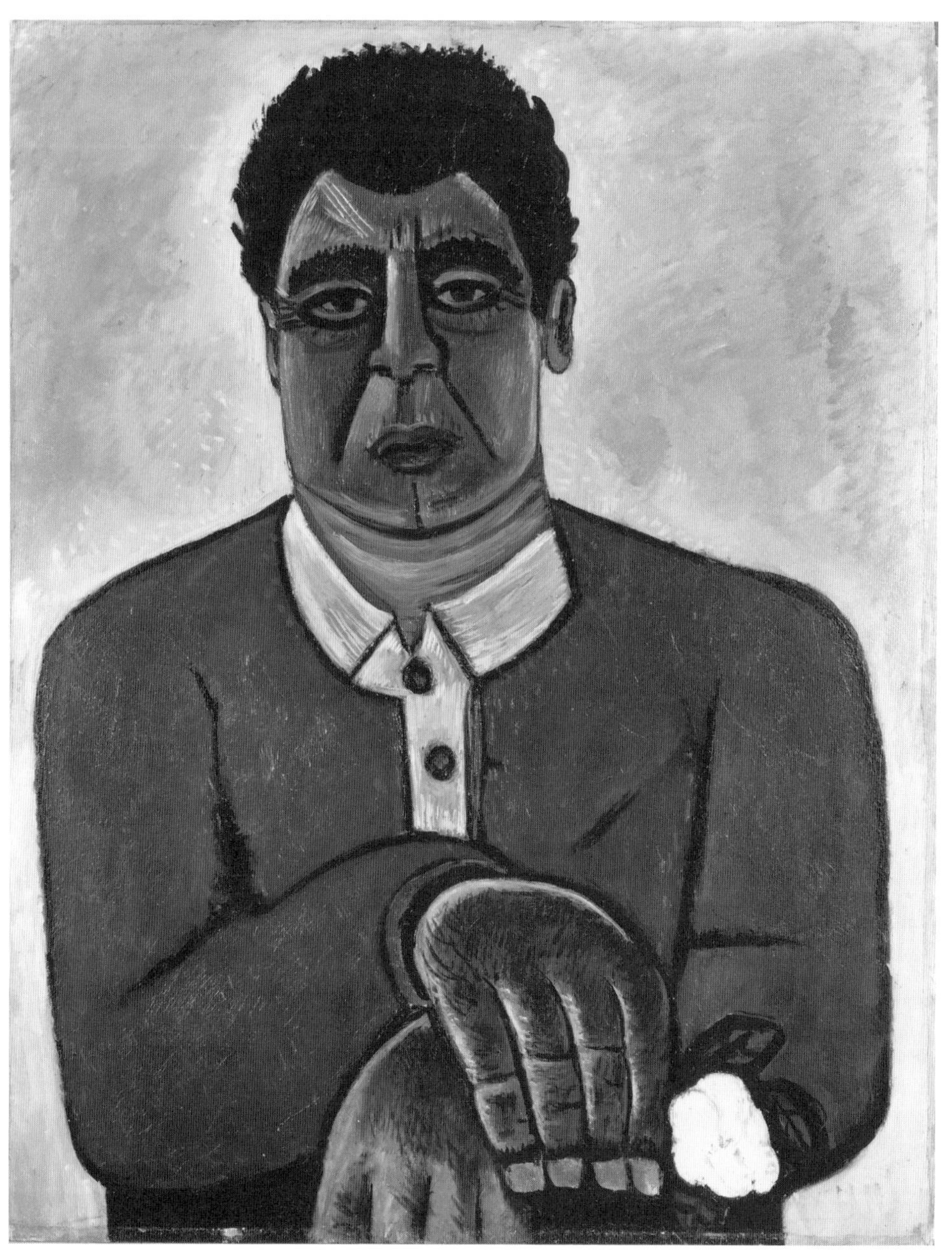

59. Marsden Hartley, *Cleophas, Master of the Gilda Gray,* oil on board, 28 × 22 in., 1938–39. Walker Art Center, Minneapolis; gift of Bertha H. Walker, 1971.

It is significant that the flower in Alty/Adelard's hair has been transferred to Cleophas's hand. Hartley writes that when Cleophas first picked the rose, he thought "he was going to put the rose in his cap, as his giant sons would have done, but he put the petals in his mouth and ate them." Alty and Donny are impetuous and vain—they display and waste their energy while their father stores it up. But for all the wisdom and grandeur of the father, Hartley is most drawn to the two sons. In late 1935, he wrote to Adelaide Kuntz of the Mason sons: "Well I love both Alty & Donny, & If I were a woman I'd have a time choosing—for Alty is wild and all flair, all demonstrative. Donny is shy as a thrush and never ventures out of the deep forests of his being until he is sure he is safe—but being a man I have them both in the ways men have of being for each other, & its all lovely, & I assure you, if I did murals, I'd do one of the family at supper or Noon meal." Here Hartley indulges for a moment in the fantasy of being a woman, as he did at the ball in Berlin, but concludes that male comradeship is better than male-female relationships. He has them in the "ways men have of being for each other."[40] His letters to Adelaide suggest a platonic relationship with the boys, but to his old friend Rönnebeck he hinted at a sexual component: "The boys build their own boats and just finished a speed boat before I left and I was first passenger—they get wildly drunk every now and then—& my god—well you know—simply wild."[41] It is hard to know just how to take this "well you know." Hartley's vagueness hides as it boasts, leaving the nature of his relationship to Alty and Donny to his friend's imagination.[42] Yet I think that Hartley wanted to believe that Alty/Adelard was consciously homosexual. In *Cleophas and His Own* he describes Adelard as having "no common codes, no inhibitions":

> . . . he will give as much love to a man as to a woman. He was totally loved by all of them up and down the coast, and because he was thrown over by the first woman, I think he has transferred his affections to his men friends, for he loves them and will do anything for them, and with this comes no mercy, love for him being the outpouring of his devastating energy . . .

Adelard's attraction to men does not make him soft. But underneath the masculinity is a young girl's heart:

> Wrists thick as the butt end of an ox-yoke and for whatever it takes two to tear or lift, he says "nonsense—give it to me" and if it is a rock out comes half of the world with it, the entrails of the earth lie bare, and beneath all his strength lies a heart as tender and as beautiful as that of a young girl.[43]

This merging of genders is suggested in Hartley's portrait of Alty. Like a woman's, Alty's hair is unusually long, but this connotation is countered by his facial hair—he has a mustache—and his hairy chest. The rose in Alty's hair is meant, presumably, to suggest that Alty's heart is like that of a young girl. But the "femininity" of the rose is paired with the "masculinity" of the pipe that pokes phallically out of Adelard's shirt pocket.

As I have argued, Hartley's *Christ Held by Half-Naked Men,* in which the discovery of Alty's dead body is converted into an all-male pietà, continues this swapping and confusion of gender roles. "I don't want to tell what I have to tell," he wrote Adelaide Kuntz, "but a terrible tragedy has fallen on our home here, & the two big lovely boys of the family & their pretty young cousin were drowned Saturday night in the teeth of the gale that swept up from Florida all along the Atlantic seaboard."[44] *Christ Held by Half-Naked Men* is Hartley's rendition of what he had been told about finding the bodies of the men—Hartley himself could not bear to look at the dead: "Dear Donny came to the surface finally last Tuesday morning, and if I had gone in the boat that was on its way to town I would have been subjected to the awful experience of seeing him, since being described to me abjectly—disfigured, as was poor little Allen (the cousin) also—less in Alty's case they said."[45] In *Marsden Hartley and Nova Scotia* the authors claim that this painting "is a metaphor of the unwavering faith of men like Francis Mason, who sustain and support a vulnerable Christ, and for Hartley, give viability to Christianity in the modern world."[46] Ferguson and company are certainly right to take seriously Hartley's lifelong search for a religious belief that would sustain his life and his art. In his last years he seemed to have settled on Christianity. Whatever the exact nature of his religious faith, he used Christian iconography to express his personal sorrow in terms that were basic to Western culture. Where I differ with the catalogue is the way religion seems to be introduced, as an explanatory category, *in order to desexualize* his paintings. In the case of the crucial *Christ Held by Half-Naked Men,* the catalogue has nothing to say—and in a sense can have nothing to say—about the partial nudity of the figures or their emphatic, idealized bodies.

In the exaggerated musculature of the lobstermen's chests in *Christ Held by Half-Naked Men,* Hartley endows the figures with the sensuousness of *Madawaska—Acadian Light-Heavy* (fig. 60, pl. 13), which also dates from around 1940. This painting depicts a torso of a standing man wearing nothing but a scant jock strap. Light falls on his body from the left, accentuating his enormous frame. Hartley's model was an amateur prizefighter originally from Madawaska, a town on the Canadian border founded by Acadians in the nineteenth century. Like Alty, he is supermasculine: "god so powerful" but "sweet." Hartley claimed that the Madawaskan asked him to "drive up to his home in Maine." Hartley wrote a friend that if he went "you can imagine the possible rest." It is probable that this prizefighter was the model for several of Hartley's figure paintings from this period, including the *Christ Held by Half-Naked Men.* The lobstermen in *Christ Held by Half-Naked Men,* all bare to the waist and big-framed, standing with their arms to their sides, staring directly at the viewer, mimic the pose of the Madawaskan. Hartley also executed several drawings of this model that were sketched either directly from life or from memory.

In its depiction of bare-chested men who stand behind their dead companion, *Christ Held by Half-Naked Men* combines mourning with desire. As in the earlier Berlin paintings, death allows Hartley to own up to his attraction for men even as it results in that attraction being largely unfulfilled. But the process of distancing is not as complete as it was in the Berlin paintings. Christ lies in the arms of another of Hartley's Canadian giants. The eroticism of the painting is held in check, however, by the strangeness of Christ's body. Christ's head is much too small—almost as if the head were attached, as an afterthought, to the body of Alty. The eroticism of the scene is more pronounced in the drawings for the painting. In the sketch *Badly Bruised—Who Is He?* (fig. 61), the dead figure does not have a beard. The only signs that the figure is Christ are the marks of the stigmata and the crown on the ground.

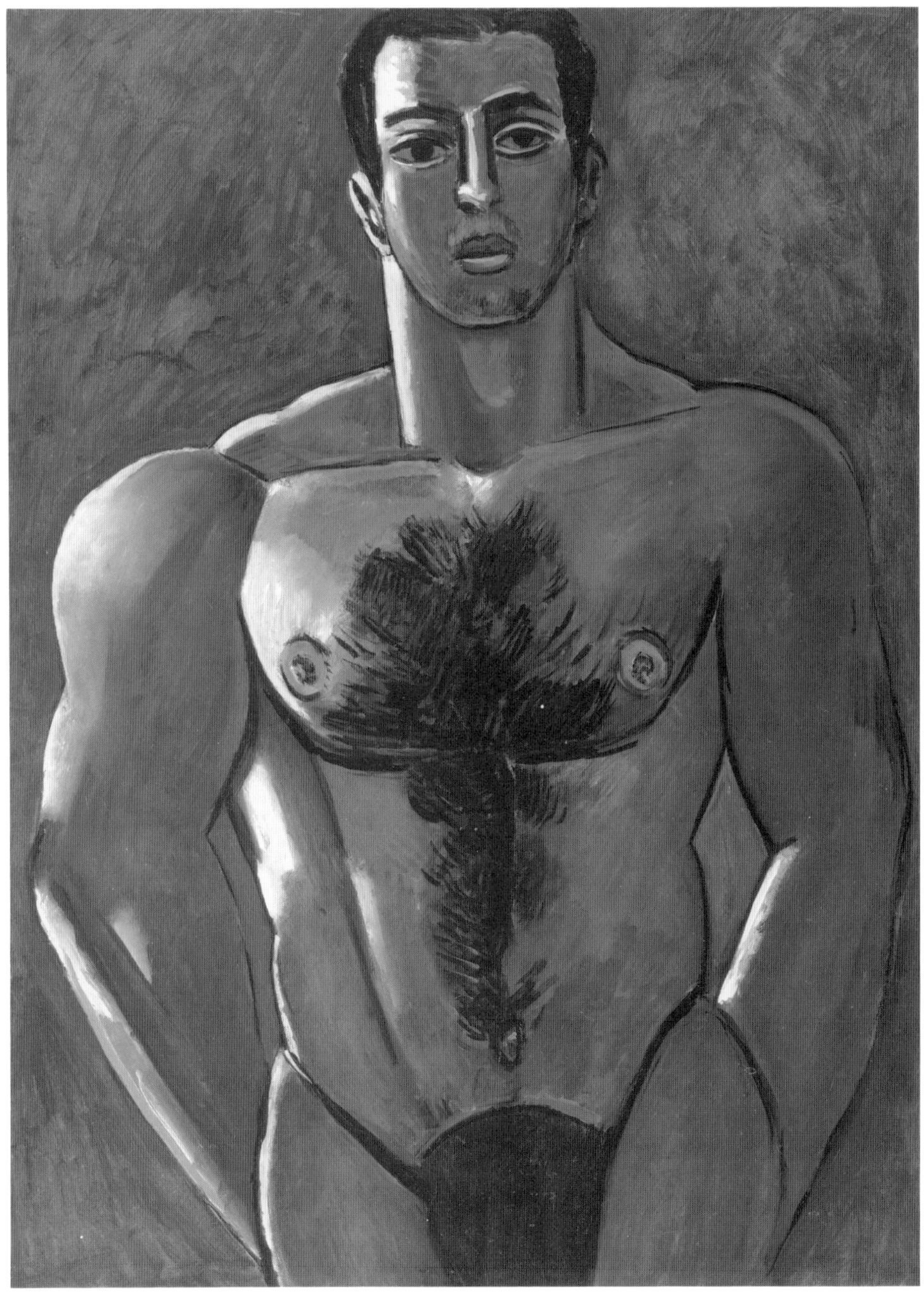

60. Marsden Hartley, *Madawaska—Acadian Light-Heavy (2nd Arrangement),* oil on hardboard, 40 × 30 in., 1940. Art Institute of Chicago, Chicago; bequest of A. James Speyer.

61. Marsden Hartley, *Badly Bruised—Who Is He?* pen and ink on paper, $10\frac{5}{8} \times 8\frac{1}{4}$ in., ca. 1940. Bates College Museum of Art, Lewiston, Maine; Marsden Hartley Memorial Collection.

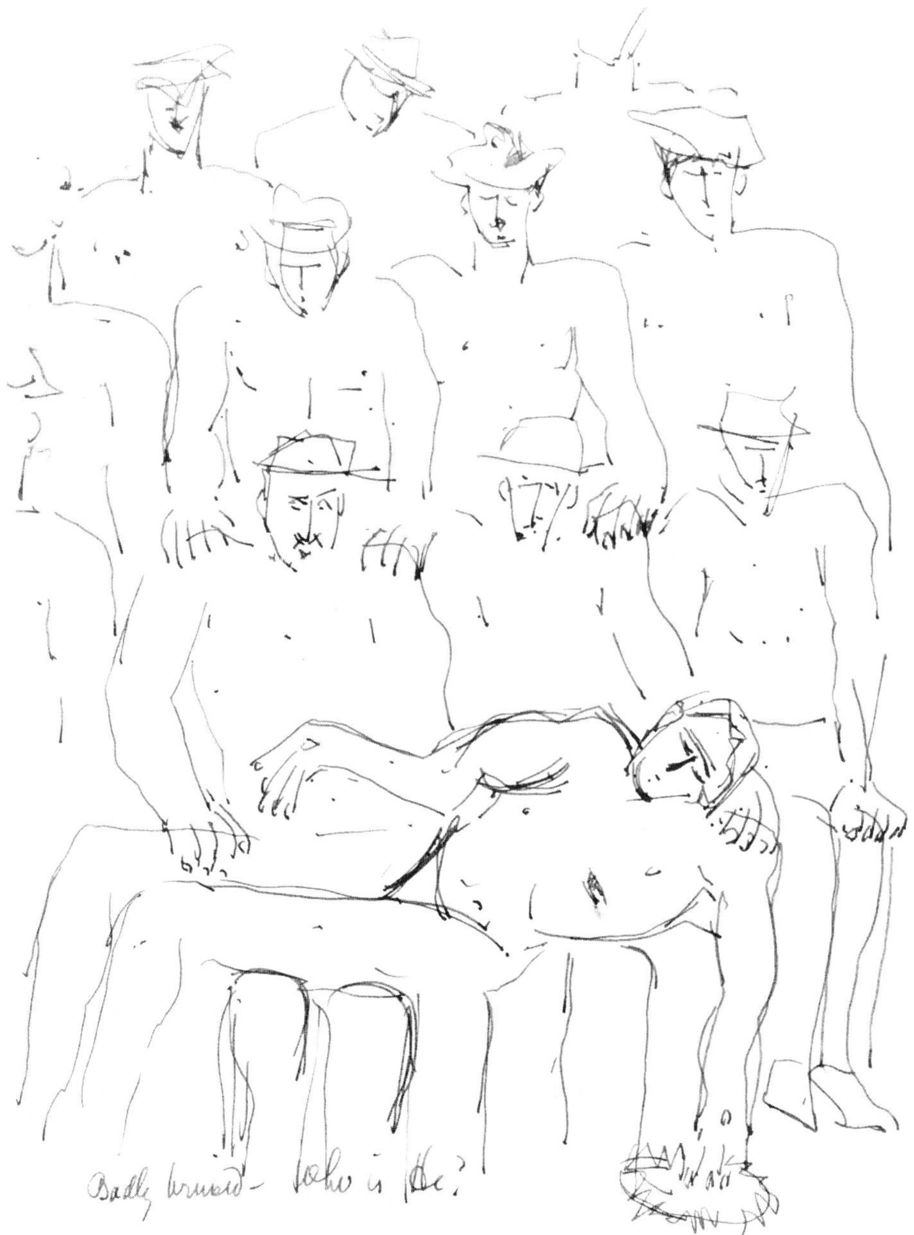

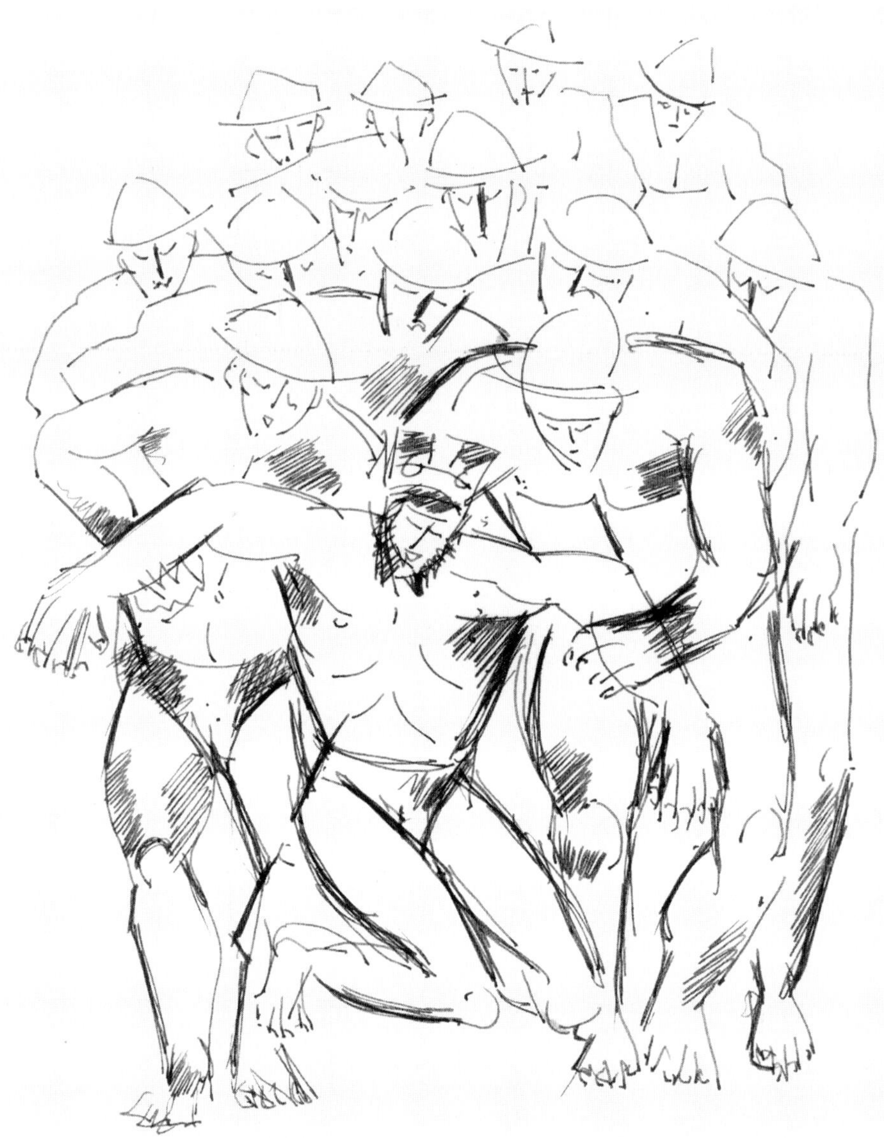

62. Marsden Hartley, *Untitled: Subject: Thirteen Lobstermen and Christ Figure—Deposition Concept,* pen and ink on paper, 10 × 8⅛ in., ca. 1940. Bates College Museum of Art, Lewiston, Maine; Marsden Hartley Memorial Collection.

The men are placed much closer together. One of the men puts his arm over the shoulder of his companion, even as they both put a hand on the shoulders of two men in the first row. In another of the studies for the painting, *Untitled: Subject: Thirteen Lobstermen and Christ Figure—Deposition Concept* (fig. 62), the figures are almost completely naked. Instead of the somber and motionless poses of the painting, the men are animated as if taking part in some weird dance. They close in on the muscular Christ as if to lift him.

It is not unusual, of course, for the Christ in a pietà to function at some level as an object of desire. As I wrote in chapter 2, what makes *Christ Held by Half-Naked Men* homosexual is not so much the sensuousness of its individual figures as its rigorous exclusion of women. The half-naked lobstermen take the holy women's place as Christ's chief mourners. A similar gender reversal occurred in Hartley's life as he took for himself the traditional role of mourning usually given to women of the fishing villages he lived in. In paintings like *Inside the Bar,* Winslow Homer had focused on the women who wait in the storm for their men to return—or not to return—from sea. Hartley does not repeat Homer's motif directly, but several of his seascapes of the Maine coast are clearly related to Homer's paintings of the ocean. Compare, for example, *Evening Storm, Schoodic, Maine* (fig. 63) with Homer's *Northeaster* (fig. 64). We might say that finally Hartley internalizes Homer's image of women, even as he takes up Homer's characteristic position at the edge of the ocean.

If Hartley was a mourner, he also identified with victims. Freyburg, Crane, and Alty were all martyrs—and Hartley thought of himself as a martyr as well. *Sustained Comedy—Portrait of an Object* (fig. 65, pl. 12) is a strange painting that seems to express Hartley's feelings of martyrdom directly. According to Mervin Jules, who purchased the work from Hartley's dealer, Hudson Walker, the painting was meant to be a self-portrait.[47] Clearly the likeness is not to be taken literally. What we are shown ostensibly is a young sailor wearing a gold earring and covered with tattoos of a rose, butterfly, stars, and a sinking ship. He wears a tank top with the curious image of a man holding a globe over the head of the crucified Christ. There is a mask over the eyes of the portrait—not unlike the kind that Hartley described wearing during the Berlin costume ball—but the openings for the eyes are punctured with arrows.

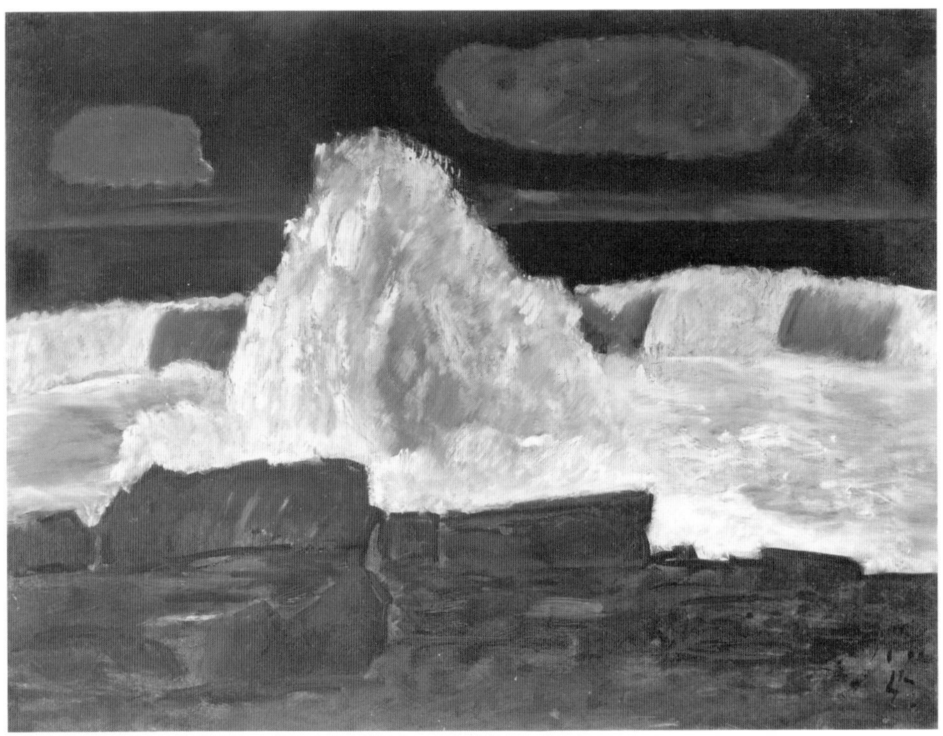

63. Marsden Hartley, *Evening Storm, Schoodic, Maine,* oil on composition board, 30 × 40 in., 1942. Museum of Modern Art, New York; acquired through the Lillie P. Bliss Bequest, 1943.

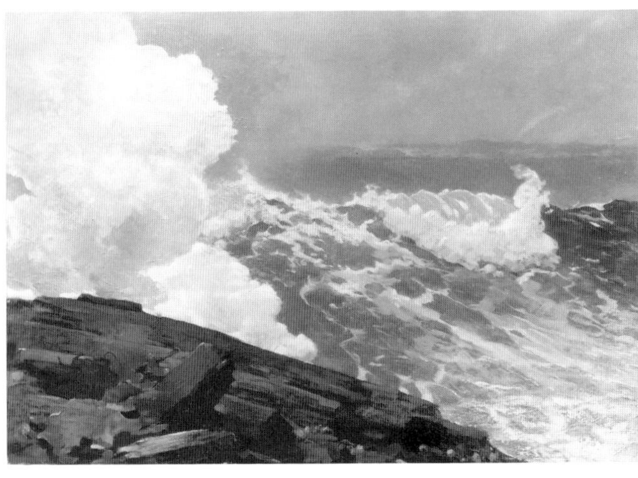

64. Winslow Homer, *Northeaster,* oil on canvas, 34⅜ × 50¼ in., 1895. Metropolitan Museum of Art, New York; gift of George A. Hearn, 1910.

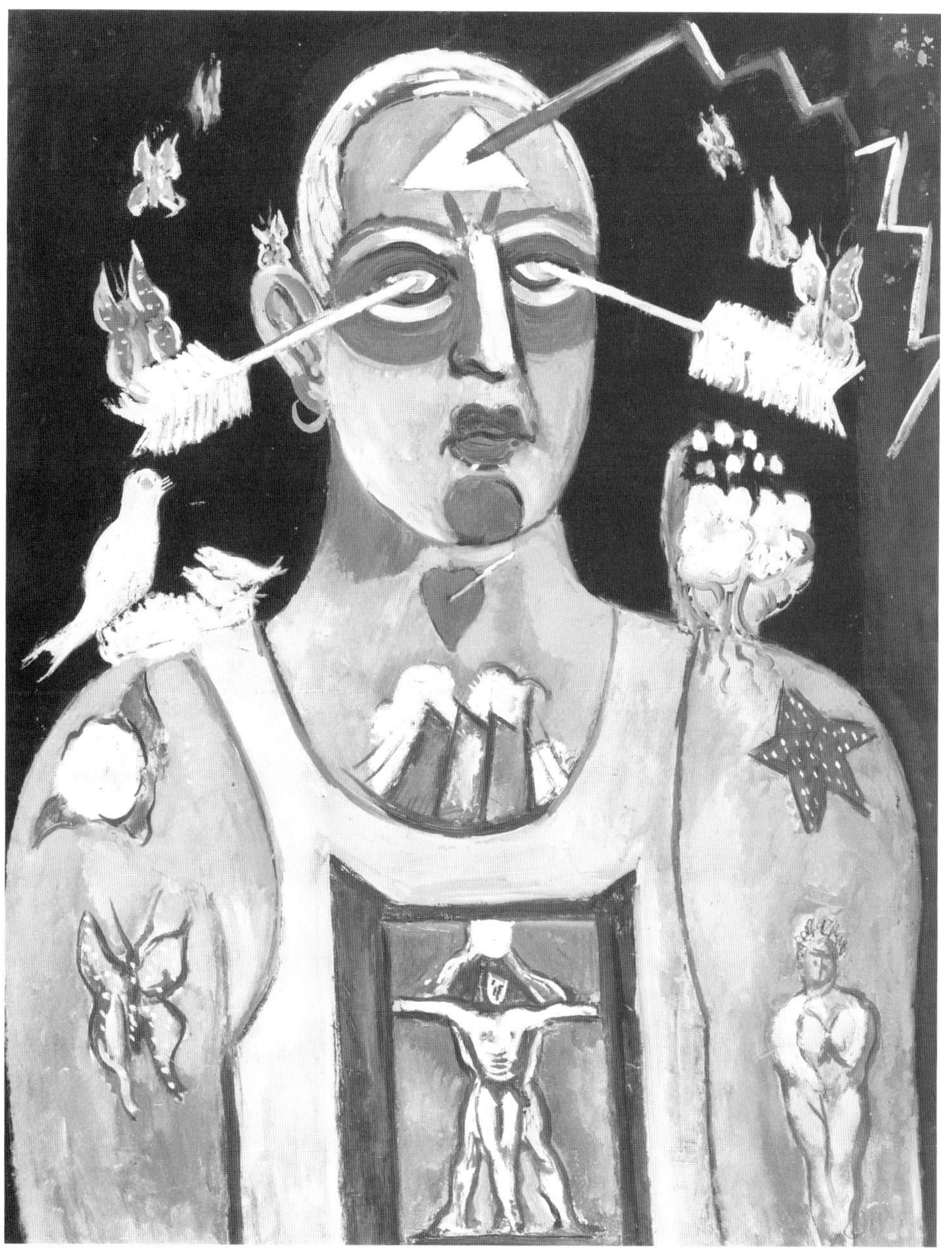

65. Marsden Hartley, *Sustained Comedy—Portrait of an Object,* oil on board, 28⅛ × 22 in., 1939. Carnegie Museum of Art, Pittsburgh, Pa.; gift of Mervin Jules in memory of Hudson Walker.

Hartley's poem "He Too Wore a Butterfly" shares the odd iconography of the picture. The poem describes a man who

> wore a butterfly upon his flanks,
> upsetting the woman and the ship in their angles,
> and down his midrib the image of Christ, the feet
> and the nails, touching his navel.

The butterfly is a sign that he "felt the fear of being musclebound." Instead of arrows, however, it is "as if the sea crowded all its waves within his eyes."[48] Although the painting may have been suggested by the memory of a real man that Hartley met in his travels, *Sustained Comedy* is actually a compendium of images from other pictures. The sinking ship on the sailor's shoulder recalls *Eight Bells Folly* and Crane's death; the rose on his shoulder and the Christ figure recall the various paintings associated with the Mason family.[49] The form of the painting, with a single figure placed in the center against a dark background, over which the various symbols are collaged, is a reprise of the war motif series.

The title of the painting, *Sustained Comedy—Portrait of an Object,* appears to be ironic, since its mood is so dark. Still, the exaggerated lips of the figure and the mask suggest a clownlike face. Perhaps Hartley sees himself as an object of ridicule. Or perhaps the word *object* is meant to suggest the way he has fashioned a portrait of himself out of other paintings. On the back of the painting Hartley wrote "Travesty," a word that Ferguson and the authors of the catalogue entry in *Marsden Hartley and Nova Scotia* claim Hartley equated with death.[50] Death is most forcefully suggested in the painting by the arrows that blind the figure. The arrows are an obvious allusion to St. Sebastian, who has traditionally served in the gay subculture as a kind of patron saint of homosexuality.[51] And on the sailor's neck is a small heart and arrow, which suggests that the arrows are weapons of love. The pierced heart is the perfect symbol for Hartley's relationship to men. (Hartley's very name contains

66. Marsden Hartley, *Finnish-Yankee Sauna,* oil on academy board, 24 × 18 in., 1938–39. Frederick R. Weisman Museum of Art, University of Minnesota, Minneapolis; bequest of Hudson Walker from the Ione and Hudson Walker Collection.

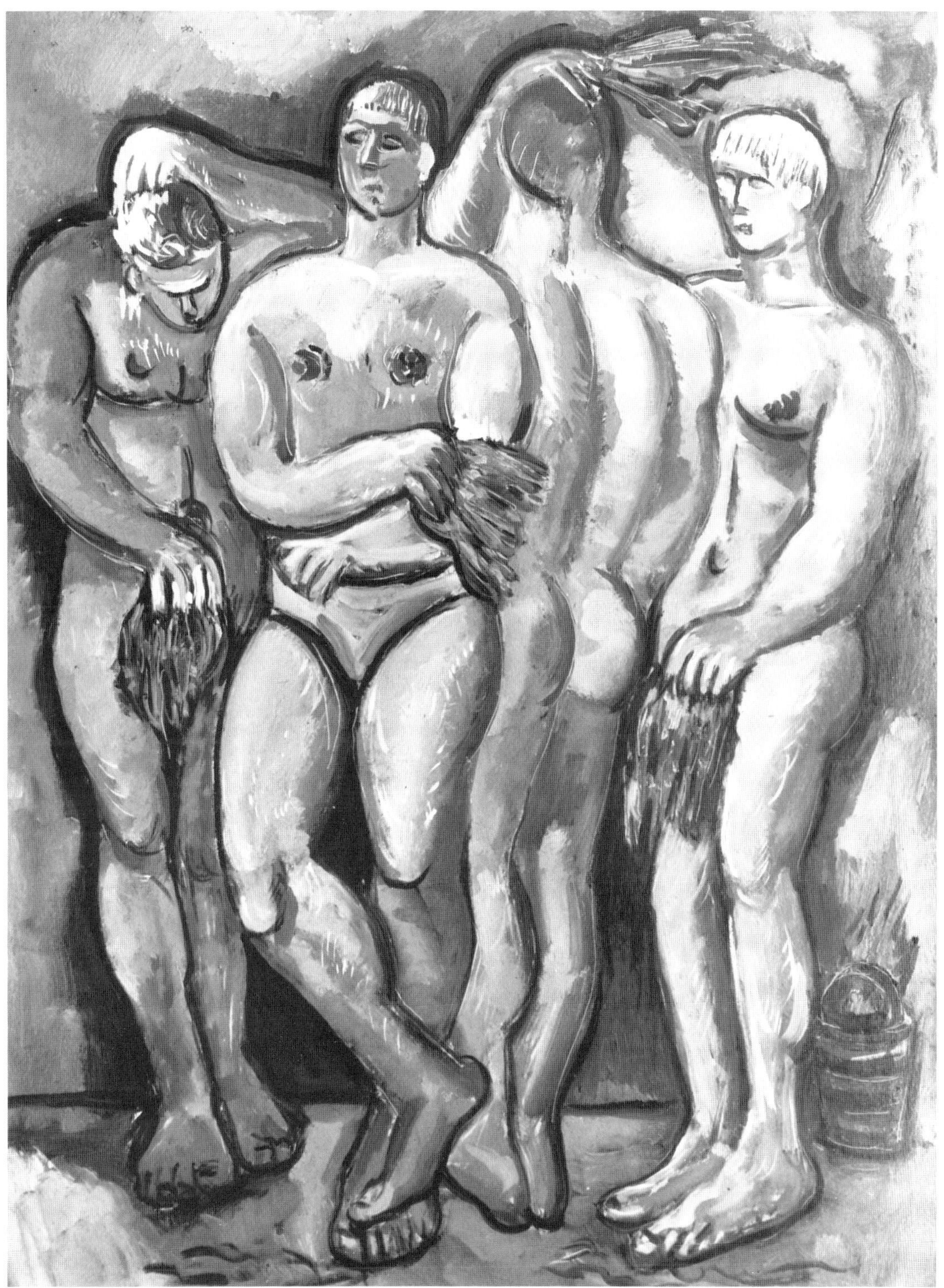

within it the word for this supposed organ of affection.) It recalls that similar tattoo on the sailor in Charles Demuth's *Three Sailors on the Beach.* The heart and arrow conflate desire and death. Hartley and Demuth both used the motif to acknowledge their homosexual love, even as it suggests the fatality of that love in the face of societal prejudice and personal inhibitions.

The meaning of *Sustained Comedy* remains obscure, yet Hudson Walker was supposedly alarmed enough by the signs of homosexuality in the picture—the makeup, the allusion to St. Sebastian, and perhaps the earring—to convince Hartley not to exhibit it. He sold the picture to Mervin Jules on condition that it not be shown publicly during Hartley's or Walker's lifetime.[52] Hartley, who was usually so discreet about his sexual taste, was now willing to risk exposure. Hartley's late paintings—*Christ Held by Half-Naked Men, Cleophas, Master of the Gilded Gray, Adelard the Drowned,* and the two versions of the *Fishermen's Last Supper*—have rightly been understood as attempts to come to terms with the Mason tragedy. But contemporaneous with these elegiac canvases is a series of paintings and drawings that join *Sustained Comedy* in focusing on the male body as an object of desire. We have already seen that Hartley's letters from the late 1930s and early 1940s are far more open about homosexuality than his earlier correspondence. It is as if the death of the Mason sons released the inhibitions Hartley had placed on the expression of his sexuality. Or perhaps, as with Demuth, Hartley's increasingly poor health made discretion seem less important.

Although Hartley's paintings of young men never depict sexual acts in the manner of Demuth's erotic watercolors, they mirror the same locations—the beach and the bathhouse. *Finnish-Yankee Sauna* (fig. 66) depicts four men beating their naked bodies with branches. In comparison to Demuth's bathhouse scenes, however, Hartley's painting is tame. One figure wears a bathing suit, while the others, though naked, hold bunches of leaves in front of their genitals. The figure on the left soaps his hair, as if to signal that the men are there for the water and the heat, and not

67. Marsden Hartley, *Canuck Yankee Lumberjack at Old Orchard Beach, Maine,* oil on fiberboard, 40⅛ × 30 in., 1940–41. Hirshhorn Museum and Sculpture Garden, Smithsonian Institution, Washington, D.C.

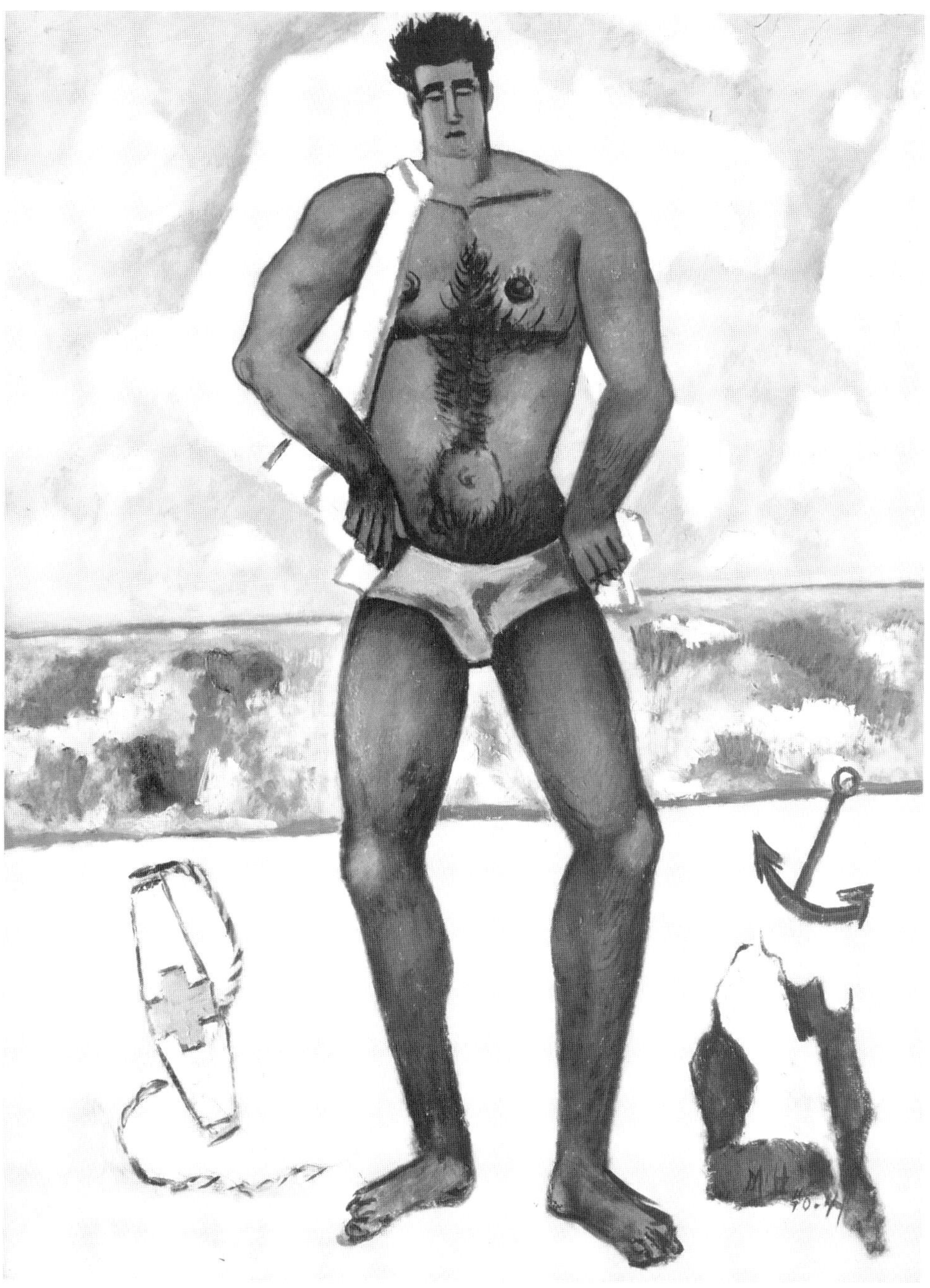

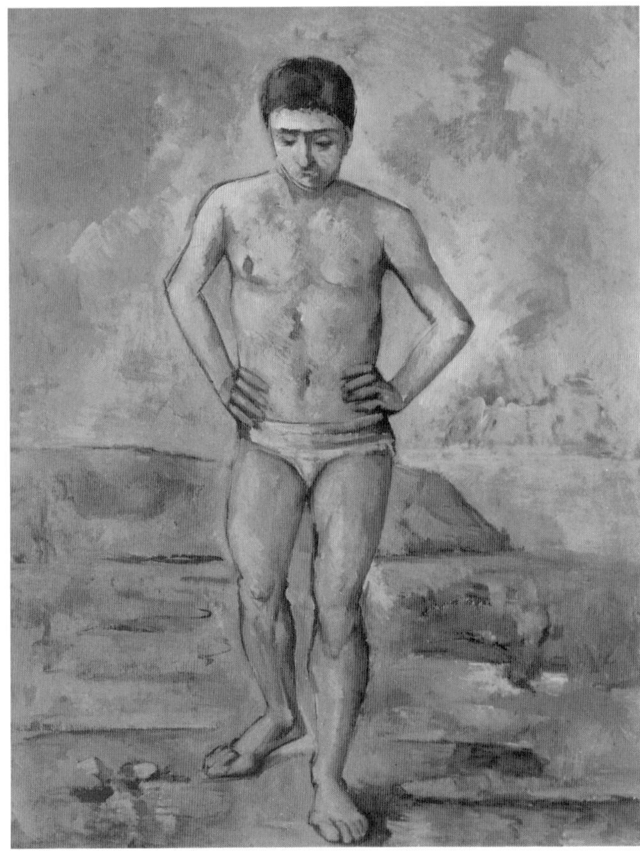

68. Paul Cézanne, *The Bather,* oil on canvas, 50 × 38⅛ in., ca. 1885. Museum of Modern Art, New York; Lillie P. Bliss Collection.

for sexual pleasures. Yet their bodies are closely packed within the rectangle of the frame. As with Demuth's *Turkish Bath Scene with Self-Portrait,* the physical closeness in Hartley's painting might seem to go beyond the decorum of heterosexual male bonding.

Finnish-Yankee Sauna is an unusual subject for Hartley. In the late paintings he focuses more frequently on a male swimmer standing or sitting on the beach, as in *Canuck Yankee Lumberjack at Old Orchard Beach, Maine* (fig. 67). The motif of the standing swimmer, hands on his hips, facing the viewer, signals the return of Cézanne to Hartley's painting, now not in the form of reworking Cézanne's motif of Mt. St. Victoire but in the form of *The Bather* (fig. 68) in the Museum of Modern Art.[53]

Whereas Hartley in his Mt. St. Victoire series of 1928 seemed to swallow Cézanne's subject whole, Hartley now blatantly eroticizes Cézanne's male figure. He exaggerates the size of the lumberjack's chest and arm muscles. Whereas Cézanne hides the bather's genitals under his bathing suit, Hartley emphasizes the bulge of his subject's crotch, making Cézanne's body overtly sexual. Hartley's transformation is an expression of his attraction to men but also indicates a desire for the practice of an earlier artist. Hartley's painting eloquently suggests that that influence—the passing on of a subject from one artist to another—is itself an erotic relationship.

Hartley's working-class bathers—lifeguards and lumberjacks—are his final attempt to merge the art of Cézanne and Whitman. These Yankees—unembarrassed by their undress, facing the viewer directly, and above all "authentic" and "masculine"—are Whitman's heroes recast in Cézanne's form. Indeed, in these late paintings Hartley makes concrete the connection he had theorized in his essay "Whitman and Cézanne." At the time Hartley was painting his bathers, he also completed *Young Worshiper of the Truth* (fig. 69), a portrait of Lincoln, Whitman's great hero and the subject of "O Captain! My Captain!" That famous poem, which is so often anthologized, conceives of Lincoln and the Union in nautical terms. Lincoln is the captain who does not survive to see his ship safely to shore, and so the poet is left "to walk the deck" where the "Captain lies, / Fallen cold and dead."[54] Whereas Whitman mourns walking the deck, Hartley mourns walking the beach. He focuses in his late paintings on the bathers, the sea, and the dead birds, on the shells, rope, and buoys that have washed up on the sand.[55] Hartley shares with Whitman themes of loneliness, death and, finally, homosexuality, but also a sense that such themes in their very interconnectedness are somehow distinctly American. The national and the homosexual are fused in the two artists' work. The same song that mourns the death of a great American president is also a love poem written by one man for another; the same painting that makes a hero out of a simple Yankee fisherman is also a declaration of homosexual desire.

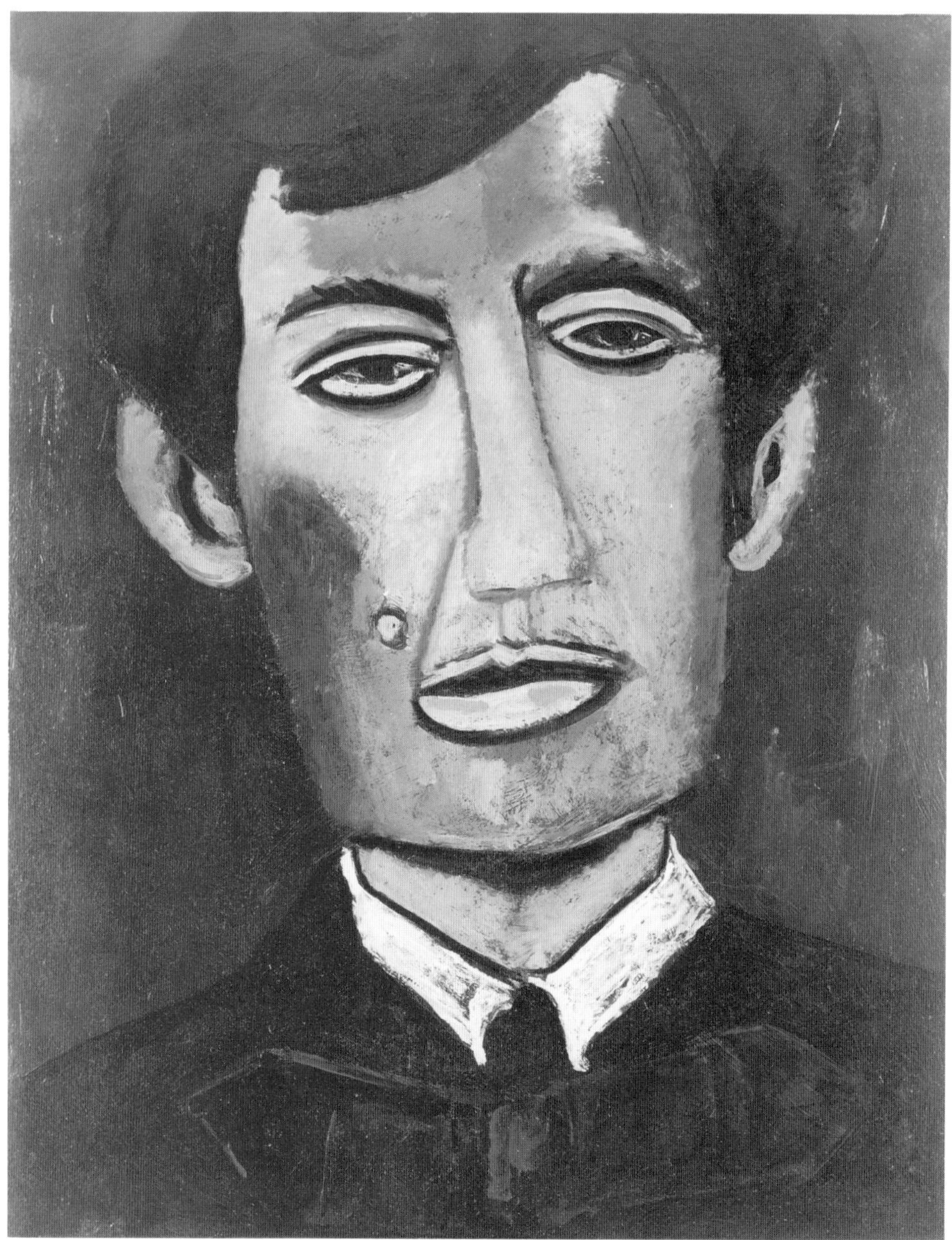

69. Marsden Hartley, *Young Worshiper of the Truth,* oil on academy board, 28 × 22 in., 1940. Sheldon Memorial Art Gallery, University of Nebraska, Lincoln; Nebraska Art Association, Nelle Cochrane Woods Memorial Collection.

9 Coming Home: Homosexuality and the American Avant-Garde

Earlier I discussed the ways Charles Demuth separated his art into discrete modes: the consciously avant-garde poster portraits and cityscapes, the conservative flowers and still lifes, and the sometimes erotic illustrations and nightlife scenes. But as Ray Gerard Koskovich has noticed, there is one watercolor in which Demuth allowed his private, figurative manner to clash with his public, abstract style: *Distinguished Air* (fig. 70).[1] The painting depicts a gallery in which a large phallus—an obvious caricature of Constantin Brancusi's *Princess X* (fig. 71)—is on display. At the center of the picture, a sailor and a gentleman in top hat, their backs turned toward us and their arms around each other's waists, stand before this strange work of art. The only figure looking at the sculpture is a woman dressed in a low-cut red evening dress. As if to protect herself from the enormous phallus, she holds a small fan in front of her vagina. On the left is another couple: a well-dressed woman and a man with a bowler hat and cane. Instead of looking at the sculpture, the woman looks across at the lady with the fan, while her male companion longingly gazes at the sailor's nether region.

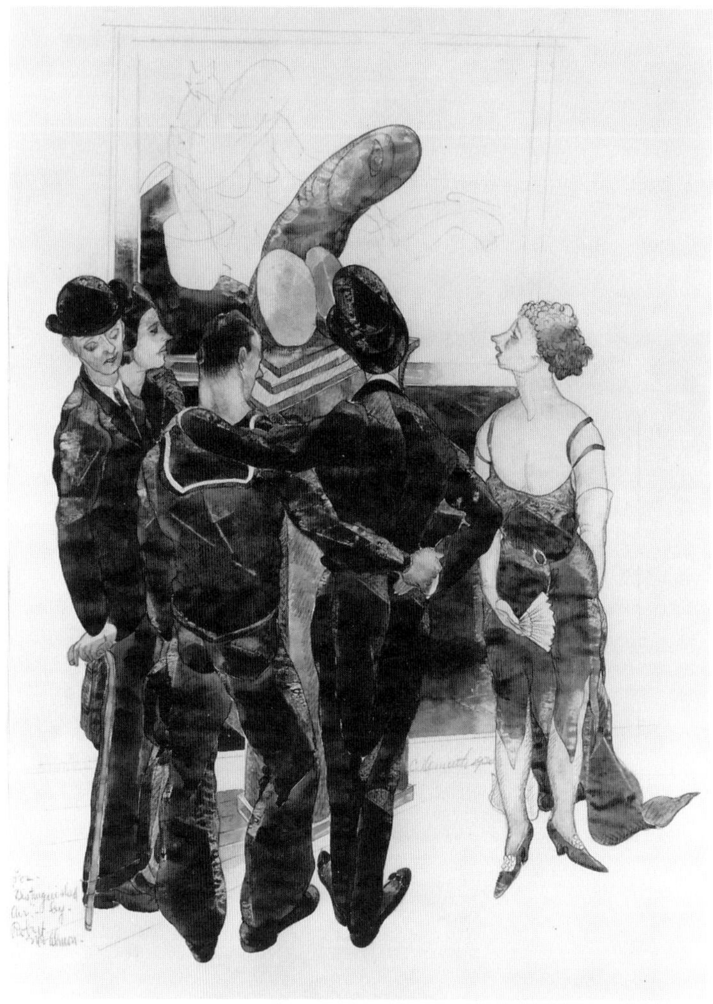

70. Charles Demuth, *Distinguished Air,* watercolor on paper, 14 × 12 in., 1930. Whitney Museum of American Art, New York; gift of the Friends of the Whitney Museum, Charles Simon (and purchase).

Although he had not done so with his other erotic drawings, Demuth risked exhibiting *Distinguished Air* publicly and allowed its reproduction in a monograph produced by the Whitney Museum.[2] For this reason, Ray Gerard Koskovich sees *Distinguished Air* "as a kind of 'coming out' " for Charles Demuth. Barbara Haskell supports such an interpretation with her conjecture that the man with the cane, who appears more interested in the sailor than in his female friend, is a self-portrait. Haskell feels that with the exhibition of *Distinguished Air* Demuth was for the first time "aesthetically overt" about his homosexuality.[3] Is *Distinguished Air* Demuth's "coming out" painting? Is Demuth unambiguously declaring his alliance with the world of the sailor and the top-hatted gentleman? And if Demuth was declaring his homosexuality in the watercolor, why did the staid Whitney Museum of the 1930s publish the picture?

Written in the lower left corner of the watercolor are the words "For 'Distinguished Air' by Robert McAlmon," suggesting that the McAlmon story might provide an explanation. Once again, an autobiographical reading of Demuth's imagery is potentially derailed by placing responsibility for the picture onto a text that the painter did not write. In his earlier illustrations Demuth could count on his audience's knowing the chosen author's work, but "Distinguished Air"—one of three

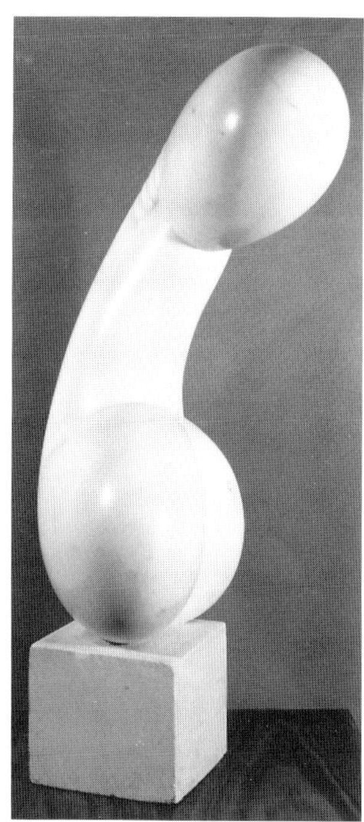

71. Constantin Brancusi, *Princess X,* marble, 1916. Sheldon Memorial Art Gallery, University of Nebraska, Lincoln; gift of Mrs. A. B. Sheldon.

short stories in a collection of the same title—was little known to anyone outside Demuth's avant-garde circle.

The collection *Distinguished Air* was published in Paris in 1925 in an edition of only 115 copies and then anthologized in Carl Van Doren's *Americana Esoterica,* also a limited edition.[4] The three stories record McAlmon's impressions of Weimar Berlin in a flat, nonjudgmental style that prefigures the more famous Berlin stories of Christopher Isherwood. The book is subtitled "Grim Fairy Tales"—the fairies in question being homosexuals and their presumed cohorts within Berlin nightlife: lesbians, transvestites, prostitutes, drug addicts, and dealers. In Demuth's illustrations, there is typically a close connection between image and text. But the meaning of Demuth's *Distinguished Air* is actually obscured when we compare it with the story it is supposed to illustrate, for the scene depicted in the watercolor does not occur in McAlmon's story. Although the homosexual couple at the center and the other ambiguous couple would be at home in McAlmon's description of inflation-ridden Berlin, it is impossible even to fix the characters' names in the text. Dickran Tashjian suggests that Demuth's illustration is meant to *augment* McAlmon's work. He claims that it "brilliantly depicts that which McAlmon omitted from the title story."[5] The story begins when the narrator runs into Foster Graham, an expatriate painter and overt homosexual who has become dissipated through reveling in Berlin's entertainments. Graham, whose behavior is clearly meant to be scandalous, makes no attempt to hide his homosexuality. He camps, that is, he makes purposely effeminate gestures and calls the male narrator by a female name. His mannerisms are so extreme that he earns the disapproval of a fellow homosexual who claims that although Foster had once had "an air—real distinction . . . life has become just too much one thing for him."[6] That one thing is the pursuit of sex.

Early in "Distinguished Air," the narrator asks Graham if he wants to go to a gallery:

> "I'm just heading for Der Sturm, to see what new has been hung in the exhibition rooms there. Do you want to come along? Some of the paintings are apt to be as frenzied as you are, and it'll pass away an hour."

> "Goodness me, Marjorie, I just love art. I love art," Foster minced, unable to be direct for over a moment. "Will there be some pretty pictures of naked boys? I just love art. It's too exquisite. So glad you asked me along."[7]

The satire here, such as it is, rests comfortably on stereotypes. The narrator's confidence that the paintings in the gallery will be as frenzied as Graham is a familiar commentary on modern art. In Graham's hope that there might be "pretty pictures of naked boys" is the suggestion that avant-garde painting is just another one of the entertainments of modernity, not unlike the pleasures provided by the nightclubs and hustlers of Berlin. Indeed, perhaps one of the reasons Demuth was able to risk the potential scandal of *Distinguished Air* was that his image, for all its seeming "obscenity," reaffirms a popular conception of modern art. In response to the question of what type of person looks at avant-garde sculpture and painting, Demuth seems to give the familiar answer "fags" and their rich women friends.

Demuth's focus on the visitors to the gallery, who had been mentioned only fleetingly in McAlmon's text, shifts the emphasis from the dissipations of Berlin to the larger question of what type of persons comprise the avant-garde and its audiences. In a number of ways, Demuth's image is a satire on the very avant-garde of which he counted himself a member. It is significant that Stieglitz gave Brancusi his first one-man show in the United States. And Stieglitz's close associate, the artist and gallery director Marius De Zayas, exhibited the sculpture in both its marble and bronze versions in his Modern Gallery in 1917.[8] Yet the watercolor is not just a spoof on the high seriousness of the Stieglitz circle. The satire is partly self-directed. Brancusi's *Princess X* had a direct influence on the brazen phallic quality of Demuth's own *Paquebot Paris*. And Brancusi's sculptures of women, particularly the Mme. Pogany series, were no doubt among the precedents that Demuth had in mind when he embarked on his series of portraits constructed from purely abstract forms (*Princess X* was also called simply *Portrait*). In this way, *Distinguished Air* can be seen as a confrontation between the kind of abstract portraiture Demuth made to establish his credentials as a member of the Stieglitz circle and the more traditional rendering of his figurative style, which contributed to the unwillingness of Stieglitz to accept him fully as one of the "select." More important to the meaning of Demuth's work is the notoriety of Brancusi's sculpture—its crucial role in the history of the reception of modern art. In a famous incident, customs officials almost taxed a Brancusi marble entering the United States, refusing to believe it was a work of art. In 1917, *Princess X* was exhibited in New York at the Society of Independent Artists to considerable negative comment. But *Princess X*'s place in the annals of avant-garde scandals was assured when, because of its phallic shape, it was removed from the Paris Salon des Indépendants in 1920.[9] *Distinguished Air,* then, presents us with a "scandalous" homosexual couple contemplating a particularly "scandalous" work of art. Demuth invites us to compare two kinds of social transgression: the breaking of codes of sexual conduct by men who have sex with other men and those strategies of avant-garde representation that purposely upset, distance, or dismay their audience. Demuth's insistent exaggeration of the penislike quality of the Brancusi sculpture, converting bronze to flesh tones and clearly marking out testicles and shaft, seems to ask whether there is some sort of equivalence between individual acts of nonconformity and public avant-garde scandal. But is homosexuality just one more scandal to put alongside the other kinds associated with the avant-garde? Can we properly compare the gesture of a man's arm around another man to the shock of the abstractness of Duchamp's *Nude Descending a Staircase,* or to the banality of his *Fountain,* or to the supposed obscenity of Brancusi's *Princess X?* How was homosexuality received by the New York avant-garde? Is it best seen as just one sort of bohemian behavior, equivalent to drinking too much, taking drugs, or committing adultery?

An answer to these questions would involve a complex study of the day-to-day habits of the avant-garde circles in New York. Such a study would require sifting through the letters, journals, and published memoirs of not only artists but also gallery owners, curators, and critics. What is really needed is an anthropology of the New York avant-garde, but such a project is beyond the boundaries of this book. I would nonetheless like to suggest certain directions such an answer, or answers, might take by focusing on a few key examples of homosexuality in the work of literary and visual artists who associated with Demuth and Hartley.[10]

Interestingly, Demuth and Hartley served as models for literary depictions of homosexuals. As the name implies, Charles Marsden, Eugene O'Neill's character from the play *Strange Interlude* of 1926, is a composite of qualities drawn from both Demuth and Hartley. Charles Marsden is an artist, but a novelist rather than a painter. Like Demuth, Marsden lives with his mother, but in his "Anglicized New England" manner he is closer to Hartley. Just as Hartley seemed uncomfortable with his own sexuality, Charles Marsden is sexually ambivalent. O'Neill describes him as having an "indefinable feminine quality."[11] Another character in the play "thinks" (the characters of *Strange Interlude* speak their thoughts in asides to the audience) Charles Marsden to be "one of those poor devils who spend their lives trying not to discover which sex they belong to!"[12] Early in the play, Marsden remembers going to a brothel at the age of sixteen with a friend named Jack Frazer: "Jack, the dead game sport . . . how I admired him! . . . afraid of his taunts . . . he pointed to the Italian girl . . . 'Take Her!' . . . daring me . . . I went . . . miserably frightened . . . what a pig she was! . . . pretty vicious face under caked powder and rouge." The incident leaves Marsden feeling that he has "defiled" his mother and himself "forever."[13]

The central character of *Strange Interlude* is Nina, who begins the play mourning a lover who has recently died in World War I. The play ends with her asking Marsden to marry her, but only after her relationships with all the other men in her life have collapsed. Her final "thoughts" are "God bless dear old Charlie . . . who, passed beyond desire, has all the luck at last!"[14] Charles Marsden's homosexuality—and I think it is clear from the Freudian implications of the relationship with his mother and the scene in the brothel that O'Neill means us to think he is homosexual—is a kind of absence of sexuality. All the men in *Strange Interlude* are flawed—unable to love and be loved—but only Charles Marsden's flaws are located in sexual deviancy. O'Neill conceptualizes homosexuality not as a defiant stance of otherness but as dysfunction. O'Neill's Charles Marsden is unable to act, unable to express his feeling for Nina—he wins her only by default. He is, in the end, not a complete man.

Robert McAlmon also used Marsden Hartley as a model for characters in two separate works. In the autobiographical *Post-Adolescence,* Hartley is given the name Brander Ogden. Whereas O'Neill's Charles Marsden is clearly a work of fiction, McAlmon's Ogden is recognizably his good friend Hartley. Ogden strolls "with deliberate eaglelike dignity, his great cold blue eyes staring about him." The stand-in for McAlmon, Peter, is "amused at what someone had called his dowager gestures, and noted his high beaklike nose, and his face with its fierce grandmother's profile."[15] Like Hartley, Ogden complains bitterly of New York and dreams of returning to Europe: "Nothing happens. I go around, but nothing happens. Surely I remember that things were not that way in Paris, or Germany when I was there before the war, but these New York people just get together and stand around dumb." Ogden is a sexually frustrated homosexual who "gets most of his erotic satisfaction through his eyes."[16]

A similar Hartley-inspired character reappears in *Distinguished Air,* this time with the name Carrol Timmons. The narrator runs into Timmons "admiring a perfumery bottle display with a great air of connoisseurship."[17] Unlike the other Americans in the story, who have come to Berlin for the first time because of favorable exchange rates, Timmons has spent long periods in Germany in flight from "New England, and that absurd moral bugaboo pursuing me for so many years." Timmons shares with Hartley an ambivalence about the sexual pleasures of Berlin. Arriving at a nightclub where men are dancing with men, he tells the narrator that the "place is too erotically upsetting . . . as a steady diet."[18] But McAlmon's description of Timmons as a homosexual who romanticizes casual relationships with young men is the most reminiscent of Hartley. Carrol's monologue about a male prostitute could almost be a satire of Hartley's characteristic relationship with younger men: " 'Such a nice boy, too; just the type that attracted me most. Such a gentle face, and so rich physically. I was quite upset about him last week, because he came home with me one night, and the experience was wonderful—wonderful. . . .' Carrol rolled his fiercely spinsterly eyes expressively, 'but he disappeared the next day. . . . Of course he is German, and has no money, and has to do things he doesn't want for money. . . . Must support his mother you know.' " He adds pathetically, " 'Well perhaps he does care for me a little for myself, you know. It's so comforting to think that anyway.' " With frustration the narrator burst out, "Why try to make romantic affairs out of these ten-mark-bought bitches?"[19] Carrol Timmons is a deluded and aging "Countess," to use another character's description of the unhappy man.

Although it is interesting that both Hartley and Demuth were considered representative of the "unhappy homosexual," these passages from O'Neill and McAlmon are less significant for their biographical information than for what they tell us about avant-garde attitudes toward homosexuality. We can take McAlmon and O'Neill to be sympathetic voices. Both were close friends of Hartley and Demuth. Yet their conceptions of homosexuality are not all that different from the stereotypes. In *Strange Interlude,* O'Neill sees homosexuality as a weakness, as an arrested, rather than alternative, sexuality. The first scene of the play sets the tone and provides the key: Charles Marsden's failure at the whorehouse is offered as sufficient explanation for his inability to be fully sexual. In contrast, McAlmon's homosexuals are oversexed. For Foster Graham and all the queers in "Distinguished Air," "life has become just too much one thing." Homosexual men desire but they are not desirable. The hero of *Post-Adolescence* winces at Ogden's touch, asking himself, "Who would want to touch skin and flesh that was so big pored and old looking?"[20] "Distinguished Air" parades homosexuals as so many unattractive oddities: "At various tables were scattered the queer types of Berlin, many of them painted up, two or three in women's clothes, and a great number of types who were not obvious."[21] Homosexuals are cast as one of the tourist sights of inflation-ridden Berlin; their otherness is neither seductive nor liberating. The attitudes of both O'Neill and McAlmon toward homosexuality amount to regarding it as disease. Both see homosexuality as a sick confusion of gender—Charles Marsden is an old lady and McAlmon's gay men frequently dress as women. Both writers use homosexuality as a metaphor for societal sickness. Their representations do not undermine middle-class conceptions of the normal. In fact, they rely on such conceptions to fix the decadence of homosexuality. O'Neill's and McAlmon's characterizations of homosexuals force us to question the clichéd view of the avant-garde as a free space in which sexual experimentation and difference were accepted and even encouraged. In fact, avant-garde artists were as capable of homophobia as the general public. In the journal *291,* Marius De Zayas characterized the New York art world as having "the mentality of homosexuals," adding that "they are flowers of artificial breeding." "Mentality of homosexuals" is meant to suggest both a lack of masculinity and an inability to procreate. According to De Zayas, New York intellectuals "wish to impregnate you, believing themselves stallions when they are but geldings."[22] De

Zayas's statement lends support to my interpretation of Demuth's *Distinguished Air* as reliant on the stereotype that the audience for modern art is made up of homosexuals. (Remember that Brancusi's *Princess X* was exhibited in Zayas's gallery.)

As Georges-Michel Sarotte states in his study of homosexuality in twentieth-century literature, *Like a Brother, Like a Lover,* homophobia pervaded the avant-garde novel of the 1920s and 1930s. F. Scott Fitzgerald's *Tender Is the Night,* published in 1933, expresses a typical bohemian attitude toward homosexuality.[23] The Divers, whose relationship was supposedly modeled after Fitzgerald's relationship with his wife, Zelda, include among their circle a gay man, Luis Campion, jester to the Divers' court. As his name implies, he camps. Jilted by a lover, he is found "weeping hard and quietly and shaking in the same parts as a weeping woman."[24] Campion is valued not as a human being—his effeminacy makes him less than human—but as a kind of comic relief. While witnessing a duel, for example, he is the only one in the party to faint. The sole difference between Fitzgerald's depiction and the 1930s Hollywood film stereotype of the effeminate homosexual interior designer or dance instructor is Fitzgerald's directness in addressing Campion's homosexuality. Later in *Tender Is the Night,* Dr. Diver, a psychiatrist, examines a troubled youth whom he suspects is homosexual. Diver warns him of his future as a homosexual: "It's a hole-and-corner business at best. . . . You'll spend your life on it, and its consequences, and you won't have time or energy for any other decent or social act. If you want to face the world you'll have to begin by controlling your sensuality."[25]

The homophobia of Fitzgerald's friend and colleague Ernest Hemingway was legendary. It was therefore no revelation when he admitted in his memoir *A Moveable Feast* that he "had prejudices against homosexuality since [he] knew its more primitive aspects." A great surprise, however, is his memory of a discussion he had with his mentor, Gertrude Stein. As Hemingway remembers it, Stein told him that "the main thing is the act male homosexuals commit is ugly and repugnant and afterwards they are disgusted with themselves. They drink and take drugs, to palliate this, but they are disgusted with the act and they are always changing partners and cannot be really happy."[26] Whether or not Hemingway invented the words he put into Stein's mouth, the cliché of the homosexual who hates himself because homosexuality is intrinsically hateful appears repeatedly in the writings of the American avant-garde. As we have seen, if Fitzgerald and McAlmon bring homosexuality "out of the closet," they do so only to confirm society's sense of the rightness of its own gender categories. Although, arguably, one could not generalize about the attitudes of such a complex phenomenon as the American avant-garde based on these few examples of homophobia, they are sufficient to raise doubts about the automatic connection between artistic notoriety and the undermining of a dominant culture's value systems. The bleak view of homosexuality of De Zayas, O'Neill, McAlmon, Fitzgerald, and perhaps even Stein returns us to the question raised by Demuth's *Distinguished Air* about the equivalence between public acts of deviancy and their representation. The exhibition of an overtly erotic work of art or the frank description of a gay bar in Berlin, however shocking, does not necessarily add up to a rebellion against the value system that marginalizes homosexuality. Such frankness may even end up reaffirming that marginalization.

These examples of internalization of homophobic stereotypes by the avant-garde does not mean that gay artists such as Hartley and Demuth were not taken seriously or admired by their straight friends. What it does suggest, however, is that friendships with homosexuals—the day-to-day knowledge of their complexity and individuality—did not interfere with a one-dimensional conceptualization of homosexuality as diseased. Sadly, we have seen that Hartley and Demuth sometimes reinforced these stereotypes in their paintings and writings. Certainly these stereotypes colored their sense of their own self-worth. Such attitudes continued to be pervasive in the New York art world throughout the 1930s and 1940s. In 1949, six years after Hartley's death, Frank Lloyd Wright, speaking at the Western Round Table on Modern Art, unembarrassedly equated homosexuality and degeneracy. And in an attempt to discredit modern art in its entirety, he asked the participants "if this movement which we call modern art and painting has been greatly, or is greatly in debt to homosexualism?" Marcel Duchamp replied, "I admit it, but not in your terms. . . . I believe that the homosexual public has shown more interest or curiosity for modern art than the heterosexual."[27]

Among the panel of experts, Duchamp alone unambiguously insisted that "homosexuality was not degenerate." Why did Wright think Duchamp was an expert on the relationship of homosexuality to modern art? Of course, there was the matter of drag: in 1920, Duchamp first donned female attire and took on a new persona, Rrose Sélavy.[28] Whereas many of the members of the early American avant-garde merely reproduced the dominant culture's prejudices in their representations of gay men, Duchamp found a far more subversive use of homosexuality. Duchamp's transvestism, first displayed publicly in photographs by Man Ray, has been discussed at length in the extensive literature on the artist. Such discussions usually tie Duchamp's feminine persona to his larger project of questioning gender boundaries. Duchamp's use of a pseudonym is traced to his undermining of the role of authorship in his art, while his use of drag is compared to similar Dadaist gestures or to the theatrical tradition of cross-dressing. The issue of Duchamp's homosexuality, though not entirely avoided, is usually dealt with only in psychoanalytic terms, as in Arturo Schwarz's massive *Complete Works of Marcel Duchamp*. Missing from these accounts is any connection to the sociology of homosexuality in the 1920s. Yet by publicly wearing women's clothing, Duchamp was borrowing from the gay subculture of his period its most public form of expression.

According to George Chauncey, Jr., drag balls proliferated in New York during the 1920s. Masquerades were held in such prominent places as Madison Square Garden and the Astor Hotel. Chauncey writes of the balls: "The drag queens who paraded there—and the effeminate homosexual men, usually called 'fairies' who managed to be flamboyant even in a suit—were the most visible element of gay life. They not only dominated public stereotypes but set the tone within the gay world much more in the 1920s than they do today."[29] Gay men would spend months designing their costumes for these public events. It is crucial to note here that many of the men who attended these balls were not habitual transvestites like Earl Lind, who felt most comfortable in women's clothing. Often drag was a costume of difference that allowed homosexuals to express their affection for other men in public. Earlier I discussed Hartley's delight in wearing an androgynous disguise and dreaming that a man might confuse him with a beautiful woman. The mask of another gender (or ambiguous gender) provided Hartley and other members of the homosexual subculture with temporary freedom. Dressed in elaborate costumes—as Marie Antoinette or Martha Washington—gay men could dance with other men. Significantly, as Chauncey points out, the masquerades were celebrations. Homosexuality was presented not as a depressing, shameful disease but as a potentially glamorous and desirable way of life. Yet it should be pointed out that the success of the drag ball was predicated on the mask. Gay men, even as they declared difference, still hid behind their costumes.

That Duchamp was aware of the drag balls is suggested by an invitation in *The Blind Man,* the 1917 magazine he unofficially edited. Duchamp designed an advertisement that invited people to a "new-fashioned hop, skip and jump to be held on Friday, May 25, at the Prehistoric, ultra-bohemian Webster Hall." The copy insisted that the guests wear a costume: "There is a difference between a tuxedo and a Turk and guests not in costume must sit in bought-and-paid for boxes."[30] Although Duchamp's ball was not exclusively for cross-dressing, the existence of the boxes suggests that the organizers expected a large drag contingent. The boxes provided those who did not want to be implicated in the possible immorality of the ball with a safe place from which to watch. Webster Hall continued to be a popular site for drags during that period. A similar invitation for a "Greenwich Village Ball" held at Webster Hall in 1923 read, "Come when you like, with whom you like—wear what you like. . . . Unconventional? Oh, to be sure—only do be discreet."[31]

From the beginning Rrose was conceived in terms of marginalization. Duchamp said that in creating a pseudonym, he originally considered taking on a Jewish identity, but he found it easier to turn himself into a woman.[32] Cross-dressing was perhaps more appealing to Duchamp because it was more visible and more aesthetic. Taking a Jewish name would not involve a physical transformation, or if it did involve such a transformation—let us say, wearing a yarmulke or donning a mask with a hooked nose—Duchamp would find himself implicated in the anti-Semitism he was trying to mock. In any case, his metamorphosis into a woman did double service; it allowed Duchamp to link his practice to two oppressed groups: homosexuals and women.

Given the prevalence of drag balls in New York City, and in particular in Greenwich Village and Harlem, the two major haunts of the avant-garde, was Duchamp's adoption of drag a radical gesture? It has been argued that drag balls were tolerated by the general New York public because they confirmed stereotypes about homosexuals. Chauncey writes: "Much evidence suggests that the 'fairy,' so long as he kept his place, was tolerated in both working class and aristocratic society—regarded as an anomaly, certainly, but as more amusing than abhorrent, and only rarely as threatening to the gender order because he was so obviously a 'third sexer': his very effeminacy confirmed the masculinity of other men."[33] In other words, cross-dressing, even as it celebrated difference, also kept difference in its place. But Duchamp's adoption of a characteristic mask of the gay subculture upset this formula. Duchamp had affairs with women, and he was not obviously effeminate. He wore women's clothing not on the way to a masquerade but on the cover of an art magazine, *New York Dada.* The drag queen was not a harmless anomaly but an artist, curator, and editor, the alter ego of a key mover of the New York art world.

Rrose was not Duchamp's first excursion into the territory of homosexuality. His cross-dressing had been to some extent anticipated by his application of a moustache to Leonardo's *Mona Lisa,* turning a woman into a man. Schwarz and others have noted Duchamp's fascination with Leonardo and his knowledge of Freud's reading of Leonardo's sexuality. Yet homosexuality is rarely mentioned in connection with one of Duchamp's most notorious works, *The Fountain* (fig. 72). In 1989, William Camfield published an exhaustive analysis of *The Fountain* and a historical survey of its critical reception over the years. Although he includes an elaborate discussion of plumbing and eroticism, he fails to mention the use of public urinals as the site of homosexual encounters.

Did Duchamp know that public urinals were used by homosexuals for clandestine sex? Robert McAlmon's character, Foster, confesses to the narrator that he "was too married to the pissoir," adding that "one must have a tea engagement now and then."[34] McAlmon's *Distinguished Air* was written eight years after *The Fountain* controversy, yet the fact that McAlmon never explains what is meant by the phrase "tea engagement" suggests a widespread knowledge among his avant-garde friends of the homosexual practices that go on in tearooms, that is, public toilets. Foster's remark about being "married to the pissoir" is interesting given Duchamp's odd note in *The Box of 1914:* "One only has: for *female* the public urinal and one lives by it."[35] William Camfield writes that Duchamp's remark "is obscure, but . . . it transforms an object for use by males into a female, uterine-like shape which receives injec-

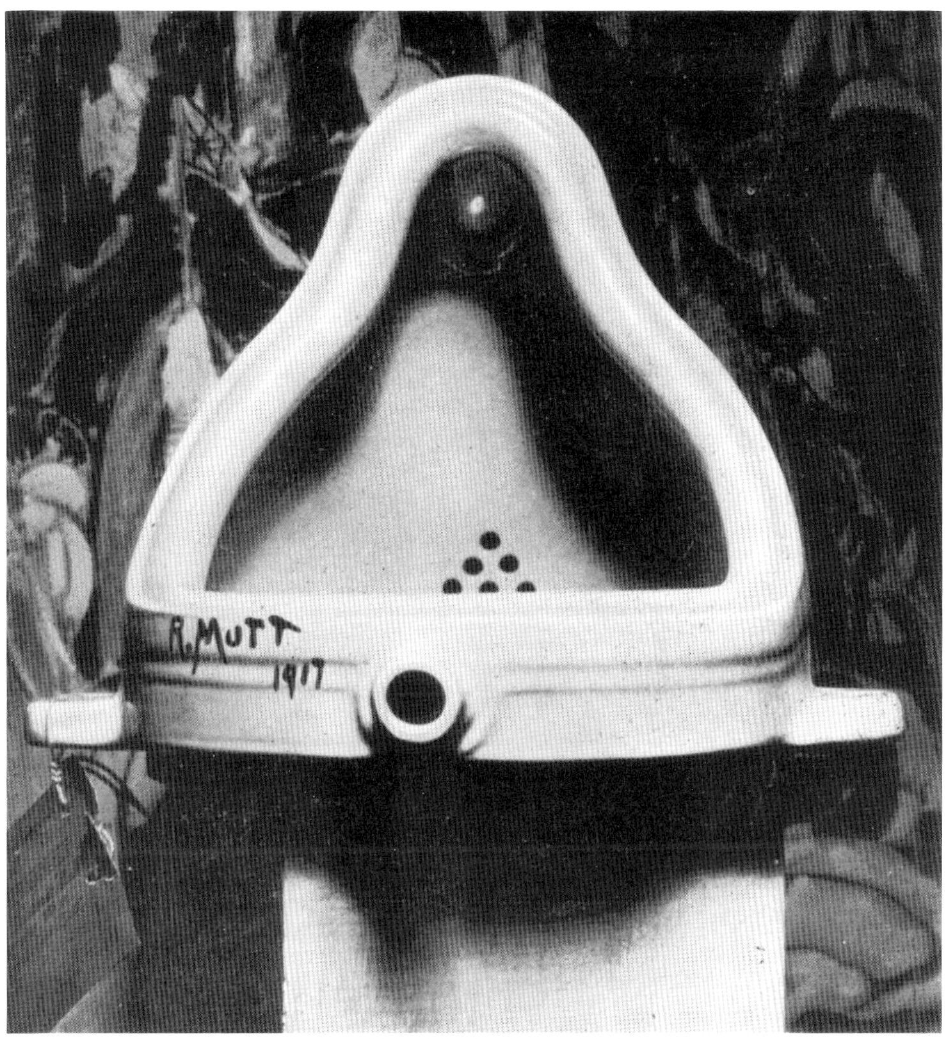

72. Marcel Duchamp, *The Fountain,* photograph by Alfred Stieglitz, from the *Blind Man* 2 (May 1917): 4. Philadelphia Museum of Art, Philadelphia; Louise and Walter Arensberg Collection.

tions of a male fluid."[36] Camfield ignores the last part of the sentence: "one lives by it," which suggests pleasure (or at least sustenance). It would be unwise to conclude from this cryptic sentence that Duchamp used public bathrooms for sex. It does suggest, however, that Duchamp knew about such practices and, more important, was not afraid that someone might make such a biographical connection. Duchamp's use of homosexuality was not accompanied by disclaimers; he never seemed anxious about his audience reaching the wrong conclusions about his private life.[37]

Camfield argues that art historians have ignored the aesthetic qualities of Duchamp's readymade. In defending its visual significance, Camfield ties the forms of *The Fountain* to works by Brancusi and takes Duchamp's contemporaries at their word when they associate Duchamp's sculpture with Buddhas and other objects of religious worship. This is not the place for a discussion of the aesthetic qualities of *The Fountain*. There is, however, an unfortunate consequence of Camfield's use of the standard techniques of art historical analysis—comparison with canonical works of art, iconographic allusions, critical context—on Duchamp's readymades. Camfield wants us to believe that *The Fountain* was not intended solely to disrupt aesthetic systems but instead was meant to reveal the latent aesthetic properties of ordinary objects. Camfield's analysis normalizes Duchamp's act of attempting to exhibit a toilet fixture as a work of art. But the connection to homosexuality, which Camfield ignores, or suppresses, suggests the danger of Duchamp's act. Camfield sees Duchamp widening the field of art, longing for a tolerant audience that is sympathetic to aesthetic expression wherever it be found. But I think *The Fountain* is better understood as questioning the mechanism of tolerance itself.

Tolerance is a power relation. It is something that those in control bestow on those who are not in control. As the filmmaker Pier Paolo Pasolini wrote, tolerance is really nothing more than "a more refined form of condemnation."[38] Such a power relation was at the center of *The Fountain* controversy. *The Fountain* was submitted to test the supposed freedom of the first exhibition of the American Society of Independent Artists. According to the bylaws of the society, "There are no requirements for admission to the Society save the acceptance of its principles and the payment of the initiation fee of one dollar and the annual dues of five dollars."[39] There were supposedly no jury and no prizes, yet *The Fountain,* submitted by

"R. Mutt," was refused. But Duchamp's sculpture was not rejected by a conservative or hostile jury. In fact, several of Duchamp's closest New York allies were key players in the society. The initial audience for Duchamp's sculpture, therefore, was not the average middle-class viewer (that vague construct of avant-garde scandals) but members of the avant-garde itself. They were the only ones who saw the original urinal, and after considerable argument, it was they who decided that it not be shown. Duchamp's *Fountain* gave the lie to the jury's refusal to judge. It revealed that claiming to tolerate difference is not the same as welcoming difference.

Some forty years after its exhibition, Duchamp remembered that *The Fountain* was technically part of the society's exhibition, after all. So as to conform to its own bylaws, the society placed the work in the exhibit hall but behind a curtained partition, presumably alongside miscellaneous refuse, cleaning supplies, and extra frames.[40] Camfield disputes Duchamp's story and presents several accounts of the sculpture being taken from the scene. Yet it is significant that in Duchamp's memory his sculpture was not excluded from the exhibit but only hidden. In his mind it was forced into the closet. Just as homosexuality was tolerated as long as it was discreet, in Duchamp's story, the urinal is allowed as long as it cannot be seen. Demuth defended Duchamp's *Fountain* with a poem, "For Richard Mutt," which is self-consciously Dada and opaque. But in describing *The Fountain* in terms of knowledge and hiding ("One must say everything—then no one will know. / To know nothing is to say a great deal"), Demuth suggests something of the predicament of the homosexual in a society that either outlaws or ignores his existence.[41]

Art historians have discussed the friendship between Demuth and Duchamp at length. The two often went to bars and nightclubs in the Village and Harlem. Duchamp remembered that it was Demuth who first gave him a tour of New York's nightclubs: "Demuth took me to Harlem for the first time, to Barron Wilkin's Cafe there in Harlem. Marshall's, another Negro night club, was at 53rd Street. It wasn't in Harlem. I believe that Florence's was located near Marshall's there on 53rd Street. It was fun to be with Demuth because he didn't care where he belonged or was in the social scale. He was not at all what you would call a climber."[42] Demuth painted a portrait of himself sitting with Duchamp at a Greenwich Village bar in the watercolor *At the Golden Swan* (fig. 29). Duchamp was more than just a drinking companion for Demuth, he was a major artistic influence. Although Demuth wrote Stieglitz that he thought Duchamp's *Large Glass* was the "great picture of our time," Kermit Champa rightly singles out *The Fountain* as crucial for Demuth's art.[43] Champa notes its "outlandish eroticism" and its "potential for stirring in a situation of unaccustomed isolation, erotic as well as scatological associations."[44] Yet he fails to draw a direct connection between Duchamp's urinal and Demuth's late watercolors of sailors urinating.

In Demuth's *Three Sailors Urinating* (fig. 44), urine is being aimed in the general direction of the viewer, and in *Two Men Urinating*, the viewer actually stands where the urinal should be. Marcel Duchamp turned a urinal into a work of art: Demuth converted his audience into a urinal. Like Duchamp's *Fountain*, Demuth's homosexual art needs to be understood in terms of the social mechanism of tolerance and repression.

For the most part, the shock of Demuth's art has been understood almost exclusively in terms of a generalized, puritanical audience rather than the worldly patrons, critics, artists, and associates who made up his social circle. One of the clichés of Demuth criticism is to see him as a decadent prisoner of an almost chaste provincial town, Lancaster. Barbara Haskell insists that Demuth's Lancaster "remained impervious to the psychic disjunctions that beset other nineteenth-century American cities as they joined the modern age."[45] An idyllic Lancaster provides the foil to Demuth's unnatural imagery. It implies that Demuth's representations of homosexuality were foreign to his hometown, even as his sexuality was somehow fundamentally un-Lancasterian. Yet with the exception of his illustrations, which were based on texts, Demuth stayed surprisingly close to experiences he had in his hometown. In his beautiful still lifes and flower studies, he depicted the fruits and vegetables that were available in Lancaster's farm markets and the flowers that he picked from his mother's garden. Betsy Fahlman has documented how closely most of Demuth's cityscapes, for all their seeming abstraction, conform to scenes that were within walking distance of his house in Lancaster.[46] Similarly, his pictures of vaudevillians and circus performers were probably modeled on performances he saw at a local theater. And Demuth made his most overtly homosexual paintings in Lancaster. Are his erotic watercolors, therefore, as far removed from Lancaster life as his biographers have suggested?

Haskell describes Lancaster as a city without psychic disjunctions, but like so many cities in the United States during the 1910s, its social problems were considered serious enough to merit a vice commission, established in 1913 to deal with prostitution and related criminal activity. The commission counted fifty-three "vice resorts" in the town, twenty-seven of which were "parlor houses" or brothels. Even homosexual prostitution was reported to the committee—though its agents thought it too terrible to write about in detail: "Considerable evidence (impossible to print) of the practice of perversion in Lancaster by inmates of houses, by street walkers, by charity girls, and by men perverts or 'fairies,' and degenerates, has been reported to the Committee."[47] The very existence of the report makes it clear that even Lancaster had its share of social problems. Indeed, given the different classes that made up Lancaster life—from the Amish farmers, who severely limited their contact with modern civilization, to the workers who ran the factories that Demuth painted, to the patrician families who owned some of those factories—how could it be otherwise?

Undoubtedly, Demuth's representation of homosexuality arose to some degree from a wish to flout exactly the kind of prudery that produced the vice-commission reports in Lancaster and across the country. But more profoundly, his literary illustrations and erotic watercolors were a coming to terms with his own social milieu—the elite who ran the local companies and controlled the newspapers. Members of such a class might go to church on Sunday and even support laws meant to uphold the morals of the poor, but these public duties did not keep them from leading a very different kind of life in private. Even in the provinces, a kind of sexual explicitness and a mockery of social mores, both usually associated with the avant-garde in New York and Paris, were permissible as long as they remained within the confines of a well-to-do patron's immediate circle. The coat of arms that I discussed earlier was a direct result of this private tolerance. Commissioned by J. F. and Blanca Steinman, owners of one of the major Lancaster newspapers, as a gift to the owners of the farmhouse, Demuth's coat of arms was actually a later addition to an existing mural that covered four walls in a ten-by-fifteen-foot room.[48]

The mural (fig. 73) tells the story, as one Lancaster resident put it, of an Amish woman "getting into trouble,"[49] or in franker terms, her seduction by a farmer, captioned with signposts displaying once more those infamous local town names—Bird-in-Hand, Intercourse, and Fertility. This sophisticated equivalent of the modern

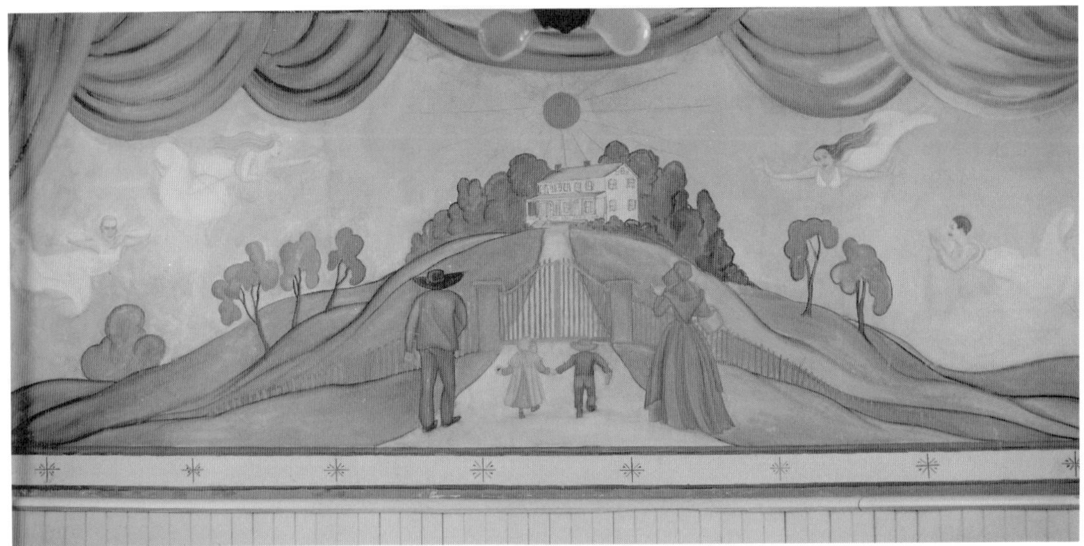

73. Thomas Farrar and Ellen Goldsborough, with additions by Charles Demuth, Henry McBride, George Biddle, and Adolphe Borie, *Mural,* 1930. Private collection.

tourist T-shirt emblazoned with the words "I've Been Through Intercourse" was painted largely by two friends of Demuth, Thomas Farrar and Ellen Goldsborough, with last-minute additions by the realist painters George Biddle and Adolphe Borie and the critic Henry McBride. The muralists painted their patrons as draglike angels (who would be quite at home at a Webster Hall masquerade) hovering prominently over the composition. Essential to the joke of the work is not only its affront to the religious principles of the Amish but also its spoofing of the public moral standards of establishment Lancaster—an establishment the Steinman newspaper represented. Certainly the obvious sexual content of the mural, produced for the amusement of wealthy patrons, forces us to revise the old chestnut of a Lancaster gentry deeply ingrained with a stern puritanism and horrified by any act of sin.

Demuth's painting *Welcome to Our City* (fig. 74) is perhaps a direct piece of sniping at the hypocrisy of the Lancaster ruling elite. The painting focuses on the

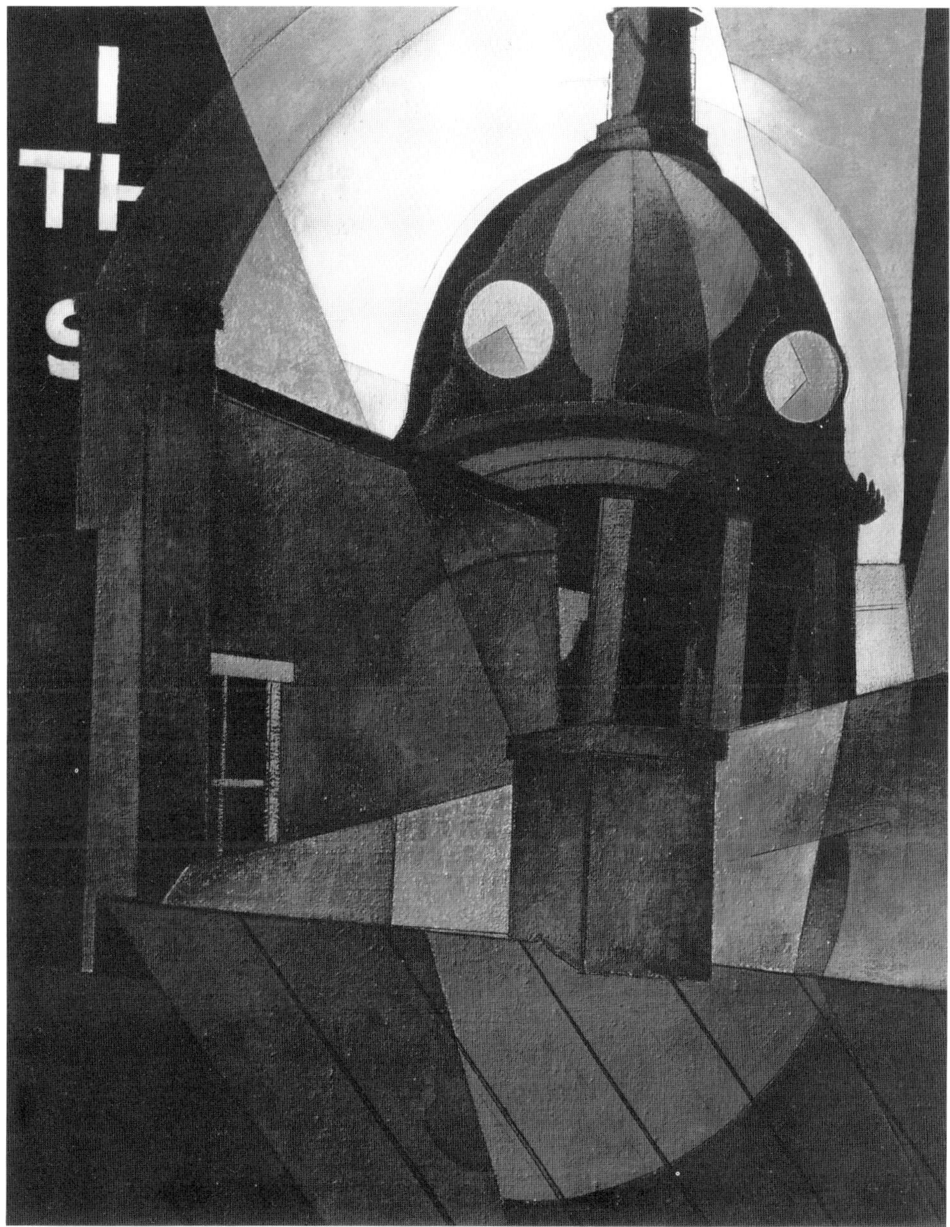

74. Charles Demuth, *Welcome to Our City,* oil on canvas, 24½ × 19⅜ in., 1921. Private collection.

dome of the Lancaster County Courthouse, the symbol of the very laws that force homosexuality underground, and of the government that his patrons, the Steinmans, controlled. To the left of the dome are the letters TIHS. The floating letters invite reassembly for possible ways they might add up: the most obvious solution is the word SHIT, which would act as a suitable counterpoint to the falsely chamber-of-commerce-like title. On one level this obscene word might be seen as Demuth raging against the prison of Lancaster's provincialism—the courthouse is, after all, a place for trying alleged criminals. But the painting, it seems to me, has a wider scope. Its subject is hypocrisy in general: the suspicion that Lancaster's "Welcome" may be no such thing. According to several interviews I conducted in Lancaster, town society in the period between the wars was a kind of mirror of Philadelphia's more-famous closed aristocracy. A few large families controlled the economy of the city as well as its social life. These families were extremely protective of their social position and disdainful of outsiders or of those not considered of the same social class. Demuth's family was a member of this social elite, so he knew how it functioned to keep out those who were considered undesirable. Just as Duchamp's scatology undermined the myth of the tolerant avant-garde, Demuth's SHIT questions the sincerity of the city and its supposed friendliness. His covert message brands Lancaster not so much for its puritanism (though this is part of its message) but for its hypocrisy. It attacks a politeness and gentility that, similar to the gridlike structure of vertical and horizontal lines in *Welcome to Our City,* regiments social interactions.

In much of this book, I have attempted to analyze the representation of marginalization—the placing of homosexuality on the edges of American society—in the red-light districts or on the waterfronts of the cities. Yet the marginal turns out to be about the center after all. Demuth's erotic work is not exclusively about the evils of New York City, which itself is often seen as outside the mainstream of American life, but also represents aspects of a fairly typical American town. Helen Henderson, an old friend of the artist, remembered running into Demuth on his way back to Lancaster. He told her about "a crusade against vice"—most likely a reference to the vice commission discussed above—and said that he was "going home to speak for vice."[50] The interesting point of this quote is that Demuth does not say he will be a carrier of vice to Lancaster, transferring it like a virus from decadent New York, Paris, or Berlin. Vice is already there, it is *home.* Demuth goes home to speak for it. Of course, his painting is his own particular speech. Rather than a speech aimed against Lancaster and against home, it is a speech *about* home, and home is where homosexuality lives.[51]

Returning from Paris in 1921, Demuth wrote Stieglitz that he was strangely "glad to be home": "At the moment I feel that I wish to grow fast—even to Lancaster. I am so tired,—maybe it is my health, but, I suspect it is more from hearing so often,—'I must go to Berlin, or, Rome, or Vienna, or, Florence, or,. the East, or, the South Seas,—I know there must be something there for *me.*' I so often wished at hearing them,—that some would, or all would go to hell. What work I do will be done here; terrible it is to work in this 'our land of the free.' "[52] Demuth decides that he will work in the United States, a place terrible for work because of its cultural backwardness. But for all his horror of American life, the United States is where he feels he belongs, and his art is as much about belonging *in difference* as it is about not belonging because of difference.

Demuth grows to Lancaster to the degree that he ceases to be like his old friend Marsden Hartley, a wanderer who searches in vain for a place conducive to art and love. Yet Hartley too ended up coming home. His late paintings share with Demuth's an attempt to place the homosexual experience within the sphere of the native. But where Demuth's late work is largely divided between public and private modes—between the sexually neutral and the homosexual—there is no such division in Hartley's art. The pictures in which Hartley expresses his desire for men—the paintings of the Mason sons and father, the lifeguards and wrestlers—are not done in a manner different from his other late paintings, such as the seascapes of Maine and Nova Scotia, the still lifes of objects found along the New England shore, and the late portraits of his heroes Abraham Lincoln and Albert Pinkham Ryder. Although he shared Demuth's sense of estrangement from American society, Hartley located that estrangement in a characteristically American landscape. And he expressed homosexual desire using the iconography of mainstream American faith.

Whereas Demuth's homosexual images expose a sexuality that lies beneath the surface of American life, Hartley tried to find a place for homosexuality out in the open. In the letter to Stieglitz quoted above, Demuth seems reconciled to the sterility and hypocrisy of Lancaster culture. He did not seek, or thought he would ever obtain, acceptance by his neighbors. He kept his homosexual fantasies largely private. But Hartley always dreamed of acceptance—not tolerance and the patronization it may involve, but love. The catalogue *Marsden Hartley in Nova Scotia* focuses on Hartley's search for family in his last years. It does so, however, at the expense of neutralizing the homosexual component in that search. It never comes to terms with the possibility that the family for which Hartley was searching might include a male lover. A subtext of the catalogue (and a basic assumption of much of society, then and today) is the idea that homosexuality and family are mutually exclusive terms. I think Hartley wanted a family, but one in which homosexuality would be accepted as a possible expression of love. This, too, would have been the power of the Christian model for Hartley—the idea of Christ and the twelve Apostles being a kind of family that did not follow the heterosexual model.

Michel Foucault thought that the hostility homosexuality provoked in society was due to the "common fear that gays will develop relationships that are intense and satisfying even though they do not at all conform to the ideas of relationship held by others. It is the prospect that gays will create as yet unforeseen kinds of relationships that many people cannot tolerate."[53] It seems to me that whatever the nature of Hartley's attachments to the Mason sons and their father (whether or not he had sex with Alty does not matter), he tries to construct in his late paintings and poetry exactly the kind of relationships Foucault suggests are so threatening.

In the poem *Cleophas and His Own* and the two paintings entitled *Fishermen's Last Supper* (fig. 75), Hartley gives us an image of familial love that is remote from the usual social norm. The family Hartley imagines is one that would unite him with two sons in a physical and emotional relationship, even as that relationship would be sanctioned by the embrace of the father and mother he had never had. Before the death of the two sons, he wrote of his intention to paint this wonderful, if unusual, family: "The table is long and narrow. I'm in the center, Donny right, Alty left, and sister on the other side—walls blue, furniture black—Mama always in black with white apron—boys and papa in overalls and dark and mystic looking."[54] Hartley

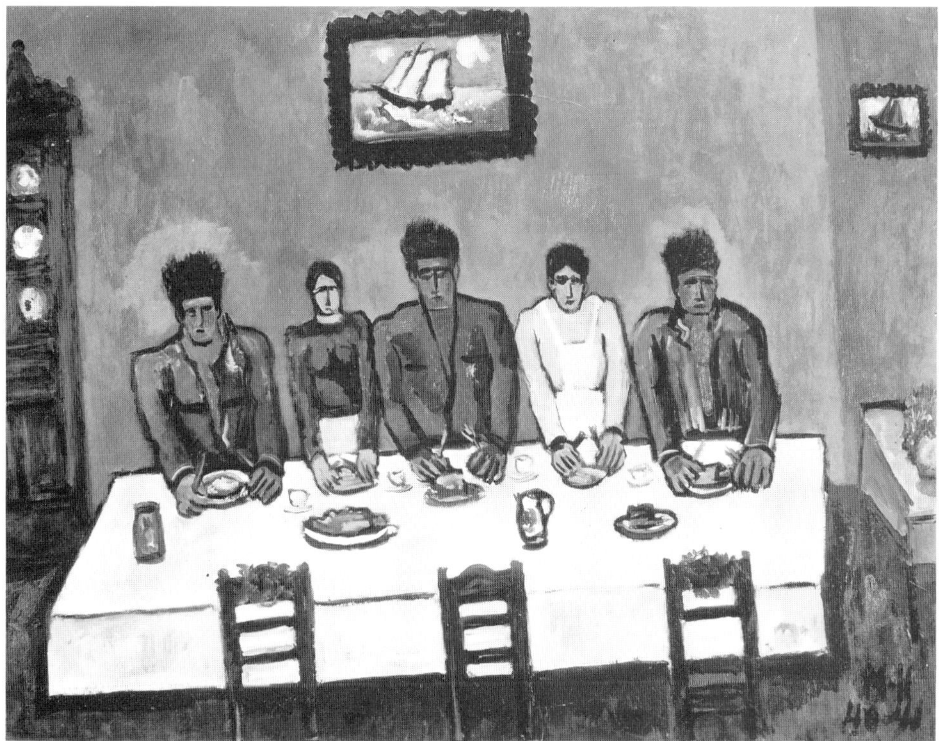

75. Marsden Hartley, *Fishermen's Last Supper,* oil on board, 29⅞ × 41 in., 1940–41. Collection of Mr. and Mrs. Roy R. Neuberger.

longed for the fixed, stable, supportive roles of a conventional family. But he also wanted that family to be transformed and extended to include the forbidden and the "marginal." Hartley was a family man, a lover of hierarchy: that was his pathos and his strength. But the family he came to need would never be complete without union with Alty in a kind of homosexual marriage. He wrote a friend a few years before he died: "[If] they had not been drowned I would have done what one of them asked me to do, to build a house and live in it with him, as he was such a dear even though he had spells of drinking hard, but even then he was more delightful."[55]

Notes

Introduction

1 Marcel Duchamp, "Interview with Marcel Duchamp at New York City, January 21, 1956," in Emily Farnham, "Charles Demuth: His Life, Psychology and Works" (Ph.D. diss., Ohio State University, 1959), 973.

2 Henry McBride, "An Underground Search for Higher Moralities," *New York Evening Sun,* 25 November 1917, 8–9.

3 Henry McBride, "American Society Exhibits," *New York Sun,* 20 May 1939; as quoted in Lincoln Kirstein, *Paul Cadmus* (San Francisco: Pomegranate, 1992), 41.

4 Jeffrey Weeks, "Discourse, Desire and Sexual Deviance: Some Problems in a History of Homosexuality," in *The Making of the Modern Homosexual,* ed. Kenneth Plummer (Totowa, N.J.: Barnes and Noble, 1981), 86.

5 Jeffrey Weeks, *Sex, Politics and Society: The Regulation of Sexuality since 1800* (New York: Longman, 1981), 97.

6 John W. Aldridge, *After the Lost Generation: A Critical Study of the Writers of Two Wars* (New York: McGraw-Hill, 1951), 101–02.

1 Who Is a Homosexual?

1 See, for example, Barbara Haskell's *Charles Demuth* (New York: Whitney Museum of American Art, 1987), 204–08. For the first nonhomophobic discussion of Demuth's erotic work, see Ray Gerard Koskovich, "A Gay Modernist: Homosexuality in the Life and Art of Charles Demuth," *Advocate* (25 June 1985): 50–52.

2 Michael Lynch, in an article in the newspaper *Body Politic,* was the first to introduce the issue of gay themes in the interpretation of the art of Marsden Hartley (Michael Lynch, "A Gay World After All: Marsden Hartley [1877–1943]," *Our Image: The Body Politic Review Supplement* 6 [December–January 1976–77]: 1–3). Barbara Haskell followed in 1980 with her catalogue for the Whitney Museum's Hartley retrospective (Barbara Haskell, *Marsden Hartley* [New York: Whitney Museum of American Art, 1980]).

3 Jeffrey Weeks in discussing the English law against "buggery," which dates back to the reign of Henry VIII, writes that the "law was directed against a series of sexual acts, not a particular type of *person,* although in practice most people prosecuted under the buggery laws were probably prosecuted for homosexual behavior (sodomy). It seems likely that homosexuality was regarded not as a

particular attribute of a certain type of person but as a potential in all sensual creatures. The prime task seems to have been protection of reproductive sex in marriage" (Jeffrey Weeks, *Sex, Politics and Society: The Regulation of Sexuality since 1800* [London: Longman, 1981], 99). For a further discussion of the history of English law dealing with sodomy—and therefore the bases for much American law as well—see H. Montgomery Hyde, *The Love That Dared Not Speak Its Name* (Boston: Little, Brown, 1970). Both Weeks and Hyde point out that sodomy was often used as a catchall to describe any sexual act that did not involve procreation. It is interesting to note that homosexuality per se was not forbidden by English law until 1885, and then only in an amendment to a bill that was otherwise concerned with protecting young women from prostitution (Hyde, 5).

4 See Michel Foucault, *The History of Sexuality,* vol. 1: *An Introduction,* trans. Robert Hurley (New York: Vintage, 1978).

5 G. Frank Lydston, "Sexual Perversion, Satyriasis, and Nymphomania," *Medical and Surgical Reporter* 61, no. 10 (November 1889): 253–58.

6 William Lee Howard, "Sexual Perversion in America," *American Journal of Dermatology and Genito-Urinary Diseases* 8, no. 1 (1904): 11.

7 George F. Shrady, "Perverted Sexual Instinct," *The Medical Record* 26 (19 July 1884): 70–71. I was directed to this article, as well as to most of the early American medical literature on homosexuality, by Jonathan Ned Katz, *Gay American History* (New York: Avon, 1976), and *Gay/Lesbian Almanac: A New Documentary* (New York: Harper and Row, 1983). Katz's pioneering work is an attempt to write a history of American male and female homosexuals by presenting in chronological order annotated excerpts from primary sources drawn from newspapers, journals, diaries, court transcripts, and books. Katz's books, along with Vern L. Bullough, W. Dover, Barret W. Elcano, James Kepner, *An Annotated Bibliography of Homosexuality* (New York: Garland Publishing, 1976), and William Parker, "Homosexuality in History, an Annotated Bibliography," in *Historical Perspectives on Homosexuality,* ed. Salvatore J. Licata and Robert P. Petersen, special issue of *Journal of Homosexuality* 6, nos. 1, 2 (Fall–Winter 1980–81): 191–210, were the starting point for my research in this chapter. Unless otherwise noted, when I quote from or discuss documents cited by Katz, I verified the information in the original source. For one of the first articles on medical discussions of homosexuality in late nineteenth-century America, see John Burnham, "Early References to Homosexual Communities in American Medical Writings," *Medical Aspects of Human Sexuality* 7, no. 8 (August 1973): 34–49, and Vern L. Bullough, *Sexual Variance in Society and History* (Chicago: University of Chicago Press, 1980).

8 Howard, "Sexual Perversion in America," 10.

9 See Phyllis Grosskurth, *Havelock Ellis: A Biography* (New York: Alfred Knopf, 1980), 184. According to Grosskurth, Ellis's *Studies in the Psychology of Sex* (New York: F. A. Davis, 1936), which included *Sexual Inversion,* was not published in England during Ellis's lifetime.

10 Ellis, *Sexual Inversion,* 87–88.

11 A. A. Brill, "Introduction," in *The Basic Writings of Sigmund Freud,* trans. and ed. A. A. Brill (New York: Modern Library, 1938), 3.

12 Steven Watson, *Strange Bedfellows: The First American Avant-Garde* (New York: Abbeville, 1991), 137.

13 A. A. Brill, "The Conception of Homosexuality," *Journal of the American Medical Association* 61, no. 5 (2 August 1913): 336. Brill was chief of the Clinic of Psychiatry at Columbia University when he wrote this article.

14 Ibid., 338.

15 Ibid.

16 Trigant Burrow, "The Genesis and Meaning of 'Homosexuality' and Its Relation to the Problem of Introverted Mental States," *Psychoanalytic Review* 4 (1917): 272.

17 Brill, "Conception of Homosexuality," 337.

18 Sigmund Freud, *Three Essays on the Theory of Sexuality,* trans. and ed. James Strachey (New York: Basic, 1975), 31.

19 Ibid., 10 n. 1.

20 George W. Henry, "Psychogenic and Constitutional Factors in Homosexuality: Their Relation to Personality Disorders," *Psychiatric Quarterly* 8 (1934): 264. Studies like Henry's represent a strong desire on the part of many of the American psychiatrists influenced by Freud to try and reach a compromise between those who argued for primarily somatic origins to perversion and the Freudian developmental position.

21 Edward J. Kempf, *Psychopathology* (St. Louis: C. V. Mosby, 1921), 477.

22 Ibid., 720.

23 Ibid., 724.

24 Mary Douglas, *Purity and Danger: An Analysis of Concepts of Pollution and Taboo* (London: Routledge and Kegan Paul, 1966), 96.

2 The Homosexual Point of View

1 Ellis, *Sexual Inversion,* vol. 2 of *Studies in the Psychology of Sex,* 173–90. Wayne Koestenbaum suggests in his *Double Talk: The Erotics of Male Literary Collaboration* (New York: Routledge, 1989) that Symonds's role in the collaboration has not been given enough significance. Indeed, Symonds initially proposed the idea of a book on homosexuality to Ellis, and in the ill-fated first edition, Ellis shared authorship with Symonds (Symonds's horrified family bought up almost every extant copy and had them burned, insisting, in addition, that Symonds's name be removed from subsequent editions). Koestenbaum would prefer that Symonds's name be returned to the title page, arguing that although Symonds died before the book was finished, his input was crucial to its final form. Yet because Ellis actually wrote *Sexual Inversion*—with the exception of the case histories—and because it was best known by the later versions that he alone revised, I shall follow (somewhat reluctantly) the practice of referring to him alone as the author of *Sexual Inversion.*

2 Steven Marcus, in his introduction to Freud's *Three Essays on the Theory of Sexuality,* points out that it was written on the basis of virtually no contact with homosexual patients: "What goes without saying, and what does not quite get said, is that in 1905 Freud had as yet had no direct psychoanalytic experience of homosexual patients or adults who practice some form of perverse sexual behavior." But Marcus continues, almost with admiration: "This lack of first hand empirical evidence appears to have been in no way a deterrent to Freud's theoretical inclinations and energies" (xxv).

3 Edward Carpenter, *Intermediate Sex: A Study of Some Transitional Types of Men and Women* (London: G. Allen and Unwin, 1908); reprinted in Edward Carpenter, *Selected Writings,* vol. 1: *Sex* (London: GMP Publishers, 1984), 211.

4 Edward Stevenson (Xavier Mayne, pseud.), *The Intersexes: A History of Similisexualism as a Problem in Social Life* (privately printed, 1908; reprint, New York: Arno Press, 1975), 16–17.

5 See George Chauncey, Jr., "Christian Brotherhood or Sexual Perversion? Homosexual Identities and the Construction of Sexual Boundaries in the World War One Era," *Journal of Social History* 19 (Winter 1985): 189–211.

6 Earl Lind, *Autobiography of an Andrögyne,* ed. Alfred W. Herzog (New York: The Medico-Legal Journal, 1918; reprint, New York: Arno Press, 1975), 8–9.

7 Stevenson, *The Intersexes,* 79.

8 Richard Weyand, "Interview with Richard Weyand at Lancaster, Pennsylvania, January 5–18, 1956," cited in Farnham, "Charles Demuth: His Life, Psychology, and Works," 927. Richard Weyand was the live-in lover of Robert Locher. It has been suggested that Demuth and Locher may have also been lovers.

9 Kermit Champa, "Charlie Was Like That," *Artforum* 12, no. 6 (March 1974): 55.

10 Milton Brown, *American Painting from the Armory Show to the Depression* (Princeton: Princeton University Press, 1972), 33.

11 Stevenson, *The Intersexes,* 438–39.

12 Ibid., 440.

13 F. K., " 'Report from America,' A Raid on the Lafayette Baths," from "Der Bericht aus America," *Blätter für Menshenrecht* 7, no. 5 (May 1929): 8–9, trans. James Streakley; cited by Jonathan Ned Katz, ed., *Gay/Lesbian Almanac: A New Documentary* (New York: Harper and Row), 453.

14 See *Sketch for Turkish Bath,* in *Selection of Watercolors and Drawings by Charles Demuth* (New York: Parke-Bernet, 1976), no. 8, which appears to be a study for the self-portrait. There is also an uncompleted version of the scene in the Yale University Art Gallery (fig. 42).

15 This is according to Richard Hopf, who told me that he was given the work by Larsen. Hopf later sold it to the Kennedy Galleries.

16 See Eunice Lipton, *Looking into Degas: Uneasy Images of Women and Modern Life* (Berkeley: University of California Press, 1987), and Charles Bernheimer, "Degas's Brothels: Voyeurism and Ideology," *Representations* 20 (Fall 1987): 158–86.

17 Barbara Haskell, *Charles Demuth* (New York: Whitney Museum of Art, 1987), 62.

18 *Eight O'Clock (Morning #2)* was exhibited at the Wadsworth Atheneum in the 1928 show "Loan Exhibition of Contemporary American Watercolors." Mrs. John D. Rockefeller purchased *Eight O'Clock (Morning #1)* directly from the artist. It was included in the 1938 Whitney Memorial Show. See Farnham, "His Life, Psychology and Works," 508–09 nn. 255 and 256.

19 Gerald Ferguson, *Marsden Hartley and Nova Scotia,* ed. Gerald Ferguson (Halifax, Nova Scotia: Mount Saint Vincent University Art Gallery, 1987), 15.

20 Charles Gardner, *The Doctor and the Devils: A Startling Expose of Municipal Corruption* (New York: Warren Publishing, 1894; reprint, New York: Vanguard Press, 1931), 21, 52.

21 Ellis, *Sexual Inversion,* 299.

22 "Bans CWA Picture as Insult to Navy," *New York Times,* 19 April 1934, 1.

23 *New York Times,* 18 April 1937, 1, 9.

24 Philip I. Eliasoph, "Paul Cadmus: Life and Work" (Ph.D. diss., State University of New York at Binghamton, 1975). See also his museum catalogue, *Paul Cadmus: Yesterday and Today* (Oxford, Ohio: Ohio Miami University, 1981). Although Eliasoph does not deal directly with the homosexual subtheme of this picture, I am indebted to his rehearsal of the events of the scandal and his bibliography of primary documents.

25 Thomas W. Sokolowski, *The Sailor, 1930–1945: The Image of an American Demigod* (Norfolk, Va.: Chrysler Museum, 1983).

26 Lincoln Kirstein, *Paul Cadmus* (New York: Pomegranate, 1992), 25.

27 For a discussion of the Newport scandal and its implications for the definition of homosexual subcultures, see Chauncey, "Christian Brotherhood or Sexual Perversion?" 189–211. Lawrence R. Murphy provides a simple

recounting of the events with little analysis in his "Cleaning Up Newport: The U.S. Navy's Persecution of Homosexuals After World War I," *Journal of American Culture* 7, no. 3 (11 February 1984): 57–64, and a far more detailed account in his *Perverts by Official Order: The Campaign Against Homosexuals by the United States Navy* (New York: Harrington Park Press, 1988).

28 *New York World-Telegram,* 19 April 1934, 1, 5.

29 *Newsweek,* 28 April 1934, 25.

30 *New York World-Telegram,* 19 April 1934, 1, 5.

31 Lewis Mumford, untitled column, *New Yorker* 13, no. 8 (10 April 1937): 66–67.

32 "Should Sailors Be Sissies?" editorial, *New York Daily News,* 20 April 1934, 37; cited in Eliasoph, "Paul Cadmus: Life and Work," 49.

3 Charles Demuth and "Some Unknown Thing"

1 As a condition of receiving permission to photograph the mural, I agreed to keep its location and present owners private.

2 Charles Demuth, "Across a Greco Is Written," *Creative Art* (29 September 1929): 629–34.

3 Marsden Hartley, "Farewell Charles," in *On Art,* ed. Gail R. Scott (New York: Horizon Press, 1982), 99. Originally printed in *New Caravan,* ed. Alfred Kreymborg, Lewis Mumford, and Paul Rosenfeld (New York: W. W. Norton, 1935), 552–62.

4 Charles Demuth, "The Voyage Was Almost Over," unpublished manuscript of a short story included in what Emily Farnham refers to as the Richard Weyand Scrapbook No. 1, 90–92. A transcript was first published in the appendix of Farnham's Ph.D. dissertation. See Farnham, "Charles Demuth: His Life, Psychology and Works," 925–28.

5 Pamela Edwards Allara, "The Watercolor Illustrations of Charles Demuth" (Ph.D. diss., Johns Hopkins University, 1970), 65.

6 Farnham, "Charles Demuth: His Life, Psychology and Works," 951–58.

7 George Biddle, "Demuth Questionnaire, with the Answers Given by George Biddle," in Farnham, "Charles Demuth: His Life, Psychology and Works," 951–52.

8 William Carlos Williams, "Interview with William Carlos Williams at Rutherford, New Jersey, 26 Jan. 1956," in Farnham, "Charles Demuth: His Life, Psychology and Works," 990.

9 Stuart Davis, "Interview with Stuart Davis at New York City, 20 Jan. 1956," in Farnham, "Charles Demuth: His Life, Psychology and Works," 971.

10 Barbara Haskell, *Charles Demuth* (New York: Whitney Museum of American Art, 1987), 24–25.

11 Robert Locher was a well-known interior designer and illustrator in the 1930s. For a short biography, see Betsy Fahlman, "Modern as Metal and Mirror: The Work of Robert Evans Locher," *Arts Magazine* 59, no. 8 (April 1985): 108–13.

12 Charles Demuth, letter to Alfred Stieglitz, 12 October 1930, Beinecke Library, Yale University, New Haven, Ct.; cited in Haskell, *Charles Demuth,* 204.

13 Charles Daniel, "Interview with Charles Daniel at New York City, January 27, 1956," in Farnham, "Charles Demuth: His Life, Psychology and Works," 990–91.

14 Susan Watts Street, "Interview with Susan Watts Street at New York City, 21 January 1956," in Farnham, "Charles Demuth: His Life, Psychology and Works," 975.

15 Hartley, "Farewell Charles," 100.

16 Charles Demuth, "Confessions: Replies to a Questionnaire," *Little Review* 12, no. 2 (May 1929): 30–31.

17 Hartley, "Farewell Charles," 93–94.

18 Charles Demuth, *"You Must Come Over," A Painting: A Play,* from the so-called Weyand scrapbook; reprinted in Haskell, *Charles Demuth,* 41–42, and in Farnham, "Charles Demuth: His Life, Psychology and Works," 929–31.

19 In arguing with the reading of Demuth's art as "fin de siècle" or "decadent," I do not mean to acquiesce in a one-dimensional interpretation of Wilde's and Huysmans's art. The term *decadent* does not convey the complexity of their writings—for example, Wilde's socialism or Huysmans's naturalism and later religious conversion—nor does it acknowledge the modernism of many of their themes.

20 Kermit Champa, " 'Charlie Was Like That,' " *Artforum* 12, no. 6 (March 1974): 55.

21 Haskell, *Charles Demuth,* 182.

22 Paul Rosenfeld, "American Painting," *Dial* 71, no. 6 (December 1921): 662–63.

23 Hartley, "Farewell Charles," 101.

24 Until recently *God* was supposed to be the creation of Morton Schamberg with perhaps the assistance of Baroness Freytag-Loringhoven. Robert Reiss contests that attribution, hypothesizing that Freytag-Loringhoven may have actually constructed the sculpture and that Schamberg only photographed it. See Robert Reiss, " 'My Baroness': Elsa von Freytag-Loringhoven," in *New York Dada,* ed. Rudolf E. Kuenzli (New York: Willis Locker and Owens, 1986), 88.

25 For a short discussion of these cases, see Vern Bullough, *Sexual Variance in Society and History* (Chicago: University of Chicago Press, 1980), 573–78. Bullough writes that although the United States did not have equivalent scandals, "Americans were well informed about what was taking place in England and Europe, and American laws about sex were modeled on those of England" (278).

26 Gide writes: "Oh, victims! As many victims as you like—but not martyrs. They all denied—they always will deny." A few sentences later he adds: "Strange! we have the courage of our opinions, but never of our behavior. We're quite willing to suffer, but not to be disgraced." André Gide, *Corydon,* trans. Richard Howard (New York: Farrar, Straus, and Giroux, 1983), 8.

27 Edward Stevenson, *The Intersexes: A History of Similisexualism as a Problem in Social Life* (privately printed, 1908; reprint, New York: Arno Press, 1975), 478.

28 Davis, cited in Farnham, "Charles Demuth: His Life, Psychology and Works," 972.

4 Illustrating Difference

1 Henry McBride, "Notes and Comments in the World of Art: Charles Demuth and Edward Fiske," *New York Sun,* 3 December 1916, sec. 5, p. 12.

2 Henry James, *The Golden Bowl* (1905; reprint, London: Macmillan, 1923), x; cited and discussed by John L. Sweeney in "The Demuth Pictures," *The Kenyon Review* 5, no. 4 (Autumn 1943): 522–32.

3 Emile Zola, *L'assommoir,* in *The Masterpieces of Emile Zola,* trans. Arthur Symons (London: Lutetian Society, n.d.), vol. 2, p. 56. "Le visage de Nana apparut à la porte vitrée du cabinet, derrière un carreau. La petite venait de se réveiller et de se lever doucement, en chemise, pâle de sommeil. Elle regarda son père roulé dans son vomissement; puis, la figure collée contre la vitre, elle resta là, à attendre que le jupon de sa mère eût dis-

paru chez l'autre homme, en face. Elle était toute grave. Elle avait de grands yeux d'enfant vicieuse, allumés d'une curiosité sensuelle" (Emile Zola, *L'assommoir,* in *Oeuvres complètes* [Paris: Cercle de Livre Précieux, 1966], 812).

4 Pamela Edwards Allara, "The Watercolor Illustrations of Charles Demuth" (Ph.D. diss., Johns Hopkins University, 1970), 108.

5 Zola, *L'assommoir,* trans. Arthur Symons, 60. "Ce qu'il y a de plus dégoûtant, c'est que Nana aurait pu entendre. . . . Elle a été agitée toute la nuit, elle qui d'habitude dort à poings fermés; elle sautait, elle se retournait, comme s'il y avait eu de la braise dans son lit" (Zola, *L'assommoir,* 814).

6 T. J. Clark has suggested to me an alternative reading in which the phallus and lampshade present Nana as already penetrated. In either interpretation, Nana can be seen as appropriating the phallus.

7 In my article " 'Some Unknown Thing': The Illustrations of Charles Demuth," I wrongly assumed that the kneeling figure in the illustration was Georges. Actually, as Emily Farnham points out ("Charles Demuth: His Life, Psychology and Works," 489 n. 206), the figure is the maid.

8 Emile Zola, *Nana,* trans. George Holden (Baltimore: Penguin, 1985), 425. "Ce fut tout. Nana s'était assise, dans sa stupeur, encore gantée et son chapeau sur la tête. L'hôtel retombait à un silence lourd, la voiture venait de partir; et elle demeurait immobile, n'ayant pas une idée, la tête bourdonnante de cette histoire"; and "Depuis un instant, la femme de chambre, qui avait pris dans le cabinet une serviette et une cuvette d'eau, frottait le tapis pour enlever une tache de sang, pendant que c'était frais" (Emile Zola, *Nana* [Paris: Livre de Poche, 1984], 422).

9 Demuth did two versions of this illustration. The so-called second version (it is impossible to tell in which order Demuth did them) is in the Museum of Fine Arts, Boston. The Boston picture includes Muffat's entrance on the scene.

10 For an illustration, see Barbara Haskell, *Charles Demuth* (New York: Whitney Museum of American Art, 1987), fig. 36, p. 96.

11 Zola, *Nana,* trans. George Holden, 470. "Nana restait seule, la face en l'air, dans la clarté de la bougie. C'était un charnier, un tas d'humeur et de sang, une pelletée de chair corrompue. . . . Toute une croûte rougeâtre partait d'une joue, envahissait la bouche, qu'elle tirait dans un rire abominable. Et, sur ce masque horrible et grotesque du néant, les cheveux, les beaux cheveux, gardant leur flambée de soleil, coulaient en un ruissellement d'or. Vénus se décomposait" (Zola, *Nana,* 467).

12 Honoré de Balzac, "The Girl with the Golden Eyes," in *The Thirteen,* trans. Ellen Marriage (Boston: Dana Estes, 1901), 354. "De Marsay grimpa lestement l'escalier qu'il connaissait et reconnut le chemin du boudoir. Quand il en ouvrit la porte, il eut le frissonnement involontaire que cause à l'homme le plus déterminé la vue du sang répandu. Le spectacle qui s'offrit à ses regards eut d'ailleurs pour lui plus d'une cause d'étonnement. La marquise était femme"; and "expirait noyée dans le sang" (Honoré de Balzac, "La fille aux yeux d'or," in *Histoire des treize* [Paris: Gallimard, 1951], 320).

13 Demuth's censoring of the horror of Balzac's description coupled with its stylistic closeness to the *Nana* series is probably responsible for Andrew Ritchie's failure to connect "The Girl with the Golden Eyes" to the proper text: he called it *Satin's Frenzy* in his Museum of Modern Art catalogue (*Charles Demuth* [New York: The Museum of Modern Art, 1950]). Pamela Edwards Allara correctly connected the image to what was previously thought to be a lost illustration; see Allara, "The Watercolor Illustrations of Charles Demuth," 109.

14 Charles Demuth supposedly told the story to Helen Henderson. She in turn recorded it in her memoirs of her friend, which were preserved in the Weyand Scrapbooks; one of the scrapbooks, which is mostly made up

of photographs of Demuth's works, has surfaced in the Beinecke Library at Yale University. See Farnham, "Charles Demuth: His Life, Psychology and Works," 56.

15 Henry James, "The Turn of the Screw," in *The Turn of the Screw and Other Short Stories* (New York: New American Library, 1962), 400.

16 Ibid., 295, 403.

17 Allara, "The Watercolor Illustrations of Charles Demuth," 81.

18 For an overview of psychoanalytic theory on homosexuality, see Ronald Bayer, *Homosexuality and American Psychiatry: The Politics of Diagnosis* (New York: Basic, 1981).

19 Because of estate litigations over its ownership, I was not able to obtain permission to illustrate *The Animal Tamer Presents Lulu*. For an illustration, see my "'Some Unknown Thing': The Illustrations of Charles Demuth," *Arts Magazine* 61, no. 4 (December 1986), fig. 8, p. 20.

20 The Lulu series consists of illustrations for two sequential plays by Wedekind, *Earth Spirit* and *Pandora's Box*, which follow the career of Lulu and her unhappy suitors. I quote in English here because it is clear that Demuth used the highly anglicized translation of Samuel A. Eliot, Jr., first published in *The Glebe* in 1914 and 1918. It is the only one that includes the name "Charlie." See Allara, "The Watercolor Illustrations of Charles Demuth," 133.

21 Henry James, "The Beast in the Jungle," in *The Turn of the Screw and Other Short Stories* (New York: New American Library, 1962), 413.

22 There is a letter in the archives of the Whitney Museum of American Art from Frank Osborn, who owned the illustration before it went into the collection of the Philadelphia Museum of Art. Demuth told Osborn that the figure was meant to be a portrait of Henry James (Demuth claimed not to know at the time that James was overweight). Frank Osborn, letter to Herman More, Whitney Museum of American Art Archives, New York, as cited in Haskell, *Charles Demuth,* 110 n. 23.

23 James, "The Beast in the Jungle," 417.

24 Eve Kosofsky Sedgwick, "The Beast in the Closet: James and the Writing of Homosexual Panic," *Sex, Politics, and Science in the Nineteenth-Century Novel,* ed. Bernard Yeazell (Baltimore: Johns Hopkins University Press, 1986), 174.

25 James, "The Beast in the Jungle," 409.

26 Ibid., 450.

27 Ibid., 448.

28 Walter Pater, "A Prince of Court Painters," in *Imaginary Portraits,* ed. William E. Buckley (New York: Macmillan, 1887), 35.

29 Ibid., 26.

30 Ibid., 42.

31 Haskell, *Charles Demuth,* 111.

32 Allara, "The Watercolor Illustrations of Charles Demuth," 131.

33 Watteau's fascination with the shoe in Demuth's illustration seems to call for a psychoanalytic interpretation, particularly Freud's theory of fetishism. For Freud the fetish object becomes a replacement for the female genitals while "remain[ing] a token of triumph over the threat of castration and a safeguard against it; it also saves the fetishist from being a homosexual by endowing women with the attribute which makes them acceptable as sexual objects." See Sigmund Freud, "Fetishism (1927)," in *Collected Papers,* ed. James Strachey (New York: Basic, 1959), 200.

34 Pater, "A Prince of Court Painters," 32.

35 Ibid., 48.

5 Demuth's Erotic Watercolors

1 Marsden Hartley, "Farewell Charles," in *On Art,* ed. Gail R. Scott (New York: Horizon Press, 1982), 98.

2 Ibid., 94.

3 Perhaps "openly" should be qualified. Stein did not announce to the world that she and Toklas were lovers—it was simply understood that their relationship was a marriage.

4 The first edition, published in 1911, included only a bit more than the first two dialogues. Gide greatly expanded the book for its general publication in 1925. See Richard Howard, "Translator's Note," in André Gide, *Corydon,* trans. Richard Howard (New York: Farrar, Straus, and Giroux, 1983).

5 Fedja Anzelewsky, *Dürer: His Art and Life,* trans. Helde Grieve (New York: Alpine Fine Arts, 1980), 58.

6 Erwin Panofsky, *The Life and Art of Albrecht Dürer* (Princeton: Princeton University Press, 1955), 50.

7 For an illustration, see Henry Adams, *The Beal Collection of Watercolors by Charles Demuth* (Pittsburgh: Museum of Art, Carnegie Institute, 1983), fig. 3, p. 23.

8 I have seen only a fuzzy photocopy of this work, which Barbara Haskell provided me at the time of the Whitney retrospective. Emily Farnham describes the painting in her catalogue of works from the Weyand Estate whose locations are unknown: "On left, nude male figure seated on bench. Before him toward right, standing figure of man with towel wrapped around his torso. Second figure is turning faucet located in upper right. First figure has two heart shapes and a star tattooed on his right arm" (Farnham, "Charles Demuth: His Life, Psychology and Works," 686 n. 721).

9 Alvord L. Eiseman, *Charles Demuth* (New York: Watson-Guptill, 1982), pl. 13, p. 47.

10 According to Emily Farnham, the 1917 version of *Dancing Sailors* was included in this exhibition, entitled *Paintings by Nineteen Living Americans* (New York: Museum of Modern Art, 1929). See Farnham, "Charles Demuth: His Life, Psychology and Works," 507 n. 253.

11 David Copp and Susan Wendell, eds., *Pornography and Censorship* (Buffalo, N.Y.: Prometheus, 1983), 196. The committee was appointed in 1977 by the British Government to review the various laws concerning obscenity.

12 David Copp, "Pornography and Censorship: An Introductory Essay," in *Pornography and Censorship,* ed. Copp and Wendell, 18. Obviously, both these definitions leave enormous leeway for confusion and debate in regard to reconstructing intentions and determining whether the standards of a culture have been violated by a given depiction.

13 Havelock Ellis, *Sexual Inversion,* vol. 2 of *Studies in the Psychology of Sex* (New York: F. A. Davis, 1936), 140.

14 John Addington Symonds, *The Memoirs of John Addington Symonds: The Secret Homosexual Life of a Nineteenth-Century Man of Letters,* ed. Phyllis Grossworth (New York: Random House, 1984), 21, 62.

15 Ellis, *Sexual Inversion,* 148–49.

16 Havelock Ellis, *My Life: An Autobiography of Havelock Ellis* (Boston: Houghton Mifflin, 1939), 84.

17 Havelock Ellis, *Erotic Symbolism,* vol. 3 of *Studies in the Psychology of Sex,* book 1 (New York: Random House, 1936), 59.

18 Ellis, *My Life,* 84.

19 Ellis, *Erotic Symbolism,* 70.

20 New York, *Report of Mayor's Committee for Study of Sex Offenses* (New York: City of New York, c. 1940), 66.

21 The New York City statute of 1915 reads: "A person who carnally knows in any manner any animal or bird; or carnally knows any male or female person by the anus or by or with the mouth; or voluntarily submits to

such carnal knowledge; or attempts sexual intercourse with a dead body is guilty of sodomy and is punishable with imprisonment for not more than twenty years. Any sexual penetration, however slight, is sufficient to complete the crime specified in the last section" (Arthur B. Spingarn, *Laws Relating to Sex Morality in New York City* [New York: Century, 1915], 10). As with many of the sodomy laws in the United States, the definition of sodomy is wide-ranging; acts common among heterosexuals are included with bestiality and necrophilia, two forms of perversion that are not associated with homosexuality. The original law is directed not against homosexuality in itself but against all forms of sexual relationships that are not part of procreation.

22 For a sociological study of the uses of bathrooms for homosexual sex, see Laud Humphreys, *Tearoom Trade: Impersonal Sex in Public Places* (Chicago: Aldine, 1970). Humphreys made his study in the 1960s but includes some history of the phenomenon; some of his general observations about the popularity of this form of public sex are, I think, valid for an earlier period.

23 James O'Higgins, "Sexual Choice, Sexual Act: An Interview with Michel Foucault," *Salmagundi* 58–59 (Fall–Winter 1983): 18–19.

6 Numbering the Dead

1 Timothy Anglin Burgard has provided the first extensive discussion of this drawing in "Charles Demuth's *Longhi on Broadway:* Homage to Eugene O'Neill," *Arts Magazine* 58, no. 5 (January 1984): 110–13. Burgard calls the anthurium a calla lily. Yet the flower of the calla lily does not open flat as in the Demuth sketch, nor is its long stamen as visible. Furthermore, Demuth writes the word "red" on the flower, and calla lilies are limited to white, yellow, and pink varieties.

2 The sexual allusions of his still lifes were not lost on Hartley's contemporaries. Indeed, in 1921 one of Hartley's strongest supporters, Paul Rosenfeld, noticed that "a cold and ferocious sensuality seeks to satisfy itself in the still lifes" (Paul Rosenfeld, "American Painting," *Dial* 71 [December 1921]: 657). And in 1924 Rosenfeld described Hartley's paintings in terms of a man striving to exert sexual dominance: "Large phallic shapes brandish themselves over the spectator as heavy crucifixi might be brandished, in all dignity and still with indubitable fanaticism, by zealous priests over dying sinners or burning heretics. Great full-sailed flaunting shapes take possession, with a certain insolence not entirely obliterated by grace, of the entire situation" (Paul Rosenfeld, *Port of New York: Essays on Fourteen American Moderns* [New York: Harcourt, Brace, 1924; reprint, Urbana: University of Illinois Press, 1961], 91).

3 Ronald Paulson, "Marsden Hartley's Search for the Father(land)," in *Marsden Hartley and Nova Scotia,* ed. Gerald Ferguson (Halifax, Nova Scotia: Mount Saint Vincent University Art Gallery, 1987), 19.

4 Barbara Haskell, *Marsden Hartley* (New York: Whitney Museum of American Art, 1980), 18.

5 Robin Jaffe Frank, "Study for Poster Portrait: Marsden Hartley," lecture given at the Whitney Museum of American Art Symposium, New York City, 29 April 1991.

6 According to Robert Burlingame, "Hartley seldom referred to any writing project more often than he did to *Letters Never Sent*" (Robert Northcutt Burlingame, "Marsden Hartley: A Study of His Life and Creative Achievement" [Ph.D. diss., Brown University, 1953], 276). Hartley first mentioned the letters as early as 1917, and the project was still not finished at his death.

7 Marsden Hartley, "Farewell Charles," in *On Art,* ed. Gail R. Scott (New York: Horizon Press, 1982), 91.

8 For a biography of Marsden Hartley, see Townsend Ludington, *Marsden Hartley: The Biography of an American*

Artist (Boston: Little, Brown, 1992). The author generously shared with me an early draft of his chapter on Hartley and homosexuality.

9 Marsden Hartley, "Somehow a Past," in *A Life in the Arts,* ed. Gail R. Scott, typescript, 220–23. Hartley's original manuscript is in the Beinecke Library, Yale University, New Haven, Conn. Gail R. Scott, who edited the volume of Hartley's essays, entitled *On Art,* as well as *The Collected Poems of Marsden Hartley,* graciously provided me with a copy of the unpublished manuscript of her second volume of Hartley papers.

10 In another manuscript, Hartley writes that he has "little or no recollection" of his mother: "I see the face labored with agonies of last illness—but I hear no voice and see no gesture" (Marsden Hartley, "Prologue to Imaginative Living," in *A Life in the Arts,* ed. Scott, 335).

11 Hartley, "Somehow a Past," 224.

12 William Carlos Williams, *The Autobiography of William Carlos Williams* (New York: Random House, 1951), 173.

13 Marsden Hartley, letter to Mabel Dodge Luhan, 1916, Beinecke Library, Yale University. He seemed to think so highly of these words that he kept a carbon of the letter.

14 Marsden Hartley, letter to Robert McAlmon, 21 September 1942, Beinecke Library, Yale University.

15 Marsden Hartley, letter to Robert McAlmon, 3 October 1942, Beinecke Library, Yale University.

16 Marsden Hartley, letter to Robert McAlmon, 31 August 1942, Beinecke Library, Yale University.

17 Alfred Kreymborg, *Troubadour* (New York: Sagamore Press, 1957), 84–85.

18 "Pub Debs Make Society Bow," *New York Dada* (1921, only issue): 3.

19 Marsden Hartley, letter to Madelaine Rice, 11 March 1922, Archives of American Art, Smithsonian Institution, Washington, D.C.

20 Marsden Hartley, "The Business of Poetry," in *A Life in the Arts,* ed. Scott, 82–83.

21 Marsden Hartley, letter to Alfred Stieglitz, 15 March 1915, Beinecke Library, Yale University.

22 Marsden Hartley, letter to Alfred Stieglitz, received 12 July 1912, Beinecke Library, Yale University.

23 Andrew Field, *Djuna: The Formidable Miss Barnes* (Austin: University of Texas Press, 1985), 61.

24 Ludington does not believe what he calls the "minor legend" of an affair between Barnes and Hartley. Ludington, *Marsden Hartley,* 36–37.

25 Marsden Hartley, letter to Leon Tebbetts, 27 October 1942, Beinecke Library, Yale University.

26 Hartley, letter to Alfred Stieglitz, 15 March 1915.

27 Marsden Hartley, letter to Arnold Rönnebeck, 8 November 1936, Beinecke Library, Yale University.

28 Compare the "commoner elements" of his letter to Mabel Dodge Luhan. The way sex and class intersect so thoughtlessly in Hartley's discourse is itself significant.

29 Marsden Hartley, "The Element of Absolutism in Leonardo's Drawings," in *On Art,* ed. Scott, 292, 288, 290, 291.

30 Paul Valéry, "Introduction to the Method of Leonardo da Vinci," in *Variety,* trans. Malcolm Cowley (New York: Harcourt, Brace, 1927), 179–282.

31 Marsden Hartley, letter to Shaemus O'Sheel, 25 December 1906, Beinecke Library, Yale University.

32 Both Hartley's and Freud's essays center on Leonardo's *Madonna and Child with St. Anne* (Hartley emphasizes the London cartoon, whereas Freud discusses both the cartoon and the painting in the Louvre). Another indication that Hartley knew of Freud's essay is the phrase "if he was not the complete man psychologically, he was the complete man intellectually," which suggests that Hartley was at least aware that Leonardo's homosexuality was the subject of psychoanalytic interest. Finally, the two essays share a view of Leonardo as detached from interpersonal relationships and sexuality. The passages of Hartley's I quoted above, in which

Renaissance sensuality is opposed to Leonardo's asceticism, echo Freud's words: "In an age which saw a struggle between sensuality without restraint and gloomy asceticism, Leonardo represented the cool repudiation of sexuality." And later Freud adds: "The stormy passions of a nature that inspires and consumes, passions in which other men have enjoyed their richest experience, appear not to have touched him" (Sigmund Freud, *Leonardo da Vinci and a Memory of His Childhood* [1910; reprint, New York: Norton, 1964], 25).

33 Freud, *Leonardo da Vinci,* 49–50. Freud is careful to warn that not all homosexuality can be attributed to the absence of the father in the early stages of childhood: "What is for practical reasons called homosexuality may arise from a whole variety of psychosexual inhibitory processes; the particular process we have singled out is perhaps only one among many, and is perhaps related to only one type of 'homosexuality' " (51).

34 Ibid., 30–31, 51–52.

35 Of the name Edmund he wrote, "I should have I think never been proud of this name as it was that of an uncle who appears vaguer to me in vision than my father but by the aid of photography I recognize a handsome man" (Hartley, "Prologue to Imaginative Living," in *A Life in the Arts,* ed. Scott, 335).

36 Haskell, *Marsden Hartley,* 12.

37 Freud, *Leonardo da Vinci,* 64 n. 1.

38 Hartley, "The Element of Absolutism in Leonardo's Drawings," in *On Art,* ed. Scott, 286.

39 Walter Pater, "Leonardo da Vinci, Homo Minister et Interpres Naturae," in *Selected Writings of Walter Pater,* ed. Harold Bloom (New York: Columbia University Press, 1974), 46.

40 For a discussion of Hartley's working habits see Scott, *Marsden Hartley,* 149–55.

41 Kreymborg, *Troubadour,* 84–85.

42 As quoted in Elizabeth McCausland, "The Return of the Native: Marsden Hartley," *Art in America* 40, no. 2 (Spring 1952): 74.

43 Marsden Hartley claimed to have done pictures of two of Whitman's houses—the house on 328 Mickle Street, which I discuss, and the one on Steven Street (Marsden Hartley, "Peter Doyle," handwritten manuscript, n.p., Beinecke Library, Yale University). Haskell claims that the Mickle Street painting is the only work of Hartley's extant from this period (Haskell, *Marsden Hartley,* 12).

44 Bryan Jay Wolf suggested this idea to me.

45 Hartley, "Peter Doyle," n.p.

46 Burlingame, "Marsden Hartley," 14. Traubel gave Hartley a letter from Whitman (Haskell, *Marsden Hartley,* 138 n. 23).

47 Robert K. Martin, *The Homosexual Tradition in American Poetry* (Austin: University of Texas Press, 1979), 3.

48 John Addington Symonds, *The Memoirs of John Addington Symonds: The Secret Homosexual Life of a Leading Nineteenth-Century Man of Letters,* ed. Phyllis Grosskurth (New York: Random House, 1984), 246–47.

49 Ibid., 20. Symonds asked Whitman whether his conception of "comradeship" included "the possible intrusion of those semi-sexual emotions and actions which no doubt do occur between men." Whitman replied with a claim that has never been substantiated: "Tho' always unmarried" he "had six children" (Justin Kaplan, *Walt Whitman* [New York: Simon and Schuster, 1980], 47).

50 William Sloan Kennedy, "Whitman's Letters to Peter Doyle," *The Conservator* 8, no. 4 (June 1897): 60–61. Elsewhere articles in *The Conservator* tried to determine what Whitman's relationship with women was, debating the merits of Whitman's claim that he had an affair in New Orleans and fathered six children. Laurens Maynard decided that despite the celebration of the "comradeship of man with man" of *Calamus,* Whitman also glorified the love of men for women. Yet John Burroughs claimed in an interview that in "the thirty

years of his intimate acquaintance with Whitman there were no entanglements, or suspicion of any such, with women, so far as he knew." He concluded that Whitman "in his private social character" was "more a man's man than a woman's man" (John Burroughs, "Walt Whitman and the Younger Writers," *The Conservator* 7, no. 5 [July 1896]: 70–71).

51 Hartley, "Peter Doyle," n.p.

52 Walt Whitman, "In Paths Untrodden," *Calamus,* in *Leaves of Grass,* ed. Gay Wilson Allen (New York: New American Library, 1958), 112.

53 Walt Whitman, "We Two Boys Together Clinging," *Calamus,* 124.

54 Walt Whitman, "To the East and To the West," *Calamus,* 126.

55 Kennedy writes that "in the Doyle letters the wistful, yearning Christ-love, passionate as that of mother for child or man for woman, takes us into still deeper and more sacred recesses of the soul" (Kennedy, "Whitman's Letters to Peter Doyle," 61).

56 Marsden Hartley, letter to Seumas (later Sheamus) O'Sheel, postmarked 19 October 1908, Beinecke Library, Yale University. Green Acre was an artistic and philosophical retreat and school of Baha'i faith founded by Sarah Farmer in Eliot, Maine. Hartley was a guest of Mosher there during the summer of 1907 (Haskell, *Marsden Hartley,* 13).

57 Marsden Hartley, "To Horace Traubel," postmarked 10 February 1907, in Marsden Hartley and Horace Traubel, *Hearts Gate: Letters Between Marsden Hartley and Horace Traubel, 1906–1915,* ed. William Innes Homer (Highlands, N.C.: Jargon Society, 1982), 25.

58 Marsden Hartley, "To Horace Traubel," postmarked 2 September 1907, *Hearts Gate,* 41.

59 Horace Traubel, "To Marsden Hartley," 3 September 1907, *Hearts Gate,* 42.

60 Marsden Hartley, letter to Anne Traubel, postmarked 21 April 1911, *Heart's Gate,* 78.

61 Marsden Hartley, letter to Franz Marc, no date, probably 26 July 1913; letter courtesy of Thomas Gaehtgens.

62 Marsden Hartley, "Whitman and Cézanne," in *Adventures in the Arts: Informal Chapters on Painters, Vaudeville and Poets* (New York: Boni, Liveright, 1921; reprint, New York: Hacker, 1972), 30–41.

63 Hartley, "The Business of Poetry," in *A Life in the Arts,* ed. Scott, 82–83.

7 German Warriors

1 Hartley, "Somehow a Past," in *A Life in the Arts,* ed. Gail R. Scott, typescript, 257.

2 Hartley, "Farewell, Charles," in *On Art,* ed. Gail R. Scott (New York: Horizon Press, 1982), 95.

3 Marsden Hartley, letter to Alfred Stieglitz, February 1913, Beinecke Library, Yale University, New Haven, Ct.

4 Hartley, "Somehow a Past," 260.

5 Marsden Hartley, letter to Alfred Stieglitz (typescript copy), 3 November 1913, Beinecke Library, Yale University.

6 Marsden Hartley, letter to Alfred Stieglitz, February 1913, Beinecke Library, Yale University.

7 Arnold Rönnebeck, letter to Duncan Phillips, no date (after March 1944), Beinecke Library, Yale University.

8 Barbara Haskell, *Marsden Hartley* (New York: Whitney Museum of American Art, 1980), 31.

9 James D. Steakley, *The Homosexual Emancipation Movement* (New York: Arno Press, 1975), 27.

10 Hartley, "Somehow a Past," 264.

11 Gertrude Stein, *Autobiography of Alice B. Toklas* (New York: Vintage, 1961), 101–02.

12 See the discussion of this caricature as well as of Hartley's relationship to Marc and Kandinsky in Gail Levin, "Marsden Hartley and the European Avant-Garde," *Arts Magazine* 54, no. 1 (September 1979): 158–63.

13 Hartley, "Somehow a Past," 265.

14 Marsden Hartley, letter to Rockwell Kent, no date (March 1913), Archives of American Art, Smithsonian Institution, Washington, D.C.; cited by Gail Levin, "Hidden Symbolism in Marsden Hartley's Military Pictures," *Arts Magazine* 54, no. 2 (October 1979): 157.

15 George Mosse, *Nationalism and Sexuality: Respectability and Abnormal Sexuality in Modern Europe* (New York: Fertig, 1985), 45–46.

16 Ibid., 47.

17 As quoted in Steakley, *The Homosexual Emancipation Movement,* 48.

18 Benedict Friedländer, *Renaissance des Eros Uranios* (Berlin-Schmargendorf: Verlag "Renaissance" Otto Lehmann, 1904), 258; quoted in Steakley, *The Homosexual Emancipation Movement,* 43.

19 Mosse, *Nationalism and Sexuality,* 58–59.

20 Marsden Hartley, letter to Alfred Stieglitz, 15 March 1915, Beinecke Library, Yale University.

21 Marsden Hartley, "Letters Never Sent," in *A Life in the Arts,* ed. Scott, 48–49.

22 Stefan George, "Prayer I," in *Maximin: The Works of Stefan George,* ed. and trans. Olga Marx and Ernst Morwitz (Chapel Hill: University of North Carolina Press, 1974), 266. "Dir gehör ich: nimm und fodre/Dass ich fliesse dass ich lodre/Ganz in deiner weissen flamme!" (Stefan George, "Gebete I," in *Maximin: Der Siebente Ring* [Berlin: Erschienen bei Georg Bondi, n.d.], 115).

23 Stefan George, "Incarnation," in *Maximin,* 268. "Mein verlangen hingekauert/Labest du mit deinem seime./ Ich empfange von dem keime/Von dem hauch der mich umdauert:/Dass aus schein und dunklem schaume/ Dass aus freudenruf und zähre/Unzertrennbar sich gebäre/Bild aus dir und mir im traume" (Stefan George, "Einverleibung," in *Maximin,* 119).

24 Marsden Hartley, letter to Alfred Stieglitz, 13 February 1913, Beinecke Library, Yale University.

25 Marsden Hartley, "Notes on the Rilke-Jacobsen Relation," manuscript, Beinecke Library, Yale University.

26 Arnold Rönnebeck, letter to Duncan Phillips, no date (after March 1944), Beinecke Library, Yale University.

27 Hartley, "Notes on the Rilke-Jacobsen Relation."

28 Marsden Hartley, letter to Alfred Stieglitz, 2 September 1914, Beinecke Library, Yale University.

29 Marsden Hartley, letter to Alfred Stieglitz, 15 March 1915, Beinecke Library, Yale University.

30 Ibid.

31 "American Artist Astounds Germans," *New York Times,* 19 December 1915, sec. 6, p. 4.

32 Marsden Hartley, *Paintings by Marsden Hartley* (New York: Photo Secession Galleries, 1916), foreword; reprinted in *Camera Work* 48 (October 1916): 12.

33 [Henry McBride], "Current News of Art and the Exhibitions," *The Sun,* 9 April 1916, sec. 6, p. 8; reprinted in *Camera Work* 8 (October 1916): 58–59.

34 Edward Stevenson, *The Intersexes: A History of Similisexualism as a Problem in Social Life* (privately printed, 1908; reprint, New York: Arno Press, 1975), 87.

35 Marsden Hartley, letter to Madelaine Rice, 11 March 1922, Beinecke Library, Yale University.

36 Marsden Hartley, letter to Alfred Stieglitz, received 12 July 1912, Beinecke Library, Yale University.

37 Gail Levin discusses this letter and Picasso's painting in "Marsden Hartley and the European Avant-Garde," 158.

38 For example, see Haskell, *Marsden Hartley,* 44.

39 W. H. Auden, *The Age of Anxiety: A Baroque Eclogue* (New York: Random House, 1947), 111; cited in Paul Fussell, *The Great War and Modern Memory* (Oxford: Oxford University Press, 1975), 270–72.

40 Fussell, *The Great War and Modern Memory,* 270–72.

8 Hartley's Late Paintings

1 Robert K. Martin, "Painting and Primitivism: Hart Crane and the Development of an American Expressionist Esthetic," *Mosaic* 14, no. 3 (Summer 1981): 49–62.

2 As quoted in John Unterecker, *Voyager: A Life of Hart Crane* (New York: Farrar, Straus and Giroux, 1969), 283.

3 Hart Crane, letter to two individuals whose names are not given, 27 March 1928, in *The Letters of Hart Crane,* ed. Brom Weber (Berkeley: University of California Press, 1965), letter 300.

4 Marsden Hartley, "Hart Crane—in Mexico," typescript, Beinecke Library, Yale University, New Haven, Conn.

5 Marsden Hartley, letter to Adelaide Kuntz, no date (1932–33), Archives of American Art, Smithsonian Institution, Washington, D.C.

6 Alfred Stieglitz, letter to Marsden Hartley, 10 February 1929, Beinecke Library, Yale University.

7 Marsden Hartley, "Somehow a Past," in *A Life in the Arts,* ed. Gail R. Scott, typescript, 318.

8 Marsden Hartley, letter to Adelaide Kuntz, 5 December 1933, Archives of American Art, Smithsonian Institution.

9 Marsden Hartley, letter to Alfred Stieglitz, August 1913, Beinecke Library, Yale University.

10 Unterecker, *Voyager,* 594.

11 Hart Crane, letter to Otto H. Kahn, 12 September 1927, in *The Complete Poems and Selected Letters and Prose of Hart Crane,* ed. Brom Weber (Garden City, N.Y.: Doubleday, 1966), 252.

12 Hart Crane, "Cutty Sark," *The Bridge,* in *The Complete Poems and Selected Letters and Prose of Hart Crane,* 82.

13 Crane, "The River," *The Bridge,* 68.

14 Crane, "Cape Hatteras," *The Bridge,* 89.

15 Marsden Hartley, "Un Recuerdo—Hermano—Hart Crane," in *Collected Poems of Marsden Hartley,* ed. Gail R. Scott (Santa Rosa, Calif.: Black Sparrow, 1987), 123.

16 *The Tempest,* act 1, sc. 2, line 399.

17 Hartley, "Hart Crane—in Mexico," 1.

18 See Allen Tate, "Introduction," in Hart Crane, *White Buildings: Poems by Hart Crane* (New York: Boni and Liveright, 1926); reprinted in *Hart Crane: A Collection of Critical Essays,* ed. Alan Trachtenberg (Englewood Cliffs, N.J.: Prentice-Hall, 1982), 18–22.

19 Yvor Winters, "The Progress of Hart Crane," *Poetry* 36 (June 1930); reprinted in *Hart Crane: A Collection of Critical Essays,* 23–31.

20 Hartley, "Hart Crane—in Mexico," 5.

21 There were also publicity considerations in Hartley's remaking of Homer. With the increasing popularity of regionalism, Hartley thought that it would be an advantageous way to market his painting, even though many of his landscapes from the late 1930s and all of his figure paintings were based on experiences taken from outside his native state (Hartley seemed to be under the impression, rightly, that the New York art world would not really differentiate between Maine, Massachusetts, and even Nova Scotia—they were all seen as part of the same Yankee landscape).

22 Gerald Ferguson, ed., *Marsden Hartley and Nova Scotia* (Halifax, Nova Scotia: Mount Saint Vincent University Art Gallery, 1987), 12.

23 Marsden Hartley, letter to Adelaide Kuntz, 6 October 1935, Archives of American Art, Smithsonian Institution; reprinted in Ferguson, ed., *Marsden Hartley and Nova Scotia,* 35.

24 Marsden Hartley, *Cleophas and His Own: A North Atlantic Tragedy,* original typescript, Beinecke Library, Yale University; reprinted in Ferguson, ed., *Marsden Hartley and Nova Scotia,* 90.

25 Marsden Hartley, letter to Adelaide Kuntz, 6 October 1936, Archives of American Art, Smithsonian Institution; reprinted in Ferguson, ed., *Marsden Hartley and Nova Scotia,* 36.

26 Marsden Hartley, "Marsden Hartley's Journal Entries, Nova Scotia, 1936," in Ferguson, ed., *Marsden Hartley and Nova Scotia,* 75.

27 Marsden Hartley, letter to Arnold Rönnebeck, 29 April 1936, Beinecke Library, Yale University.

28 For the first extensive discussion of Hartley's interest in Nazi Germany, see Gail Levin, *Marsden Hartley in Bavaria* (Clinton, N.Y.: Emerson Gallery, Hamilton College, 1989), 42–44.

29 Marsden Hartley, letter to Adelaide Kuntz, 12 July 1933, Archives of American Art, Smithsonian Institution; excerpted in "Letters from Germany 1933–1938," *Archives of American Art Journal* 25, nos. 1, 2 (1985): 4.

30 Marsden Hartley, letter to Adelaide Kuntz, 16 May 1933, Archives of American Art, Smithsonian Institution; excerpted in "Letters from Germany," 4.

31 Marsden Hartley, letter to Edith Halpert, 12 July 1933, Archives of American Art, Smithsonian Institution; excerpted in "Letters from Germany," 6–7.

32 Marsden Hartley, letter to Adelaide Kuntz, 15 November 1933, Archives of American Art, Smithsonian Institution; excerpted in "Letters from Germany," 9–10.

33 Marsden Hartley, letter to Adelaide Kuntz, 3 February 1934, Archives of American Art, Smithsonian Institution; excerpted in "Letters from Germany," 4.

34 Marsden Hartley, letter to Adelaide Kuntz, 28 December 1933, Archives of American Art, Smithsonian Institution; excerpted in "Letters from Germany," 11.

35 I should note that Hartley's attraction to Germany and Hitler is an individual case and should be kept separate from the issue of sexuality and the rise of the National Socialist movement, which George Mosse discusses in *Nationalism and Sexuality.* It was a cliché after World War II to attribute the rise of Hitler to the degeneracy of the Weimar period, particularly its comparative tolerance of homosexuality. Although it is true that Hitler's early counselors included gay men, homosexuals were violently rooted out of the party and exterminated along with the Jews (see Richard Plant, *The Pink Triangle: The Nazi War Against Homosexuals* [New York: Henry Holt, 1986]).

36 Hartley, *Cleophas and His Own,* in *Marsden Hartley and Nova Scotia,* ed. Ferguson, 94.

37 Ibid., 95.

38 Ferguson, ed., *Marsden Hartley and Nova Scotia,* 168.

39 Hartley's last painting, *Roses,* is now in the Walker Art Center in Minneapolis. For a photograph of his studio at the time of his death, see Ferguson, ed., *Marsden Hartley and Nova Scotia,* 168.

40 Marsden Hartley to Adelaide Kuntz, 6 November 1935, Archives of American Art, Smithsonian Institution; reprinted in Ferguson, ed., *Marsden Hartley and Nova Scotia,* 43.

41 Marsden Hartley, letter to Arnold Rönnebeck, 29 April 1936, Beinecke Library, Yale University.

42 The kind of sexual relationship to which Hartley alludes suggests fellatio—with the boys so plied with liquor that they do not care who is servicing them. In *Cleophas and His Own* he focuses on Adelard's sexual appe-

tite, insisting that the gender of his partner did not matter: "He lives utterly for the consummate satisfaction of the flesh, the kind of flesh/making no difference" (98). The discussion of the Newport Scandal in chapter 2 demonstrated that such sexual play would not necessarily be considered "perverse" by young working-class males.

43 Hartley, *Cleophas and His Own,* 98.

44 Marsden Hartley, letter to Adelaide Kuntz, 23 September 1936, Archives of American Art, Smithsonian Institution; reprinted in Ferguson, ed., *Marsden Hartley and Nova Scotia,* 47.

45 Marsden Hartley, letter to Adelaide Kuntz, 5 October 1936, Archives of American Art, Smithsonian Institution; reprinted in Ferguson, ed., *Marsden Hartley and Nova Scotia,* 50.

46 Ferguson, ed., *Marsden Hartley and Nova Scotia,* 160.

47 Author's interview with Mervin Jules, 17 July 1988, Provincetown, Mass.

48 Marsden Hartley, "He Too Wore a Butterfly," *Collected Poems,* 171.

49 The picture on the tank top is related to the painting *Adelard Ascending* (for an illustration, see Ferguson, ed., *Marsden Hartley and Nova Scotia,* pl. 2, p. 165), which shows Adelard crucified, with wings rising up over a Nova Scotia seascape. In this way, the image on the sailor's chest may stand for Adelard and Christ.

50 Ferguson, ed., *Marsden Hartley and Nova Scotia,* 162.

51 See Louis Réau, *Iconographie de l'art chrétien* (Paris: Presses Universitaires de France, 1959), vol. 3, p. 1192. James Saslow provided me with this citation.

52 Author's interview with Mervin Jules, 17 July 1988, Provincetown, Mass.

53 Gail Scott notes the relationship of *Canuck Yankee Lumberjack at Old Orchard Beach, Maine* to Cézanne's *The Bather* (Gail R. Scott, *Marsden Hartley* [New York: Abbeville, 1988], 136–38).

54 Walt Whitman, "Oh Captain! My Captain!" *Leaves of Grass,* ed. Gay Wilson Allen (New York: New American Library, 1958), 243.

55 As T. J. Clark reminds me, this imagery of beach and flotsam is profoundly Whitmanesque as well. See Whitman's poem "As I Ebb'd with the Ocean of Life" and other poems from the *Sea Drift* section of *Leaves of Grass.*

9
Coming Home

1 Ray Gerard Koskovich discusses *Distinguished Air* in "A Gay American Modernist: Homosexuality in the Life and Art of Charles Demuth," *Advocate* (25 June 1985): 50–52, and in his longer unpublished paper, "Ambiguity, Ideality and Otherness: Homosexuality and Ideological Strategies in the Art of Charles Demuth," which he wrote as an independent project for Professor Wanda Corn at Stanford University in 1982.

2 William Murrell, *Charles Demuth* (New York: Whitney Museum of American Art, 1931).

3 Barbara Haskell, *Charles Demuth* (New York: Whitney Museum of American Art, 1987), 206.

4 According to Koskovich, the anthology *American Esoterica,* ed. Carl Van Doren (New York: privately printed by Macy-Masius, 1927), was published in an edition of three thousand (Koskovich, "Ambiguity, Ideality and Otherness," n. 65).

5 Dickran Tashjian, *William Carlos Williams and the American Scene* (New York: Whitney Museum of American Art, 1978), 70–71. As Barbara Haskell points out, Tashjian wrongly identifies the Brancusi sculpture as *Mme. Pogany* (Haskell, *Charles Demuth,* 205–06).

6 Robert McAlmon, "Distinguished Air," in *Distinguished Air (Grim Fairy Tales)* (Paris: Contact Editions, 1925), 15.

7 Ibid., 14.

8 William Camfield, *Marcel Duchamp Fountain* (Houston, Tex.: The Menil Collection and Houston Fine Art Press, 1989), 55.

9 Sidney Geist, *Constantin Brancusi, 1876–1957: A Retrospective Exhibition* (New York: Guggenheim Museum, 1969), 78–79.

10 I realize that even using the term *avant-garde* to describe the practices and philosophies of the artists in the circle of Demuth and Hartley is problematic. I use it here without making any claims about the quality or complexity of the art of the early American modernists. It suggests a loose community of artists including Stieglitz, Strand, Duchamp, Picabia, O'Keeffe, Demuth, and Hartley, as well as writers like O'Neill, Stein, and Williams, all of whom were searching for new forms in their art. But the term is also used to express a supposedly communal sense of alienation from traditional middle-class values. New York avant-gardism often involved an assertion of difference—differences of style, morality, and taste. The question is, how did homosexuality fit in among these stances of difference?

11 Eugene O'Neill, *Strange Interlude* (1928), in *Three Plays* (New York: Vintage, 1959), 61–62.

12 Ibid., 86.

13 Ibid., 63–64.

14 Ibid., 222.

15 Robert McAlmon, *Post-Adolescence* (Paris: Contact Publishing, n.d.); reprinted in *McAlmon and the Lost Generation: A Self-Portrait* (Lincoln: University of Nebraska Press, 1962), 114.

16 Ibid., 124, 125.

17 McAlmon, "Distinguished Air," 14.

18 Ibid., 30, 28.

19 Ibid., 29–30.

20 McAlmon, *Post-Adolescence,* 25.

21 McAlmon, "Distinguished Air," 26.

22 Marius de Zayas, *291,* 5–6 (July–August 1915). I wish to thank Steven Watson for leading me to this quote.

23 Sarotte discusses Fitzgerald's sexuality at length, suggesting that he was latently homosexual. Sarotte also includes a short analysis of Hemingway's attitude to homosexuality. See Georges-Michel Sarotte, *Like a Brother, Like a Lover: Male Homosexuality in the American Novel and Theater from Herman Melville to James Baldwin,* trans. Richard Miller (Garden City, N.Y.: Anchor Books, Doubleday, 1978), 212–28, 262–78.

24 F. Scott Fitzgerald, *Tender Is the Night* (New York: Scribner's, 1962), 41.

25 Ibid., 245.

26 Ernest Hemingway, *A Moveable Feast* (New York: Collier, 1964), 18–20.

27 "Excerpts from 'The Western Round Table on Modern Art'" (1949), in *Modern Artists in America,* ed. Bernard Karpel, Robert Motherwell, and Ad Reinhardt (New York: Wittenborn Schultz, 1951), 30.

28 I do not mean to imply here that Duchamp was an early advocate for homosexual rights or that he was immune from prejudice. As his remark about Demuth's "perverse tendencies" (which I discuss in my introduction) suggests, he was even capable of unconsciously homophobic characterizations. Arturo Schwarz writes: "Duchamp's attitude toward homosexuality is consistent with his noncommittal outlook, his 'suspending judgment'; he neither approves of it nor condemns it, he simply acknowledges its existence" (Arturo Schwarz, *The Complete Works of Marcel Duchamp* [New York: Harry Abrams, 1969], 91 note). Whatever Duchamp's statements or personal feelings about homosexuality, his art had certain ramifications. His don-

ning of drag, a costume of the gay subculture, seems to me to negate such a noncommittal outlook. For this discussion of Duchamp, I am indebted to Alison Tilghman for her work during my fall 1989 seminar at Yale University on the Stieglitz Circle and for her resulting paper, "Why Not See Rrose Sélavy?"

29 George Chauncey, Jr., "The Way We Were: Gay Male Society in the Jazz Age," *Village Voice,* 1 July 1986, 29.

30 *The Blind Man* 2 (May 1917): 2.

31 Chauncey, "The Way We Were," 30.

32 Pierre Cabanne, *Dialogues with Marcel Duchamp,* trans. Ron Padgett (New York: Viking Press, 1971), 64.

33 Chauncey, "The Way We Were," 29.

34 McAlmon, "Distinguished Air," 13.

35 "On n'a que: pour *femelle* la pissotière et on en vit." Marcel Duchamp, *Marchand du Sel: Ecrits de Marcel Duchamp,* ed. Michel Sanouillet (Paris: Le Terrain Vague, 1958), 31; translated under the title *Salt Seller: The Writings of Marcel Duchamp,* ed. Michel Sanouillet and Elmer Peterson (New York: Oxford University Press, 1973), 23. Cited in William A. Camfield, *Marcel Duchamp Fountain* (Houston: The Menil Collection and Houston Fine Art Press, 1989), 50.

36 Camfield, *Marcel Duchamp Fountain,* 50.

37 Indeed, Arturo Schwarz's *The Complete Works of Duchamp,* which was written with Duchamp's participation, includes discussions of homosexuality in relationship to Duchamp's work.

38 Pier Paolo Pasolini, "Gennariello," in *Lutheran Letters,* trans. Stuart Hood (Manchester, Eng.: Carcanet New Press, 1983), 21–22; cited by Douglas Crimp, "Mourning and Militancy," *October* 51 (Winter 1989): 11.

39 Camfield, *Marcel Duchamp Fountain,* 19.

40 Cabanne, *Dialogues with Marcel Duchamp,* 55.

41 Charles Demuth, "For Richard Mutt," *The Blind Man* 2 (May 1917): 6.

42 Marcel Duchamp, "Interview with Marcel Duchamp at New York City, January 21, 1956," in Emily Farnham, "Charles Demuth: His Life, Psychology and Works" (Ph.D. diss., Ohio State University, 1959), 973–74.

43 Charles Demuth, letter to Alfred Stieglitz, 5 February 1928 or 1929, Beinecke Library, Yale University, New Haven, Ct.

44 Kermit Champa, " 'Charlie Was Like That,' " *Artforum* 12, no. 6 (March 1974): 58.

45 Barbara Haskell, *Charles Demuth* (New York: Whitney Museum of American Art in association with Harry Abrams, 1987), 12.

46 Betsy Fahlman, "Charles Demuth's Paintings of Lancaster Architecture: New Discoveries and Observations," *Arts Magazine* 61, no. 7 (March 1987): 24–29.

47 Lancaster, Pa., *Report on the Conditions in the City of Lancaster, Pa.* (Lancaster, Pa.: City of Lancaster, 1913), 44.

48 For a discussion of the vast holdings of the Steinman family in Lancaster, see John H. Brubaker, *The Steinmans of Lancaster: A Family and Its Enterprises* (Lancaster, Pa.: Steinman Enterprises, 1984).

49 Author's interview with Dorothea Demuth, Charles Demuth's cousin by marriage (his father's nephew's wife), 28 May 1986, Lancaster, Pa.

50 Helen Henderson, "Charles Demuth," paper, Junior League, Lancaster, Pa., 10 November 1947; copy in the archives of the Whitney Museum of American Art.

51 As T. J. Clark has pointed out to me, the scabrousness of *Welcome to Our City* is an exception to Demuth's insider role. Its denunciation—speaking *against* from *outside, coding* its real feelings—is avoided in Demuth's other Lancaster paintings. Critics have debated whether Demuth's Precisionism is meant to idealize or cas-

tigate Lancaster, falling back on the catchall term *ambivalence* to express his characteristic attitude toward his home. See Karal Ann Marling's "*My Egypt:* The Irony of the American Dream," *Winterthur Portfolio* 15 (Spring 1980): 25–39; Fahlman, "Charles Demuth's Paintings of Lancaster Architecture: New Discoveries and Observations"; and Haskell, *Charles Demuth,* 135.

52 Charles Demuth, letter to Alfred Stieglitz, 28 November 1921, Beinecke Library, Yale University; reprinted in Farnham, "Charles Demuth: His Life, Psychology and Works," 944.

53 James O'Higgins, "Sexual Choice, Sexual Act: An Interview with Michel Foucault," *Salmagundi* 58–59 (Fall-Winter 1983): 22.

54 Marsden Hartley, letter to Adelaide Kuntz, 6 November 1935, Archives of American Art, Smithsonian Institution, Washington, D.C.

55 Marsden Hartley, letter to Isabel Lachaise, 26 August 1940, Beinecke Library, Yale University.

Selected Bibliography

Abrams, Albert. "Homosexuality: A Military Menace." *Medical Review of Reviews* 24 (1918): 528–29.

Ackerley, J. R. *My Father and Myself.* London: Penguin, 1971.

Ackroyd, Peter. *Dressing Up, Transvestism and Drag: The History of an Obsession.* New York: Simon and Schuster, 1979.

Adams, Henry. *The Beal Collection of Watercolors by Charles Demuth.* Pittsburgh: Museum of Art, Carnegie Institute, 1983.

Adler, Alfred. "The Homosexual Problem." *Alienist and Neurologist* 38, no. 3 (August 1917): 268–87.

Agee, William C. "Demuth at the Whitney." *New Criterion* 6, no. 10 (June 1988): 41–48.

Aldridge, John W. *After the Lost Generation: A Critical Study of the Writers of Two Wars.* New York: McGraw-Hill, 1951.

Allara, Pamela Edwards. "The Watercolor Illustrations of Charles Demuth." Ph.D. diss. Johns Hopkins University, 1970.

Anthony, Francis W. "The Question of Responsibility in Cases of Sexual Perversion." *Boston Medical and Surgical Journal* 139, no. 12 (22 September 1898): 288–91.

"Art at Home and Abroad: Exhibitions of Modern Painting." *New York Times Magazine,* 28 January 1917, p. 13.

"Art at Home and Abroad: News and Comment, At the Daniel Gallery." *New York Times,* 1 November 1914, sec. 5, p. 11.

"Art Notes: Demuth and Fiske." *New York Times,* 27 November 1917, p. 12.

Ashbury, Herbert. *The Barbary Coast.* Garden City, N.Y.: Garden City Publishing, 1933.

Barbedette, Gilles. *Paris Gay, 1925.* Paris: Presses de la Renaissance, ca. 1981.

Barnett, Vivian Endicott. "Marsden Hartley's Return to Maine." *Arts Magazine* 54, no. 2 (October 1979): 172–76.

Barry, Roxanna. "The Age of Blood and Iron: Marsden Hartley in Berlin." *Arts Magazine* 54, no. 2 (October 1979): 166–71.

Baruch, S. *Public Baths in New York (City).* New York: City of New York, 1918.

Bayer, Ronald. *Homosexuality and American Psychiatry: The Politics of Diagnosis.* New York: Basic, 1981.

Becker, Howard S. *Outsiders: Studies in the Sociology of Deviance.* New York: Free Press of Glencoe, 1963.

Becker, Raymond de. *The Other Face of Love.* New York: Grove Press, 1969.

Benjamin, Walter. *Charles Baudelaire: A Lyric Poet in the Era of High Capitalism*. Translated by Harry Zohn. London: Verso, 1983.

Benstock, Shari. *Women of the Left Bank, Paris, 1900–1940*. Austin: University of Texas Press, 1987.

Bentley, Eric. "The Homosexual Question." In *Hidden Heritage*. Edited by Byrne Fone. New York: Avocation, 1982.

Bérubé, Allan. "Marching to a Different Drummer: Lesbian and Gay GI's in World War II." In *Powers of Desire*. Edited by Ann Snitow, Christine Stansell, and Sharon Thompson. New York: Monthly Review Press, 1983.

Biddle, George. *An American Artist's Story*. Boston: Little, Brown, 1939.

Blair, Niles. *Strange Brothers*. New York: Liveright, 1931. Reprint. New York: Arno, 1975.

Blanchard, P. M. "Homosexuality: Ancient and Modern." In *Our Neurotic Times*. Edited by S. D. Schmalhausen. New York: Farras, 1932.

Bloch, Iwan. *The Sexual Life of Our Time in Its Relation to Modern Civilization*. Translated by M. Eden Paul. New York: Allied, 1928. Reprint. New York: Falstaff Press, 1937.

———. *Strange Sexual Practices*. Translated by Keene Wallis. New York: Anthropological Press, 1933.

———. *Strangest Sex Acts in Modes of Love of All Races*. New York: Falstaff Press, 1935.

Bodenheim, Maxwell. *My Life and Loves in Greenwich Village*. New York: Bridgehead, 1954.

Boswell, John. *Christianity, Social Tolerance, and Homosexuality: Gay People in Western Europe from the Beginning of the Christian Era to the Fourteenth Century*. Chicago: University of Chicago Press, 1980.

Boulton, Agnes. *Part of a Long Story*. Garden City, N.Y.: Doubleday, 1958.

Bowie, Theodore, Otto Bendel, and Paul Gebhard. *Studies in Erotic Art*. New York: Basic, 1970.

Breeskin, Dohme. *Romaine Brooks in the National Museum of American Art*. 1971. Washington, D.C.: Smithsonian Institution Press, 1988.

Brian, Doris. "The Passing Shows: Hartley." *Art News* 41 (15–31 March 1942): 27.

Brill, A. A. "The Conception of Homosexuality." *Journal of the American Medical Association* 61 (2 August 1913): 335–40.

———. "Introduction." In *The Basic Writings of Sigmund Freud*. Translated and edited by A. A. Brill. New York: Modern Library, 1938.

Broder, Patricia Janis. *The American West: The Modern Vision*. Boston: Little Brown for the New York Graphics Society, 1984.

Bronski, Michael. *Culture Clash*. Boston: South End Press, 1984.

Brown, Milton. *American Painting from the Armory Show to the Depression*. Princeton: Princeton University Press, 1972.

Brubaker, John H. *Steinmans of Lancaster: A Family and Its Enterprises*. Lancaster, Pa.: Steinman Enterprises, 1984.

Bruesendorff, Ove, and Paul Hennington. *Love's Picture Book: The History of Pleasure and Moral Indignation*. Translated by H. R. Ward. Copenhagen: Veta Publishers, 1963.

Bryant, Clifton D., ed. *Sexual Deviancy in Social Context*. New York: New Viewpoints, 1977.

Buchen, Irving, ed. *The Perverse Imagination: Sexuality and Literary Culture*. New York: New York University Press, 1970.

Bullough, Vern. *Homosexuality, A History: From Ancient Greece to Gay Liberation*. New York: New American Library, 1979.

———. "Homosexuality and the Medical Model." *Journal of Homosexuality* 1, no. 1 (Fall 1974): 99–110.

———. "Sex in History." *Tangents* 4 (January–March 1972): 4–5, 22–28.

———. "Sex in History: A Virgin Field." *Journal of Sex Research* 8, no. 2 (May 1972): 101.

———. *Sexual Variance in Society and History.* Chicago: University of Chicago Press, 1980.

Bullough, Vern, W. Dover, Barreet W. Elcano, and James Kepner. *An Annotated Bibliography of Homosexuality.* New York: Garland Publishing, 1976.

Bullough, Vern, and Martha Voght. "Homosexuality and Its Confusion with the 'Secret Sin' in Pre-Freudian America." *Journal of History of Medicine and the Allied Sciences* 28 (1973): 143–55.

Burg, B. R. *Sodomy and the Pirate Tradition: English Sea Rovers in the Seventeenth-Century Caribbean.* New York: New York University Press, 1984.

Burgard, Timothy Anglin. "Charles Demuth's *Longhi on Broadway:* Homage to Eugene O'Neill." *Arts Magazine* 58, no. 5 (January 1984): 110–13.

Burlingame, Robert Northcutt. "Marsden Hartley: A Study of His Life and Creative Achievement." Ph.D. diss., Brown University, 1953.

Burnham, John. "Early References to Homosexual Communities in American Medical Writings." *Medical Aspects of Human Sexuality* 7, no. 8 (August 1973): 34–49.

Burrow, Trigant. "The Genesis and Meaning of Homosexuality." *Psychoanalytic Review* 4 (1917): 272–84.

Butts, W. H. "Boy Prostitutes of the Metropolis." *Journal of Clinical Psychopathology* 8 (1947): 674.

Cabanne, Pierre. *Dialogues with Marcel Duchamp.* Translated by Ron Padgett. New York: Viking Press, 1971.

Caffin, Charles H. "New and Important Things in Art: Emotional 'Experiences' Shown by Hartley Paintings." *New York American* 6 (January 1914): 6; reprinted in *Camera Work* 45 (January 1914): 22.

———. "New and Important Things in Art: Latest Work by Marsden Hartley." *New York American* 8 (17 April 1916); reprinted in *Camera Work* 48 (October 1916): 59–60.

Camfield, William A. *Marcel Duchamp Fountain.* Houston: The Menil Collection and Houston Fine Art Press, 1989.

Carpenter, Edward. *Intermediate Sex: A Study of Some Transitional Types of Men and Women.* London: G. Allen and Unwin, 1908. Reprinted in Edward Carpenter, *Sex.* Vol. 1 of *Selected Writings.* London: GMP Publishers, 1984.

———. *Intermediate Types Among Primitive Folk.* London: G. Allen, 1914.

———. *Love's Coming of Age: A Series of Papers on the Relations of the Sexes.* London: privately printed, 1896. Reprint. New York: Vanguard Press, 1928.

———. *My Days and Dreams: Being Autobiographical Notes.* New York: Scribner's, 1916.

———. "On the Connection Between Homosexuality and Divination and the Importance of the Intermediate Sexes Generally in Early Civilizations." *American Journal of Religious Psychology and Education* 4 (1910–11): 219–43.

———. *Sex.* Vol. 1 of *Selected Writings.* London: GMP Publishers, 1984.

———. "Some Friends of Walt Whitman." *British Society for the Study of Sex Psychology,* 1924.

Chaddock, Charles Gilbert. "Sexual Crimes." In *A System of Legal Medicine.* Edited by Allan McLane and Lawrence Godkin. New York: E. M. Treat, 1894.

Champa, Kermit. " 'Charlie Was Like That.' " *Artforum* 12, no. 6 (March 1974): 54–59.

Chapman, John Jay. *Lucien, Plato, and Greek Morals.* Boston: Houghton Mifflin, 1931.

"Charles Demuth: Intimate Gallery." *Art News* 24, no. 5 (10 April 1926): 7.

Chauncey, George, Jr. "Christian Brotherhood or Sexual Perversion? Homosexual Identities and the Construction of Sexual Boundaries in the World War One Era." *Journal of Social History* 19 (Winter 1985): 189–211.

———. "From Sexual Inversion to Homosexuality: Medicine and the Changing Conceptualization of Female Deviance." *Salmagundi,* nos. 58–59 (Fall 1982–Winter 1983): 114–46.

———. "Gay Male Society in the Jazz Age." *Village Voice,* 1 July 1986: 29–32.

Chester, L., D. Leitch, and C. Simpson. *The Cleveland Street Affair.* London: Weidenfeld and Nicholson, 1976.

Churchill, Allen. "What Is a Homosexual?" *Argosy* 329, no. 2 (August 1949): 28–97.

Clark, Kenneth. *The Nude: A Study in Ideal Form.* New York: Pantheon, 1953.

Cocteau, Jean. *The Difficulty of Being.* New York: Coward McCann, 1967.

Cole, Robert J. "Studio and Gallery: Chinese and Russian Collections; Marsden Hartley's Heraldic Devices." *New York Evening Sun,* 25 April 1916, p. 13; reprinted in *Camera Work* 48 (October 1916): 60.

A Collection of Drawings and Watercolors by Charles Demuth. New York: Sotheby Parke-Bernet Inc., 1976.

Collins, Joseph. *The Doctor Looks at Love and Life.* New York: Geo. H. Doran, 1926.

Cooper, Emmanuel. *Sexual Perspective: Homosexuality and Art in the Last One Hundred Years in the West.* London: Routledge and Kegan Paul, 1986.

Copp, David, and Susan Wendell, eds. *Pornography and Censorship.* Buffalo, N.Y.: Prometheus, 1983.

Coriat, Isador. "Homosexuality: Its Psychogenesis and Treatment." *New York Medical Journal* 97, no. 12 (22 March 1913): 589–94.

Cory, Donald Webster. *The Homosexual in America.* New York: Greenberg, 1951.

Crane, Hart. *The Letters of Hart Crane.* Edited by Brom Weber. Berkeley: University of California Press, 1965.

Craven, Thomas. *American Art.* New York: Simon and Schuster, 1934.

Croft-Cooke, R. *The Unrecorded Life of Oscar Wilde.* London: W. H. Allen, 1972.

Crow, Thomas. "Modernism and Mass Culture in the Visual Arts." In *Modernism and Modernity, the Vancouver Conference Papers.* Edited by Benjamin H. D. Buchloh, Serge Guilbaut, and David Solkin. Halifax, Nova Scotia: Nova Scotia College of Art and Design Press, 1983. Reprinted in Francis Frascina, ed., *Pollock and After.* New York: Harper and Row, 1985.

"Cubism Has Share in Demuth Exhibit." *New York Sun,* 1 December 1918, p. 11.

Curry, Larry. *Eight American Masters of Watercolor.* Los Angeles and New York: Los Angeles County Museum of Art and Frederick Praeger, 1968.

Daniel, F. E. "Castration of Sexual Perverts." *Texas Medical Journal* 27, no. 10 (April 1912): 371–72, 376–81.

Daniel, Marc. "A Methodology for the Study of Historical Aspects of Homosexuality." *One Institute Quarterly: Homophile Studies* 3, no. 4 (Fall 1960): 268–80.

Danto, Arthur C. "Charles Demuth." *Nation* 246, no. 3 (23 January 1988): 101–04.

Davidson, Abraham A. "Demuth's Poster Portraits." *Artforum* 17, no. 3 (November 1978): 54–57.

———. *Early American Modernist Painting, 1910–1935.* New York: Harper and Row, 1981.

Davidson, Michael. *The World, the Flesh and Myself.* London: David, Bruce and Watson, 1962.

De Zayas, Marius. "How, When, and Why Modern Art Came to New York." *Arts Magazine* 54, no. 8 (April 1980): 96–126.

Dean, Andrea. "He Was an Acrobat on the Leading Edge of Jazz Age Art." *Smithsonian* 18, no. 7 (October 1987): 58–67.

Dean, Dawson F. *Significant Characteristics of the Homosexual Personality.* Ph.D. diss., New York University, 1936.

Demuth, Charles. "Across a Greco Is Written." *Creative Art* 29 (September 1929): 629–34.

———. *The Azure Adder. The Glebe* 1 (December 1913): 5–31.

———. "Confessions: Replies to a Questionnaire." *The Little Review* 12, no. 2 (May 1929): 30–31.

———. "For Richard Mutt." *The Blind Man* 2 (May, 1917): 6.

Denneng, Michael, ed. *The Christopher Street Reader.* New York: Wideview/Penger, 1984.

Deutsch, Albert, ed. *Sex Habits of American Men: A Symposium on the Kinsey Report.* New York: Prentice Hall, 1948.

Devree, Howard. "A Reviewer's Notebook." *New York Times,* 6 March 1938, sec. 11, p. 8.

———. "A Reviewer's Notebook: Brief Comment on Some Recently Opened Group and One Man Shows in Galleries: Hartley Drawings." *New York Times,* 18 October 1942, sec. 8, p. 9.

———. "A Reviewer's Notebook: In Galleries, Brief Comment on Some Recently Opened Shows—Paintings by Marsden Hartley—Karl Mattern's Debut—Other Attractions." *New York Times,* 15 March 1942, sec. 8, p. 3.

Dijkstra, Bram. *The Hieroglyphics of a New Speech: Cubism, Stieglitz, and the Early Poetry of William Carlos Williams.* Princeton: Princeton University Press, 1969.

Documents of the Homosexual Rights Movement in Germany, 1836–1927. New York: Arno Press, 1975.

Dodge, Mabel. "Foreword for 1914 Exhibition at 291." *Camera Work* 45 (January 1914): 16–18.

Douglas, Mary. *Purity and Danger: An Analysis of Concepts of Pollution and Taboo.* London: Routledge and Kegan Paul, 1966.

Duberman, Martin. *About Time: Exploring the Gay Past.* New York: Gay Presses of New York, 1986.

Duberman, Martin, Martha Vicinus, and George Chauncey, Jr., eds. *Hidden from History: Reclaiming the Gay and Lesbian Past.* New York: Meridan, 1990.

Du Bois, Guy Pène. "Among the Art Galleries." *The [New York] Evening Post Magazine,* 7 December 1918, p. 21.

Duchamp, Marcel. *Salt Seller: The Writings of Marcel Duchamp.* Edited by Michel Sanouillet and Elmer Peterson. New York: Oxford University Press, 1973.

———. "A Tribute to the Artist." *Charles Demuth.* New York: Museum of Modern Art, 1950.

"Early Hartley Drawings on View." *Art Digest* 17 (15 October 1942): 11.

Edwinson, Edmund [pseud.]. *Men and Boys: An Anthology.* 1924. Reprint. New York: Coltsfoot Press, 1978.

Eiseman, Alvord L. *Charles Demuth.* New York: Watson-Guptill, 1982.

———. "A Study of the Development of an Artist: Charles Demuth." Ph.D. diss., School of Education, New York University, 1975.

Eldorado: Homosexuelle Frauen und Männer in Berlin 1850–1950, Geschichte, Alltag und Kultur. Berlin, West Germany: Frölich and Kaufmann, 1984.

Eliasoph, Philip I. "Paul Cadmus: Life and Work." Ph.D. diss., State University of New York, 1978.

———. *Paul Cadmus: Yesterday and Today.* Oxford, Ohio: Miami University Art Gallery, 1981.

Ellis, Havelock. *Erotic Symbolism.* Vol. 3 of *Studies in the Psychology of Sex.* Part 1. New York: Random House, 1936.

———. "Freud's Influence on the Changed Attitude Toward Sex." *American Journal of Sociology* 45 (1939): 309–17.

———. *My Life: An Autobiography of Havelock Ellis.* Boston: Houghton Mifflin, 1939.

———. *Sexual Inversion.* Vol. 2 of *Studies in the Psychology of Sex.* New York: F. A. Davis, 1936.

———. "Sexual Inversion in Man." *Alienist and Neurologist* 17 (April 1896): 115–50.

———. "Sexual Inversion: With an Analysis of Thirty-three Cases." *Medico-Legal Journal* 13 (December 1895): 254–67.

———. "Study of Sexual Inversion." *Medico-Legal Journal* 12 (1894): 148–57.

"Exhibitions in New York." *Art News* 29, no. 10 (18 April 1931): 10–11.

"Exhibitions of Painting in Great Variety: Art at Home and Abroad." *New York Times,* 1 December 1918, sec. 7, p. 11.

Fahlman, Betsy. "Charles Demuth's Paintings of Lancaster Architecture: New Discoveries and Observations." *Arts Magazine* 61, no. 7 (March 1987): 24–29.

———. "Charles Demuth Retrospective at the Whitney." *Arts Magazine* 62, no. 7 (March 1988): 52–54.

———. "Modern as Metal and Mirror: The Work of Robert Evans Locher." *Arts Magazine* 59, no. 8 (April 1985): 108–13.

———. *Pennsylvania Modern: Charles Demuth of Lancaster.* Philadelphia: Philadelphia Museum of Art, 1983.

Farnham, Emily. "Charles Demuth: His Life, Psychology and Works." 3 vols. Ph.D. diss., Ohio State University, 1959.

———. *Charles Demuth: Behind a Laughing Mask.* Norman: University of Oklahoma, 1971.

Ferguson, Gerald, ed. *Marsden Hartley and Nova Scotia.* Halifax, Nova Scotia: Mount Saint Vincent University Art Gallery in association with the Press of the Nova Scotia College of Art and Design and the Art Gallery of Ontario, 1987.

Fiedler, Leslie A. *An End to Innocence.* Boston: Beacon, 1952.

———. *Love and Death in the American Novel.* New York: Criterion, 1960.

Field, Andrew. *Djuna: The Formidable Miss Barnes.* Austin: University of Texas Press, 1985.

Flint, Austin. "A Case of Sexual Inversion, Probably with Complete Sexual Anaesthesia." *New York Medical Journal* 94, no. 23 (2 December 1911): 1111–12.

Ford, Charles Henri, and Parker Tyler. *The Young and Evil.* New York: Arno Press, 1975.

Foucault, Michel. *The Archeology of Knowledge and the Discourse on Knowledge.* Translated by A. M. Sheriden Smith. New York: Pantheon, 1972.

———. *An Introduction.* Vol. 1 of *The History of Sexuality.* Translated by Robert Hurley. New York: Vintage, 1980.

———. *Madness and Civilization: A History of Insanity.* Translated by Richard Howard. New York: Vintage, 1982.

———. *The Order of Things: An Archeology of Human Sciences.* New York: Vintage, 1970.

———. *The Use of Pleasure.* Vol. 2 of *The History of Sexuality.* Translated by Robert Hurley. New York: Pantheon, 1985.

Freud, Sigmund. "Certain Neurotic Mechanisms in Jealousy, Paranoia, and Homosexuality (1922)." In *Sexuality and the Psychology of Love.* New York: Collier, 1963.

———. *Collected Papers.* Edited by James Strachey. New York: Basic, 1959.

———. *Leonardo da Vinci and a Memory of His Childhood.* 1910. Reprint. New York: Norton, 1964.

———. "The Psychogenesis of a Case of Homosexuality in a Woman (1920)." In *Sexuality and the Psychology of Love.* New York: Collier, 1963.

———. *Three Essays on the Theory of Sexuality (1905).* Translated and edited by James Strachey. New York: Basic, 1975.

Fussell, Paul. *The Great War and Modern Memory.* Oxford: Oxford University Press, 1975.

G., C. K. "A Homosexual History." *Journal of Sexology and Psychoanalysis* 2 (1924): 12–15.

Gagnon, J. H., and William Simon. *Sexual Conduct: The Social Sources of Human Sexuality.* London: Hutchinson, 1973.

Gallichan, Walter M. *Human Love.* New York: Walden Publications, 1939.

Galloway, Thomas W. *Sex and Social Health.* New York: The American Social Hygiene Association, 1924.

Gambone, Robert L. *Marsden Hartley: Pastels.* Minneapolis: University Art Museum, University of Minnesota, 1986.

Garber, Eric. "A Spectacle in Color: The Lesbian and Gay Subculture of Jazz Age Harlem." In *Hidden from History: Reclaiming the Gay and Lesbian Past.* Edited by Martin Duberman, Martha Vicinus, and George Chauncey, Jr. New York: Meridan, 1990.

Gardner, Charles W. *The Doctor and the Devil: A Startling Expose of Municipal Corruption.* New York: Warren Publishing, 1894. Reprint. New York: Vanguard Press, 1931.

Gedhard, David, and Phyllis Plous. *Charles Demuth: The Mechanical Encrusted on the Living.* Santa Barbara: Art Galleries, University of California, 1971.

Gerber, Henry. "The Society for Human Rights—1925." *ONE* (Sept. 1962): 5–8.

Gerber, Israel. *Man on a Pendulum.* New York: American Press, 1955.

Gerhard, W. P. *Modern Baths and Bath Houses.* New York: City of New York, 1908.

———. *Public Bath Houses and Swimming Pools.* New York: New York City, n.d.

Gide, André. *Corydon.* New York: Farrar Straus, 1950.

———. *The Journals of André Gide, 1889–1949.* 4 vols. Translated and edited by Justine O'Brien. New York: Knopf, 1947–51.

Gillette, Paul J. *An Uncensored History of Pornography.* Los Angeles: Holloway House, 1965.

Gilmore, Donald H. *Sex and Censorship in the Visual Arts.* San Diego, Calif.: Greenleaf, 1970.

Gordon, A. "History of a Homosexual: His Difficulties and Triumphs." *Medical Journal and Record* 131, no. 3 (5 February 1930): 152–56.

Green, Julian. *Diary, 1928–1957.* Translated by Anne Green. New York: Helen and Kurt Wolf, 1964.

Green, Martin. *Children of the Sun: A Narrative of "Decadence" in England after 1910.* New York: Basic, 1976.

Greenberg, Clement. "Marsden Hartley." *Nation* 59, no. 27 (30 December 1944): 810–11.

Greenfeld, Howard. *The Devil and Dr. Barnes: Portrait of an American Art Collector.* New York: Viking Penguin, 1987.

Grosskurth, Phyllis. *Havelock Ellis: A Biography.* New York: Alfred A. Knopf, 1980.

Hagen, Angela. "Demuth Watercolors and Oils at 'An American Place.' " *Creative Arts* 8 (June 1931): 441–43, 449.

Haire, Norman, ed. *World League for Sexual Reform: Reform Congress London, 1929.* London: Kegan Paul-Trench-Trubner, 1930.

Hale, Eunice Mylonas. "Charles Demuth: His Study of the Figure." Ph.D. diss., New York University, 1974.

Hall, Radclyffe. *The Well of Loneliness.* 1928. Reprint. New York: Avon, 1980.

Halperin, David. *One Hundred Years of Homosexuality and Other Essays on Greek Love.* New York: Routledge, 1990.

Hamilton, Gilbert Van Tassel. *An Introduction to Objective Psychopathology.* St. Louis: C. V. Mosby, 1925.

Hammond, William A. "The Disease of the Sythians (Morbus Feminarum) and Certain Analogous Conditions." *American Journal of Neurology and Psychiatry* 1, no. 3 (August 1882): 339–55.

———. *Sexual Impotence in the Male.* New York: Birmingham, 1883.

Hapgood, Hutchins. *A Victorian in the Modern World.* New York: Harcourt, Brace, 1939.

Hartland, Claude. *The Story of a Life.* St. Louis: Medical Fraternity, 1901. Reprint. San Francisco: Grey Fox, 1985.

Hartley, Marsden. *Adventures in the Arts: Informal Chapters on Painters, Vaudeville and Poets.* New York: Boni, Liveright, 1921. Reprint. New York: Hacker, 1972.

———. *Androscoggin.* Portland, Maine: Falmouth Publishing, 1940.

———. "Cleophas and His Own: A North Atlantic Tragedy and Related Poems." In *Marsden Hartley and Nova Scotia.* Edited by Gerald Ferguson. Halifax, Nova Scotia: Mount Saint Vincent University Art Gallery in association with the Press of the Nova Scotia College of Art and Design and the Art Gallery of Ontario, 1987.

———. *Cleophas and His Own: A North Atlantic Tragedy.* Edited by Gerald Ferguson. Halifax, Nova Scotia: A Press Publication, 1982.

———. *Collected Poems of Marsden Hartley.* Edited by Gail R. Scott. Santa Rosa, Calif.: Black Sparrow, 1987.

———. "Foreword for 1914 Exhibition at 291." *Camera Work* 45 (January 1914): 16–18.

———. "Letters from Marsden Hartley to Adelaide Kuntz, 1935–36." In *Marsden Hartley and Nova Scotia.* Edited by Gerald Ferguson. Halifax, Nova Scotia: Mount Saint Vincent University Art Gallery in association with the Press of the Nova Scotia College of Art and Design and the Art Gallery of Ontario, 1987.

———. *A Life in the Arts.* Edited by Gail R. Scott. Typescript.

———. *On Art.* Edited by Gail R. Scott. New York: Horizon Press, 1982.

———. *Recent Works by Marsden Hartley.* New York: Paul Rosenberg, 1942.

———. *Sea Burial: Poems by Marsden Hartley.* Portland, Maine: Leon Tebbetts, 1941.

———. *Selected Poems.* New York: Viking, 1945.

———. *Twenty-five Poems*. Paris: Contact Press, 1923.

Hartley, Marsden, and Horace Traubel. *Hearts Gate: Letters Between Marsden Hartley and Horace Traubel, 1906–1915*. Edited by William Innes Homer. Highlands, N.C.: Jargon Society, 1982.

Marsden Hartley: First Exhibition in Four Years. New York: An American Place, 1936.

Marsden Hartley: Paintings and Drawings. New York: Salander-O'Reilly Galleries, 1985.

Marsden Hartley: Recent Painting of Maine. New York: Hudson Walker Gallery, 1938.

Marsden Hartley: Twenty-fifth One Man Show. New York: Hudson Walker Gallery, 1929.

"Marsden Hartley's Journal Entries, Nova Scotia." In *Marsden Hartley and Nova Scotia*. Edited by Gerald Ferguson. Halifax, Nova Scotia: Mount Saint Vincent University Art Gallery in association with the Press of the Nova Scotia College of Art and Design and the Art Gallery of Ontario, 1987.

Haskell, Barbara. *Charles Demuth*. New York: Whitney Museum of American Art in association with Harry Abrams, 1987.

———. *Marsden Hartley*. New York: Whitney Museum of American Art in association with New York University Press, 1980.

Hebdige, Dick. *Subculture: The Meaning of Style*. London: Methuen, 1983.

Hemingway, Ernest. *A Moveable Feast*. New York: Collier, 1964.

Henderson, Helen. "Charles Demuth." Paper presented at the Junior League of Lancaster, 10 November 1947. Whitney Museum of American Art. Typescript.

Hendricks, Gordon. *The Life and Work of Thomas Eakins*. New York: Grossman, 1974.

Henry, G. W. "Psychogenic and Constitutional Factors in Homosexuality: Their Relation to Personality Disorders." *Psychiatric Quarterly* 8 (1934): 243–67.

Hesnard, Angelo. *Strange Lust: The Psychology of Homosexuality*. New York: Methnol Press, 1933.

Highly Important Nineteenth- and Twentieth-Century American Paintings from the Estate of Edith Halpert. New York: Sotheby Parke Bernet Inc., 1973.

Hirschfeld, Magnus. *Men and Women: The World Journey of a Sexologist*. New York: Putnam's, 1935.

———. *Sexual Anomalies*. New York: Emerson, 1948.

———. *The Sexual History of the World War*. New York: Cadillac Publishing, 1941.

———. *Sexual Pathology*. Translated by Jerome Gibbs. New York: Emerson, 1945.

Hokin, Jeanne. "Marsden Hartley: Volcanoes and Pyramids." *Latin America* 2, no. 1 (Winter 1990): 33–36.

Holloway, Emory. "Walt Whitman's Love Affairs." *Dial* 69 (1920): 473–83.

Homer, William I. *Alfred Stieglitz and the American Avant-Garde*. New York: New York Graphic Society, 1977.

———. *Alfred Stieglitz and the Photo-Secession*. Boston: Little, Brown, 1983.

Hooker, Edith Houghton. *The Laws of Sex*. Boston: R. G. Badger, 1921.

Howard, William Lee. "Sexual Perversion in America." *American Journal of Dermatology and Genito-Urinary Disease* 8, no. 1 (January 1904): 9–14.

———. *Confidential Chats with Boys*. New York: Edward J. Clode, 1911.

Hoyt, Edwin P. *Horatio's Boys: The Life and Work of Horatio Alger, Jr.* Radnor, Pa.: Chilton, 1974.

Hughes, C. H. "Erotopathia: Morbid Eroticism." *Alienist and Neurologist* 14, no. 4 (September 1893): 531–78.

Hyde, Montgomery. *The Love That Dared Not Speak Its Name*. Boston: Little, Brown, 1970.

Ives, George Cecil. *A History of Penal Methods: Criminals, Witches, Lunatics*. New York: Stokes, 1914.

Jay, Karla. *The Amazon and the Page*. Bloomington: University of Indiana Press, 1988.

Jewell, Edward Alden. "Metamorphosis." *New York Times*, 21 December 1930, sec. 8, p. 15.

———. "Our Annual Non-Objective Field-Day: Painters." *New York Times,* 12 March 1939, sec. 11, p. 9.

———. "A Quartet of Solo Flights." *New York Times,* 25 April 1937, sec. 10, p. 10.

———. "What Is Imagination?—Doubts Surge Forward as Marsden Hartley Frames New Credo—Six Artists Work." *New York Times,* 17 June 1928, sec. 9, p. 19.

Johnson, James Weldon. *Black Manhattan.* New York: Alfred A. Knopf, 1930.

Kahn, S. *Menality and Homosexuality.* Boston: Meador, 1937.

Kalonyme, Louis. "Charles Demuth: The Magician of Water Colors Leads Art Season of Old Favorites and New Contenders." *Arts and Decorations* 26, no. 2 (December 1926): 63, 102, 108, 111.

Kaplan, Justin. *Walt Whitman.* New York: Simon and Schuster, 1980.

Karpel, Bernard, Robert Motherwell, and Ad Reinhardt, eds. *Modern Artists in America.* New York: Wittenborn Schultz, 1951.

Katz, Jonathan Ned, ed. *Gay American History: Lesbian and Gay Men in the U.S.A.* New York: Thomas Crowell, 1976.

———, ed. *Gay/Lesbian Almanac: A New Documentary.* New York: Harper and Row, 1983.

Kempf, Edward J. *Psychopathology.* St. Louis: C. V. Mosby, 1921.

Kennedy, William Sloan. "Whitman's Letters to Peter Doyle." *The Conservator,* no. 4 (June 1897): 60–61.

Kenton, Edna. "Henry James to the Ruminant Reader: The Turn of the Screw." *Arts* 6, no. 5 (November 1924): 534.

King, Lyndel. *Marsden Hartley, 1908–1942: The Ione and Hudson D. Walker Collection.* Minneapolis: University Art Museum, University of Minnesota, 1986.

Kirstein, Lincoln. *Paul Cadmus.* New York: Pomegranate, 1992.

———. *Pavel Tchelitchew.* New York: Gallery of Modern Art, 1964.

Knoll, Robert E. *Robert McAlmon: Expatriate Publisher and Writer.* Lincoln: University of Nebraska Press, 1957.

Koestenbaum, Wayne. *Double Talk: The Erotics of Male Literary Collaboration.* New York: Routledge, 1989.

Koskovich, Ray Gerard. "A Gay American Modernist: Homosexuality in the Life and Art of Charles Demuth." *Advocate* (25 June 1985): 50–52.

Krafft-Ebing, Richard von. *Psychopathia Sexualis with Especial Reference to the Antipathic Sexual Instinct: A Medico-Forensic Study.* New York: Rebman, 1906.

Krafft-Ebing, Richard von, and Alexander Hartwick. *Aberrations of Sexual Life after the Psychopathia Sexualis of Dr. Richard von Krafft-Ebing.* Translated by Arthur Vivian Burburg. New York: Capricorn, 1969.

Kreymborg, Alfred. *Troubadour.* New York: Sagamore Press, 1957.

Kronhausen, Phyllis, and Eberhard Kronhausen. *The Complete Book of Erotic Art.* New York: Bell Publishing, 1970.

Kuenzli, Rudolf E., ed. *New York Dada.* New York: Willis Locker and Owens, 1986.

Lancaster, Pa. *Report on Vice Conditions in the City of Lancaster, Pa.* Lancaster, Pa.: City of Lancaster, 1913.

Lane, James W. "Charles Demuth." *Parnassus* 8 (8 March 1936): 8–9.

———. "New Exhibitions of the Week: The Virile Paintings by Marsden Hartley." *Art News* 38 (16 March 1940): 15.

Lauritsen, John, and David Thorstad. *The Early Homosexual Rights Movement (1864–1935).* New York: Times Change Press, 1974.

Lay, Wilfrid. *Man's Unconscious Passion.* New York: Dodd, Mead, 1920.

Leeves, Edward. *Leaves from a Victorian Diary.* London: Alison Press, 1985.

Legman, George Alexander. "The Language of Homosexuality; an American Glossary." In *Sex Variants.* Edited by G. W. Henry. New York: Hoeber, 1941.

Lenz, Ludwig L. *Discretion and Indiscretion: The Memoirs of a Sexologist.* New York: Cadillac Publishing, 1951.

Levin, Gail. "Hidden Symbolism in Marsden Hartley's Military Pictures." *Arts Magazine* 54, no. 2 (October 1979): 154–58.

———. "Marsden Hartley and the European Avant-Garde." *Arts Magazine* 54, no. 1 (September 1979): 158–63.

———. *Marsden Hartley in Bavaria.* Clinton, N.Y.: Emerson Gallery, Hamilton College, distributed by University Press of New England, 1989.

———. "Wassily Kandinsky and the American Avant-Garde, 1912–1950." Ph.D. diss., Rutgers University, 1976.

Lewis, David Levering. *When Harlem Was in Vogue.* New York: Vintage, 1982.

Licata, Salvatore. *Gay Power: A History of the American Gay Power Movement, 1908–1974.* Ph.D. diss., University of Southern California, 1978.

Licata, Salvatore J., and Robert P. Petersen, eds. *Historical Perspectives on Homosexuality.* Special issue of *The Journal of Homosexuality* 6, nos. 1, 2 (Fall–Winter 1980–81).

Lichtenstein, Perry M. "The Fairy and the Lady Lover." *Medical Review of Reviews* 27, no. 8 (August 1921): 369–74.

Lida, Marc. "Demuth Retrospective at Whitney." *West Side Spirit* 2, no. 90 (9 November 1987): 15.

Lind, Earl [pseud.]. *Autobiography of an Androgyne.* Edited by Alfred W. Herzog. New York: The Medico-Legal Journal, 1918. Reprint. New York: Arno Press, 1975.

———. *The Female Impersonators: A Sequel to the Autobiography of the Androgyne.* New York: The Medico-Legal Journal, 1922. Reprint. New York: Arno Press, 1975.

Lowe, Sue Davidson. *Stieglitz: A Memoir/Biography.* New York: Farrar, Straus and Giroux, 1983.

Ludington, Townsend. *Marsden Hartley: The Biography of an American Artist.* Boston: Little, Brown, 1992.

Luhan, Mabel Dodge. *European Experiences.* New York: Harcourt Brace, 1935.

Lydston, G. Frank. "Sexual Perversion, Satyriasis, and Nymphomania." Parts 1, 2. *Medical and Surgical Reporter* (Philadelphia) 61, no. 10 (November 1889): 253–58, no. 11 (September 14, 1889): 281–84.

Lynch, Michael. "A Gay World After All: Marsden Hartley (1877–1943)." *Body Politic* (December–January 1977): 1–3.

McAlmon, Robert. *Being Geniuses Together, 1920–1930.* San Francisco: North Point Press, 1984.

———. *Distinguished Air (Grim Fairy Tales).* Paris: Contact, 1925.

———. *Post-Adolescence.* Paris: Contact, n.d. Reprinted in *McAlmon and the Lost Generation: A Self-Portrait.* Lincoln: University of Nebraska Press, 1962.

McBride, Henry. "Charles Demuth." *Creative Art* 5 (September 1929): 635.

———. "Charles Demuth, Artist." *Magazine of Art* 31 (January 1931): 21–23, 58.

———. *Charles Demuth, Memorial Exhibition.* New York: Whitney Museum of American Art, 1938.

———. "Current News of Art and the Exhibitions." *Sun,* 9 April 1916, sec. 6, p. 8; reprinted in *Camera Work* 48 (October 1916): 58–59.

———. "Demuth: Phantoms from Literature." *Art News* 49 (March 1950): 18–21.

———. *The Flow of Art: Essays and Criticism of Henry McBride.* Edited by Daniel Catton Rich. New York: Atheneum, 1975.

———. "Modern Art." *Dial* 71 (December 1921): 718–20.

———. "Modern Art." *Dial* 73 (December 1922): 690–92.

———. "Modern Art." *Dial* 74 (February 1923): 217–19.

———. "News and Comment in the World of Art: Charles Demuth and Edward Fisk." *New York Sun,* 3 December 1916, sec. 5, p. 12.

———. "An Underground Search for Higher Moralities." *New York Evening Sun,* 25 November 1917, sec. 5, pp. 8–9.

———. "What Is Happening in the World of Art." *New York Sun,* 18 January 1914, sec. 6, p. 2; reprinted in *Camera Work* 45 (January 1914): 19–21.

———. "What Is Happening in the World of Art." *New York Sun,* 1 November 1914, sec. 6, p. 5.

McCausland, Elizabeth. "The Daniel Gallery and Modern American Art." *Magazine of Art* 44 (November 1951): 280–85.

———. *Marsden Hartley.* Minneapolis: University of Minnesota Press, 1952.

———. "The Return of the Native: Marsden Hartley." *Art in America* 40, no. 2 (Spring 1952): 55–79.

McCausland, Elizabeth, and Mary Bartlett. "Marsden Hartley: A Transcript of a Taped Interview with Hudson Walker." *Journal of the Archives of American Art* 8, no. 1 (January 1968): 9–21.

McCoy, Garnett, ed. "Letters from Germany: 1933–1938." *Archives of American Art Journal* 25, nos. 1, 2 (1985): 3–28.

McDougall, William. *Outline of Abnormal Psychology.* New York: Scribner's, 1926.

MacGowan, Christopher J. *William Carlos Williams's Early Poetry: The Visual Arts Background.* Ann Arbor, Mich.: UMI Research Press Studies in Modern Literature, 1984.

Marcus, Steven. "Introductory Essay to Freud's Three Essays on the Theory of Sexuality." In Sigmund Freud, *Three Essays on the Theory of Sexuality.* New York: Basic, 1975.

———. *The Other Victorians.* New York: Basic, 1966.

Marcuse, Herbert. *Eros and Civilization.* Boston: Beacon Press, 1955.

Marling, Karal Ann. "*My Egypt:* The Irony of the American Dream." *Winterthur Portfolio* 15 (Spring 1980): 25–39.

Marling, William. "Marsden Hartley and William Carlos Williams: The Figure of a Friendship." *Arts Magazine* 55, no. 10 (June 1981): 103–07.

———. *William Carlos Williams and the Painters, 1909–1923.* Athens: Ohio University Press, 1982.

Martin, Robert K. *The Homosexual Tradition in American Poetry.* Austin: University of Texas Press, 1979.

———. "Homosexuality in Whitman." *Partisan Review* 42, no. 1 (1975): 80–96.

———. "Painting and Primitivism: Hart Crane and the Development of an American Expressionist Esthetic." *Mosaic* 14, no. 3 (Summer 1981): 49–62.

Matthiessen, F. O., and Russell Chaney. *Rat and the Devil: Journal Letters of F. O. Matthiessen and Russell Chaney.* Edited by Louis Hyde. Boston: Alyson Press, 1988.

May, Geoffrey. *Social Control of Sex Expression.* New York: William Morrow, 1931.

Miller, Alvan V. *Directory of the International Association of Lesbian and Gay Archives and Libraries.* Toronto, Ontario: Canadian Gay Archives, 1979.

Mitchell, Juliet. *Psychoanalysis and Feminism.* London: Allen Lane, 1974.

Mitchell, Roger Sherman. *The Homosexual and the Law.* New York: Arco, 1969.

Mitchell, William J. *Ninety-nine Drawings by Marsden Hartley.* Lewiston, Maine: Bates College Art Department, 1970.

Mosse, George. *Nationalism and Sexuality: Respectability and Abnormal Sexuality in Modern Europe.* New York: Fertig, 1985.

Mulvey, Laura. "Visual Pleasure and Narrative Cinema." *Screen* 16, no. 3 (Autumn 1975): 6–18; reprinted in Brian Wallis, ed., *Art After Modernism: Rethinking Representation.* New York and Boston: New Museum of Contemporary Art in association with David R. Godine, 1984.

Mumford, Lewis. Untitled column. *New Yorker* 13, no. 8 (10 April 1937): 66–67.

Murphy, Lawrence R. "Cleaning Up Newport: The U.S. Navy's Persecution of Homosexuals After World War I." *Journal of American Culture* 7, no. 3 (Fall 1984): 57–64.

———. *Perverts by Official Order: The Campaign Against Homosexuals by the United States Navy.* New York: Harrington Park Press, 1988.

Murrell, William. *Charles Demuth.* New York: Whitney Museum of American Art, 1931.

New York (City). *Report of Mayor's Committee for Study of Sex Offenses.* New York: City of New York, c. 1940.

———. *Report on Public Baths and Public Comfort Stations by the Mayor's Committee.* New York: City of New York, 1897.

New York (State). *New York City Investigative Committee Report of the Special Committee of the Assembly Appointed to Investigate the Public Offices and Departments of the City of New York . . . Transmitted by the Legislature January 15, 1900.* 5 vols. Albany, N.Y.: James Lyon, 1900.

Nordus, Simon. *Degeneration.* London: W. Heinemann, 1895.

Norman, Dorothy, Waldo Frank, Harold Odway Rugg, Lewis Mumford, and Paul Rosenfeld, eds. *America and Alfred Stieglitz: A Collective Portrait.* New York: Doubleday, Doran, 1934. Reprint. New York: Aperture, 1975.

Norton, Rictor. *The Homosexual Literary Tradition: An Interpretation.* New York: Revisionist Press, 1974.

O'Higgins, James. "Sexual Choice, Sexual Act: An Interview with Michel Foucault." *Salmagundi* 58–59 (Fall–Winter 1983).

O'Neill, Eugene. *Strange Interlude.* In *Three Plays.* 1928. Reprint. New York: Vintage Books, 1959.

"Paintings by Marsden Hartley." *New York Times,* 31 January 1915, sec. 3, p. 2.

Parker, William. *Homosexuality Bibliography: Supplement, 1970–75.* Metuchen, N.J.: Scarecrow Press, 1977.

———. "Homosexuality in History: An Annotated Bibliography." *The Journal of Homosexuality* 6, nos. 1–2 (Fall–Winter 1980–81): 191–210.

———. *Homosexuality: A Selective Bibliography of Over Three Thousand Items.* Metuchen, N.J.: Scarecrow Press, 1971.

Pater, Walter. "Leonardo da Vinci, Homo Minister et Interpres Naturae." In *Selected Writings of Walter Pater.* Edited by Harold Bloom. New York: Columbia University Press, 1974.

———. "A Prince of Court Painters." In *Imaginary Portraits.* New York: Macmillan, 1887.

Paulson, Ronald. "Marsden Hartley's Search for the Father(land)." In *Marsden Hartley and Nova Scotia.* Edited by Gerald Ferguson. Halifax, Nova Scotia: Mount Saint Vincent University Art Gallery in association with the Press of the Nova Scotia College of Art and Design and the Art Gallery of Ontario, 1987.

Peterson, Houston. *Havelock Ellis: Philosopher of Love.* Boston: Houghton Mifflin, 1928.

Petruck, Peninah R. *American Art Criticism.* New York: Garland, 1981.

Plant, Richard. "Nazis and Gays." In *Christopher Street Reader.* Edited by Michael Denneng, Charles Ortleb, and Thomas Steele. New York: Wideview/Penger, 1984.

———. *The Pink Triangle: The Nazi War Against Homosexuals.* New York: Henry Holt, 1986.

Plummer, Kenneth, ed. *The Making of the Modern Homosexual.* Totowa, N.J.: Barnes and Noble, 1981.

Posner, David. "Caravaggio's Homoerotic Early Works." *The Art Quarterly* 34, no. 2 (Summer 1971): 301–24.

Potter, La Forest. *Strange Loves.* New York: Padell, 1933.

Raffety, W. Edward. *Brothering the Boy.* Philadelphia: Griffith and Rowland Press, 1913.

Reade, Brian, ed. *Sexual Heretics: Male Homosexuality in English Literature from 1850–1900.* New York: Coward McCann, 1970.

Rector, Frank. *The Nazi Extermination of Homosexuals.* New York: Stein and Day, 1981.

Reid, Kenneth E. *Other Voices: The Style of a Male Homosexual Tavern.* Novato, Calif.: Chandler and Sharp, 1980.

Rice, Lee C. "Review of Men and Boys: An Anthology." *GPU News* (May 1979): 41–44.

Ritchie, Andrew Carnduff. *Charles Demuth.* New York: The Museum of Modern Art, 1950.

Rivers, W. C. *Walt Whitman's Anomaly.* London: George Allen, 1913.

Robbins, Bernard S. "Psychological Implications of the Male Homosexual Marriage." *Psychoanalytic Review* 30, no. 4 (October 1943): 428–37.

Rosenfeld, Paul. "American Painting." *Dial* 71, no. 6 (December 1921): 661–70.

———. "Charles Demuth." *Nation* 133 (7 October 1931): 371–73.

———. "Marsden Hartley." *Nation* 157 (18 September 1943): 326–27.

———. *Men Seen*. New York: Dial Press, 1925.

———. *Port of New York: Essays on Fourteen American Moderns*. New York: Harcourt, Brace, 1924. Reprint. Urbana: University of Illinois Press, 1961.

Ruggiero, Guido. *The Boundaries of Eros: Sex Crime and Sexuality in Renaissance Italy*. London: Oxford University Press, 1985.

Sagarin, Edward. *Structure and Ideology in an Association of Deviants*. New York: Arno Press, 1975.

Sarotte, Georges-Michel. *Like a Brother, Like a Lover: Male Homosexuality in the American Novel and Theater from Herman Melville to James Baldwin*. Translated by Richard Miller. Garden City, N.Y.: Anchor, Doubleday, 1978.

Saslow, James M. *Ganymede in the Renaissance: Homosexuality in Art and Society*. New Haven: Yale University Press, 1986.

Schnakenberg, H. E. "Charles Demuth." *Arts* 17 (May 1931): 581.

Schwarz, Arturo. *The Complete Works of Marcel Duchamp*. New York: Harry Abrams, 1969.

Scott, Colin. "Sex and Art." *American Journal of Psychology* 7 (January 1896): 198–226.

Scott, Gail R. "Cleophas and His Own: The Making of a Narrative." In *Marsden Hartley and Nova Scotia*. Edited by Gerald Ferguson. Halifax, Nova Scotia: Mount Saint Vincent University Art Gallery in association with the Press of the Nova Scotia College of Art and Design and the Art Gallery of Ontario, 1987.

———. *Marsden Hartley*. New York: Abbeville, 1988.

———. "Marsden Hartley at Dogtown Common." *Arts Magazine* 54, no. 2 (October 1979): 159–65.

Scott, George Riley. *Sex Problems and Dangers in War-Time: A Book of Practical Advice for Men and Women on the Fighting and Home Fronts*. London: T. W. Laurie, 1940.

———. *Story of Baths and Bathing*. London: T. W. Laurie, 1939.

Sedgwick, Eve Kosofsky. "The Beast in the Closet: James and the Writing of Homosexual Panic." In *Sex, Politics, and Science in the Nineteenth-Century Novel*. Edited by Bernard Yeazell. Baltimore: Johns Hopkins University Press, 1986.

———. *Between Men: English Literature and Male Homosocial Desire*. New York: Columbia University Press, 1985.

———. *Epistemology of the Closet*. Berkeley: University of California Press, 1990.

Selection of Watercolors and Drawings by Charles Demuth. New York: Parke-Bernet, 1976.

Shively, Charley, ed. *Calamus Lovers: Walt Whitman's Working-Class Camerados*. San Francisco: Gay Sunshine Press, 1987.

Shrady, George F. "Perverted Sexual Instinct." *Medical Record* (New York), 26 (July 1884): 70–71.

Shufeldt, Robert. "Biography of a Passive Pederast." *American Journal of Urology and Sexology* 13, no. 10 (October 1917): 451–60.

Simon, Carleton. "Homosexualists and Sex Crimes." Paper presented before the International Association of Chiefs of Police, 21–25 September 1947, Deluth, Minn.

Smith, Timothy d'Arch. *Love in Earnest: Some Notes on the Lives and Writings of English "Uranian" Poets from 1889–1930*. London: Routledge and Kegan Paul, 1970.

Socarades, Charles W. *Beyond Sexual Freedom*. New York: Quadrangle, 1975.

———. *Homosexuality*. New York: Jason Aronson, 1978.

———. *The Overt Homosexual*. New York: Grune and Stratton, 1968.

Sokolowski, Thomas W. *The Sailor, 1930–45: The Image of an American Demigod*. Norfolk, Va.: The Chrysler Museum, 1983.

Spender, Stephen. *World within World: The Autobiography of Stephen Spender*. London: H. Hamilton, 1951.

Spingarn, Arthur B. *Laws Relating to Sex Morality in New York City*. New York: Century, 1915.

Stambolin, Georges, and Elaine Marks, eds. *Homosexualities and French Literature: Cultural Contexts/Critical Texts.* Ithaca, N.Y.: Cornell University Press, 1979.

Steakley, James D. *The Homosexual Emancipation Movement.* New York: Arno Press, 1975.

Stebbins, Theodore E., and Carol Troyen. *The Lane Collection: Twentieth Century Paintings in the American Tradition.* Boston: Museum of Fine Arts, 1983.

Stein, Gertrude. *Autobiography of Alice B. Toklas.* New York: Vintage, 1961.

———. "From a Play by Gertrude Stein" (Foreword for 1914 exhibition at 291). *Camera Work* 45 (January 1914): 16–18.

Steiner, George, and Robert Boyers, eds. *Homosexuality: Sacrilege, Vision, Politics.* Special issue of *Salmagundi* 58–59 (Fall–Winter 1983).

Stekel, William. *Bi-sexual Love: The Homosexual Neurosis.* Boston: R. G. Badgly, 1922.

———. "Masked Homosexuality." Translated by S. A. Tannenbaum. *American Medicine* (Burlington, Vt.) 9, no. 8 (August 1914): 530–37.

Stevenson, Edward [Xavier Mayne, pseud.]. *The Intersexes: A History of Similisexualism as a Problem in Social Life.* Privately printed, 1908. Reprint. New York: Arno Press, 1975.

Sweeney, John L. "The Demuth Pictures." *Kenyon Review* 5, no. 4 (Autumn 1943): 522–32.

———, ed. *Painter's Eye: Notes and Essays on the Pictorial Arts by Henry James.* London: Rupert Hart-Davis, 1956.

Symonds, John Addington. *The Memoirs of John Addington Symonds: The Secret Homosexual Life of a Nineteenth-Century Man of Letters.* Edited by Phyllis Grossworth. New York: Random House, 1984.

———. *A Problem in Greek Ethics.* London: Privately printed, 1891.

———. *Studies in Sexual Inversion.* London: Privately printed, 1928.

Symonds, John, and Kenneth Grant, eds. *The Confessions of Aleister Crowley.* New York: Hill and Wang, 1969.

Symons, Arthur. *Confessions: A Study in Pathology.* New York: Fountain Press, 1930.

Talbot, E. S., and Havelock Ellis. "A Case of Developmental Degenerative Insanity, with Sexual Inversion, Melancholia, Following Removal of Testicles, Attempted Murder and Suicide." *Journal of Mental Science* 42, no. 177 (n. s. no. 141) (April 1896): 341–44.

Tarnowsky, Benjamin. *Pederasty in Europe.* Translated by Paul Gardner. New York: Falstaff Press, 1933. Reprint. Hollywood, Calif.: Brandon House, 1967.

Tashjian, Dickran. *Skyscraper Primitives: Dada and the American Avant-Garde.* Middletown, Conn.: Wesleyan University Press, 1975.

———. *William Carlos Williams and the American Scene, 1920–1940.* New York and Berkeley: Whitney Museum of American Art in association with the University of California Press, 1978.

Tickner, Lisa. "Feminism, Art History, and Sexual Difference." *Genders* 3 (Fall 1988): 113.

Tyler, Parker. *The Divine Comedy of Pavel Tchelitchew.* London: Fleet, 1967.

———. *Screening the Sexes: Homosexuality in the Movies.* New York: Holt, Rinehart and Winston, 1972.

Unterecker, John. *Voyager: A Life of Hart Crane.* New York: Farrar, Straus, and Giroux, 1969.

United States Government. *Government vs. Homosexuals.* New York: Arno Press, 1975.

Vacha, Keith, and Cassie Damewood. *Quiet Fire: Memoirs of Older Gay Men.* Trumansburg, N.Y.: Crossing Press, 1985.

Valéry, Paul. "Introduction to the Method of Leonardo da Vinci." In *Variety.* Translated by Malcolm Cowley. New York: Harcourt, Brace, 1927.

Vechten, Carl van. *Blind Boy Bow-Boy.* New York: Alfred Knopf, 1923.

———. *Nigger Heaven.* New York: Alfred Knopf, 1928.

———. "Pastiches et Pastiches: Charles Demuth and Florine Stettheimer." *Reviewer* 2 (February 1922): 269–70.

———. *Sacred and Profane Memoirs*. 1932. Freeport, N.Y.: Books for Libraries Press, 1971.

Vice Commission of Chicago. *The Social Evil in Chicago: A Study of Existing Conditions/With Recommendations*. Chicago: Gunthorp-Warren, 1911.

Walker, Kenneth. *Sex and Society*. London: Muller, 1955.

Warner, Marina. "Homoeroticism on High." Review of *Ganymede in the Renaissance*, by James M. Saslow. *Times Literary Supplement*, 19 September 1986, p. 1038.

Washburn Gallery. *Charles Demuth, The Early Years: Works from 1909–1917*. New York: Washburn Gallery, 1975.

"Water-color: A Weapon of Wit." *Current Opinion* 66, no. 1 (January 1919): 51–52.

Watercolors and Paintings by Charles Demuth: Part One of the Collection Belonging to the Estate of the Late Richard W. C. Weyand, Lancaster, Pennsylvania. New York: Parke-Bernet Galleries, 1957.

Watercolors and Paintings by Charles Demuth: Part Two [Final] of the Collection Belonging to the Estate of the Late Richard W. C. Weyand, Lancaster, Pennsylvania. New York: Parke-Bernet Galleries, 1957.

Watson, Forbes. "Charles Demuth." *Arts* 3, no. 1 (January 1923): 77–78.

———. "Prints and Paintings in Great Variety Feature December Exhibitions." *Arts and Decorations* 14, no. 3 (January 1921): 214–15, 230.

Watson, Steven. *Strange Bedfellows: The First American Avant-Garde*. New York: Abbeville, 1991.

Waugh, Tom. "Photography, Passion and Power." *Body Politic*, no. 101 (March 1984): 20–33.

Weeks, Jeffrey. "Capitalism and the Organization of Sex." In *Homosexuality: Power and Politics*. Edited by Gay Left Coalition. London: Allison and Busby, 1980.

———. *Coming Out: Homosexual Politics in Britain from the Nineteenth Century to the Present*. London: Quartet, 1977.

———. *Sex, Politics and Society: The Regulation of Sexuality Since 1800*. New York: Longman, 1981.

Weinberg, Jonathan. "Cruising with Paul Cadmus." *Art in America* 80, no. 11 (November 1992): 102–09.

———. "Demuth and Difference." *Art in America* 76, no. 4 (April 1988): 188–95, 221, 223.

———. "Homosexual Art and Artists." *Art in America* 75, no. 10 (October 1987): 23–25.

———. " 'Some Unknown Thing': The Illustrations of Charles Demuth." *Arts Magazine* 61, no. 4 (December 1986): 14–21.

Weinberg, Martin S., and Allan P. Bell. *Homosexuality: An Annotated Bibliography*. New York: Harper and Row, 1972.

Wellman, Rita. "Pen Portraits: Charles Demuth, Artist." *Creative Art* 9 (December 1931): 484.

Whitemore, Hugh. *Breaking the Code*. London: Amber Lane Press, 1987.

Whitman, Walt. *Calamus: A Series of Calamus Letters Written During the Years 1868–1880 by Walt Whitman to a Young Friend (Peter Doyle)*. Boston: Maynard, 1897.

———. *Leaves of Grass*. Edited by Gay Wilson Allen. New York: New American Library, 1958.

Williams, William Carlos. *The Autobiography of William Carlos Williams*. New York: Random House, 1951.

———. *A Recognizable Image: William Carlos Williams on Art and Artists*. Edited by Bram Dijkstra. New York: New Directions, 1978.

Wilson, Edmund. "The Ambiguity of Henry James." *The Triple Thinkers*. Oxford: Oxford University Press, 1963.

Wolff, Adolph. "Excerpt from a Review in the *International*." *Camera Work* 45 (January 1914): 23.

Woods, Gregory. *Articulate Flesh: Male Homo-eroticism and Modern Poetry*. New Haven: Yale University Press, 1987.

Wright, Willard Huntington. "Modern Art." *International Studio* (January 1918): 98.

———. "Revised Excerpt from *The Forum*." *Camera Work* 48 (October 1916): 58–59.

Young, Ian. *Gay Resistance: Homosexuals in the Anti-Nazi Underground*. Toronto: Stubblejumper Press, 1985.

———. *The Male Homosexual in Literature*. Metuchen, N.J.: Scarecrow Press, 1975.

Index

Page numbers in italics refer to illustrations. Numbers following "pl." refer to plate numbers.